FAITH CRISIS
VOLUME 2
Behind Closed Doors

LEONARD ARRINGTON & THE
PROGRESSIVE REWRITING
OF MORMON HISTORY

JOSEPH SMITH®
FOUNDATION

FAITH CRISIS
VOLUME 2
Behind Closed Doors

Leonard Arrington & the Progressive
Rewriting of Mormon History

Joseph Smith Foundation®

Joseph Smith Foundation is an organization focused on supporting and contributing to projects founded in the words of Jesus Christ. Those contributing to *Joseph Smith Foundation* projects are members of The Church of Jesus Christ of Latter-day Saints, but the foundation is not sponsored by the Church. *Joseph Smith Foundation* projects include documentary films, Latter-day Answers, ZionTube, InspiraWiki, FAQs, Papers, Audio, Ebooks and much more.
www.JosephSmithFoundation.org

Published by:
Joseph Smith Foundation®
Salem, UT, USA

2nd printing

Interior Design: Leah M. Stoddard, Isaiah M. Stoddard, Ephraim J. Stoddard

Cover Design: Leah M. Stoddard, James F. Stoddard III

Thanks & Contribution: Jim F. & Margaret J. Stoddard, Russell H. & Heidi S. Barlow, Cameron & Kimberly W. Smith, Julie A. & Natalie Smith, Ezra B. & Mary D. Stoddard

Library of Congress Control Number: 2020946107
ISBN: 978-1-64871-407-8

Printed in the USA

FAITH CRISIS
VOLUME 2
Behind Closed Doors

LEONARD ARRINGTON & THE PROGRESSIVE REWRITING OF MORMON HISTORY

L. Hannah Stoddard

James F. Stoddard III

To Ezra Taft Benson, for remaining true to the Restoration

Russell H. Barlow . . . . Assistant Writer, Senior Editor

Leah M. Stoddard . . . . .Citation Editor

Kimberly W. Smith . . . . Senior Researcher

Jill Limburg Korajac. . . . . Senior Editor

Emma Katherine Korajac. . . . . Editor

Margaret J. Stoddard . . . . .Editor, Researcher

Isaiah M. Stoddard. . . . . Layout Editor

Threesa L. Cummings . . . . Researcher

Beverly J. Arbon . . . . Editor

Emily Dayley . . . . Researcher

Rebecca Connolly . . . . Researcher

Lloyd E. Ward . . . . Assistant Editor

Ephraim J. Stoddard. . . . . Assistant Editor

Luke William Mulder . . . . Assistant Editor

Benjamin G. Mulder. . . . . Assistant Editor

Joseph Smith Foundation®

Seer Stone v. Urim & Thummim
Book of Mormon Translation on Trial

Seer Stone v. Urim and Thummim places the Book of Mormon translation on trial, presenting the latest research in one of the most comprehensive treatments of the translation process to date—providing encouragement for Latter-day Saints who fear they have been "betrayed" by the translation history taught by the Church for over 190 years.

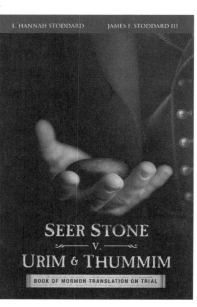

- Has The Church of Jesus Christ of Latter-day Saints covered up its history for nearly 200 years?
- Did Joseph Smith translate the Book of Mormon using a dark seer stone in a hat?
- Why are progressive historians creating a new history using sources from a man who vowed to wash his hands in the blood of Joseph Smith, while boasting that he had deceived the Prophet and his God?
- Was Joseph Smith a treasure digger? During his life, did the Prophet artfully suppress his alleged treasure digging past?
- Did Joseph Smith cover up his use of a seer stone during the translation, feigning use of the Urim and Thummim?
- What new information has The Joseph Smith Papers Project uncovered that challenges our understanding of the translation process?
- Is David Whitmer a credible witness of the Book of Mormon translation? Did you know that David Whitmer consulted a witch and occultic seer stones, denounced Joseph Smith as a false prophet, and aided the mob in the persecution of the Missouri Saints?
- Was Joseph Smith involved in sorcery, astrology, and ritual magic?
- Did Joseph Smith study and master the Nephite language? Did the Prophet tutor some of the early Brethren in ancient Nephite characters?

Order now at www.JosephSmithFoundation.org

CONTENTS

CONTENTS (CONTINUED)

FOREWORD

The history of The Church of Jesus Christ of Latter-day Saints is captivating. The persecutions, trials, definitive personalities, and introduction of strange doctrines to the general public—all set in lawless frontier settlements—make for exciting reading. Typical of New Englanders of the period, the Smith family fit well into the panorama. They were hard-working, upright, and intent on persevering in the mission that was entrusted to them by the Father and the Son. It was a straightforward and transparent history.

As a young convert to the Church, I read and pondered the early stories regularly. Joseph Smith, his family, and other leaders were heroes and models. Later, after teaching in the Church Education System for a few years and receiving continual inspiration from reading and teaching courses in Church History, I determined to pursue further graduate work, centered on pioneer Utah and the expanding Church.

My studies at the University of Utah during the 1970s were timely. It was an era of some inner turmoil, unnoticeable to lay membership, as the 'new history' began to show itself in various books and articles. *Faith Crisis* is the first book to unwrap the influence of the new history and its impact on coming to an understanding of historical Mormonism. Prior to the calling of Leonard Arrington to act as the first professional Church Historian, the office had remained the purview of general authorities, and had generally promoted a positive, faith-promoting image of The Church of Jesus Christ of Latter-day Saints. It was not a false image, but one that emphasized the Lord's hand in the Church's creation and expansion. With the professionalization of the office, however, doors were opened to the new history.

What was the new history? In academic circles it was called "revisionist" history. It was a retelling of events with greater emphasis on the 'why' of events—their imputed motives and surmisings—rather than the 'what.' About the time of new history's appearance in the Church—at the nation's bicentennial—President Ezra Taft Benson wrote:

❝ Today, students are subjected in their textbooks and classroom lectures to a subtle propaganda that there is a natural or rational explanation for all causes and events. Such a position removes the need for faith in God or belief in His interposition in the affairs of men. Events are only—and I purposely stress that word—explained from a humanistic frame of reference.

Historians and educational writers who are responsible for this movement are classified as 'revisionists.' Their purpose has been and is to create a 'new history.' By their own admission they are more influenced by their own training and other humanistic and scientific disciplines than any religious conviction. This detachment provides them, they say, with an objectivity that the older historians did not have.[1]

Revisionism is notorious for little-known sources and acceptance of dubious references. Under the newness of including material that was 'off limits' to former researchers, but charging forward to uncover motives behind events, revisionism frequently dictated that what historically took place was not as important as why certain events occurred. Accepting source material that was formerly debunked, the new historian's investigation could uncover tidbits of personal information and thought patterns about historical figures. Armed with assumed facts, the revisionist historian then often impugned men's personal motives for events, doctrines, or beliefs. Key to the new history of the Church were little-known supposed imperfect characteristics and motivations of decision-making personalities, and a subsequent lessening of testimony-producing information.

Taken to an extreme, anti-Mormon writers latched on to sundry tidbits: Joseph was a womanizer, Brigham an autocrat, the temple was Masonic, the roots of plural marriage were founded in sensuality, and so on. In general, the historical emphasis shifted from revelation and divine direction toward assumed personality flaws and general anti-Mormon sentiment of the period.

It must be said that the new historians within the Church were not malicious or self serving in their intent. The historians I worked with were loyal Church members with sound testimonies of the

---

1   Ezra Taft Benson, *This Nation Shall Endure* (Salt Lake City, Utah: Deseret Book Co., 1977), 14.

truthfulness of The Church of Jesus Christ of Latter-day Saints; and most held responsible ecclesiastical positions. Serving with Church Historian Leonard Arrington were two Assistant Church Historians—one of whom was a close personal friend on my doctoral committee; while the other was a major professor with whom I worked. I must admit that at the time, I was academically naive of the new history, and found that I was somewhat of an anomaly among other Church historians because I was a staunch supporter of Ezra Taft Benson—soon to become the next President of the Church.

The aim of James and Hannah Stoddard in writing *Faith Crisis* is to show that far-reaching consequences of the new history have led to misunderstandings and one-sided interpretations concerning the historical base of The Church of Jesus Christ of Latter-day Saints. Various statements or singular events taken out of their original context—taken from source material intentionally antagonistic—or taken from their original historical setting, are easily misunderstood. Frequently, such trivia and assumed facts have received attention at the expense of faith-promoting activity.

Unfortunately, others opposed to the Church have also used the new history to weaken the faith of Latter-day Saints, and many 'good' Mormons, including recently-returned missionaries, have fallen into the trap of gaining "a little knowledge." Much of this has come to the forefront because of the internet and ease of pursuing anti-Mormon themes while surfing the web. Intrigued by assumed new knowledge, often a member of the Church is drawn into curiosities about his religion. Tantalizing comments and innuendos are taken out of context; and the reader, having a limited background in historical fact, searches further. The 'rabbit hole' of his knowledge leads into little-known—or contrived—events written intentionally to create distrust and doubt of his beliefs.

Several have become perplexed over what appear to be historical anomalies. Often, revisionism has overshadowed the Restoration, and inordinate emphasis has been placed on the flaws of the messenger or incorrect information—at the expense of the divine message. Questions frequently arise concerning the character of Joseph Smith and the perceived motives of 'modern-Mormonism.' Joseph, they have read, was lustful—he was a money digger, a dreamer, a trickster, a believer in the occult, and a plagiarizer. Brigham Young was overbearing, was responsible for murders, and confiscated much of the Saints' earnings. Polygamy has been presented as a trademark of the sensuality of Church leaders. In fine, the contemptible and abhorrent issues surrounding the Church—although seemingly objective and readable—have presented a lopsided and incorrect view of Mormonism that has infected many.

Were all leaders of The Church of Jesus Christ of Latter-day Saints without fault? Certainly not. There were personalities that were out of step with gospel practice, and whose behaviors reflected badly on the greater Church movement. Today, just as in the early Church, bishops have been excommunicated for adultery and absconding with tithing funds; there are abusive family situations following temple sealings; members of the Church commit felonies; there is a host of sinning that brings disgrace to members, their families, and the Church. To say that those things are nonexistent is naive folly. A reliable historian, however, tells the story of The Church of Jesus Christ of Latter-day Saints using trusted sources—without capitalizing and accentuating dubious references and personal foibles.

The Stoddards have documented the entry of revisionism into Latter-day Saint history, and shown the clear distinction between printed historical accounts appearing in the popular press—the realities of truthful journalism. In *Faith Crisis*, they have done groundbreaking work in squarely facing the new history of The Church of Jesus Christ of Latter-day Saints. It is a necessary read for those who have been confused or demoralized by revisionism, past or present.

John D. (Jack) Monnett, Ph.D.
Author, historian, and former Church Educational System instructor

INTRODUCTION

"Daddy, can you please tell us a story?"

As a little nine-year-old girl, I can remember afternoon sunlight streaming through our family room windows as my dad returned from work for his long lunch break every day, and I gathered with my siblings to listen—enraptured—to stories from Church history. The story of Parley P. Pratt's daring 4th-of-July jailbreak, the moving healings performed by the Prophet on the banks of the Mississippi in Nauvoo, and the many accounts of miracles stimulated our imaginations and aroused our faith. I'll never forget snuggling under a blanket in the back of our suburban during a family road trip, listening to the eyewitness accounts of those who personally knew Joseph Smith. My siblings and I wrote plays telling the stories of our ancestors who served as Joseph Smith's bodyguards; we dressed up as pioneers for the ward costume party, and we loved to read the original journals and histories of our faithful forebears.

Moving to Utah when I was ten, my first memories of the sparkling, twinkling lights surrounding Utah Lake—while

bouncing along beside my dad and brother in the moving van—are inseparably connected with the voice of Lucy Mack Smith's autobiography playing through the van's sound system. My first book was my very own prized set of Joseph Fielding Smith's *Answers to Gospel Questions*.

Since my dad taught at the MTC and served as a released-time seminary instructor, we grew up watching all of the movies, from "Zion's Camp," to "How Rare a Possession," to "Ensign to the Nations." My father was one who *never* turned down a Church calling, who never missed his Sunday meetings (unless health issues intervened) and who instilled in us a desire to serve and to build up the foundation established by our forefathers. Scripture study was non-negotiable in our home, and service within the Church was a given. As we jokingly commented growing up, "In our family, the question for boys isn't 'Are you going on a mission?' It's 'Where are you at in preparing for one?" There was just never a question about "if" they should serve.

Two of my siblings were named after Joseph Smith's grandparents, who are my own ancestors, Asael and Mary Duty Smith; and each Stoddard child was named after a Gospel hero or heroine. When we remembered our names, we remembered *them* in the spirit of Helaman's counsel to his sons, Nephi and Lehi: "when ye remember them ye may remember their works; and when ye remember their works ye may know how that it is said, and also written, that they were good."[1]

As I grew up, animated by the legacy of the Restoration and continually drawing strength from these heroes and heroines, I never dreamed that these narratives would incite such conflict, and would develop into an intense battleground that would prove to be one of the most decisive wars—not of guns and swords, but of spirit—of the 21st-century. Never did I imagine that I would live to daily witness _my_ generation, my millennial peers, falling away in droves. What happened? And what could I do to help?

New 'Mormon Stories'

In 2005, incidentally, the same year our family launched what would become the Joseph Smith Foundation, John Dehlin started a podcast

---

1   Helaman 5:6.

he titled "Mormon Stories." With 23.5k YouTube subscribers and nearly 17.5k Facebook likes to date, Dehlin's work has become one of the most effective weapons driving members to abandon their testimonies and leave the Church. What was—and still is—his strategy? It is actually quite simple: claim the Church lied about its origins, its history, and its doctrine. Why would you devote your life, your tithing, your energy, and your faith to an institution and to a man (Joseph Smith) who deceived you?

Dehlin's strategy is becoming increasingly effective because the most vocal response has been from sheepish progressives who are effectively surrendering to Dehlin's outlook. Yes, they argue, past leaders did lie about our history; the truth is not what you were told. But, they say, Mormon culture has a lot of goodness and cultural perks to offer—so stay with it. Because of a carefully spun, new narrative, a few progressive thought leaders are convincing our generation that a new interpretation of our history—and therefore our doctrine—is imperative. Growing numbers of thoughtful members are becoming increasingly uneasy, and some are perplexed. We claim to be the true Church; but if we are changing our narrative, how can we be considered credible?

Progressive historians, authors, and speakers are falling in line with Dehlin's clarion call as they rewrite our history and reshape our faith. In 2016, New Mormon Historian Ron Barney announced that we are in a "new era" of Latter-day Saint history.[2] Sadly, the result of this "new era" is the most catastrophic faith crisis in the history of the Church—and we are only seeing the very *beginning*.

Are the progressives right? Did we cover up our true history? Did we inherit lies from our past leaders? These are questions we Millennials need answered!

Traditionalists vs. Progressives

Informed traditionalists attribute today's faith crisis largely to the shifting narrative of progressive history. Progressives insist that the crisis is the result of traditionalists holding on too tightly to

---

2 Benchmark Books, "Laura Hales & Contributors (A Reason for Faith)-- Benchmark Books, 5/11/16," YouTube video, 00:21:30, May 18, 2016, https:// youtu.be/zlVGqk5hjlI?t=1290.

the "dominant narrative"[3] for far too long, and for not allowing progressive voices to be heard earlier. On either side stand opposing worldviews—rival solutions and conflicting interpretations. Regardless of which side one embraces, this is the pivotal battle—the decisive conflict—of our generation.

Our position—my position—is a resounding testimony that we were not betrayed. Our dominant narrative is true! There have been 'warts' and misunderstandings, but those warts do not affect our underlying foundational story. Primary sources and solid research affirm that our traditional origins are true—there is no need to transform or accommodate in behalf of the raging deconstructionist voice.

In Volumes 1 and 2 of the *Faith Crisis* series, we mention specific names, dates, events, and organizations in our retelling of the conflict between progressivism and traditionalism in the Church over the past century. Specifically, the storyline has necessitated that we name prominent historians and scholars. But is our work meant as an attack on the reputation of these men and women? Are we attempting to malign their character? Absolutely NOT. The men and women we have highlighted are those who advocated their position with pride, and publicly promoted their viewpoint. We have done our best to represent their position correctly, without overstating or undermining. We have exercised great care in verifying and documenting direct quotations from their own writings, speeches, or comments. The *Faith Crisis* series is *not* an exposé of any individual personality. It is not a denunciation of these individuals; nor is it intended as a smear campaign against any person's character.

Leonard Arrington is not our personal enemy. Those who knew him individually remember him as a man who always had a "big grin," and who lacked any airs of "pretense" or "pompousness."[4] Arrington loved people, he built bridges for the progressive movement, and was remembered by many as someone who "insisted . . . in seeing the best in everyone."[5] He told his employees to skip the titles (Doctor,

---

3   James F. Stoddard III, "'The dominant [Church history] narrative is not true . . .' LDS scholars encourage new history, new policy, new Church," Latter-day Answers, October 1, 2016, https://ldsanswers.org/dominant-church-history-narrative-not-true-lds-scholars-encourage-new-history-new-policy-new-church/.

4   Gregory A. Prince, *Leonard Arrington and the Writing of Mormon History* (Salt Lake City, UT: Tanner Trust Fund and J. Willard Marriott Library, 2016), 89.

5   Ibid., 90.

Professor, Brother), and simply call him "Leonard." His son, James, remembered that his father "always had a book but the children never minded because he would always put it down and without saying, 'Let me finish this chapter first.'"[6] All of this is commendable!

We also want to be absolutely clear that *Faith Crisis* is not about belittling or criticizing Leonard Arrington as a person. If he was broken down by the side of the road, we would be among the first to stop and give him a lift. The message of this book is not a consideration of whether Leonard Arrington, Richard Bushman, and other progressive evangelists were—or as the case may be, still are—nice, friendly, congenial individuals.

Faith Crisis is about two divergent worldviews—about ideology and history—but most importantly, its core intent is to clarify the issues and bring discussions that occurred 'behind closed doors' into the light. Every member should be given the opportunity to judge and choose what they wish to believe. True choice requires the possession of correct information. Some members might ask, *Do I have a right to make such a decision concerning what is right and what is wrong? Should I not defer to the opinion of a trained historian, or should I not relinquish my sentiment to an ecclesiastical leader?*

In a revelation given to the Prophet Joseph Smith on September 11, 1831, the Lord charged every member of The Church of Jesus Christ of Latter-day Saints with a sacred duty—the duty to judge for themselves:

> ❚❚ I, the Lord, have made my church in these last days like unto a judge sitting on a hill, or in a high place, to judge the nations. For it shall come to pass that the *inhabitants of Zion shall judge all things* pertaining to Zion.[7]

Now, more than ever, we believe that members need to hear both sides; they need all of the information—all of the data, theories, and interpretations provided to them for their own review, without fear of repercussion. How else can the inhabitants of Zion judge concerning matters in Zion, as the Lord has instructed? Without open dialogue, truth cannot be weighed against falsehood. Both sides in this debate

---

6   "In Memoriam, Leonard J. Arrington," *Journal of Mormon History* 25, no. 1 (February 15, 1999), 8.

7   Doctrine and Covenants 64:37-38; emphasis added.

must be *honest* and *open* about where they stand. The discussion must come out from behind closed doors. Then, and *only* then, will each and every member be empowered with the choice and the freedom to decide as the Lord has instructed.

Shall the Youth of Zion Falter?

William Wilberforce is reported to have said: "You may choose to look the other way but you can never say again that you did not know."[8] Regardless of the original author, these words still resonate with us. Once we became aware of the shattered lives, broken hearts, divided homes, and dwindling numbers of faithful members, we knew what we must do—and there was no looking back. For the past decade and a half, I have been working with my father, sometimes day and night, to produce documentaries, deliver presentations, write books, and engage in online discussion with those who are struggling. We have received thoughtful and encouraging feedback that our efforts are making a difference, helping to strengthen the feeble knees of many who have succumbed to misleading propaganda. But we know we have only begun to scratch the surface, to tap the tip of the iceberg. The organization (Joseph Smith Foundation) that began as a few families has grown to include many volunteers who consecrate their free hours and energy to defend the Restoration.

What has motivated these sacrifices? Why do we care? Throughout the world today, there is a serious welfare mentality that is wreaking havoc in our government, in our culture, in our families, and even in our Church. Far too many sit back in ease, assuming, and sometimes even exclaiming, that "The government will fix it. The Church will fix it. The government will set up a program. The Church will set up a program. If my neighbor is hungry, the government will help them, and if not, the Church will feed them."

However, in direct opposition to this attitude and mindset, President Ezra Taft Benson gave an excellent talk in 1965 entitled, "Not Commanded in All Things." Speaking of the freedom issue, he counseled:

---

8 *William Wilberforce: Greatest Works* (Alachua: Bridge-Logos, 2007), 15.

Joseph Smith by David Lindsley

" . . . the last neutralizer that the devil uses most effectively—it is simply this: "Don't do anything in the fight for freedom until the Church sets up its own specific program to save the Constitution." This brings us right back to the scripture I opened with today—to those slothful servants who will not do anything until they are "compelled in all things." Maybe the Lord will never set up a specific church program for the purpose of saving the Constitution. . . .

The Prophet Joseph Smith declared it will be the elders of Israel who will step forward to help save the Constitution, not the Church. And have we elders been warned? Yes, we have. And have we elders been given the guidelines? Yes indeed, we have.

. . . The longer we wait, the heavier the chains, the deeper the blood, the more the persecution and the less we can carry out our God-given mandate and world-wide mission. The war in heaven is raging on earth today. Are you being neutralized in the battle?[9]

This timeless principle applies to the faith crisis erupting among millennials, returned missionaries, and even the older generation. Are we going to wait for someone else to stand and defend Joseph Smith? Shall we bury our heads in the sand while our friends, our children, and our grandchildren abandon the faith? Are we to pretend that all is well in Zion until it is too late, and we wake up to the realization that the Restoration is lost?

True to the Faith

For our part, this is our witness—our cherished testimony that the Gospel of Jesus Christ has been restored to the Earth, that Joseph Smith stood as a righteous prophet of God, that there are answers to every difficult faith crisis issue, and that the Restoration of the Gospel holds the **answers** to solve even the world's deepest doubts, its severest trials, and its most complicated dilemmas. This is *our* Gospel. This is *our* home. This is *our* Church—the Church we love— and we will not stand idly by in this war.

If the Constitution is saved, if the Prophet Joseph Smith's character is defended, and if the Restoration is preserved, it will be because we, the people, "the inhabitants of Zion," the members of the Church, the remnant of Latter-day Israel, are willing to draw a line in the sand, and to rise up, speak, and act. The time is now. *We* are the Church, and *we* are Latter-day Israel. The Gospel of Jesus Christ is being trampled in the dust; and we, as members, have made sacred covenants to stand "as witnesses of God at all times and in all things, and in all places."[10] How are you keeping that covenant?

L. Hannah Stoddard
Author, film producer, speaker, educator
Executive Director, Joseph Smith Foundation®

---

9   Ezra Taft Benson, *Conference Report*, April 1965, 125.

10 Mosiah 18:9.

1

Unlocking Sealed Diaries

A New Voice From the Dust

In October 2001, a group of employees from the Church Historian's Office descended on the Special Collections and Archives at Utah State University. For three weeks these researchers spent over 1,000 hours collectively, searching intently and poring over Leonard J. Arrington's papers housed at USU. The vast accumulation included xerox scans and typescripts of historical documents—books, pamphlets, magazines, newspaper clippings, scrapbooks, research notes, correspondence, and personal papers—a veritable time capsule of the Arrington epoch. In all, "The Leonard J. Arrington Papers, 1839-1999" contained 727 boxes, grouped into 13 series or categories.

One portion of those 727 boxes, however, was locked from public view: Leonard Arrington's diaries. In contrast to a typical personal record, Arrington's extensive writings, consisting of over 40,000 pages,[1] filled 50 boxes and occupied 26 linear feet of shelving—all of it locked away from the roving eyes of the research team presently searching the USU repository.

Leonard Arrington's Diary

Leonard Arrington had passed away two years prior to this gathering, leaving strict instructions that his diaries were not to be read until ten years subsequent to his death. Furthermore, when a microfilm

---

1   Leonard J. Arrington and Gary James Bergera, *Confessions of a Mormon Historian: The Diaries of Leonard J. Arrington, 1971-1997*, vol. 1 (Salt Lake City: Signature Books, 2018), vii.

copy of entries he penned, dictated, and typed while functioning as Church Historian (1972-1982) was created by the Church Historical Department, Arrington "explicitly forbade any church official from reading them for a period of twenty-five years past his death, which would have been 2024."[2] Arrington had recorded his sentiments for future Latter-day Saints and fellow historians, but did not feel comfortable having these entries examined directly. "Because it is frank and candid and aimed at helping historians in the future," Arrington wrote, "some of its contents might be damaging to persons still alive."[3]

For decades, Arrington kept copious records with the specific purpose of narrating the story of progressive struggle and triumph for future generations of Latter-day Saints. His daughter, Susan Arrington Madsen, reflected:

> Some may wonder if Leonard Arrington intended for the general public to read his private writings. That can be answered with a resounding, *Yes!* . . . he fully intended for his diary to be made available to the public after a reasonable amount of time had passed.[4]

The entries typed out while Arrington served as Church Historian document his perspective on the battle he waged and generalled as he sought to introduce and establish New Mormon History into the mainstream historical narrative of the Church.

Writing to future members, Arrington recorded his lament regarding "the relentless, sometimes crippling ire of his faith's most conservative leaders—from apostle Boyd K. Packer to eventual

---

2   Gregory A. Prince, *Leonard Arrington and the Writing of Mormon History* (Salt Lake City, UT: Tanner Trust Fund and J. Willard Marriott Library, 2016), 464. The microfilm copy of Leonard Arrington's diaries, given to the Church Historical Department, was given with the agreement that "forbade any church official from reading them for a period of twenty-five years past his death." The original diaries housed at Utah State University were originally given the same 25-year restriction. However, after a discussion with his children, the embargo on the USU originals was amended to ten years, resulting in their release in September 2010.

3   Genevieve Draper, "Knowing the Man in History," (2010), Arrington Student Writing Award Winners, Paper 4, 6, https://digitalcommons.usu.edu/cgi/viewcontent.cgi?article=1005&context=arrington_stwriting.

4   Leonard J. Arrington and Gary James Bergera, *Confessions of a Mormon Historian: The Diaries of Leonard J. Arrington*, 1971-1997, vol. 1 (Salt Lake City: Signature Books, 2018), ix.

"Leonard J. Arrington, the 'Dean of Mormon History" photographed in the 1950s" by Susan Arrington Madsen under CC BY-SA 3.0.

church President Ezra Taft Benson."[5] Arrington documented private meetings with general authorities, including his interactions with the President of the Church. He recorded personal conversations with friends, and sometimes spent time venting page after page— detailing his frustrations, giving life to his lament over the present state of affairs, and expressing his hope for change in the future. In addition to revealing many of his personal thoughts, beliefs, and hopes for Latter-day Saint history, Arrington documented specific names and conversations with many of his colleagues, associates, and disputants, some of whom are still alive today, and who continue working in influential positions.

Understanding the controversial nature of these behind-closed-doors conversations, Arrington intended that his diaries would remain entirely locked up and inaccessible for at least a decade. However, in 2001, just two years after his passing, it was revealed

5   Bob Mims, "New collection of Leonard Arrington's vast journals shows battles the Mormon historian had with LDS leaders over telling the truth about the church's past," *The Salt Lake Tribune*, May 9, 2018, https://www.sltrib.com/religion/2018/05/09/new-collection-of-leonard-arringtons-vast-journals-shows-battles-the-mormon-historian-had-with-lds-leaders-over-telling-the-truth-about-the-churchs-past/.

that someone from the Church's offices had broken the agreement and read the diaries.

Controversy over the Archives

The Utah State University Leonard J. Arrington Papers archive, excepting Arrington's diaries, was opened to the public in 2001, allowing individuals to access his research projects, teaching files, correspondence, speeches, and his extensive scrapbook-like collection. Once the collection was released, employees from the Church Historian's Office began scouring the contents. They were not permitted to access the personal diaries, also housed at USU; but the rest of Arrington's collection contained files the Church suspected belonged to them.

Gregory A. Prince, Arrington's biographer, recorded a pivotal event that created a storm of controversy:

> One afternoon . . . Steven Sorensen, an administrator in the Church Historical Department, went outside the search room of USU Special Collections and used a [public] phone to call someone at Church headquarters. He apparently used phrases during this phone conversation such as "church ownership," "controversial," and "censorship."[6]

Sorensen had not realized that a USU student had been standing quietly behind him, eavesdropping and taking in every word. After relaying the sensitive information to the student newspaper, an article shortly appeared, "questioning what the Church was looking for and why, and the whole controversy then exploded into virtually every newspaper in the state of Utah."[7] *The Herald Journal* in Logan, Utah reported:

> An introduction to the Arrington exhibit on the USU Special Collections website describes his tenure as historian as controversial. He gained a reputation for promoting open access to church documents but also came into conflict with church authorities for not promoting faith-affirming history,

---

6   Gregory A. Prince, *Leonard Arrington and the Writing of Mormon History* (Salt Lake City, UT: Tanner Trust Fund and J. Willard Marriott Library, 2016), 461; brackets in original.

7   Ibid.

the introduction states. Arrington was given full access to the private archives of the church. Now church officials say that privilege has been misused.[8]

When *The Herald Journal* met with Richard E. Turley, Jr., managing director of the Family and Church History Department, Dale Bills, Church public relations official, and Berne S. Broadbent, attorney for the Church—Turley, speaking for the group, argued: "The written agreement between the church and Arrington was clear . . . Leonard Arrington expressly agreed that historical documents or copies of historical documents that he used in his work should be returned to the church and not copied or distributed to anyone else."[9] The Church's legal department sent letters to USU, insisting that over 60% of Arrington's papers

> ## The legal department insisted over 60% of Arrington's papers were Church property

were the property of the Church—and they wanted the documents released and delivered to them immediately.

In an attempt to avoid the brewing storm, negotiations between the Church and the University ensued as both sides began to work out a settlement. The discussion began to unravel on Friday, the week before Thanksgiving, when someone from the Church complained that "there are some things in Leonard's journals that we are not very comfortable with, and we think ought to be taken out."

Dr. F. Ross Peterson, a USU professor present at the legal-negotiation meeting, asked in surprise, "Have you read the journals?" The exchange intensified:

❚❚ They [the Church's spokesperson] said, "Well, when we receive things, we have to read them." I said, "Well, have you read the journals? And how many of you have read them?" Then all of

---

8   Arrin Brunson, "LDS papers for a few eyes only? Church determined to keep documents out of public domain," *The Herald Journal News*, October 26, 2001, https://www.hjnews.com/lds-papers-for-a-few-eyes-only-church-determined-to-keep-documents-out-of-public/article_3d564804-7af9-5dca-85b6-0afeef59ce0d.html.

9   Ibid.

a sudden, George Daines, the lawyer for the Arringtons, said, "This meeting is over."[10]

When Daines, the Arrington family attorney, learned that a Church employee had read the sealed diaries, he rushed out of the legal conference to call Arrington's daughter, Susan, who hastily provided a copy of the agreement entered into between the Church and her father. In essence, it stated that the microfilm copies of Arrington's diaries held in the Church Historical Library would not be read for 25 years.[11]

Daines knew they had a solid case when he announced to all those presently convened: "It's over. With that, in and of itself, it's over."[12] As Arrington's biographer, Greg Prince, noted: "By acknowledging in the meeting that they had violated the terms of the agreement, the church representatives had placed themselves not only in a very awkward position, but also one of potential legal liability."[13]

The Church had read the diaries although the contract strictly forbade them from doing so. In searching the diaries, multifarious troubling entries were discovered. According to author and editor Gary James Bergera,[14] forty specific entries that "offend[ed] church sensibilities" were requested to be removed:

❝ ... the church told the family it should remove forty entries from the diaries that risked offending church sensibilities. After some discussion, the number of entries the church took exception to was reduced to fifteen, with the following rationales given:

10　Gregory A. Prince, *Leonard Arrington and the Writing of Mormon History* (Salt Lake City, UT: Tanner Trust Fund and J. Willard Marriott Library, 2016), 463.

11　The diaries located at Utah State University were locked for 10 years. However, "when Leonard allowed the Historical Department to make a microfilm of his diaries up to the time that he was released as church historian—1982—he explicitly forbade any church official from reading them for a period of twenty-five years past his death, which would have been 2024." Ibid., 464.

12　Ibid., 463.

13　Gregory A. Prince, *Leonard Arrington and the Writing of Mormon History* (Salt Lake City, UT: Tanner Trust Fund and J. Willard Marriott Library, 2016), 464.

14　Progressive author and editor Gary Bergera has served as a director of *Dialogue* and former managing director of Signature Books. Bergera is presently the managing director of the Smith-Pettit Foundation, Salt Lake City and served as the editor for the published edition of Leonard Arrington's diaries spanning from his years as Church historian and up to his death, *Confessions of A Mormon Historian: The Diaries of Leonard J. Arrington, 1971-1999.*

Six entries that have to do with temple ordinances, temple garments[,] and an untrue story about Joseph Smith: March 9, 1981; March 26, 1979; December 3, 1974; October 8, 1974; January 15, 1973; and June 22, 1972.

Nine entries that have incomplete, unfair[,] or untrue stories about the Brethren: March 6, 1981; June 30, 1980; March 10, 1980; January 6, 1978; April 11, 1977; February 4, 1975; March 29, 1973; February 8, 1973; February 13, 1973.[15]

In all, the Church was seeking over 60% of the Arrington collection and the redaction of likely 40 or so entries in the diaries. However, this new revelation gave the Arrington family grounds for cause of action, and the Church's legal department knew it. It would not take long to finalize negotiations; and when finished, the Church left with a single, half-filled box of documents—a mere trifle, representing less than one half of one percent of the massive collection. Moreover, the Church withdrew its request to redact the offending entries from Arrington's diary.

Arrington's Biography

"Leonard had a way of stirring things up,"[16] observed progressive historian and mentored friend of Leonard Arrington, Thomas G. Alexander. Alexander referred specifically to Arrington's article, "An Economic Interpretation of 'The Word of Wisdom,'" carried in *BYU Studies,* which caused the journal's year-long suspension. However, one could reasonably apply the comment directly to many incidents and circumstances during Arrington's long tenure with Mormon history. This is owing to his ambition to liberalize and intellectualize the Church.

Arrington's apprehension over the premature publication of his story was a nagging concern for some time before his death in February of 1999. Years earlier, in 1981, he had commissioned Lavina Fielding Anderson to compile his memoirs. Anderson completed and submitted a draft of her biographical sketch of Arrington's life, titled *Doves and Serpents: The Activities of Leonard Arrington as Church Historian, 1972-1982.* Arrington entrusted a few copies to

---

15   Leonard J. Arrington and Gary James Bergera, *Confessions of a Mormon Historian: The Diaries of Leonard J. Arrington*, 1971-1997, vol. 3 (Salt Lake City: Signature Books, 2018), 666; brackets in original.

16   Ibid., 671.

close friends and family, but was insistent that it "must not become public knowledge":

> **❝** It's a pretty intimate history, and MUST NOT BECOME PUBLIC KNOWLEDGE because it essentially gives the story of THE GOOD GUYS and THE BAD GUYS. The General Authorities, in that work are the Bad Guys, and it would have been a far more fair approach to have made it a story of The Good Guys v. the Good Guys. After all, one must consider the point of view of the Defenders of the Faith. Good men, betrayed to some extent by their own limitations.[17]

In 1988, Arrington's son Carl urged him to write his own autobiography, explaining to his father that he stood "at the fulcrum of the intellectual mind of a major religious movement,"[18] and that "The Army needs a leader with charisma to awaken and mobilize them. I say this not to flatter you, but perhaps to plant a seed."[19]

Arrington began writing and compiling his experiences. But when former Assistant Church Historian R. Davis Bitton reviewed his first draft in 1993, he warned Arrington that his account would be seen as an "attack," and cautioned him: "I have to say that I don't think the time is ripe for going public with a naming of names. (And for you to shield them with phrases like 'a certain general authority' would take the punch out of it.)"[20] Carol Lynn Pearson recalled: "He tells everything like it was, recounts run-ins with Boyd Packer and others. He said they won't like that."[21] Historian D. Michael Quinn remembered Arrington saying "he was expecting to be excommunicated because

"I don't think the time is ripe for going public with a naming of names."

---

17   LJA to Children, November 30, 1982; LJAHA, Series X, Box 102, fd. 11.

18   Gregory A. Prince, *Leonard Arrington and the Writing of Mormon History* (Salt Lake City, UT: Tanner Trust Fund and J. Willard Marriott Library, 2016), 439.

19   Ibid., 440.

20   Ibid.

21   Ibid., 441.

of what he had published in the book."[22] In the end, however, Arrington decided to temper the telling of his story, making it "decidedly less candid than his diary entries, letters to his children, and conversations with friends and colleagues as reflected in subsequent interviews."[23] He would save his journals for a future generation of members who, Arrington anticipated, would not be antagonistic to the New Mormon Historians.[24] Arrington's daughter Susan recalled:

/// When times were tough, especially while he was serving as LDS Church Historian, Dad was painfully frank in his personal journals in ways he was not when composing his autobiography, *Adventures of a Church Historian*. He did not hesitate to document his frustrations with those who opposed his projects and who would sometimes resort to seemingly petty comments and actions. . . .

It was wise of my father to restrict access to the diary from any and all except his three children until ten years had elapsed since his death, during which time most of the issues that had paralyzed his ability to meet his original goals as Church Historian had become less sensitive and enough people had passed away . . .

. . . he saw himself as part of a broader movement, rather than as a lone voice in the wilderness.[25]

With the arrival of 2010 and the passage of a decade following the death of Leonard Arrington in 1999, his diaries were opened to the public. The microfilm copy of Leonard Arrington's diaries, given to the Church Historical Department, was given with the agreement that "forbade any church official from reading them for

---

22   Ibid., 442.

23   Ibid., 443.

24   According to a *Salt Lake Tribune* interview with Susan Arrington Madsen, "the diary includes some rich nuggets that will interest researchers, her father did not record history 'warts and all.' 'He had this wisdom,' she says. 'He was cautious what he put in there [the diary] because he knew it would be read.'" Kristen Moulton, "Diary of famed Mormon historian reveals more of the man," *The Salt Lake Tribune*, September 24, 2020, https://archive.sltrib.com/article. php?id=50275670&itype=cmsid; brackets in original.

25   Leonard J. Arrington and Gary James Bergera, *Confessions of a Mormon Historian: The Diaries of Leonard J. Arrington*, 1971-1997, vol. 1 (Salt Lake City: Signature Books, 2018), viii-x.

a period of twenty-five years past his death."[26] The original diaries housed at Utah State University were originally given the same 25-year restriction. However, after a discussion with his children, the embargo on the USU originals was amended to ten years, resulting in their release in September 2010.

What would be the response of Church members? Were they ready to know of the decades-long battle between progressive scholars and traditionalist leaders—a battle for the heart and head of the faith? This was combat between the old and the new historians—a struggle held almost exclusively behind closed doors. Arrington's archenemy, President Ezra Taft Benson, preceded Arrington's passing by five years and had now been dead for about sixteen years. How had his conservative viewpoint and traditionalist teachings on history held up—had they become outdated and abandoned in favor of progressivism? How would the Latter-day Saints react when forced to face the details of the unabridged Leonard Arrington narrative?

The *Salt Lake Tribune* carried the announcement: "The newly opened diary of Leonard J. Arrington, Mormonism's most influential historian of the late 20th century, reveals a life imbued with the sense that he was chosen by heaven to help the LDS Church and its people truthfully tell the Mormon story."[27] In 2018, Signature Books published an edited edition of Arrington's diaries, *Confessions of a Mormon Historian*, covering the time he was working at Church headquarters, from 1972-1982, acclaimed as revealing "battles the Mormon historian had with LDS leaders over telling the truth about the church's past."[28]

What were these intense battles, and why the passionate, protracted struggle? How does this war impact each and every Latter-day Saint today?

---

26   Gregory A. Prince, *Leonard Arrington and the Writing of Mormon History* (Salt Lake City, UT: Tanner Trust Fund and J. Willard Marriott Library, 2016), 464.

27   Kristen Moulton, "Diary of famed Mormon historian reveals more of the man," *The Salt Lake Tribune*, September 24, 2020, https://archive.sltrib.com/article.php?id=50275670&itype=cmsid.

28   Bob Mims, "New collection of Leonard Arrington's vast journals shows battles the Mormon historian had with LDS leaders over telling the truth about the church's past," *The Salt Lake Tribune,* May 9, 2018, https://www.sltrib.com/religion/2018/05/09/new-collection-of-leonard-arringtons-vast-journals-shows-battles-the-mormon-historian-had-with-lds-leaders-over-telling-the-truth-about-the-churchs-past/.

2

REJECTING THE FAITH
Mormonism's Lost Generation

The Church of Jesus Christ of Latter-day Saints was established in 1830 by the Prophet Joseph Smith upon what some have termed "traditionalist" ideals and doctrines. As the Restoration of the Gospel began to unfold, the Prophet warned the Saints in Nauvoo of a counterfeit gospel and kingdom that would unfold in contradiction to the Lord's system and plan. "In relation to the Kingdom of God, the devil always sets up his Kingdom at the very same time in opposition to God." The Prophet additionally taught, "False prophets *always* arise to oppose the true prophets, and they will prophesy so very near the truth that they will deceive almost the very chosen ones."[1] The Prophet Joseph's prediction that the adversary would establish his converse, counter-gospel to deceive even "the humble followers of Christ"[2] was essentially forgotten by the Saints—and for some at least, a tower for watching the enemy was never constructed, making it impossible to set a watchman on that tower.[3]

---

1   Joseph Smith, May 12, 1844, History, 1838–1856, volume F-1, p. 18, The Joseph Smith Papers.

2   "They wear stiff necks and high heads; yea, and because of pride, and wickedness, and abominations, and whoredoms, they have all gone astray save it be a few, who are the humble followers of Christ; nevertheless, they are led, that in many instances they do err because they are taught by the precepts of men." 2 Nephi 28:14.

"And my vineyard has become corrupted every whit; and there is none which doeth good save it be a few; and they err in many instances because of priestcrafts, all having corrupt minds." Doctrine & Covenants 33:4.

3   Doctrine & Covenants 101:46-51.

In the ensuing decades, as progressive and liberal philosophies swept the United States of America during the latter 19th and early 20th centuries, the children and grandchildren of Latter-day Saint pioneers were not immune to the shifting culture. Desperate for their children to benefit from the educational opportunities they had not personally received, many well-meaning fathers and mothers sent their unsuspecting and trusting youth to receive tutelage at universities and institutions increasingly dominated by secular, anti-traditional, progressive ideals.

However, the sacrifices for worldly prestige, credentialed schooling, and sophistication came at a heavy price: Young men and women were returning from their experience with higher learning; and yet they were disgruntled with traditionalist doctrines, practices, and the presumably outdated culture within the Church. Many abandoned their faith, while still others became closet nonbelievers. This cynical, doubting group became known as "Mormonism's Lost Generation." Progressive Latter-day Saint author L. T. Downing commented:

> As Mormonism rounded the bend of the early 20th century, children who had not known Joseph Smith or experienced the pioneer trek came to adulthood—and many of them began leaving the church, earning for themselves the nickname "the lost generation." These were people who didn't experience the miracles of early Mormonism, nor did they understand their parents' testimonies against the gritty reality of the industrial age.[4] The old shoe didn't fit.[5]

Others among this new group of unbelievers sought opportunities to change the Church by acquiring influential positions at institutions such as Brigham Young University. In a story outlined in the first volume of this series, *We Were NOT Betrayed!*, a group of progressive academics—most of them members of the Church who

---

4   "Now it came to pass that there were many of the rising generation that could not understand the words of king Benjamin, being little children at the time he spake unto his people; and they did not believe the tradition of their fathers . . . For it came to pass that they did deceive many with their flattering words, who were in the church, and did cause them to commit many sins . . ." Mosiah 26: 1,6.

5   Lisa Torcasso Downing, "Today's Lost Generation and the Crisis of Trust," Life Outside The Book of Mormon Belt, February 6, 2019, https:// outsidethebookofmormonbelt.com.

jokingly called themselves "the Swearing Elders"—began meeting in the 1950s. These 'intellectuals' hailed from BYU, Utah State University, the University of Utah, and even the Institute of Religion in Salt Lake City. As one member, University of Utah professor Ray Canning, noted:

*// *Nobody cared about the "swearing," and nobody cared about the "elders," but the name sort of said that this was a group of people who were more relaxed in Mormonism, and certainly more on the liberal side than on the ultraconservative side of the Mormon and political and theological spectrum, and therefore more apt to look at Mormonism naturalistically[6] as well as supernaturalistically.[7]

A frequent host and primary organizer of the Swearing Elders, Sterling M. McMurrin held a University of Utah professorship, taught formerly under the Church's Education System (CES), and acted as United States Commissioner of Education under President John F. Kennedy. Despite McMurrin's long affiliation and extensive influence within the Church, he did not believe Adam and Eve ever existed, that the First Vision literally occurred, that Jesus Christ was divine, that the Book of Mormon was historical, or that the spiritual realm existed as traditionalists maintain.[8]

William (Bill) Mulder, a co-founder of this unorthodox, high-minded, and intellectual circle, commented: "I think if anything marks the Swearing Elders, it was a healthy skepticism about anything that the Brethren—early or late—uttered, and the last resort was always a sense of rationality, the attempt to be rational

---

6   "The philosophical belief that everything arises from natural properties and causes, and supernatural or spiritual explanations are excluded or discounted." "naturalism," Oxford Dictionary, https://www.lexico.com/en/definition/naturalism.

"The great majority of contemporary philosophers would happily accept naturalism ... they would both reject 'supernatural' entities, and allow that science is a possible route (if not necessarily the only one) to important truths about the 'human spirit'." "Naturalism," Stanford Encyclopedia of Philosophy, https://plato.stanford.edu/entries/naturalism/.

7   Thomas A. Blakely, "The Swearing Elders: The First Generation of Modern Mormon Intellectuals," *Sunstone* 10 (September 1985): 10-11.

8   Sterling M. McMurrin and L. Jackson Newell, *Matters of Conscience* (Salt Lake City: Signature Books, 1996), http://signaturebookslibrary.org/heresies-and-criticism/.

about everything . . . ."[9] It is worth noting that traditionalists would disagree with Mulder's definition of "rational," especially as he used it in this context. The Swearing Elders believed that to be rational, one must of necessity employ the philosophy of 'rationalism.'[10]

Hugh W. Nibley served for over fifty years as a professor at BYU, and had his own experience with the Swearing Elders. Nibley's biography, *Hugh Nibley: A Consecrated Life*, details his interaction with the Swearing Elders during a meeting at the University of Utah:

> At some point before his 1955 debate with Sterling McMurrin, Hugh was invited to speak to a meeting at the University of Utah, of the "Swearing Elders"—a group of liberal Mormons associated with Utah universities. After giving his presentation, Hugh says they took him aside and told him "You're among friends now, you can say what you really feel about the Book of Mormon." Hugh simply bore his testimony that the Book of Mormon is, in fact, a true record of an ancient people and that Joseph Smith was a prophet. "Oh, were they mad," Hugh states. "They were just boiling." He recalls one member of the group launching into a harangue about the Book of Mormon and how "we have to get rid of it. It's driving the best minds out of the church! You can't see it, but with my training, I know it. Joseph Smith was a deceiver, but he was a sly deceiver." Hugh was chilled by such reactions: "They had a real active hatred of the Book of Mormon." These were, for the most part, members of the Church in good standing.[11]

When Nibley returned home that night, his wife Phyllis encountered a "visibly rattled"[12] husband due to the evening's entanglements.

Thomas A. Blakely observed in a *Sunstone* article, "The Swearing Elders: The First Generation of Modern Mormon Intellectuals":

---

9   Thomas A. Blakely, "The Swearing Elders: The First Generation of Modern Mormon Intellectuals," *Sunstone* 10 (September 1985): 11.

10   Rationalism, "The practice or principle of basing opinions and actions on reason and knowledge rather than on religious belief or emotional response." "Rationalism," Lexicon, https://www.lexico.com/definition/rationalism.

11   Boyd J. Petersen, *Hugh Nibley: A Consecrated Life* (Salt Lake City, UT: Greg Kofford Books, 2002), 160.

12   Ibid., footnote 52.

// Eventually, the probing and questioning of the intellectuals like the Swearing Elders attracted the attention of Church authorities, who regarded the meeting with suspicion and probably some confusion. Such intellectuals posed a potential threat, the officials felt, because as professors they could corrupt the youth of the Church.

> ... one of the most important factors appears to be the degree of secular education attained by the members of the study group. The Swearing Elders was the first generation of educators who in large numbers had studied at secular universities. Consequently, several of these individuals began to apply their scholarly methods and academic skepticism to their religion.[13]

While some progressive scholars experiencing intellectual or philosophical dissonance and disagreement with the traditional faith abandoned the Church and the Gospel, others sought to find a compromise—a way to blend their progressive skepticism and scholarly methods taught in the higher echelons of academia with the traditional tenets of Mormonism. Every academic field was subject to the stroke of progressive reinterpretation: civil law, philosophy, economics, archaeology, anthropology, political science, psychology, biology, geology, music, art—and particularly, history.

Driven, in part, by a desire to produce history that would be acceptable among their secular, irreligious, non-Mormon colleagues, a growing number began seeking for a new progressive approach to the writing of Latter-day Saint history. Nearly all credentialed Latter-day Saint historians began shifting their approach from a traditionalist narrative to one more accepted by their progressive, non-Mormon colleagues. This had become the new trend in writing the history of the Church, and only a courageous few stood up to challenge the surge of change and capitulation.[14]

---

13 Thomas A. Blakely, "The Swearing Elders: The First Generation of Modern Mormon Intellectuals," *Sunstone* 10 (September 1985): 11, 13.

14 For example, Hyrum Andrus was a Ph.D. historian, author, and professor at Brigham Young University. Andrus believed "the plan of life revealed to Joseph Smith could solve the social, economic and political problems of the world." He would specialize in the life and teachings of the Prophet Joseph Smith, authoring many works including *They Knew the Prophet, Doctrines of the Kingdom,* and *Joseph Smith and World Government.* He is considered by traditionalists to be a solid historian. "About Dr. Andrus," HyrumAndrus.com, http://www.hyrumandrus. com/about-dr-andrus.html.

Leonard J. Arrington—author, historian, and economist—a man revered by many as the father of New Mormon History, earned the moniker, "dean of Mormon historians." Arrington would play the primary role as mentor, leader, and inspiration behind countless historians and authors in his own era; and his influence continues and has been magnified in intensity today. Arrington's advocates and devotees occupy influential roles throughout the Church: leaders of the Joseph Smith Papers project, prominent biographers, Church historians, and professors at the Brigham Young Universities, as well as other institutions. These prominent influencers comprise the primary and essentially solo voice of modern Latter-day Saint history.

Leonard Arrington was a personal friend of Sterling McMurrin and attended several of the Swearing Elders meetings, noting in his journal:

" ... I did not see this group as anti-mormon or anti-gospel or anti-religion in any sense. To me, the discussions provided intellectual support for our traditional beliefs and practices. To say this another way—and it may sound incredible—my own testimony was bolstered as the result of attending these sessions. . . . I learned much from these brethren. Basically these discussions were an early example of what Dialogue was to do later, to provide a forum of Mormon intellectuals and to help intellectuals with gospel questions and problems. I did not at any time see this as a subversive group or as a destructive influence.[15]

As detailed in *Faith Crisis, Volume 1,* Arrington embraced, crafted, and sponsored the new progressive approach to Latter-day Saint history while eschewing the traditional foundations of the Church and Gospel in this latter-day dispensation. He recorded that he had read the Book of Mormon and Bible all the way through only once, when he was 13 years old—but never did so entirely again, admitting in his diary that he had "never been an avid student of the scriptures."[16] His father encouraged Leonard to serve a mission, offering to shoulder the entire expense himself,

---

15   Leonard J. Arrington Diaries, August 18, 1978; Leonard J. Arrington and Gary James Bergera, *Confessions of a Mormon Historian: The Diaries of Leonard J. Arrington*, 1971-1997, vol. 2 (Salt Lake City: Signature Books, 2018), 603.

16   Leonard J. Arrington Diaries, September 25, 1978; Ibid., 632.

even in the face of financial hardship during the Great Depression. However, Leonard declined, choosing instead to attend college at the University of Idaho.[17] While working through a faith crisis at the U of I, Arrington converted to an ideology based on Darwinian Evolution, abandoned Creationism, embraced Biblical Criticism,[18] and accepted the supposition that the narratives in the Bible represented primarily myth and allegory, and that the "Scriptures are *not* themselves divine revelation."[19]

Arrington initially pursued economics; but during the winter of 1950, he experienced what he termed an "epiphany" wherein he felt God had called him to write a new history for the Latter-day Saints consistent with his personal progressive understanding.[20] He felt called of God to change the direction of both the Church and its people. He went on to write his dissertation, *Great Basin Kingdom,* reinterpreting the history of the Latter-day Saints in Utah through a critical economic and liberal perspective. In this and other works,

---

17   James and Hannah Stoddard, *Faith Crisis, Volume 1: We Were NOT Betrayed!* (Joseph Smith Foundation, 2020), 115.

18   Biblical Criticism is the academic analysis of the Bible which attempts to determine whether the text is historically accurate, who originally authored the texts, when the Bible was written, and whether portions were copied from earlier oral traditions—such as stories, legends, myths, etc. Since "biblical criticism generally treats the Bible as a human book, rather than accepting it as the inspired Word of God," Biblical Criticism has led many scholars to determine that the Creation, the story of Adam and Eve, Noah's worldwide Flood, the account of Jonah and the whale, Moses' Exodus, and other miraculous events, are merely fictional stories with an allegorical purpose. See more in *Faith Crisis, Volume 1: We Were NOT Betrayed!*, Chapter 10, "Criticism Leads the Camel's Nose Into the Tent."

19   James and Hannah Stoddard, *Faith Crisis, Volume 1: We Were NOT Betrayed!* (Joseph Smith Foundation, 2020), 137; Leonard J. Arrington Diaries, July 15, 1977; Leonard J. Arrington and Gary James Bergera, *Confessions of a Mormon Historian: The Diaries of Leonard J. Arrington*, 1971-1997, vol. 2 (Salt Lake City: Signature Books, 2018), 390.

20   During the winter of 1950, Arrington received what he described as a "peak experience" while working on his doctoral dissertation. Also known as his "third epiphany," Arrington recorded that the event "sealed my devotion to Latter-day Saint history." While he was reviewing notes from "letters, diaries, and personal histories of the hundreds of past church leaders and members," Arrington recalled that he felt "a feeling of ecstasy" come over him, and in mystic language reminiscent of his earlier epiphany, he wrote of "an exhilaration that transported me once again to a higher level of consciousness." Arrington interpreted the experience as God telling him that his "research efforts were compatible with the divine restoration of the Church." With this, he felt that it was his mission to "write about their [19th-century Mormon] story." Leonard J. Arrington, *Adventures of a Church Historian* (University of Illinois Press, 1998), 28.

he strongly criticized President Brigham Young for his presumably failed economic directives, and took on the role of defending and promoting excommunicated dissenters, including spiritualists like William S. Godbe.[21]

A man of great energy, Arrington began to seek out, organize, network, and mentor progressive thought leaders throughout the Church and in the broader historical communities. He began hiring and mentoring recruits to write Mormon biographies and history. He made a point of attending historical conventions where he could connect with Mormon studies scholars, and through those connections, initiate discourse and exchange. In 1965, Arrington helped found the liberal Mormon History Association, and he anxiously supported the progressive Mormon studies publication, *Dialogue: A Journal of Mormon Thought,* co-founded by his friend, Eugene England. Arrington taught as a professor of economics at Utah State University, and as a professor of history at University of California, Los Angeles.[22]

By 1966, Arrington had been involved in discussions with Church leaders over scholarly history and other historiography projects. However, when President David O. McKay passed away in 1970, significant changes in the organization of the Church Historian's Office came under discussion. Elder Joseph Fielding Smith would assume the leadership of the Church, necessitating that he relinquish the office of Church Historian—a title he had held for forty years. During most of President Smith's approximately two-year service as President of the Church, Elder Howard W. Hunter would occupy the leadership position in the Historian's office; but that was soon destined to change. Leonard Arrington's influence within the Church would undergo a substantial boost and transformation, beginning with an invitation involving a phone call from Salt Lake City one cold January morning in 1972.

---

21   James and Hannah Stoddard, *Faith Crisis, Volume 1: We Were NOT Betrayed!* (Joseph Smith Foundation, 2020), 153.

22   Leonard Arrington also served as a Fulbright Professor of American Economics at the University of Genoa in Italy from 1958-1959 and a professor of Western American History at BYU from 1972 to 1987. He was involved in the founding of the Western Historical Quarterly and served as president of the Western History Association (1968–69), the Agricultural History Society (1969–70), and the Pacific Coast Branch of the American Historical Association (1981–82).

3

The New 'Undercover Liberal'
Church Historian

The sharp staccato of a telephone ring broke the silence in Leonard Arrington's office on a January morning in 1972.

"When will you next be in Salt Lake City?"

On the other end of the line, Arrington heard the voice of President N. Eldon Tanner, Second Counselor in the First Presidency to President Joseph Fielding Smith.

"I could come whenever [you wish] it," Arrington replied.

"How about yesterday?" President Tanner chuckled.[1]

Thus would begin one of the most transformative and controversial periods in Latter-day Saint Church History. Traditionalists would regard this period as a liberal era fraught with disconcerting progressive narratives and fractious agendas. Progressives would nostalgically remember the age as nothing less than Camelot—a title chosen comparing the era of the progressive control of the History Division to the majestic, mythical, and romanticized icon of the legendary King Arthur's realm.

The Beginning of Camelot

Thursday—the day after Leonard Arrington's January 5, 1972, phone conversation—the unsuspecting, 55-year-old professor drove to Salt Lake City to meet with President Tanner. Sitting in a large, well-appointed, leather easy chair, President Tanner came straight to the point:

1   Leonard J. Arrington Diaries, January 7, 1972; Leonard J. Arrington and Gary James Bergera, *Confessions of a Mormon Historian: The Diaries of Leonard J. Arrington*, 1971-1997, vol. 1 (Salt Lake City: Signature Books, 2018), 96.

" ... Brother Arrington, we need a Church Historian. You know that Brother [A. William] Lund died last February, and we have not replaced him. We would like to initiate a reorganization of the Church Historian's Office. ... Will you accept the position of Church Historian under such an arrangement?[2]

Elder Howard W. Hunter had been serving as Church Historian for two years after Joseph Fielding Smith relinquished the role to become President of the Church in 1970. Now, however, Church leaders were looking for what they saw as an upgrade to the department—both academically and professionally. "We are under obligations to write our history for the benefit of the generations to come," President Tanner told Arrington as they chatted in his office at Church Headquarters. "[W]e want it to be done in a thoroughly professional way, and we have confidence that you can do it."[3] In a letter to his son, Arrington mentioned the excitement he noticed among some members over this "departure from tradition."[4]

Overall, the entire Church administration was in the midst of receiving a thorough makeover. The First Presidency hired the consulting firm Cresap, McCormick & Paget to complete a thorough analysis and provide advice on structuring the bureaucratic and corporate side of the Church. During this period of change, the Church Historian's Office would officially become the Historical Department, comprised of three separate divisions, with Leonard Arrington as the new Church Historian and head of the History Division.

Events moved quickly; one week after Arrington's conversation with President Tanner, Howard W. Hunter was released, and the Church announced that Leonard J. Arrington would become the new Church Historian. During the following General Conference, his name was presented to the body of the Church for a sustaining vote.

Interestingly, reactions to the appointment included surprise from non-member critics of the Church, Jerald and Sandra Tanner. Jerald, a fifth-generation Latter-day Saint and descendant of John Tanner, along with his wife Sandra, a descendant of Brigham Young, resigned from the Church in 1960. Together, they began publishing

2   Ibid., 97; brackets in original.

3   Ibid., 98.

4   Gregory A. Prince, *Leonard Arrington and the Writing of Mormon History* (Salt Lake City, UT: Tanner Trust Fund and J. Willard Marriott Library, 2016), 160.

documents and research intended to impugn the character of Joseph Smith, to challenge the integrity of his revelations, and to criticize the Church and its history. The reaction of the Tanners to Arrington's appointment as Church Historian also included curiosity about the direction the Church was headed:

> *"* While Dr. Arrington is an active Mormon, many people consider him to be very liberal. . . .
>
> While the appointment of Leonard Arrington as Church Historian was certainly a surprise, the choice of James B. Allen and Davis Bitton as assistant historians made some wonder what direction the Church was headed in. Allen had previously published an article which undermined Joseph Smith's story of the First Vision, and Bitton had written an article in which he made an attack on the accuracy of Joseph Smith's *History of the Church*. Now, what could the Church leaders have had in mind when they appointed such liberals to the Church Historian's Office?[5]

Arrington himself also recognized the anomaly: "I suppose a lot of 'intellectuals' might have been pleased that an academic person who was a 'liberal' received the appointment."[6] Just how would this "liberal" change the Church's historical department? Time would tell.

Arrington Rehearses His Testimony

As Leonard Arrington walked into the new History Division, he brought with him his unique and different mindset—a primarily intellectual, even secular, approach to the Gospel. Previously, when he had been called as a high councilor in the Utah State University Stake in 1959, Arrington's ". . . speeches differed markedly from those of his peers. Theirs were generally sermons, but his were history lectures."[7] Writing to his children many years later, Arrington recalled:

---

5   Jerald and Sandra Tanner, "MORMONISM—Shadow or Reality?" http://www.utlm.org/newsletters/no47.htm#Arrington.

6   Gregory A. Prince, *Leonard Arrington and the Writing of Mormon History* (Salt Lake City, UT: Tanner Trust Fund and J. Willard Marriott Library, 2016), 160.

7   Ibid., 117.

❢❢ Today, as a by-product of a search for something else, I ran
across a box that had the cards I used in my talks on religious
themes when I was on the USU High Council and in the Stake
Presidency. Perhaps as many as forty or fifty different talks, all
delivered in Logan. I realize now that every talk I have given
since coming here was on a history topic. Not a single talk with
a religious theme.[8]

Arrington's inspiration for his "markedly different" sacrament
meeting talks came, in part, from lectures he had earlier devoured
while studying as a young college student at the University of Idaho.
He attended a lecture series titled, "Religion in Life Series,"[9] which
presented a "conscious attempt to harmonize religious thought
with secular thought." With pages of "full notes," Arrington, at
first hesitantly—then eagerly—embraced the 'modern' philosophies
taught by the lecturers. This frame of reference would influence and
predispose his thinking and approach for the next several decades.
Arrington commented that they "introduced [him] to religious
images and metaphors, and scriptures which I would never have
gotten from my <u>Mormon</u> experience . . ."[10] What specifically did these
lectures teach? Arrington noted that the equivalent could be found in
progressive publications such as *Dialogue, Sunstone, Exponent II*, and
the writings of Lowell L. Bennion (a member of the Swearing Elders),
as well as by authors Sterling B. Talmage, John A. Widtsoe, and others.

Arrington was proud of the fact that he "enjoyed preparing talks
which involved a kind of intellectualization of the gospel."[11] He
abandoned scriptural knowledge in exchange for literature, "reading
widely," and suggesting that it "makes up to some extent for my lack of
expertise in the scriptures."[12] For Arrington, his familiarity with many
"important works of fiction, philosophy, history, biography, science,
and so on" represented a strength he brought to the table. Someone
else could provide the requisite doctrine and scripture:

---

8   Ibid., 117.

9   Leonard J. Arrington Diaries, October 31, 1976; Leonard J. Arrington and
Gary James Bergera, *Confessions of a Mormon Historian: The Diaries of Leonard J.
Arrington*, 1971-1997, vol. 2 (Salt Lake City: Signature Books, 2018), 281.

10 Ibid., 282; emphasis in original.

11 Leonard J. Arrington Diaries, October 10, 1976; Ibid., 252.

12 Leonard J. Arrington Diaries, September 25, 1978; Ibid., 634.

▮▮ I am not as knowledgeable on doctrine as a Church historian ought to be. I have read a number of doctrinal works—even studied some of them carefully—but I realize every Sunday in High Priest and Sunday School classes that I do not know as much doctrine as nine-tenths of the High Priests in the Church. I feel very inadequate discussing doctrine and take the easy way out by simply telling people they ought to talk with a General Authority . . .[13]

Adjusting to his new role as Church Historian, Arrington resolved to do "some intense reading in the field of religious psychology and religious history."[14] He had determined that religious psychology would help him make sense of and better interpret the prophetic history of the Church of Jesus Christ.

Arrington's struggle to conform with what he saw as the 'orthodox' side of the Church is reflected in a story told by his son, James Arrington. When Leonard became Church Historian, he approached his son for assistance in delivering a testimony at the end of his talk. "You're a performer," he told his son. "I don't know exactly how to end my talks. It's like people want to know something, and I don't know what to tell them."[15]

James was an accomplished actor, and he eagerly coached his father through the 'perfect testimony'—even rehearsing the body language his physical actions would convey:

▮▮ . . . I [James Arrington] said, "Okay, here's what you do, Dad. When you get to the part where you start talking about these things, I want you to take off your glasses, and lean over the pulpit and talk to the people. . . .

You need to bear a testimony that no one thinks you are hiding, or that you have prepared it, or that it is anything but the real, exact truth. You get to decide what you want to say there, but when you get to that point, you whip off your glasses, carefully, gently, and lean on the pulpit, and you talk to those people.

---

13 Ibid., 633.

14 Letter from LJA to Jan Shipps, November 14, 1972, LJAHA, Series V, Box 6, Fd. 3.

15 Gregory A. Prince, *Leonard Arrington and the Writing of Mormon History* (Salt Lake City, UT: Tanner Trust Fund and J. Willard Marriott Library, 2016), 119.

You tell them that you've seen the deepest, darkest parts of the Church's history, and that it bears record of the truthfulness of the Gospel."[16]

When Arrington gave his first talk, his son was in attendance to watch his father's 'performance.' The response from the congregation was remarkably positive:

❘❘ People went out of there going, "Hallelujah! That's the greatest testimony I've ever heard."[17]

Arrington's son noted, however, that his father's delivery was still not quite perfect; that he removed his glasses "mechanically" at first. The awkward flaws in Arrington's testimony would improve with each live rehearsal until it became "very natural to him."[18] However, James Arrington noted the conflict within his father:

❘❘ He hates this. He sees that this is subterfuge. He's trying as hard as he can to do what I told him to, but with difficulty. . . .

After that first time it became very natural to him to do that. He really got what he was doing. The first time, it felt very directed; but after that, he just did it regularly and it was great. People just adored him.[19]

The Holy Ghosters

As Leonard Arrington contemplated and created a list of names he would consider inviting into the new Historical Department, his associates cautioned him not to include the names of any "Holy Ghosters." The term Holy Ghosters was a pejorative title bequeathed by progressives who saw little value in spirit-borne scholarship. Arrington recorded his thoughts regarding Holy Ghosters in his diary, lamenting that:

---

16   James Arrington interview, April 12, 2012, as quoted in Gregory A. Prince, *Leonard Arrington and the Writing of Mormon History* (Salt Lake City, UT: Tanner Trust Fund and J. Willard Marriott Library, 2016), 120.

17   Ibid.

18   Gregory A. Prince, *Leonard Arrington and the Writing of Mormon History* (Salt Lake City, UT: Tanner Trust Fund and J. Willard Marriott Library, 2016), 120-121.

19   Ibid.

ℓℓ The leading features of the Holy Ghosters is their emphasis upon obtaining the Holy Ghost as the most valuable, if not the exclusive source of truth. They are anti-intellectual in the sense that they have no faith and confidence in the traditional[20] ways of acquiring truth—reason, experimentation, etc. Through prayer and meditation, collective and private, they achieve or seek to achieve a feeling of certitude about important matters. Once they know a thing or idea to be true, by this means, they are firm in the face of logic, demonstration, and the more traditional sources of inquiry.[21]

Arrington saw members who believed in a witness born of the Holy Ghost as those who "motivate students by tears rather than by logic or evidence," and are "disgusted by attempts to intellectualize the gospel and our history."[22] Ironically, in the ultimate paradox, the same month Arrington recorded these entries disparaging "Holy Ghosters," the *New Era* published a Q&A asking, "How do you know if you have received the Holy Ghost?" The answer was written by none other than Leonard J. Arrington.[23]

Because Holy Ghosters produced history and scholarship that was not in line with progressive New Mormon History, Arrington knew he would need to bypass these fanatic devotees, and even circumvent this perceived threat. His trusted colleagues agreed, and had warned him "not to employ such persons in our department since they would not necessarily follow the canons of good historianship in the work we have to do."[24] Arrington listed the names of Presidents Joseph

---

20   Note that when Leonard Arrington refers to the "traditional ways of acquiring truth," his use of the term "traditional" is not in reference to the traditionalist worldview, but instead to the scientific method and naturalistic, secular, means for acquiring knowledge.

21   Leonard J. Arrington Diaries, June 15, 1972; Leonard J. Arrington and Gary James Bergera, *Confessions of a Mormon Historian: The Diaries of Leonard J. Arrington*, 1971-1997, vol. 1 (Salt Lake City: Signature Books, 2018), 164.

22   Leonard J. Arrington Diaries, October 22, 1976; Ibid., 2:273.

23   Leonard Arrington, "How do you know if you have received the Holy Ghost?" *New Era*, October 1972, https://www.churchofjesuschrist.org/study/new-era/1972/10/q-and-a-questions-and-answers/how-do-you-know-if-you-have-received-the-holy-ghost?lang=eng.

24   Leonard J. Arrington Diaries, June 15, 1972; Leonard J. Arrington and Gary James Bergera, *Confessions of a Mormon Historian: The Diaries of Leonard J. Arrington*, 1971-1997, vol. 1 (Salt Lake City: Signature Books, 2018), 165.

Fielding Smith and David O. McKay among the Holy Ghosters, as well as author and scholar Hyrum L. Andrus.[25] The fact that Arrington sidestepped the credentialed and acclaimed Professor Andrus in deference to progressive intellectuals is evidence that his direction was not about scholarship—but rather ideology.

Arrington's perspective on revelation and testimony differed conclusively from that of other credentialed scholars such as Andrus and Truman G. Madsen, as well as other contemporary traditionalist leaders and historians including Joseph Fielding Smith. For Arrington, revelation was merely intuition; and he claimed no understanding of direct verbal communication from God. Arrington regarded "Darwin's conception of the law of evolution" to be a leap in intellect on equal standing with Joseph Smith's revelations.[26] He also considered Emerson's experience of "being caught up in a giant eyeball," as well as the experiences shared by Jewish and Protestant mystics, as equal to, or on par with the experiences related by Joseph Smith and other prophets in scripture.[27] Arrington appears to have had no experience with the appearance of God, the appearance of angels, the gift of tongues, or inspired dreams, and his 'testimony'

---

25   Ibid., 164.

26   Leonard J. Arrington Diaries, February 13, 1980; Ibid., 2:907.

27   Leonard J. Arrington Diaries, December 25, 1979; Ibid., 2:894.

seems to have been rooted more in the intellect and possibly mystical experience, as opposed to spiritual manifestation.[28]

In distinct contrast, when speaking directly with regard to the recounting of Latter-day Saint history, President Benson explained that "No writer can ever accurately portray a prophet of God if he or she does not believe in prophecy. They cannot succeed in writing what they do not have in personal faith."[29] A few months later, in the midst of growing controversy over *The Story of the Latter-day Saints,* he warned religious educators: "We must never forget that ours is a prophetic history. Our students need to understand this prophetic history. This can only be done by teachers who themselves possess the Spirit of prophecy and revelation."[30]

President Benson advocated for the traditionalist conviction that those who do not have spiritual experience—the gift of prophecy and revelation—cannot accurately relate to or produce a true history of Joseph Smith or the Restoration. They are not qualified to speak on matters they do not understand. It requires an attorney to address law, a plumber to address plumbing, a musician to address music, and an artist to address a work of art. How can those who do not have spiritual experience possibly understand—let alone depict—a spiritual history?

The Prophet Joseph Smith himself boldly stated: "you never knew my heart no man knows my hist[ory]."[31] We must ask why. The Prophet spent his entire life enveloped in spiritual experiences and communication with God. How is it possible for a man or woman to truly grasp his life—or comprehend his character—who has not walked in his shoes?

---

28   For example, on February 26, 1979, Arrington wrote, "I've had a wide variety of dreams, of course—some sexual, a few horrible, but as I say, few that ever stayed with me or disturbed me. I have never had any dream which was a religious experience or which bore any resemblance to a beatific vision." Leonard J. Arrington Diaries, February 26, 1979; Ibid., 2:731.

29   Ezra Taft Benson, "God's Hand in Our Nation's History," Brigham Young University Devotional, 1976, https://speeches.byu.edu/talks/ezra-taft-benson/gods-hand-nations-history/.

30   Ezra Taft Benson, "Gospel Teacher and His Message," address to religious educators, September 17, 1976, 7.

31   Joseph Smith, Discourse, April 7, 1844, as reported by Thomas Bullock, p. 22, The Joseph Smith Papers.

Elder Boyd K. Packer commented on the impossibility of this in his talk, "The Mantle Is Far, Far Greater Than the Intellect." The aftermath of this discourse was a reverberating, incensed New Mormon Historian community following its delivery in 1981. The following is an excerpt from that talk:

❝ ... there is no such thing as an accurate or objective history of the Church which ignores the Spirit.

You might as well try to write the biography of Mendelssohn without hearing or mentioning his music, or write the life of Rembrandt without mentioning light or canvas or color.

If someone who knew very little about music should write a biography of Mendelssohn, one who had been trained to have a feeling for music would recognize that very quickly. That reader would not be many pages into the manuscript before he would know that a most essential ingredient had been left out. ...

If we who research, write, and teach the history of the Church ignore the spiritual on the pretext that the world may not understand it, our work will not be objective. And if, for the same reason, we keep it quite secular, we will produce a history that is not accurate and not scholarly—this, in spite of the extent of research or the nature of the individual statements or the incidents which are included as part of it, and notwithstanding the training or scholarly reputation of the one who writes or teaches it. We would end up with a history with the one most essential ingredient left out.[32]

For Arrington, this revelation-based lifestyle—with history underscored by prophecy—was entirely foreign to his naturalistic way of thinking. In consummate contrast, for a man like the Prophet Joseph who consistently conversed with heavenly beings, the path to truth was not solely by intellectual study—but through genuine spiritual experience: "The only way to obtain truth and wisdom, is not to ask it from books, but to go to God in prayer and obtain divine teaching."[33]

---

32   Boyd K. Packer, "The Mantle Is Far, Far Greater Than the Intellect," *BYU Studies Quarterly* 21, no. 3 (1981): 262-263.

33   Joseph Smith, Discourse, 3 October 1841, as reported by *Times and Seasons*, The Joseph Smith Papers.

"Joseph Smith's Last Dream," Jon McNaughton

During his third year of graduate school, Arrington wrestled with the question of whether or not God truly existed. He later noted that "My mother and father and my friends and teachers led me to emphasize study over personal revelation."[34] Following the advice given, and resorting to intellectual and academic study over personal revelation in college, Arrington eventually decided that God did exist—and he "never seriously worried about it since."[35] Arrington described his conversion as "not the product of action by the spirit," but instead, as an "experience of deciding [intellectually] whether the Church was true, whether Jesus was a great man or a Son of God, whether Joseph Smith was an inspired religious teacher and prophet or leader who deluded people into following him."[36] When

34   Leonard J. Arrington Diaries, February 13, 1995; Leonard J. Arrington and Gary James Bergera, *Confessions of a Mormon Historian: The Diaries of Leonard J. Arrington*, 1971-1997, vol. 3 (Salt Lake City: Signature Books, 2018), 635.

35   Gregory A. Prince, *Leonard Arrington and the Writing of Mormon History* (Salt Lake City, UT: Tanner Trust Fund and J. Willard Marriott Library, 2016), 111.

36   Leonard J. Arrington Diaries, November 29, 1975; Leonard J. Arrington and Gary James Bergera, *Confessions of a Mormon Historian: The Diaries of Leonard J. Arrington*, 1971-1997, vol. 2 (Salt Lake City: Signature Books, 2018), 122.

Arrington did tackle the question of spiritual experiences, he used words such as "mystical experiences" and "mystical illumination" to describe his own "personal religious experiences."[37]

Ultimately, Arrington also declared that he did have a testimony; but his definition of 'testimony' differed altogether from those claiming Spirit-borne witnesses. The economic aspects of the Gospel—the influence of art, music, and nature, as well as the general goodness of the people, and his new techniques toward Mormon history—all shaped his intellectualized approach to truth, authority, and faith.

A belief in goodness—as opposed to spiritual knowledge—characterizes liberal progressives. When Arrington's friend, Richard L. Bushman, answered questions regarding his own testimony—especially after a faith crisis during college—with John Dehlin on Mormon Stories Podcast, he responded similarly: "Well, I probably never recovered it [his "believingness"] all. I'm not someone who has a simple faith that just everything is absolutely true beyond any doubt. . . . The big word for me is goodness. I, above all things, want to go where things are good. . . . I just get that over and over in the Church . . . I can't deny that, so I stick with it. . . ."[38]

On another occasion, Richard Bushman was asked by a Catholic friend: "How can you believe in Joseph Smith? You're a scholar. How can you accept his fantastic story?" Bushman's response was not that he had a witness of the Prophet and his calling—but instead: "I find that when I live the Mormon way, I'm the kind of man I want to be."[39]

---

37   Leonard J. Arrington Diaries, August 17, 1996; Ibid., 3:656.

38   John Dehlin and Richard L. Bushman, "047-051: Richard Bushman — Experiences as a Mormon Historian (Part 1)," Mormon Stories Podcast, 12:44-15:25, January 22, 2007, https://www.mormonstories.org/podcast/ richard-bushman-and-rough-stone-rolling-part-1-experiences-as-a-mormon-historian/. Bushman also explains, "During the mission, you know I worked like crazy. If you've read that little essay of mine, you know that I worked like crazy to figure out whether or not I could believe the Book of Mormon. And finally after some weighing everything that I had at hand, which was limited, I just had this affirmation. . . . It wasn't a proof, it wasn't a set of historical proofs. It was just an affirmation that yes, this is *right*. I didn't even say this is *true*, I said this is *right*."

39   On June 17-18, 2016, Richard L. Bushman gave the keynote address, "Finding the Right Words: Speaking Faith in Secular Times," sponsored by the Neal A. Maxwell Institute for Religious Scholarship. Maxwell Institute, "Mormonism in the Academy, Keynote—Richard L. Bushman, 'Speaking Faith in Secular Times," July 14, 2016, video, at 28:45, https://youtu.be/nX9NLYVtuM0?t=1725.

When recalling the story later on the Reddit forum "exmormon," Bushman explained that, "when I live the Mormon way, I am lifted up. . . . I don't use the word 'know' a lot, but I do know I am a better person for being a Mormon."[40]

Two Alternative Understandings of God

Although the religious beliefs of traditionalists baffled him, Leonard Arrington found kinship among other Latter-day Saints who shared his own paradigm. One of those was Jack H. Adamson, a professor of English at the University of Utah. Arrington remembered his friend Jack as a "cultural Mormon" who had publicly announced on television that he did not "take the Bible literally but regard[ed] it as a great folk tradition and piece of literature," and considered himself a universalist[41] "as for basic philosophy and theology."[42] Arrington shared Adamson's doubts as to the historical viability and credibility of the Bible.

---

40   Richard Bushman, "AMA Series: Richard Bushman - Dec 16, 3:00 - 4:00 PM EST.," Reddit, https://www.reddit.com/r/exmormon/comments/1sp4mi/ama_series_richard_bushman_dec_16_300_400_pm_est/ce3huif/.

41   Universalist, "A person who believes that all humankind will eventually be saved. 'Ultimately he is a universalist who believes that all souls will be reconciled to God, including the souls of Satan and his minions.'" Lexico, "Universalist," https://www.lexico.com/en/definition/universalist. According to Wikipedia, "The fundamental idea of Christian universalism is universal reconciliation – that all humans will eventually be saved. They will eventually enter God's kingdom in Heaven, through the grace and works of the lord Jesus Christ. Christian universalism teaches that an eternal Hell does not exist, and that it was not what Jesus had taught." "Universalism," Wikipedia, last modified July 14, 2020, https://en.wikipedia.org/wiki/Universalism.

Claudia Bushman expressed her subscription to 'universalism' in 2016: ". . . I'm really a universalist religionist. I think everyone will be saved. I think that some move through the system more quickly than others, but I can't believe that a third of the host of heaven was just discarded. I think that they went into some remedial program and then were shipped off and are now peopling other earths and working out their salvation somewhere else. I even have my doubts about the sons of perdition. They're important players in the scheme of things, and certainly spirits of merit and ability. They too will be saved." Maxwell Institute, "Mormonism in the Academy, Session 6—Armand Mauss, Laurel Thatcher Ulrich, Claudia Bushman, Grant Wacker," July 14, 2016, YouTube video, 54:11, https://www.youtube.com/watch?v=ws1cGMW8g58&feature=youtu.be&t=3251.

42   Leonard J. Arrington Diaries, December 18, 1972; Leonard J. Arrington and Gary James Bergera, *Confessions of a Mormon Historian: The Diaries of Leonard J. Arrington*, 1971-1997, vol. 1 (Salt Lake City: Signature Books, 2018), 389.

Upon Adamson's death in 1975, Arrington wrote a tribute to the man he felt was, "in many ways . . . like myself"[43]:

❝❝ Jack is surely one of the greatest teachers in Utah history. . . . a great human being. He was brilliant with some characteristics of the bon vivant. He has been outspoken on some issues and has had the reputation of not being very churchy. . . . he had his problems with the church, mostly intellectual and doctrinal.

When Jack went to the University of Idaho in the fall of 1936 he joined a fraternity and partook of the life of fraternity boys which included occasional smoking, drinking and partying. After two years he went on a mission and was a good missionary from all reports. . . .

[After returning] He permitted exploration of unorthodox ideas and this caused church authorities (I think Apostle Harold B. Lee) to advise the bishop that he be released. I heard him myself make a public statement in response to a question that he did not believe in a personal God and he did not regard himself as an orthodox Mormon. I think he did not believe in a future life. Nevertheless, he never became bitter or rebellious and did not like people who did. He was proud to call himself a Mormon in a cultural and social sense—in every sense except orthodox in theology.[44]

Upon Adamson's passing, Arrington also expressed regret that "it will now be impossible for us to use him in a collaborative way in doing a biography of Brigham Young."[45] He further opined in a letter to his children:

❝❝ In many ways he was like myself . . . [he] found positive values in [M]ormonism but not always the ones that the so-called orthodox thought paramount and was often warned about

---

43   Leonard J. Arrington to his children, September 12, 1975. "Correspondence From Leonard Arrington to His Children and Grandchildren - 1975," Utah State University, USU Special Collection, LJAHA 1, Series 10, Box 102, Fd. 4.

44   Leonard J. Arrington Diaries, September 12, 1975; Leonard J. Arrington and Gary James Bergera, *Confessions of a Mormon Historian: The Diaries of Leonard J. Arrington*, 1971-1997, vol. 2 (Salt Lake City: Signature Books, 2018), 88-89.

45   Ibid., 89.

his Sunday School teaching. . . . I wish we had more inside the faith who had his humanity and his love of beautiful thoughts and imagery.[46]

While Arrington felt a kinship with Adamson, he felt like a fish out of water when trying to relate to some of the religion faculty at BYU: "I do not see anyone in the school of religion at BYU who is studying the Bible in the context of Higher Criticism. And how can one obtain the real meaning of the Gospels without Higher Criticism?" On the other hand, Arrington felt "so encouraged that a number of . . . bright young intellectuals, primarily those influenced by Jack Adamson, I suspect . . . have gone to Harvard Divinity School"[47] and other intellectual institutions critical of the Bible. In his personal diary, Arrington pleaded with God that intellectuals critical of revelation and scripture would one day teach and be welcomed in the BYU religion department. Not many years would pass before Arrington's dream would be fully realized.

Many Latter-day Saint progressives, and even celebrated apologists, share Jack Adamson's unorthodox views of God. David H. Bailey—outspoken anti-creationist member, mathematician, and author—was asked by John Dehlin on a Mormon Stories podcast whether he believed in an anthropomorphic God—or in other words, a God with a perfected body and perfected human characteristics—as opposed to a force in the universe:[48]

❝❝ *John Dehlin:* There's the "big G" God, as I've heard it described, which is a God that's all powerful, omniscient, all-knowing and intimately involved in even the smallest minute details of human life. The sparrow doesn't fall without God knowing it, you know. "God sends the hurricane" because in His

---

46   Leonard J. Arrington to his children, September 12, 1975. "Correspondence From Leonard Arrington to His Children and Grandchildren - 1975," Utah State University, USU Special Collection, LJAHA 1, Series 10, Box 102, Fd. 4.

47   Leonard J. Arrington Diaries, February 18, 1978; Leonard J. Arrington and Gary James Bergera, *Confessions of a Mormon Historian: The Diaries of Leonard J. Arrington*, 1971-1997, vol. 2 (Salt Lake City: Signature Books, 2018), 471.

48   Anthropomorphic: "described or thought of as having a human form or human attributes" or "ascribing human characteristics to nonhuman things." Merriam-Webster, "Anthropomorphic," https://www.merriam-webster.com/dictionary/anthropomorphic.

supreme wisdom He knows the balance of justice and mercy and maybe He wants to punish some people or maybe just He needs a certain amount of misery to be inflicted on earth for whatever reason and that's all it is. Infinite wisdom, His ways are higher than our ways. So that's sort of the "big G."

Then we've got the "small G" God, [which] is this God who maybe is limited in its powers, scope and maybe he loves us and has lots of power but some laws that he's obeying. He just can't interfere with nature. Or with adversity. Or whatever and so he can't intervene in lots of things but he still can give whisperings or promptings or occasionally intervene in people's lives in a limited fashion.

And then there's this just really loose interpretation of a god which is just like, "God is some force or some power and I don't know if it's the promoter figure or not but you know if all it is is a hope that there's some power or influence out there . . . or some meaning or purpose to this existence then that's God for me."

Where do you stand in your belief or are you open to any and all of those options or something else?

David Bailey: Well, I think there's something to be said for all of them. . . . I'm more of a minimalist person in the sense of that I don't really put a lot of stock in theology. I don't see that there's any point in going off into speculation . . .

I'm willing to just leave a lot of those questions unanswered. I'm willing to have a somewhat vague but [at] least not clearly defined concept and I can see, again, a lot of value in many different points of view . . . [I don't] feel that any one particular definition is the full answer.[49]

Dehlin again clarified during the 2010 interview: "You're saying that it's within your realm of possibility that all this literalistic

---

49   John Dehlin and David Bailey, "160-162: Dr. David Bailey on Science and the LDS Church, and How Science Has Strengthened his Faith in God and the Church," Mormon Stories, June 17, 2010, 00:03:24, https://www.mormonstories. org/podcast/160-162-dr-david-bailey-on-science-and-the-lds-church-and-how-science-has-strengthened-his-faith/.

anthropomorphic stuff that we can tie back to Joseph [Smith] doesn't necessarily have to be a pillar for your belief as a Mormon." Bailey responded, "Exactly. I don't see any need to hold to any particular definition."[50]

David Bailey is often applauded as an apologist by progressives for his 'reconciliation' of science and religion. For traditionalists, the fact that Bailey, Arrington, and other progressives have all but given up the doctrine of an anthropomorphic God is further evidence for the fulfillment of President Joseph Fielding Smith's testimony: "those who insistently follow the evolutionary theories, cannot at the same time accept and worship an intelligent anthropomorphic God!"[51]

David H. Bailey by Raul654
under CC-BY-SA-3.0

"Liberal" Mormonism

In 1980, Leonard Arrington summarized in his diary what he saw as "two schools of LDS theology and philosophy." He noted that the "progress or liberal school of thought" was "best expressed in our day by Sterling McMurrin and Lowell Bennion," and conceded that this was "the view I was brought up on—it was commonly expressed by LDS intellectuals and teachers during the 1930s and 1940s."[52]

---

50   Ibid., June 17, 2010, 00:08:05.

51   Joseph Fielding Smith, *Man, His Origin and Destiny* (Salt Lake City: Deseret Book Company, 1954), 85.

52   Leonard J. Arrington Diaries, December 13, 1980; Leonard J. Arrington and Gary James Bergera, *Confessions of a Mormon Historian: The Diaries of Leonard J. Arrington, 1971-1997*, vol. 3 (Salt Lake City: Signature Books, 2018), 132. The full context of Arrington's statement includes his belief that Joseph Smith contradicted himself. In other words, the Book of Mormon and early revelations and teachings of the Prophet Joseph Smith contradict the later teachings of Joseph Smith in the King Follett discourse, etc. For Arrington, Joseph Smith was 'progressing' in understanding. For traditionalists, this subverts and undermines the foundation of the Restoration of the Gospel.

In contrast to this "liberal school of thought" stood traditionalist ideology that, according to Arrington's view:

II . . . derives from the Book of Mormon, early revelations, and early statements of Joseph Smith, proceeds through some statements of Brigham Young to Orson Pratt, Joseph Fielding Smith, and best expressed today by Bruce R. McConkie. This school emphasizes the dependent and depraved status of man, the absolute power and perfection of God, the importance of "works," such as temple work, ordinances, following church regulations, discipline, obedience, "narrow is the way,"[53] and so on. . . . A sort of Mormon Fundamentalism like Protestant Fundamentalism. Emphasizes Biblical literalism, rejects the Higher Criticism, the law of evolution, the New History, [and] cultural approaches to an understanding of Mormonism.

I have been all along, and continue to be, in the first school, but find the going very hard, considering the implacable opposition of Elder Benson, Elder Petersen, Elder Packer, Elder McConkie, and perhaps others who agree with them.[54]

Arrington discounted the traditionalism espoused by Ezra Taft Benson, Joseph Fielding Smith, Boyd K. Packer, Bruce R. McConkie, and others—castigating it as "Mormon Fundamentalism." Progressives often attempt to discount or attack traditionalist ideology by belittling the traditionalists directly—dubbing them with the pejorative 'fundamentalist' moniker, hinting that they are a splinter from the pillars of Mormonism. To the contrary, traditionalist doctrine and teachings were established by the Prophet Joseph Smith himself. Traditionalism is not 'fundamentalist' in the sense that it is praetorian or extremist; it is merely a hearkening back to the original foundation laid by the Prophet Joseph Smith.

---

53   Henry Eyring expressed similar views to Arrington when he commented, "He [Joseph Fielding Smith] had a different background and training on this issue. Maybe he was right. I think he was right on most things, and if you followed him, he would get you into the celestial kingdom—maybe the hard way, but he would get you there." Henry Eyring, *Reflections of a Scientist* (Salt Lake City: Deseret Book Company, 1983), 54.

54   Leonard J. Arrington Diaries, December 13, 1980; Leonard J. Arrington and Gary James Bergera, *Confessions of a Mormon Historian: The Diaries of Leonard J. Arrington*, 1971-1997, vol. 3 (Salt Lake City: Signature Books, 2018), 132.

Progressive Mormonism, alternatively, is the aberration; and as Arrington noted throughout his diary, it is a substitute theology—a revision to the Restoration narrative, and one hotly opposed by the traditional narrative and teachings of the Church for two centuries.

Fence-Sitting in Latter-day Saint History

In 1972, the year Leonard Arrington was called as Church Historian, he was scheduled to speak at Northern Arizona University—when only a few minutes from his presentation, a sudden bout of nausea caused him to rush to the restroom where he vomited from nervousness.

Arrington had been asked to visit Flagstaff, Arizona to deliver an address on "Mormonism in American history" at the Northern Arizona University campus. Arrington had carefully crafted his talk, tailoring the language and message for what he anticipated would be a small, non-Mormon audience. When he referred to the history of Joseph Smith, he chose coded phrases, including "supposed revelation" and "pretended prophet." When speaking of the First Vision, Arrington apologetically referred to it as "Joseph Smith's purported First Vision."[55]

Arrington arrived at the lecture room a few minutes before his scheduled speech, and was stunned to find an enthusiastic audience of 1200-1500 individuals already assembled. He had expected only 20 or 30 faculty members and graduate students—this was too much. Terror set in as he learned that many of the members of the local Latter-day Saint wards were there, as well as students from the Institute and LDSSA. All were eager to hear what the newly-called Latter-day Saint historian had to say.

I felt very uneasy about my talk about the scholarly approach to Mormon history but that was the talk I had. I felt so uneasy that for the only time in my life I can recall I felt both like vomiting and purging. I asked Bill Lyon where I could find a bathroom—this was about five minutes before my talk. I went to the bathroom, vomited and purged, came back white-faced ready to be introduced. Bill Lyon looked very puzzled and disturbed.

---

55   Leonard J. Arrington Diaries, February 11, 1982; Ibid., 243.

Anyway, he introduced me and I went through [with] it and once again did fine. No problems that I was ever aware of.[56]

Arrington recalled the experience ten years later in his diary, noting the conflict he and other historians felt in trying to write papers, deliver talks, or author books for very different audiences. The man who taught in Sunday School or gave a talk in Sacrament meeting was drastically different from the same man who spoke before academic audiences. Which appearance was the facade—and which was the genuine man?

Two years after Arrington's regurgitating experience at Northern Arizona University, he was preparing to deliver a paper to the American Historical Association in Atlanta, Georgia. Again, he anticipated a small non-Mormon audience of his peers; but when he arrived this was not the case, as he discovered a very different assemblage of eager listeners:

❝ ... a friend of mine without my knowledge or approval had telephoned the [LDS] Institute and Seminary teachers in the area and ecclesiastical leaders so that the audience was made up more of Mormons than non-Mormons.[57]

One of the Latter-day Saints in the audience was Joseph Fielding McConkie,[58] son of Elder Bruce R. McConkie, who would later author many books on the Restoration, ancient prophecies foretelling the mission of Joseph Smith, the Book of Mormon, and other gospel doctrinal compositions. "I knew he was a hard liner," Arrington reflected, writing in his journal that Joseph McConkie had "given trouble to Jim [James L.] Kimball and others at the University of Washington in Seattle":

---

56   Leonard J. Arrington Diaries, February 11, 1982; Ibid., 243-244.

57   Ibid., 244.

58   Joseph Fielding McConkie, Ph.D., was a BYU professor of Ancient Scripture. He authored over 25 works including *Truth and Courage: Joseph F. Smith Letters, His Name Shall Be Joseph, "Ancient Prophecies of the Latter-day Seer," Gospel Symbolism,* and *Doctrinal Commentary on the Book of Mormon.*

// Anyway, I had to go through my paper, which was not in the line of a missionary or Sacrament meeting talk. I learned afterwards that Brother McConkie had brought some investigators, that he did not think my paper was proper for investigators to hear, that he complained about what Mormon historians were doing with our history. He has never attended one of our lectures since and has been very distant and cool and his father who had demonstrated warmth and sympathy with our History Division efforts seemed at the same time to become cool towards us. I knew as I was giving the paper that I was not getting a good audience from the "faithful Mormons" there and therefore was uneasy throughout.[59]

While traditionalist historians had written history that testified of Joseph Smith as a prophet and unashamedly taught the doctrines of the Gospel, the New Mormon History was "an intellectual and historiographical movement that carried the story of the Latter-day Saints into the cultural mainstream . . ."[60] The New Mormon Historians prided themselves on maintaining their image in all circles, in gaining accolades from their secular colleagues—while at the same time, maintaining their memberships in the Church.

Joseph Fielding McConkie,
used with permission

59   Leonard J. Arrington Diaries, February 11, 1982; Leonard J. Arrington and Gary James Bergera, *Confessions of a Mormon Historian: The Diaries of Leonard J. Arrington, 1971-1997*, vol. 3 (Salt Lake City: Signature Books, 2018), 244.

60   Jan Shipps, "Richard Lyman Bushman, the Story of Joseph Smith and Mormonism, and the New Mormon History," *Journal of American History* 94 (September 2007): 498.

However, some traditionalists felt this attitude was a betrayal of testimony and a neglect of the calling to stand as a witness at all times. Truth was truth. Joseph Smith wasn't a "pretended prophet" who gave "supposed revelations" after receiving a "purported First Vision."[61]

But, the New Mormon Historians considered, *what secular university, what fellowship, what popular publisher would take them seriously if they were to write history that defended Joseph Smith or the Gospel he espoused?* Ages and times past had proven to the progressive that standing out from the crowd was not popular; so the New Mormon Historians rejected polemic history and launched into an endeavor to create an "objective, dispassionate analysis of the religion."[62] D. Michael Quinn defined New Mormon History as an "effort to avoid using history as a religious battering ram."[63] These progressive Latter-day Saint historians would claim neutrality in this eternal conflict—this millennia-old struggle between light and darkness.

However, in their very attempt to avoid conflict and 'sit on the fence,' they embroiled themselves in an intense war at Church headquarters—and rightly so. This was a war of ideologies, with Joseph Smith's character and the Restoration of the Gospel he captained weighing in the balance. Who would triumph? What interpretation of Church history and its origins would be used to train and indoctrinate the rising generation under Arrington's tutelage? And perhaps we might ask ourselves: What interpretation will we maintain today in the incomparable task and stewardship of teaching our own rising generation?

---

61   Leonard J. Arrington Diaries, February 11, 1982; Leonard J. Arrington and Gary James Bergera, *Confessions of a Mormon Historian: The Diaries of Leonard J. Arrington, 1971-1997,* vol. 3 (Salt Lake City: Signature Books, 2018), 244.

62   Kevin Opsahl, "On Arrington's shoulders: New USU Mormon history prof. recognizes late scholar's legacy while charting own course," *HJ News,* July 24, 2019, https://www.hjnews.com/features/faith/on-arringtons-shoulders-new-usu-mormon-history-prof-recognizes-late-scholars-legacy-while-charting-own/article_29e99f03-c666-5e01-bf9f-cd3b8998d189.html.

63   D. Michael Quinn, "Editor's Introduction," in *The New Mormon History: Revisionist Essays on the Mormon Past* (Signature Books, 1992), viii.

4

ARRINGTON ASSEMBLES HIS TEAM
AT CHURCH HEADQUARTERS

With the changing of the guard in the Church History Department in 1972, the traditional ways of defending the faith of the Latter-day Saints through the recounting of faithfully curated historical events began a decided change in direction—a swift 180 degrees toward intellectualism.

Arrington would enlist other progressive professionals in the new Historical Department who would become formidable allies in his quest to transition from a traditionalist headquarters to a department popularizing and defending their own new narrative with its accompanying new theology. Choosing James B. Allen and R. Davis Bitton as his 'counselors,' Arrington formed a kind of "presidency" as he would later describe them.[1] Allen co-authored *The Story of the Latter-day Saints* in 1976, a revisionist history of the Church that would disconcert President Ezra Taft Benson and other traditionalist leaders. Bitton and Arrington published *The Mormon Experience: A History of the Latter-day Saints* in 1979, presenting a new 'version' of Church history that appealed to a largely secularized non-Mormon audience.

Other inner-circle members of the group included Dean C. Jessee, Ronald K. Esplin, and Maureen Ursenbach Beecher. Jessee, a senior researcher, would later apply his well-known skill in handwriting analysis to unwittingly—and inaccurately— authenticate a number

---

1   Gregory A. Prince, *Leonard Arrington and the Writing of Mormon History* (Salt Lake City: The University of Utah Press, 2016), 162.

of Mark Hofmann's forgeries during the 1980s.[2] Ronald K. Esplin, future managing editor of The Joseph Smith Papers project, was one of Arrington's summer research fellows,[3] and he would later move the staff and the direction of the Joseph Smith Papers to the unorthodox liberal left. Maureen Beecher, a senior research associate and friend of mid-20th-century feminism, was later tasked with the development of a number of papers purposed with reconfiguring the narrative and influence of women in the Church.

There was one progressive, however, whom Leonard Arrington could not bring himself to hire—a writer who, through a twist of irony, would later be recognized as one of the founders of New Mormon History.[4] This side-stepped historian, Juanita Brooks, was the famed author of *The Mountain Meadows Massacre*. Brooks was a life-long friend of Obert C. Tanner, member of the Swearing Elders.[5] In 1950, after two decades of research and writing, Brooks published her historiography of what is considered the darkest moment in Latter-day Saint history. On September 11, 1857, a cabal of over fifty Latter-day Saint men, led by their local ecclesiastical leaders, diabolically slaughtered 120 men, women, and children in what would become known as the 'Mountain Meadows Massacre.'

Although Brooks' endeavor to approach the history of the massacre with complete honesty was commendable, some of her interpretations reflected a progressive—even revisionist tone—contradicting the traditional understanding of its genesis. Brooks viewed the causes of the Mountain Meadows tragedy in terms of "war hysteria"[6] and

---

2   Dean C. Jessee would later become the general manager of the Joseph Smith Papers project along with Richard Bushman and Ron Esplin. He also published *The Personal Writings of Joseph Smith*.

3   Leonard J. Arrington Diaries, June 12, 1972; Leonard J. Arrington and Gary James Bergera, *Confessions of a Mormon Historian: The Diaries of Leonard J. Arrington, 1971-1997*, vol. 1 (Salt Lake City: Signature Books, 2018), 160.

4   "'The New Mormon History,' for want of a better term, began with the publication of Juanita Brooks's *The Mountain Meadows Massacre* in 1950 by Stanford University Press..." D. Michael Quinn, "Editor's Introduction," in *The New Mormon History: Revisionist Essays on the Mormon Past* (Signature Books, 1992), vii.

5   Glen M. Leonard, "Revisiting the Massacre At Mountain Meadows," The Juanita Brooks Lecture Series, St. George Tabernacle, March 18, 2009, p. 3, https://library.dixie.edu/special_collections/Juanita_Brooks_lectures/2009.pdf.

6   Juanita Brooks, *The Mountain Meadows Massacre* (Norman: University of Oklahoma Press, 1950), 109, 218.

"ungrounded fears,"[7] placing much of the blame on Brigham Young, Heber C. Kimball, George A. Smith, and other leaders for their war rhetoric and so-called radical doctrinal teachings. While exonerating Brigham Young of accusations that he ordered the massacre directly, Brooks blamed him and other leaders for feverishly inciting the murderous rampage by provoking the stake presidents, bishops, and other Latter-day Saints in southern Utah to engage in the slaughter of the Baker-Fancher party.[8]

President N. Eldon Tanner and George S. Tanner—Arrington's mentor who converted him to Biblical Criticism and Darwinian Evolution while in college—were not opposed to Brooks' employment in the new History Division; but Arrington was not enthusiastic. ". . . I want somebody more malleable, less stubborn, less controversial than Juanita Brooks."[9]

Arrington desired strategic, diplomatic historians who could work within the system, not make waves, and simply follow his lead. One rising star was Richard Bushman, a Boston University professor whom Leonard Arrington proposed hiring as a part-time third Assistant Church Historian.[10] Richard Bushman would later become the chief evangelist for promoting a new, occultic, money-digging Joseph Smith through his biographies, *Joseph Smith and the Beginnings of Mormonism,* and *Rough Stone Rolling.* Already an admirer of Fawn McKay Brodie, and a dedicated devotee to the advancement of New Mormon History, Bushman viewed Brodie's anti-Mormon biography, *No Man Knows My History,* as "a classic."[11] Arrington's biographer, Greg Prince, commented on the mutual respect evident between Arrington and Bushman:

---

7   Ibid., 59.

8   For example, Ibid., 35, 219.

9   Leonard J. Arrington Diaries, July 28, 1972; Leonard J. Arrington and Gary James Bergera, *Confessions of a Mormon Historian: The Diaries of Leonard J. Arrington, 1971-1997*, vol. 1 (Salt Lake City: Signature Books, 2018), 210.

10   Leonard J. Arrington Diaries, September 15, 1972; Ibid., 278.

11   Dennis Lythgoe, "'Warts and All' in Smith Biography," *Deseret News*, October 1, 2005, https://www.deseret.com/2005/10/1/19914955/warts-and-all-in-smith-biography.

❙❙ *How* Leonard mentored was as important—and impressive—as *who* he mentored. . . . Richard Bushman, author of the most definitive biography of Joseph Smith,[12] senior statesman of Mormonism, and quite possibly Leonard's successor as networker, remembers his first encounter, which occurred in 1960 at BYU where he took his first job after graduate school. "I realized by what happened that Leonard Arrington, even at that time, had become the dean of Mormon history, as exemplified by the fact that soon after I arrived in Provo, I received a letter from him in Logan, welcoming me to Utah and sort of inviting me to join the fraternity of Latter-day Saint historians. So from that early stage he already had taken responsibility for the whole historical enterprise."[13]

Arrington and his friends formed a close group, bound together by a shared vision to bring about change as they reshaped Mormon history. Later that year, Leonard Arrington, James Allen, Davis Bitton, Dean Jessee, and another of Arrington's protégés, D. Michael Quinn, traveled to Connecticut for a Western History Association meeting and planned interaction with like minds. A "get-together of Mormon historians, either a dinner or something for Thursday afternoon around 4:30 until night so that we can get together and talk shop."[14]

Arrington frequently gathered progressive historians, authors and thought leaders together for "rump sessions." These late-night get-togethers were one of the "secrets" to Leonard's success:

❙❙ Part of Leonard's "secret," if one could call it such, was to gather people together in his hotel room in the evening for his famed "rump sessions." Robert Flanders described one such session that occured at a meeting in Montana, just as his landmark and controversial book, *Nauvoo: Kingdom on the Mississippi,*

---

12   Traditionalists do not agree that *Rough Stone Rolling* should be the "most definitive" biography on the Prophet Joseph Smith.

13   Gregory A. Prince, *Leonard Arrington and the Writing of Mormon History* (Salt Lake City, UT: Tanner Trust Fund and J. Willard Marriott Library, 2016), 220; emphasis in original.

14   Leonard J. Arrington Diaries, July 10, 1972; Leonard J. Arrington and Gary James Bergera, *Confessions of a Mormon Historian: The Diaries of Leonard J. Arrington*, 1971-1997, vol. 1 (Salt Lake City: Signature Books, 2018), 266.

was going to press. "That was my first late-night meeting with Leonard and his protégés. I was invited. Leonard was the only one, of course, who knew about *Kingdom on the Mississippi*, because he had read it in manuscript. But that's not what the meeting was about. The meeting was about the *meeting*. Here were all these young guys. I don't remember who they all were. The important thing was that I saw Leonard as the leader of this little group."

The gatherings always took the same format, as described by RLDS historian Paul Edwards. "After the sessions he would bring a bunch of people into his hotel room and they would sit around and talk. He'd point to you and say, 'What are you doing now?' Before long, everybody was offering everybody suggestions."[15]

Significant changes were in play in this fresh, avant-garde era, and opinions once frowned upon were now seeing new life. In 1959, Arrington's article, "An Economic Interpretation of 'The Word of Wisdom',"[16] had been banned, causing a suspension of the *BYU Studies* magazine for one year.[17] Thirteen years later, a high priest

15   Gregory A. Prince, *Leonard Arrington and the Writing of Mormon History* (Salt Lake City, UT: Tanner Trust Fund and J. Willard Marriott Library, 2016), 221.

16   Leonard J. Arrington, "An Economic Interpretation of the 'Word of Wisdom,'" *BYU Studies Quarterly* 1, no. 1 (Winter 1959), 37-49.

17   Greg Prince explains the context for the controversy over Arrington's paper as follows: "A second focus of Leonard's doubt was the Word of Wisdom. Noting that for decades after the revelation, 'there is considerable evidence that many Mormon leaders and members believed that the Word of Wisdom meant only a piece of good advice and nothing more,' he placed it in the context of the American Temperance Movement by quoting from a little-noticed doctoral dissertation written in 1929 . . .

"Perhaps more significantly, he coupled its gradual transition—from advice to commandment—to economic exigencies within the newly colonized Great Basin, not the least being the need to channel cash into the Perpetual Emigrating Fund. 'The way to obtain cash for the emigration fund—was to use moral sanction against the importation and use of such "wasteful" commodities as tea, coffee, tobacco, liquor, fashionable clothing, and elegant furniture.' In other words, 'It was not so much a moral principle as a matter of sound economic policy.'

"Although his views on the Word of Wisdom were clearly articulated in *Great Basin Kingdom*, they did not attract attention from the church hierarchy until a year later when, in the inaugural issue of *Brigham Young University Studies*, Leonard published an article entitled, 'An Economic Interpretation of the "Word of Wisdom."' Elder Mark Petersen of the Quorum of the Twelve, in particular, took great offense at the article, 'saw to the suspension of that publication for a full year,' and thereafter 'always had questions about my loyalty and orthodoxy and judiciousness.'" Gregory A. Prince, "Faith and Doubt as Partners in Mormon

instructor from a Salt Lake ward reached out to Davis Bitton, asking for a copy of Arrington's article because he was "going to use that article as the basis for the high priests' lesson on the Word of Wisdom." Arrington was thrilled. "I have also heard of a number of instances in which my paper in Dialogue, 'Blessed Damozels,' was used as the basis for a Relief Society lesson,"[18] Arrington recorded in his diary.

However, not all members were thrilled with Arrington's work. Greg Prince noted that Earl E. Olson "spent his entire career, beginning in 1934, working in the Church Historian's Office . . . [and] more than three decades . . . working under the direction of Joseph Fielding Smith." Olson disagreed with Leonard's vision. Interviewed in 2006, he asserted: "Leonard wanted to start a completely new history. I object to that."[19]

One evening, shortly after being called as Church Historian, Arrington was invited to speak at a study group in the wealthy Federal Heights neighborhood in Salt Lake City. During the meeting:

> One person said that he had been disturbed by the portrait of Brigham Young which he saw presented in Great Basin Kingdom [Arrington's Ph.D. dissertation]. It had disenchanted him somewhat—removed the prophetic aura from around that mighty prophet. . . .
>
> One person pointed out that Great Basin Kingdom gives no example of revelation or inspiration, and did I believe that there was any in Church history.[20]

Arrington explained he was writing for a scholarly audience who dismissed such revelation as "rubbish."[21] His audience still appeared

---

History," (2013), 19th annual Arrington Lecture, 7-8, https://digitalcommons.usu. edu/cgi/viewcontent.cgi?article=1019&context=arrington_lecture.

18   Leonard J. Arrington Diaries, August 28, 1972; Leonard J. Arrington and Gary James Bergera, *Confessions of a Mormon Historian: The Diaries of Leonard J. Arrington*, 1971-1997, vol. 1 (Salt Lake City: Signature Books, 2018), 254.

19   Gregory A. Prince, *Leonard Arrington and the Writing of Mormon History* (Salt Lake City, UT: Tanner Trust Fund and J. Willard Marriott Library, 2016), 159.

20   Leonard J. Arrington Diaries, July 10, 1972; Leonard J. Arrington and Gary James Bergera, *Confessions of a Mormon Historian: The Diaries of Leonard J. Arrington*, 1971-1997, vol. 1 (Salt Lake City: Signature Books, 2018), 185-186.

21   Ibid., 187.

tense with the discussion, prompting him to record in his diary later that night: ". . . it may have been me that was in a sense on trial. They may have been very serious in attempting to find out whether I had a testimony, whether anyone as well acquainted with Church history as I am is completely secure in his testimony. Perhaps there is a certain doubting of persons who attempt to intellectualize the gospel and look at history in naturalistic terms."[22] Arrington noted the conflict he felt as a progressive academic serving as Church Historian:

// On the one hand, I am the *Church* Historian and must seek to build testimonies, spread the Word, build the Kingdom. On the other hand, I am called to be a *historian*, which means that I must earn the respect of professional historians . . . This means that I stand on two legs—the leg of faith and the leg of reason.[23]

Dialogue Controversy

As Arrington began his work as Church Historian, he became aware that his friends at *Dialogue* were becoming a growing source of controversy among many of his ecclesiastical leaders. Elder Ezra Taft Benson reportedly commented that *"Dialogue* should be burned."[24] It was true that among many of its publications, *Dialogue* had:

// . . . given great impetus to the New History movement . . . This was a response by young Mormon intellectuals to the need for competent professional history and commentary. Though the creation of this periodical caused a degree of controversy among the conservative Mormon community, including the General Authorities, it was welcomed by many members as the fulfillment of an intellectual need in the Church.[25]

---

22   Ibid., 187.

23   Gregory A. Prince, *Leonard Arrington and the Writing of Mormon History* (Salt Lake City, UT: Tanner Trust Fund and J. Willard Marriott Library, 2016), 162.

24   Please note that this statement is coming from Paul H. Dunn. See footnote 40 in this chapter. Leonard J. Arrington Diaries, August 18, 1976; Leonard J. Arrington and Gary James Bergera, *Confessions of a Mormon Historian: The Diaries of Leonard J. Arrington, 1971-1997*, vol. 1 (Salt Lake City: Signature Books, 2018), 293.

25   Richard Stephen Marshall, "'The New Mormon History': A Senior Honors Project Summary," May 1, 1977, Department of History, University of Utah Special Collections, Marriott Library, University of Utah, 25; photocopy in our possession.

On May 1, 1973, Elder Joseph Anderson, Assistant to the Quorum of the Twelve Apostles, advised Arrington that he must "avoid giving the impression that the Church or the Historical Department sponsors or supports Dialogue."[26] This created a significant challenge for Arrington, as most of his team members were associated with *Dialogue* in some way. Arrington was an advisory editor for *Dialogue* when it was founded in 1966. *Dialogue* enjoyed mutual collaboration and support with the Mormon History Association (co-founded by Arrington). Arrington recorded in his diary on March 23, 1976, "The founders of Dialogue agreed to give special attention to running articles by historians and we agreed to submit articles to them and to support the magazine. I myself agreed to be one of their advisory editors."[27] Arrington's good friend, Richard Bushman, was a member of *Dialogue's* charter editorial staff.[28] Arrington's editor, Maureen Beecher, would be a charter subscriber of *Dialogue*—later serving as one of its editors. Davis Bitton, Arrington's assistant, was serving as the book review editor for *Dialogue* in 1973, but resigned the position after Arrington's informal warning from Elder Anderson. For the New Mormon Historians, these were acceptable sacrifices deemed necessary to enable their shrouded work inside the system to continue moving forward. However, this did not prevent them from discreetly promoting their progressive brothers and sisters whenever they could safely do so.

Association of Mormon Letters

On July 27, 1976, the First Presidency called Leonard Arrington in to discuss a request from a newly formed scholarly organization, the Association for Mormon Letters, to use the conference room of the Church Historical Department for their first official meeting in October.

Maureen Beecher, a senior researcher for Arrington's division, had conceived of and organized a meeting for the Association for Mormon

---

26   Leonard J. Arrington Diaries, May 1, 1973; Leonard J. Arrington and Gary James Bergera, *Confessions of a Mormon Historian: The Diaries of Leonard J. Arrington,* 1971-1997, vol. 1 (Salt Lake City: Signature Books, 2018), 490.

27   Leonard J. Arrington Diaries, March 23, 1976; Ibid., 2:161.

28   Gregory A. Prince, *Leonard Arrington and the Writing of Mormon History* (Salt Lake City, UT: Tanner Trust Fund and J. Willard Marriott Library, 2016), 143.

Letters (AML), and had sent invitations using paper printed with the "Historical Department letterhead" after Arrington had reportedly given her permission to do so.[29] When questioned regarding the meeting, Arrington deceptively told the First Presidency he had "nothing to do with the Association of Mormon Letters but I was glad that they [the First Presidency] called me in because I was able to find out the story on them in order to review it for the First Presidency."[30] The First Presidency had expressed specific concern about who these individuals were and, more importantly—were they planning on publishing a magazine like *Dialogue*? The truth was, those attending the Association for Mormon Letters meeting would all at some point be associated with *Dialogue,* and were essentially of one heart and one mind with the progressive agenda of *Dialogue.* Arrington was careful not to raise red flags.

Arrington did his best to appear nonchalant, allaying any concerns regarding the group's true intentions. "They were all active members of the Church," he said, "[with] no intention to start a new magazine." Some had written for *Dialogue*, he admitted—but only a "small group" of them had done so.[31]

Arrington 'neglected' to mention that not only was Eugene England—the founder of *Dialogue*—present at Beecher's first meeting, but that it was England who had, in fact, suggested the idea of the AML to begin with, after posing the question: "How could we go about organizing a group focused on the criticism of Mormon literature?"[32] Ultimately, every member present at the original AML meeting would at some point publish in, or work for, *Dialogue*. Lavina Fielding Anderson and Eugene England were "key participants in that first meeting, and would continue to be

---

29   Andrew Hall, "Spencer W. Kimball and the founding of the Association for Mormon Letters," Association of Mormon Letters, April 20, 1976, http://associationmormonletters.org/blog/2019/08/spencer-w-kimball-and-the-founding-of-the-association-for-mormon-letters/.

30   Leonard J. Arrington Diaries, July 27, 1976; Leonard J. Arrington and Gary James Bergera, *Confessions of a Mormon Historian: The Diaries of Leonard J. Arrington,* 1971-1997, vol. 2 (Salt Lake City: Signature Books, 2018), 217.

31   Ibid., 218.

32   Lavina Fielding Anderson, "Tending the Garden with Eugene England," Eugene England Foundation, http://eugeneengland.org/wp-content/uploads/sbi/articles/2001_e_003.pdf.

leading members of AML over the next two decades."[33] As the AML planned to convene their first official meeting in the Historical Department's conference room in October, Anderson commented that "the [Church] bureaucrats had an absolute fit, terrified that somebody might think Leonard was sponsoring a new, intellectual and possibly anti-Mormon organization."[34] Thus the progressive-dominated, pro-*Dialogue* group was careful to conceal their true intentions and ideals from the First Presidency.

Unaware of the progressive undertones and the questionable direction in which the group was headed, President Kimball was nevertheless still hesitant and concerned with the appearance of Church affiliation. Finally, he decided to place trust in his Church Historian, remarking: "If you [Arrington] feel that there cannot be any harm in this organization, then I see no reason why we should object. I hope you will keep us informed of it and its activities."[35] Arrington promised that "no Church officer as such would be an officer of this organization. Certainly I would not serve as an officer nor [would] either of the Assistant Church Historians."[36]

Arrington could not have been more pleased. With the welcome blessing of the President of the Church, it seemed that the camel was fully inside the tent. In spite of Arrington's deliberate attempt to minimize the relationship between the AML and *Dialogue*, the true nature of the affair revealed itself at the first meeting, when "*Dialogue* agreed to collaborate with the Association by sharing those papers with a wider audience than the seventy or so members who were near enough to attend the meeting."[37] Moreover, Arrington himself "not only heartily

---

33   Andrew Hall, "Spencer W. Kimball and the founding of the Association for Mormon Letters," Association of Mormon Letters, April 20, 1976, http://associationmormonletters.org/blog/2019/08/spencer-w-kimball-and-the-founding-of-the-association-for-mormon-letters/.

34   Ibid.

35   Leonard J. Arrington Diaries, July 27, 1976: Leonard J. Arrington and Gary James Bergera, *Confessions of a Mormon Historian: The Diaries of Leonard J. Arrington*, 1971-1997, vol. 2 (Salt Lake City: Signature Books, 2018), 219-220.

36   Ibid., 219-220.

37   Maureen Ursenbach Beecher, "Proceedings of the Association for Mormon Letters: Introduction," *Dialogue: A Journal of Mormon Thought* 11, no. 2 (Summer 1978): 13.

seconded Maureen's hosting of this meeting but delivered a paper at the first meeting."[38]

God's Hand in Our Nation's History

While Leonard Arrington and his team were busy rewriting Latter-day Saint history, in an office nearby, the President of the Quorum of the Twelve Apostles was watching the winds of change in American history—and the efforts of progressive groups like *Dialogue*—with interest and deep concern. President Ezra Taft Benson was, as yet, blind to Arrington's hidden agenda within the Church Historical Department, but he was working to impress upon the Quorum of the Twelve and First Presidency the dangers of BYU faculty publishing in journals antagonistic to the Restoration. In December 1967, Alvin R. Dyer, a member of the First Presidency, remarked "that the continued publication of the magazine, and of its liberal content, was a matter of discussion in the Quorum of the Twelve meeting on Thursday, November 30."[39] Later in 1972, Arrington recorded second hand an incident coming from a general authority:[40]

---

38   Lavina Fielding Anderson, "Tending the Garden with Eugene England," Eugene England Foundation, http://eugeneengland.org/wp-content/uploads/sbi/articles/2001_e_003.pdf.

39   Gregory A. Prince, *Leonard Arrington and the Writing of Mormon History* (Salt Lake City, UT: Tanner Trust Fund and J. Willard Marriott Library, 2016), 148, footnote 44.

40   Please note that this statement is coming from Paul H. Dunn. In 1991, Dunn stated that he had "not always been accurate" in his speeches and writings, particularly in regard to his war and baseball stories. Dunn added, "They [the Church leaders] have censured me and placed a heavy penalty upon me," and that "I [Dunn] accept their censure and the imposed penalty, and pledge to conduct my life in such a way as to merit their confidence and full fellowship." Paul H. Dunn, "An open letter to members of the Church," *Church News*, October 26, 1991, 5.

It appears clear that Paul Dunn had a serious problem with honesty and entirely fabricated most of his life stories. This is a very unfortunate and disappointing occurrence in Church History. See Lynn Packer, "Paul H. Dunn: Fields of Dreams," *Sunstone* 15, no. 3 (September 1991): 35-39.

The *Deseret News* published an Associated Press story on February 16, 1991 reporting "Elder Paul H. Dunn, one of the most popular speakers and authors in The Church of Jesus Christ of Latter-day Saints, made up many of the stories about baseball and battle he told as personal experiences . . . ." Associated Press, "Arizona paper alleges many stories were exaggerated," *Church News*, February 16, 1991, B-5.

Ezra Taft Benson, 15th Secretary of Agriculture,
January 1953 - January 1961

❝ ... Brother Benson raised the question of BYU staff members publishing in Dialogue. He thought that they should not do so—that they should be prohibited from doing so. It was clear from the discussion that about half of the brethren were in favor of supporting publishing in Dialogue and the others were opposed to it. Brother Benson saw this cleavage, this division and brought his hand down firmly on the table and said that he thought this kind of thing should [not] be done: he thought that Dialogue should be burned.[41]

---

41   Leonard J. Arrington Diaries, September 20, 1972; Leonard J. Arrington and Gary James Bergera, *Confessions of a Mormon Historian: The Diaries of Leonard J. Arrington, 1971-1997*, vol. 1 (Salt Lake City: Signature Books, 2018), 293.

If this account is true, then President Benson was attempting early on to limit the influence of the progressive history movement within the Church. Regardless, President Benson recognized the tell-tale signs of the progressive movement to revise history among American historians and scholars, even among professors employed at Brigham Young University and other Church institutions.

Ezra Taft Benson was the grandson of Ezra T. Benson, an early member of the Quorum of the Twelve and one of the first pioneers to enter the Salt Lake valley with Brigham Young in 1847. Famous for his uncompromising principles in both the political realm as well as the religious, President Benson is remembered by those who knew him best as a man who sincerely, yet uncompromisingly, cared for mankind. His biographer, Sheri L. Dew, wrote of a young man who during the 1970s received permission to have his membership and temple ordinances restored, but passed away from cancer before he had a chance to have the ordinances performed. When President Benson became aware of the dilemma, "he acquired permission to have the blessings restored by proxy, contacted the family, and drove to Logan to take care of it himself."[42]

Dew also noted that while some perceived President Benson as austere, "no one realized how frequently he slipped away, both at home and on stake conference visits, to visit the sick, perform blessings, and seek out those who were burdened in some way." Instead of seeking personal pleasure while spending time "briefly" with his family at their Midway cabin, President Benson often spent his vacation visiting and counseling with neighbors in need. One mission president wrote, "I have become very aware lately of the tremendous missionary work you have done . . . here in the South. I have met many individuals who appeared to have unusual stature who were recent converts of the Church and when inquiring what attracted them to the Church, I found that you and your [family] were very frequently mentioned."[43]

President Benson recognized that both the United States of America and The Church of Jesus Christ of Latter-day Saints were under attack, and that both constituted essential, divinely appointed

---

42   Sheri L. Dew, *Ezra Taft Benson: A Biography* (Salt Lake City, Utah: Deseret Book Company, 1987), 435.

43   Ibid., 414-415.

vehicles designed to enable the Restoration of the Gospel of Jesus Christ to roll forward. He traveled to BYU in March of 1977 to plead for the protection of traditionalist history and to enlist defenders to stand up for that crucial cause. Once everyone was seated and introductions made, he arose before the student body to issue a rallying call to "uphold, sustain and defend the kingdom of God":

❝ I will speak to you also about some mischief that has been afoot for a number of years, a mischief that intends to undermine our republic, its founders, and the Church. I address you as students and faculty of this great University; but more importantly, I speak to you as members of the "household of faith," the Lord's true church, and remind you of your solemn charge to uphold, sustain, and defend the kingdom of God.

... My purpose this evening is to help you to discern a trend that has been destructive to the faith of many of our people in our nation's founders and our country's divine origin and destiny. My purpose further is to forewarn you about a humanistic emphasis which would tarnish our own Church history and its leaders.[44]

During this public address before the student body at Brigham Young University, President Benson denounced Fawn Brodie's biography, *No Man Knows My History,* and expressed distress over the progressive-leaning portrayals of the events surrounding the Mountain Meadows Massacre.[45] Furthermore, he challenged—even censured without naming—BYU evolutionary biology professor Duane Jeffrey, pleading with the Saints to be wary, and imploring them to exercise discernment that they "[b]eware lest ye are deceived."

President Benson took a courageous stand for traditionalism without fear or compromise, leading many to exult—while at the same time, earning remonstration and even hatred of many progressives. When Greg Prince characterized President Benson's address at BYU in his biography of Leonard Arrington, he brazenly chastened President Benson, accusing him of having a "paranoid

---

44 Ezra Taft Benson, "God's Hand in Our Nation's History," Brigham Young University Devotional, 1976, https://speeches.byu.edu/talks/ezra-taft-benson/gods-hand-nations-history/.

45 Ezra Taft Benson's comments were likely in reference to Juanita Brooks' *Mountain Meadows Massacre.*

streak" of "patriotism," claiming he used "demeaning and even insulting language." Prince dramatically unloaded on President Benson's approach: "[h]ere his wrath rose to new heights" as he "dared to contextualize what he saw as sacred history":

❞❞ Ezra Taft Benson, who saw the hand of God as both the proximate and ultimate cause of the founding and development of the United States of America and of the Church of Jesus Christ of Latter-day Saints was outspoken not only in delivering that message but also in criticizing any who suggested that other factors might also have been consequential.[46]

One fact is certain: President Benson earned the ire of his progressive contemporaries, feeling the sting of opposition and persecution because he dared to stand for traditional principles. An internet search for the most hated and criticized leaders within the Latter-day Saint movement identifies Jesus Christ, Joseph Smith, Brigham Young, Ezra Taft Benson, Boyd K. Packer, and Joseph Fielding Smith. Some wonder why—but it should come as no surprise that these names represent men who figure prominently in the defense of the long-standing traditional narrative of the Church. They were men who fought unflinchingly the onslaught of revisionist redirection and reinterpretation of our sacred past.

It is interesting to note that the events of the Book of Mormon here in America, just prior to the birth of the Lord Jesus Christ, parallel this great struggle to defend traditional history. Those who believed in the traditionalist teachings handed down by the prophets and leaders of the Nephite past were put to a severe test:

❞❞ Now it came to pass that there was a day set apart by the unbelievers, that all those who believed in those **traditions** should be put to death except the sign should come to pass, which had been given by Samuel the prophet.

Now it came to pass that when Nephi, the son of Nephi, saw this wickedness of his people, his heart was exceedingly sorrowful.

---

46   Gregory A. Prince, *Leonard Arrington and the Writing of Mormon History* (Salt Lake City, UT: Tanner Trust Fund and J. Willard Marriott Library, 2016), 279-280.

> And it came to pass that he went out and bowed himself down upon the earth, and cried mightily to his God in behalf of his people, yea, those who were about to be destroyed because of their faith in the **tradition of their fathers**.[47]

The humble traditionalists among the Nephites had been accused for several decades of being unwilling to accept modern teachings. "Behold, these things which ye call prophecies, which ye say are handed down by holy prophets, behold, they are foolish traditions of your fathers." Traditionalists among the Nephites were accused of being mentally unsound, even psychologically deranged: ". . . it is the effect of a frenzied mind; and this derangement of your minds comes because of the **traditions** of your fathers . . . ."[48]

On March 1, 1953, Elder Harold B. Lee defended his fellow apostle during a stake conference in Washington D.C., stating:

// There will be men who will belittle [Brother Benson] and will try to destroy him and destroy his reputation and destroy his influence in his high place. . . . Those who do will be forgotten in the remains of Mother Earth, and the odor of their infamy will ever be with them. But the glory and majesty attached to the name of Ezra Taft Benson will never die so long as Brother Benson continues to live the gospel of Jesus Christ. . . . And you and I who are in this congregation will live one day to see what I have said verified.[49]

---

47   3 Nephi 1:9-11; emphasis added.

48   Alma 30:16; emphasis added.

49   Sheri L. Dew, *Ezra Taft Benson: A Biography* (Salt Lake City, Utah: Deseret Book Company, 1987), 276-277. Harold B. Lee's choice of words when paying tribute to President Benson is remarkably reminiscent of the stirring defense of the Prophet Joseph Smith given by President George Albert Smith after Fawn Brodie published her defamatory biography *No Man Knows My History*. "There have been some who have belittled him, but I would like to say that those who have done so will be forgotten and their remains will go back to mother earth, if they have not already gone, and the odor of their infamy will never die, while the glory and honor and majesty and courage and fidelity manifested by the Prophet Joseph Smith will attach to his name forever. So we have no apologies to make." George Albert Smith, *Conference Report*, April 1946, 181–182. It appears President Lee may have been attempting to draw a parallel between the two.

5

BUTTING HEADS

A Noticeably New Story for the Saints

"Do people ever ask why you're rewriting our early history?"
Leonard Arrington was questioned while participating in an interview with the *Ensign* staff for a story they would publish in the July 1975 edition of the magazine. "Yes, often," Arrington acknowledged. Apparently, the question of rewriting history nagged members of the Church in the 1970s just as it does today. "But one of the things they don't realize is that we have three times as much material available now,"[1] Arrington assured his interviewer. Throughout the discussion, he continued to focus on the 'new' information his department was revealing. Was Arrington's new history the result of newly-discovered documents inaccessible to previous historians—or simply a revision of the interpretation?

Arrington's department certainly was active! Arrington excitedly shared with the *Ensign* new developments on a biography of Eliza R. Snow, as well as the cataloging of Joseph F. Smith's papers. He also pitched the new 16-volume history of the Church, the histories of Latter-day Saint communities in the West, the publication of Brigham Young's letters to his sons, and the sermons of Heber C. Kimball.

As members celebrated the efforts to document and preserve the history of the Restoration, few realized that Arrington's version of "our early history" would do far more than merely provide new information. He and his department would exert substantial effort in evaluating and recombining elements of original accounts into a new, progressive understanding of our past. As Arrington recorded

---

1   "History Is Then—and Now: A Conversation with Leonard J. Arrington, Church Historian," *Ensign*, July 1975.

in his diary on January 1, 1975, "One of our primary responsibilities is to develop the implications of new findings in Church History, and to advance new *interpretations* of our history."[2] Greg Prince noted that Arrington included in his diary the acknowledgment "that there was a political game to be played."[3]

Among other announcements in 1975, Arrington eagerly shared, "Before the end of 1975, we hope to make available a one-volume history that [will] be of interest to members and general readers . . ."[4] The next year, *The Story of the Latter-day Saints*[5] was published—authored by Arrington's assistants, James B. Allen and Glen M. Leonard. Before long, *Story* would ignite a firestorm of controversy between Leonard Arrington's progressive department and traditionalist leaders of the Church—including Ezra Taft Benson, Mark E. Peterson, and others—reportedly leading President Benson to demand that *Story* be "shredded."[6]

The Story of the Latter-day Saints

During the summer of 1976, Leonard Arrington and his colleagues were in high spirits. Thirty-five thousand copies of the new survey history of the Church, *The Story of the Latter-day Saints,* had arrived hot off the press—and were made available for sale on July 12. Five thousand copies were ordered by Church Public Communications to place "in every library in the United States,"[7] and the volume was quickly placed "on required reading lists for seminaries, institutes, and classes at BYU."[8] Arrington noted that "the die is cast and I feel

---

2   Gregory A. Prince, *Leonard Arrington and the Writing of Mormon History* (Salt Lake City, UT: Tanner Trust Fund and J. Willard Marriott Library, 2016), 250.

3   Ibid.

4   "History Is Then—and Now: A Conversation with Leonard J. Arrington, Church Historian," *Ensign*, July 1975.

5   James B. Allen and Glen M. Leonard, *The Story of the Latter-day Saints* (Salt Lake City, Utah: Deseret Book Company, 1976). Hereafter referred to as "Story."

6   Richard Stephen Marshall, "'The New Mormon History': A Senior Honors Project Summary," May 1, 1977, Department of History, University of Utah Special Collections, Marriott Library, University of Utah, 38; photocopy in our possession.

7   Leonard J. Arrington Diaries, August 18, 1976; Leonard J. Arrington and Gary James Bergera, *Confessions of a Mormon Historian: The Diaries of Leonard J. Arrington, 1971-1997*, vol. 2 (Salt Lake City: Signature Books, 2018), 223, footnote 17.

8   Ibid., 223.

Story would ignite a firestorm of controversy between Leonard Arrington and President Ezra Taft Benson.

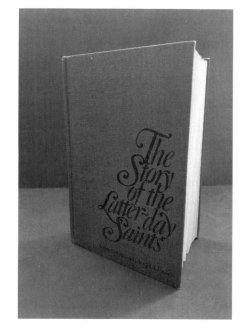

The Story of the Latter-day Saints, 1976

good about what we have done, proud of it."[9] Even with its departure from the traditionalist narrative, some progressives lamented that the book was still too apologetic toward Mormonism,[10] while others recognized it as a milestone toward ushering in progressivism. *Dialogue* hailed the book as:

> *II* . . . the most important volume yet produced in the new Mormon history. . . . the *Story of the Latter-day Saints* must be judged as a milestone—a refreshing, readable narrative which every Latter-day Saint should not only own, as an indispensable addition to his library, but should read with enthusiasm.[11]

It seemed the strength of the traditionalist voice was dying, and plans to dominate the narrative with progressive voices were finding

---

9   Leonard J. Arrington, *Adventures of a Church Historian* (University of Illinois Press, 1998), 143.

10   Gregory A. Prince, *Leonard Arrington and the Writing of Mormon History* (Salt Lake City, UT: Tanner Trust Fund and J. Willard Marriott Library, 2016), 278.

11   Dennis L. Lythgoe, "Artful Analysis of Mormonism," *Dialogue: A Journal of Mormon Thought* 10, no. 4 (1977): 135, 137.

success. There had been alleged threats that *"Dialogue* should be burned,"[12] but the *Dialogue*-supporting Church Historian continued to "fly under the radar."[13] The "camel" had made his way into the tent,[14] and the tent was now being born away. How long would it be before 'traditional Mormon History' would become an artifact for the museums—buried in the shifting sands of time, wasted in the ash heap of history?

Little did Arrington realize the extent of the storm clouds gathering. He was about to go head to head with a spiritually-seasoned man known for his earnest fealty to the Prophet Joseph Smith, his loyalty to traditional history, and his devotion to principles of liberty: Ezra Taft Benson.

Concerns Raised with *The Story of the Latter-day Saints*

One warm summer day, August 18, 1976, Arrington was alerted by "a friend" that one or two members of the Quorum of the Twelve Apostles "had perused The Story of the Latter-day Saints and did not like it."[15] The book was already published and in circulation when some of the concerned brethren turned to Ezra Taft Benson, then president of the

---

12   Please note that this statement is coming from Paul H. Dunn. See Chapter 4, footnote 40. Leonard J. Arrington Diaries, September 20, 1972; Leonard J. Arrington and Gary James Bergera, *Confessions of a Mormon Historian: The Diaries of Leonard J. Arrington, 1971-1997*, vol. 1 (Salt Lake City: Signature Books, 2018), 293.

13   Gregory A. Prince, *Leonard Arrington and the Writing of Mormon History* (Salt Lake City, UT: Tanner Trust Fund, and J. Willard Marriott Library, 2016), 51.

14   See *Faith Crisis, Volume 1: We Were NOT Betrayed!,* Chapter 10, "Criticism Leads the Camel's Nose Into the Tent." The reference to Leonard Arrington being a camel making his way into the tent comes from Elder John A. Widtsoe. When Arrington was researching for his dissertation, he reached out to Elder Widtsoe, about the possibility of writing an academic dissertation on economics in Latter-day Saint history. When Arrington moved to Utah in the summer of 1946, he met with Elder Widtsoe who suggested, unsolicited, a subtle plan to access the Church archives:

"First, he said, go in and ask to see published books. Read those a few days. Then ask for theses and dissertations. Read those a few days. Then ask for the Journal History. And when you're through with that, ask for specific documents you need. This way you will build up their confidence in you, and they will see you as a serious scholar. Like the proverbial camel, you will stick your head in the tent, gradually move fa[r]ther in, and ultimately carry the whole tent away with you." Leonard J. Arrington Diaries, September 6, 1976; Leonard J. Arrington and Gary James Bergera, *Confessions of a Mormon Historian: The Diaries of Leonard J. Arrington, 1971-1997*, vol. 2 (Salt Lake City: Signature Books, 2018), 230.

15   Leonard J. Arrington Diaries, August 18, 1976; Leonard J. Arrington and Gary James Bergera, *Confessions of a Mormon Historian: The Diaries of Leonard J. Arrington, 1971-1997*, vol. 2 (Salt Lake City: Signature Books, 2018), 222.

*Ezra Taft Benson is sworn in as secretary of agriculture under
Dwight D. Eisenhower, 1953*

Quorum of the Twelve, for help. Arrington's "friend," an informant
whose name would remain concealed in Arrington's personal diary,
had divulged confidential information that the meeting with President
Benson had resulted in a commissioned investigation into the new
book authored by James Allen and Glen Leonard.

A self-assured Arrington did not become overly anxious by the news.
In fact, he felt "very confident" that the book he had overseen would
yet become a well-accepted standard for Latter-day Saint history, and
that it would "weather the criticisms that some persons are apt to
make of it."[16] At the very worst, Arrington assumed, his department
may be required to pass their manuscripts through Correlation in
the future.[17]

At Church headquarters, President Benson was deliberating over
his own concerns with the new volume produced by Arrington's

16 "As for myself, I feel very confident about The Story of the Latter-day Saints—
that it will weather the criticisms that some persons are apt to make of it and that it
will come to be a standard and well accepted one-volume history of the Latter-day
Saints." Ibid., 223.

17 Ibid., 223.

department. For years concurrent with his full-time service for the Church, President Benson had served as a prominent cabinet member of the Dwight D. Eisenhower Presidential Administration—one of the highest political positions ever held by a Latter-day Saint. This assignment afforded him the opportunity to meet with and address audiences around the world; but it was at home, in America, where he would exert his greatest influence as he battled the growing socialist agenda intent on undermining the Constitutional Republic in the United States. He had observed and fought against the progressive rewriting of America's history, and many throughout the nation and the world loved him for his unwavering stance. He was even being considered as a presidential or vice presidential candidate for the 1968 election.[18] Elder Vaughn J. Featherstone expressed his sincere gratitude to President Benson in 1979: "I know the Lord has blessed you with a special understanding of the needs of this country. You have helped breed in my heart a love for this great nation, a love for the founding fathers, and a love for the Constitution."[19]

Now, with his attention more fully focused on his service within the Church—President Benson began to recognize the same portentous trends previously identified threatening liberty working simultaneously within the Church. He had questioned and called *Dialogue* out, challenging the progressive historians who were doggedly attempting to change Latter-day Saint history. What he did not know was that his own Church Historian, just a few doors away, was not only sympathetic to the "New Mormon History,"—he was its champion.

Rumors had reached President Benson alluding to a left-leaning element within the Historical Department, but nothing concrete enough to raise serious concern had yet come to light. James Allen related an experience he had conducting oral history interviews with President Benson before *Story* was released: "[A]t the end, Elder Benson complimented me on the interviews, saying that at first he was apprehensive because he had heard that the History Division was filled with a 'bunch of liberals,' and my treatment of him had been a pleasant surprise."[20]

---

18   Kenneth W. Godfrey, "Ezra Taft Benson," *Utah History Encyclopedia*, https://www.uen.org/utah_history_encyclopedia/b/BENSON_EZRA.shtml.

19   Sheri L. Dew, *Ezra Taft Benson: A Biography* (Salt Lake City, Utah: Deseret Book Company, 1987), 439.

20   A review by James B. Allen, "Gregory A. Prince. Leonard Arrington and the

Behind Closed Doors

A little over one week after Leonard Arrington was initially tipped off by an informant in his obscured network, he learned that President Benson's personal secretary had drafted an eight-page critique that was then being circulated and deliberated upon among members of the Twelve. Several days later, Arrington vented that as yet, no member of the Quorum had approached him or the authors to discuss their concerns. He voiced his logical misgiving in his diary:

Although apparently several members of the Twelve have been aware of the existence of the critique, and of President Benson's support of it (and apparently the support also of Elder Mark Petersen), not a person has called me up or written me, or made other contact to ask me (or Allen or Leonard) how I would defend the book, and our history writing in general. Elder Howard Hunter told me, as he walked out of our advisors' meeting on Wednesday Sept. 1 that he wanted to talk with me sometime on the subject of running all our works through Correlation, but he has made no attempt to discuss this with me.[21]

The entry in Arrington's journal reflected his wounded feelings. Why was criticism spreading behind closed doors and not broached with him directly? Why did the various players not feel that it was possible to employ appropriate, open, and honest dialogue? Resentment, when neglected, only festers in darkness, beneath the surface.[22] It seems that a significant part of the story is missing.

At the present time, we only have access to Arrington's side of the story, revealing his perspective of the struggle unfolding in Salt Lake City. This renders it difficult to ascertain the true intent of all the voices weighing in on the subject, and to know just where the fault lay.

Writing of Mormon History," *BYU Studies Quarterly* 57, no. 2 (2018): 179, footnote 1.

21   Leonard J. Arrington Diaries, September 6, 1976; Leonard J. Arrington and Gary James Bergera, *Confessions of a Mormon Historian: The Diaries of Leonard J. Arrington, 1971-1997*, vol. 2 (Salt Lake City: Signature Books, 2018), 226.

22   The Son of God divinely instructed His disciples with reference to conflict and trespasses within the Church, ". . . if thy brother shall trespass against thee, go and tell him his fault between thee and him alone: if he shall hear thee, thou hast gained thy brother. But if he will not hear thee, then take with thee one or two more, that in the mouth of two or three witnesses every word may be established. And if he shall neglect to hear them, tell it unto the church: but if he neglect to hear the church, let him be unto thee as an heathen man and a publican." Matthew 18:15-16.

Regardless, Arrington's concern with the lack of open discussion may stand as a reminder for both traditionalists and progressives engaging in the search and struggle for truth today: frank, uncensored dialogue is critical. Should not the battle between progressive and traditional history come out into the open from behind closed doors? If concerns exist, should we not all endeavor to address misgivings forthrightly?

Most of the history concerning this struggle remains inaccessible at this time. What we do know is that the general membership of the Church was not informed of the players and controversy taking place at Church headquarters in the 1970s. This controversy has continued—and still exists today—causing misunderstanding and contributing to a faith crisis of ever growing numbers. Historical narratives are changing, historians with agendas are driving the redefinition of our origins, and lay members remain inert and confused.

The following principles are common ground that should be both agreeable and achievable among honest progressives and traditionalists.

First, the Lord, in this dispensation, has judiciously counseled, "No power or influence can or ought to be maintained by virtue of the priesthood, only by persuasion, by long-suffering, by gentleness and meekness, and by love unfeigned."[23] Likewise, no individual, and no group of individuals who have stewardship over the influence of our history, should decide the final draft of any historical narrative while sequestered behind closed doors. If the issues are not generally understood by the people, and decided upon by common consent, how can persuasion—as opposed to manipulation—be considered part of the foregoing equation? At sundry times, advocates from both sides have been guilty of violating this fundamental principle, and have thus wielded unrighteous dominion.

> *Should not the battle between progressive and traditionalist history come out into the open from behind closed doors?*

There have been times when the authors of this book have personally experienced censorship by progressive groups on various social

---

23   Doctrine and Covenants 121:41.

media forums. The refusal of progressive thought leaders to engage in public dialogue prohibits members from becoming familiar with the issues for themselves. When the discussion is shut off, informed decisions are impossible.

In addition, the authors have also experienced the impact of censorship by book companies and distributors who are aligned with progressive voices—voices who seem to be afraid of opening communication beyond their own partisan points of view. Should we not seek to do away with hidden agendas and the politics of censorship or manipulation—notably when it involves influencing the information and beliefs of the Latter-day Saints?

For those who value choice, President Benson was an exemplary representative of exercising priesthood authority righteously when he took his private concerns and disclosed them publicly in speeches and published addresses—thus enlisting each member of the Church to share his or her voice. In doing so, this wise leader endured criticism and took heat from liberal progressives for representing controversial matters candidly before the people. However, his actions placed him squarely in alignment with scripture. President Benson took the principles behind revisionist history directly to the people, allowing individuals to accept or reject by exercising agency. Accordingly, the members in that generation ultimately chose the direction of the Church. In a revelation given to the Prophet Joseph Smith on September 11, 1831, the Lord charged every member of The Church of Jesus Christ of Latter-day Saints with a sacred duty—the duty to judge:

// Behold, I, the Lord, have made my church in these last days like unto a judge sitting on a hill, or in a high place, to judge the nations. For it shall come to pass that the *inhabitants of Zion shall judge all things* pertaining to Zion.[24]

In the Prophet Joseph Smith's day, he exemplified open and honest dialogue by allowing pastors and ministers of all sects to have an opportunity to speak to the Saints. Binding doctrine and scripture were presented and sustained by the membership of the Church before requiring adherence to the precepts contained therein— they were never forced upon the general membership. Leaders were

---

24 Doctrine and Covenants 64:37-38; emphasis added.

held accountable for their actions,[25] and every Latter-day Saint was allowed—even encouraged—to question freely and to search sincerely and deliberately for truth until they owned it for themselves.

---

25   On April 6, 1843, a special conference was organized in commemoration of the anniversary of the organization of the Church. On this occasion, the Prophet declared:

> "It is my object to ascertain the [standing] of the first presidency. (as I have been instructed) I present myself for trial, I shall next present my councillors [sic] for trial. . . . Are you satisfied with the first presedincy [sic], so far as I am concerned, or will you choose another? If I have done any thing to injure my character in the sight of men & angels— or men & women. come forward tell of it. & if not ever after hold your peace." Joseph Smith, "President Joseph Smith's Journal," Journal, December 1842–June 1844; Book 2, April 6, 1843, p. 50-51, The Joseph Smith Papers.

The Prophet Joseph Smith was not afraid to acknowledge shortcomings or mistakes. Joseph Smith, the prophet of the Restoration, the head of the dispensation, the President of Church and the greatest man ever to live, excepting the Son, had a better right than any man to frown on criticism. However, even he did not consider himself above the law. After requesting the Latter-day Saints to present any complaints or concerns, Brigham Young "arose & nominated Joseph Smith to continue as the President of the Church." President Young's loyalty to Joseph Smith was a theme that continued until his last breath. Orson Hyde seconded President Young's motion, and then it was put to a vote. For the first time in the history of the Church, the vote was unanimous!

> "Such a show of hands was never seen before in the church.— Joseph retur[ne]d his thanks—— to the assembly. & said he would serve them according to the best of his ability." Joseph Smith, "President Joseph Smith's Journal," Journal, December 1842–June 1844; Book 2, April 6, 1843, p. 52, The Joseph Smith Papers.

Sidney Rigdon (First Counselor) was then presented "for trial" and sustained. William Law (Second Counselor) was then presented "for trial" and sustained. Patriarch Hyrum Smith was then presented, and the congregation voted in favor of Hyrum retaining his office. At the conclusion of this action, the Prophet Joseph Smith humbly proclaimed, "I do not know any thing agai[n]st the twelve, if I did I would presnt [sic] them for trial." Joseph Smith, "President Joseph Smith's Journal," Journal, December 1842–June 1844; Book 2, April 6, 1843, p. 55, The Joseph Smith Papers.

During this same conference, Brigham Young "asked if any one knew anything against any one of the Twelve—any dishonesty. If they did, he wanted it exposed." Richard S. Van Wagoner, editor, The Complete Discourses of Brigham Young, vol. 1 (Salt Lake City: The Smith-Pettit Foundation, 2009), 23.

The Prophet Joseph understood that he and his fellow leaders were not "above the law." To Joseph Smith, "defending the Church" did not mean defending his first counselor, his second counselor, or even himself as President. Defending the Church meant defending the Gospel of Jesus Christ and pointing the Latter-day Saints to the Father and the Son. Here, and here alone, the Prophet begged his people to place their trust. If the members knew of anything he had done wrong, he asked them to "come forward tell of it" so that he might rectify the issue. Joseph Smith understood that holding leaders accountable would not threaten the Church, for the foundation he built was founded on God, and not man.

The modern tendency on both sides—the progressives and the traditionalists—to censor or suffocate open debate, discussion, and even thought, continues to prove catastrophic for the testimonies of growing numbers of members within the Church. We believe it is imperative to exchange jockeying for position and private debate with open and upfront civil discussion.[26]

Regardless of whether or not the private criticisms of *Story of the Latter-day Saints* were ideally conducted, one matter is clear—informants on both sides were leaking intelligence to their respective sympathizers. Arrington and his assistant, James Allen[27]—co-author of *The Story of the Latter-day Saints*—each knew of the growing controversy before being approached directly by those who had concerns.[28] At the same time, Arrington suspected for some unknown reason that two employees from the Library-Archives staff were secretly 'working for' President Benson. "I have a feeling based on absolutely no evidence except hunch that the critique [commissioned by President Benson] was prepared by Lauritz Petersen and Tom Truitt of our Library–Archives staff."[29] Apparently, Arrington's covert operation of changing history was being watched by his opposition's own cloaked investigators. Informants on each side relayed information to their respective handlers in an undercover, behind-the-scenes cold war. Both sides, traditionalists and progressives alike, relied on insider information.[30]

---

26   A detailed study of Arrington's diaries reveals jockeying for position, disagreement and disunity, maneuvering for position, appeasing bureaucratic superiors, authoritative supervisory and other inappropriate activity.

27   "I only wish," James B. Allen wrote in his diary, "that if some of these folks had some specific concerns, they would come and discuss them with us personally and let us know why we wrote it the way we did, before they take negative reports to the higher authorities." Leonard J. Arrington Diaries, September 6, 1976; Leonard J. Arrington and Gary James Bergera, *Confessions of a Mormon Historian: The Diaries of Leonard J. Arrington*, 1971-1997, vol. 2 (Salt Lake City: Signature Books, 2018), 227, footnote 25.

28   Ibid., 225-227.

29   Leonard J. Arrington Diaries, August 18, 1976; Ibid., 223. Arrington recorded in a later entry that the "original critique of Story of the Latter-day Saints . . . was prepared by Bill Nelson, Elder Benson's special assistant, and by Cal Rudd of the Institute of Religion at the University of Utah." Leonard J. Arrington Diaries, November 30, 1976; Ibid., 321.

30   Some may feel uncomfortable with the existence of stratagem employed by both traditionalists and progressives in furthering history according to their interpretation. The reader should note that both sides of this debate felt they were

Before Arrington was officially apprised of the Brethren's concerns, "a friend" read him the complete critique from President Benson's secretary, of which Arrington recorded an overview in his diary:

" Basically, the critique did the following:

1. Said that Joseph Fielding Smith, Essentials in Church History, should be continued in print.

2. Criticized the bibliography as containing mention of works that were anti-Church: Brodie, No Man Knows My History; articles in Dialogue, particularly by Poll, Jeffries.

3. Criticized the story of the crickets and seagulls as not bringing God into the picture.

4. Criticized the account of Zion's Camp which implies that it was a failure.

5. Criticized the account of BYU firing the evolutionists as not being sufficiently anti-evolution.

6. Said the book failed to mention the doctrinal contributions of Joseph Fielding Smith. (Didn't say what they were.)

7. Said the book was basically a secular history; did not have enough of the spiritual in this account of our history.

8. Said all of our history publications should be routed through Correlation in order to insure [sic] that they were doctrinally and historically accurate, and had the right tone and impact.[31]

Later discussions between Leonard Arrington and Ezra Taft Benson, as well as other traditionalist leaders, would reveal a few primary points of contention. Traditionalists were concerned that *Story* accepted anti-Mormon slanders against Joseph Smith as

---

called by God to further what they saw as the truth. In the Book of Mormon, Mormon deliberately clarified at least five times that stratagem should be used by the righteous as a defensive device.

"And Moroni placed spies round about . . . knowing that it was the only desire of the Nephites to preserve their lands, and their liberty, and their church, therefore he thought it no sin that he should defend them by stratagem . . ." Alma 43:28, 30. See also, Alma 52:10, 54:3, 56:30, and 58:28.

31   Leonard J. Arrington Diaries, September 6, 1976; Leonard J. Arrington and Gary James Bergera, *Confessions of a Mormon Historian: The Diaries of Leonard J. Arrington*, 1971-1997, vol. 2 (Salt Lake City: Signature Books, 2018), 225-226.

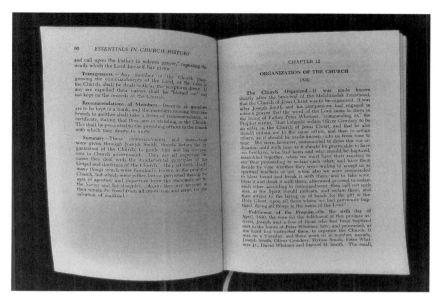

Joseph Fielding Smith devoted 4 pages to the organization of the Church in Essentials in Church History (pictured above), while the 1976 edition of Story budgeted "a paragraph."

credible historical fact; and they disputed a reinterpretation of the prophetic history of the Restoration through a secular, progressive, liberal, and evolutionary worldview. This new narrative contrasted conclusively with the traditional understanding of doctrine and scripture. Finally, the traditionalists were averse to the portrayal of miraculous events in unduly naturalistic terms and perceptions— as having been initiated and influenced purely by contemporary economic, political, and cultural climates. The traditional reverential acknowledgment of God's direct involvement through "His-story" was lacking in the progressive narrative.

Arrington began nervously anticipating a war between his department and the man who "will not stand for our 'real' history"— President Benson.[32] Arrington wrote to his children that some complaints dealt with the book being "too secular—not spiritual enough," but added that "we knew we'd have criticism from both sides. It's a tightrope we're walking."[33] Arrington blamed the criticism on

---

32   Ibid., 226.

33   Gregory A. Prince, *Leonard Arrington and the Writing of Mormon History* (Salt Lake City, UT: Tanner Trust Fund and J. Willard Marriott Library, 2016), 282.

right-wing conservatives, suggesting that "some John Bircher[34]... has complained to President Benson."[35] For over a week, Arrington fretted:

❝ ... we are in a powerless position ...

... Shall I retain the job (assuming they don't release me) and try to write history which will be approved by Correlation. Or shall I resign and continue to write 'real history.' ... I am not clear in my own mind as to the best course to pursue, but feel discouraged, sad, shook. It has been a tough few days for me since I do not dare mention all this to a soul.[36]

Leonard Arrington struggled with whether or not he should compromise his own ideals. Was his position as Church Historian really worth the sacrifice? As Arrington brooded, President Benson was deliberating on his own plan to combat the progressive historical agenda he observed facing the Church.

---

34   The John Birch Society was a conservative, anti-communist group founded in 1958 to defend the Constitution of the United States. It was named after an American Christian missionary and U.S. military intelligence officer who was killed by Chinese Communist soldiers in 1945. According to President Ezra Taft Benson, the John Birch Society was attacked in a smear campaign launched by the Communists during the 1960s. President Benson defended the group, although he was personally not a member. He supported his son Reed's appointment as a state coordinator. On June 24, 1968, Ezra Taft Benson wrote a letter to Mr. & Mrs. Gene Curtis, informing them: "You will be interested to know that President McKay encouraged my son, Reed, to stay with the John Birch Society indicating that it would be vindicated and become a powerful organization in the preservation of our freedom." (Photocopy in author's possession) The society was criticized and spurned by liberal and progressive individuals as "far-right." Leonard Arrington's diaries reveal that he shared the liberal disdain, criticizing many members who opposed his progressive history work as "John Birchers."

35   Leonard J. Arrington Diaries, August 18, 1976; Leonard J. Arrington and Gary James Bergera, *Confessions of a Mormon Historian: The Diaries of Leonard J. Arrington, 1971-1997*, vol. 2 (Salt Lake City: Signature Books, 2018), 223, footnote 23.

36   Leonard J. Arrington Diaries, September 6, 1976; Ibid., 226-227.

6

AN AWKWARD, FERVENT MEETING
WITH THE FIRST PRESIDENCY

O n Friday, September 17, 1976—a few weeks after Leonard
Arrington was apprised of the growing controversy—
President Ezra Taft Benson arose before a crowd of religious
educators in the Assembly Hall. His delivery included a strong
denunciation of progressive history and a clarification of the
inherent and sacred responsibilities of educators:

❦❦ There have been and continue to be attempts to bring (a
humanistic) philosophy into our own Church history. . . .

We would warn you teachers of this trend, which seems to be
an effort to reinterpret the history of the Church so that it is
more rationally appealing to the world. We must never forget
that ours is a prophetic history. Our students need to understand
this prophetic history. This can only be done by teachers who
themselves possess the Spirit of prophecy and revelation.[1]

The Monday following President Benson's address, Arrington
received a phone call requesting his attendance at a meeting with
the First Presidency the next morning.

"What is the meeting about? Are there any materials I should
bring or prepare myself on?"

"No," was the vague reply. "Just come to the meeting
tomorrow morning."

---

1   Ezra Taft Benson, "The Gospel Teacher and His Message," address to religious
educators, Assembly Hall, Salt Lake City, Utah, September 17, 1976, p. 7, typescript
in Leonard J. Arrington Papers, Special Collections, Merrill-Cazier Library, Utah
State University, Logan, Utah.

The next morning, a little before 8:30 a.m., Arrington shuffled outside the First Presidency Conference Room door, waiting alongside none other than Ezra Taft Benson, as well as Mark E. Petersen, Howard W. Hunter, and Bruce R. McConkie. Progressives and traditionalists lingered side by side, no doubt with some awkward uneasiness, each side understanding the brewing cold war more than each could let on.

Spencer W. Kimball, President 1973-1985

Finally, the door of the conference room opened. All were then invited to join the First Presidency, consisting of President Spencer W. Kimball and his counselors, N. Eldon Tanner and Marion G. Romney, who were already seated in the room.[2]

A smiling President Kimball set a non-confrontational tone; but he was also blunt and came straight to the point. "Serious questions [have] been raised about two books recently published, *The Story of the Latter-day Saints*[3] and *Building the City of God*." Turning to Ezra, he invited the sitting President of the Quorum of the Twelve to share his concerns.

As President Benson began, it was clear he would not be pulling any punches.[4] According to Arrington's recollection, President Benson

---

2   Leonard J. Arrington Diaries, September 21, 1976; Leonard J. Arrington and Gary James Bergera, *Confessions of a Mormon Historian: The Diaries of Leonard J. Arrington, 1971-1997*, vol. 2 (Salt Lake City: Signature Books, 2018), 238.

3   James B. Allen and Glen M. Leonard, *The Story of the Latter-day Saints* (Salt Lake City, Utah: Deseret Book Company, 1976). Hereafter referred to as "*Story.*"

4   Some progressives have criticized Ezra Taft Benson because Leonard Arrington claims in his diary that President Benson told him "he had not read all . . . but that he had read some portions of The Story of the Latter-day Saints. He [President Benson] said that one member of the Quorum of the Twelve had read The Story of the Latter-day Saints all the way through and others had read portions of it." Leonard J. Arrington Diaries, September 21, 1976; Leonard J. Arrington and

began expressing his fears that *Story* "would cause young people to lose faith," specifically because:

> **❝** . . . it tended to degrade or demean Joseph Smith; it did not give enough emphasis to important events such as the founding of the Church (only 16 lines and the names of the six persons not given); it had raised questions. It [letter from a concerned member read by President Benson] was a rather eloquent letter protesting against the "new history." Brother Benson made other statements about the book and the problems and dangers and risks and indicated that he felt very strongly that it was a mistake to have published it and that it would do great damage.[5]

By this time, President Benson fully understood that he was not confronting just one offhand history book, or its unique interpretation of Church history. He knew *Story* was only the tip of the iceberg—representing only one of many works emerging from a growing movement to revise and reinterpret history. Even progressive authors have acknowledged that for President Benson, "the real issue was not a book but a philosophy of historiography."[6]

During the meeting with Arrington and the First Presidency, President Benson stressed that he was not the only member who found *Story* troublesome. After delivering "The Gospel Teacher and His Message" the previous Friday, President Benson had been approached by a member who admitted to being quietly distressed

---

Gary James Bergera, *Confessions of a Mormon Historian: The Diaries of Leonard J. Arrington*, 1971-1997, vol. 2 (Salt Lake City: Signature Books, 2018), 239.

In a later entry, Arrington records President Benson as explaining that "He had read far more in Story of the Latter-day Saints and was equally concerned with its tone which he said to be secular, even negative, and not faith-building." Leonard J. Arrington Diaries, October 22, 1976; Ibid., 266.

Regardless of whether President Ezra Taft Benson personally analyzed the entire text of *Story,* an analysis today demonstrates that President Benson's concerns were valid, as various portions of *The Story of the Latter-day Saints* do reflect elements of the progressive New Mormon History. *The Story of the Latter-day Saints* was certainly moderate, and could even be considered a compromise between traditionalist and progressive history when compared to progressive Latter-day Saint publications today, such as *Rough Stone Rolling, A Reason for Faith, In Sacred Loneliness: The Plural Wives of Joseph Smith*, etc.

5   Ibid., 239.

6   Gregory A. Prince, *Leonard Arrington and the Writing of Mormon History* (Salt Lake City, UT: Tanner Trust Fund and J. Willard Marriott Library, 2016), 280.

by *Story*. President Benson had not mentioned the book specifically in his address to the educators, but his pleadings had prompted this member to initiate a reference to the "New Mormon History."[7]

President Benson then read a letter which had been written by this concerned member, a letter Arrington observed "was concerned not only with *Story* in particular but with the 'new history' in general." The letter went on to express concerns with the Historical Department generally, with nearly all of their books and articles, as well as fears for the upcoming 16-volume history Arrington was preparing for the sesquicentennial celebration of the Church. Arrington noted that while he had "no idea who wrote [the letter]" he was "clearly a good writer and thinker."[8]

Priority in History?

One of the concerns raised by President Benson, pertaining to *Story*, consisted in the priority given to certain events in the Church's history over others. Arrington recorded the apprehension as he understood it:

> As one illustration of his critique he [President Benson] said that the most important event in the history of modern civilization was the Restoration of the Gospel which he regarded as equivalent to the founding of the Church April 6, 1830. He found only a paragraph on that without even naming the six people involved. On the other hand he found two or three pages, maybe even three or four, on the founding of ZCMI.[9] There was very little

---

7   Leonard J. Arrington and Gary James Bergera, *Confessions of a Mormon Historian: The Diaries of Leonard J. Arrington, 1971-1997*, vol. 2 (Salt Lake City: Signature Books, 2018), 238-239, 266-267.

8   Leonard J. Arrington Diaries, October 22, 1976; Ibid., 267.

9   ZCMI (Zion's Co-operative Mercantile Institution) was a department store chain established by Brigham Young in 1868. Joseph Fielding Smith wrote about the founding of ZCMI in *Essentials in Church History*, "The attitude of local anti-'Mormons,' coupled with the proposed unfavorable and inhuman legislation, naturally drove the members of the Church closer together. It was proposed in self-protection that there be organized throughout the various settlements a chain of co-operative stores, and that the people trade with each other rather than with their enemies. And if the proposed threats were to be fulfilled, the enemies of the Church who came to Utah to do business would have to bring their customers with them, for the Saints would not patronize them. Based upon this proposition a parent institution was established in Salt Lake City, in which all the 'Mormon' people were invited to take stock. This commercial house, known as Zion's Co-

Zion's Co-operative Mercantile Institution (ZCMI), 1910

on the most glorious vision in modern times—Section 76 of the Doctrine and Covenants.[10]

Allen and Leonard conspicuously prioritized the mercantile institution ZCMI above or ahead of the organization of the Church, as well as the Vision of the Three Degrees of Glory. For President Benson, this was inconceivable.

James Allen, co-author of *The Story of the Latter-day Saints*, was mentored by progressives S. George Ellsworth, Eugene E. Campbell,

---

operative Mercantile Institution, opened its doors for business in 1869, and the following year was incorporated. In a circular announcing their intentions it was stated by the brethren that they were 'convinced of the impolicy of leaving the trade and commerce of the territory to the conduct of strangers,' and therefore 'it was advisable that the people of Utah should become their own merchants' and 'unite in a system of co-operation for the transaction of their own business.' In this way there could be a consolidation of the mercantile stores in which all the people might be interested, and receive their merchandise based on a small margin of profit. Branches were established in nearly every settlement and were beneficial to the people while that condition lasted." Joseph Fielding Smith, *Essentials in Church History* (Deseret Book, 1966), 543-544.

10   Leonard J. Arrington Diaries, October 22, 1976; Leonard J. Arrington and Gary James Bergera, *Confessions of a Mormon Historian: The Diaries of Leonard J. Arrington*, 1971-1997, vol. 2 (Salt Lake City: Signature Books, 2018), 267.

and Richard D. Poll. Allen assisted Arrington in founding the Mormon History Association (MHA) and had published his works previously in *Dialogue*. Leonard Arrington, James Allen's supervisor, was originally trained as an economist—not a historian. The life and teachings of Joseph Smith, as well as scripture and Church doctrine, were not his expertise. Arrington confessed that he "particularly lack[ed] knowledge in Church history before 1847. And in the view of many persons, that is the key period of Church history."[11] In essence, Arrington was largely unfamiliar with the history of the Prophet Joseph Smith and the origins of the Restoration and the Church—all of which comprised the most important foundation of the 'Mormon' identity.

Having read neither the Bible nor the Book of Mormon entirely through since his first attempt as a 13-year-old boy, Arrington admitted not being "an avid student" of the scriptures and feeling inadequate when discussing doctrine with other lay members.[12] Arrington's illiteracy in the Church's foundational texts is reflected in the decisions he made while writing Latter-day Saint history, and during his role as director of the Church History Department.

President Benson's frame of reference, on the other hand, was strongly imprinted by the countless hours he had spent studying the scriptures and the history of the Church from his youth. "We'd had a lot of reading of the scriptures in our home,"[13] President Benson recalled. His biographer shared, "Ezra couldn't remember his father ever going to the field without first having family prayer."[14]

Without question, Ezra Taft Benson's heart swelled with a great love for the scriptures and for Church history. His biographer noted as well that:

 His mission log, in which he accounted for every shilling spent, frequently noted the purchase of secondhand books. He . . . "eagerly devoured the Book of Mormon," read the complete *History of the Church* by Joseph Smith, and studied the life of the Prophet. . . .

---

11   Leonard J. Arrington Diaries, September 25, 1978; Ibid., 632.

12   Ibid., 632-633.

13   Sheri L. Dew, *Ezra Taft Benson: A Biography* (Salt Lake City, Utah: Deseret Book Company, 1987), 52-53.

14   Ibid., 36.

Dates of note didn't escape Elder Benson's attention. On June 27 he wrote, "78 yrs. ago today, Prophet Joseph killed." . . . [On July 14], it was a landmark of a different nature. "One year since I left the dear home in the [mountains]. Has been the most beneficial year of my life, because it has been spent in the service of the Master."

Nevertheless, the fruits of tracting and ferreting out investigators provided a meager harvest. By and large, the people were indifferent and bitter. Ezra kept himself going by "devouring the Book of Mormon," particularly the missionary experiences of the sons of Mosiah.[15]

Later, while serving as Secretary of Agriculture for U.S. President Eisenhower, President Benson eagerly shared the Gospel with his political colleagues. For eight years, all of his staff meetings began with prayer, each member taking a turn. One assistant noted that the practice caught some attendees off guard, but noticeably led to a quicker resolution of problems, less pride, and more humility among

Ezra Taft Benson presented with ancient map of
Holy Land by Levi Eshkol, Jerusalem, 1957

15   Ibid., 53, 59.

the office staff.[16] President Benson refused to work on Sunday, and his patterned adherence to living the Word of Wisdom prompted some of his aides to follow his example, an act forever benefiting their lives:

// When a third-level employee developed a drinking problem and his work suffered, his supervisor recommended dismissal. Secretary Benson called the man in and talked at length about his responsibility to his family, his job, and himself. The man became a productive employee.[17]

President Benson's deep love for the scriptures prompted him to share them often with others, even when it may have seemed unpopular:

// When a university radio station in the Midwest asked if it might broadcast his favorite scriptural reading, he selected the Joseph Smith story . . . Ezra sent Eisenhower lengthy excerpts from the Book of Mormon prophesying about America's destiny. . . . Dozens of world leaders received copies of the Book of Mormon—heads of state, ambassadors, even newspaper editors.[18]

President Benson's devotion to and knowledge of the scriptures influenced his understanding of history. For him, the Gospel of Jesus Christ was everything. When he reviewed *Story,* President Benson felt that events such as the 1830 founding of the Church or Joseph Smith's Vision of the Three Degrees of Glory, as recorded in section 76 of the Doctrine and Covenants, were not prioritized, nor given proper attention. The key difference between the two boys-become-men—Ezra and Leonard—was mindset and attitude toward remaining true to the Restoration and remaining true to those divinely directed events leading up to the reestablishment of the Gospel—namely the foundations of American liberty.

To understand the distinction and characteristic discrepancy between the traditionalist and progressive views of historical priority, an illustration is necessary. The Book of Mormon contrasts vividly

---

16   "Secretary Benson's Faith in the American Farmer," *Farm and Ranch,* September 1956, reprinted in *Reader's Digest,* October 1956, 84-88; quoted in Ibid., 268.

17   Sheri L. Dew, *Ezra Taft Benson: A Biography* (Salt Lake City, Utah: Deseret Book Company, 1987), 268-269.

18   Ibid., 292.

the difference in the Lord's prioritization of historical events, versus the world's. If someone were to ask you, what are the most important events in American history, how would you answer?

Lists compiled by contemporary authors or historians frequently list the following "most important events":[19]

- Assassination of Abraham Lincoln
- Louisiana Purchase
- Manhattan Project/Atomic Bomb
- Vietnam War
- Death of Osama bin Laden
- President Truman Orders Racial Equality in Military (1948)
- Assassination of John F. Kennedy
- New York City Teachers Go on Strike (1975)
- The American Revolution
- The Civil War & Gettysburg Address
- September 11, 2001 terrorist attacks
- Apollo 11 Moon Landing
- Explorers Bridge the Pacific (1564-1565)
- Bald Eagle Gets Federal Protection

In 2017, the *New York Post* published an article entitled, "America's most important historical dates will surprise you." The disparate list included events ranging from: "The teddy bear debuts," to "'The Tonight Show' with Johnny Carson premieres," to "Yosemite is named as the first US national park." Each presumably represents "some of our country's most important but less celebrated moments . . . that helped shape . . . our American identity."[20]

---

19   See "The 25 Moments From American History That Matter Right Now," Time.com, https://time.com/5314430/american-history-moments-matter-today/; "What Were the Most Important Events in American History?" HistoryontheNet. com, https://www.historyonthenet.com/what-were-the-most-important-events-in-american-history; "Top 10 Important Events in US History," ListVerse.com, https://listverse.com/2011/07/14/top-10-important-events-in-us-history/.

20   Susannah Cahalan, "America's most important historical dates will surprise you," *New York Post*, August 12, 2017, https://nypost.com/2017/08/12/americas-most-important-historical-dates-will-surprise-you/.

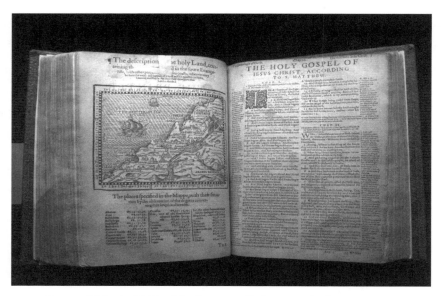

Geneva Bible, the "Bible of the Protestant Reformation," taken to America on the Mayflower, by Hi540 under CC BY-SA 4.0

While these lists may reflect the priorities of many history textbooks, newspaper headlines, magazine articles, or popular memes, traditionalists ask the question, *What does the Lord view as the most important landmarks in Latter-day history?* When Nephi was shown a vision of the last dispensation, these are the American[21] events the Lord designated in prioritization above all others:

- Pure doctrine and scripture are corrupted during Dark Ages (1 Nephi 13:26-29; Isaiah 60:2; Amos 8:11; 2 Thessalonians 2:3)

- Apostate churches founded after the Priesthood is taken from the Earth (1 Nephi 13:4-9, 26; Joseph Smith—History 1:19)

- Persecution, torture, and death of faithful Christians during Dark Ages (1 Nephi 11:34; 13:5-9; Acts 20:29-30; Matthew 24:9)

- A righteous "man among the Gentiles" is "wrought upon" by the "Spirit of God"[22] to discover America (1 Nephi 13:12)

---

21   Several leaders of the Church have commented that the Reformation and other events leading up to the colonization of America should all be considered a prologue for American liberty and the Restoration.

22   Identified as Christopher Columbus by some leaders. See Mark E. Peterson (Mark E. Petersen, *The Great Prologue* (Salt Lake City, Utah: Deseret Book Company, 1975), 24-29), James E. Talmage, and Gordon B. Hinckley. Columbus

- Pilgrims, Puritans, Scottish Covenanters, French Huegunots, Calverts, Quakers, and others, are called by God to come to America (1 Nephi 13:13-15; Isaiah 49:22-23; 1 Nephi 21:22-23; Ezekiel 34:13; 36:24)

- Lamanite descendants are scattered and driven in America (1 Nephi 13:14; 22:7)

- God blesses and prospers righteous colonists by virtue of their "humility" (1 Nephi 13:16)

- The War for Independence (1 Nephi 13:17-19)

- British defeated in War for Independence by "power of God" (1 Nephi 13:19)

- Translation and distribution of the Bible (1 Nephi 13:20-24)

- Coming forth of the Book of Mormon (1 Nephi 13:35-38)

- Joseph Smith & the Restoration of the Gospel (1 Nephi 13:34, 37; Revelation 14:6)

---

was also ordained a high priest during the visitation of the Founding Fathers, and other eminent men and women, to Wilford Woodruff in the St. George temple. (Wilford Woodruff journal, 1873 January-1880 February, p. 276-277, The Church History Library, https://catalog.churchofjesuschrist.org/assets?id=eb07ddd8-d258-43b3-82fd-1b0bc186b269&crate=0&index=275).

Orson Hyde taught that the Angel Moroni came to Columbus and gave him dreams and visions: "This same angel presides over the destinies of America, and feels a lively interest in all our doings. He was in the camp of Washington; and, by an invisible hand, led on our fathers to conquest and victory; and all this to open and prepare the way for the Church and kingdom of God to be established on the western hemisphere, for the redemption of Israel and the salvation of the world.

"This same angel was with Columbus, and gave him deep impressions, by dreams and by visions, respecting this New World. Trammeled by poverty and by an unpopular cause, yet his persevering and unyielding heart would not allow an obstacle in his way too great for him to overcome; and the angel of God helped him—was with him on the stormy deep, calmed the troubled elements, and guided his frail vessel to the desired haven. Under the guardianship of this same angel, or Prince of America, have the United States grown, increased, and flourished, like the sturdy oak by the rivers of water." Orson Hyde, "Celebration of the Fourth of July," in *Journal of Discourses*, vol. 6 (Liverpool, 1859), 368. Discourse given on July 4, 1854.

Columbus understood that it was his mission to be a preparer for the great latter-day events as recorded in scripture. (See for example: Isaiah 42:1-4; 55:5; Psalms 2:8; 18:43, 49) Columbus attributed his mission and life calling to the fulfillment of certain Biblical prophecies in Isaiah. Many of the passages he felt corresponded to his mission, were prophecies of the Latter-day Servant, Joseph Smith. Through revelation, Columbus knew his work of exploration would prepare the way for greater latter-day events.

- Revelations of the Doctrine and Covenants (1 Nephi 13:39-40; Ezekiel 37:15-20; D&C 5:9-10)
- Scattered House of Israel regathered (1 Nephi 10:14; 13:41; 14:17; 15:19-20; 19:15-16; Jeremiah 16:14-21; Jacob 5:50-74; 2 Nephi 6:11; 3 Nephi 15:15-17; 21:1-7, 26; D&C 77:9, 14)
- Latter-day Gentiles reject the gospel (1 Nephi 14:6-7, 11-12; 3 Nephi 16:10; 30:2; D&C 45:28-30; 84:49-59; 101; 103; JST Mark 9:40-48; Isaiah 24:5)
- Persecution of saints in the Last Days (1 Nephi 14:13; 22:14; Luke 21:12-19; Revelation 13:7; 16:6; 17:6; 18:24; 2 Timothy 3:12; D&C 88:94)
- Increasing wickedness and apostasy (1 Nephi 14:12; 2 Timothy 3:1-7; Mormon 8:28, 31-41; 2 Nephi 28:12, 14, 21-22; D&C 112:23-28; Moses 7:60-61; Isaiah 59:12-15)

The vast majority of the prophetic events the Lord enumerated to Nephi and highlighted as essential in the last days did not appear on the *New York Post's* list of 'top events' in any form. Those that did appear were stripped of their providential, God-honoring elements.

In 1852, John Taylor published a pamphlet entitled, "The Government of God," wherein he explained that he would skip over the history of European Reformation heroes only because the early Latter-day Saints were familiar with and conversant in the historical

Stained glass window of the signing of the Mayflower Compact, Plymouth Congregational Church, 1217 6th Avenue, Seattle, Washington by Joe Mabel under CC BY-SA 3.0

events relevant to liberty and the prophecies of the latter days: "I need not here refer to the history of the Waldenses, and Albigenses,

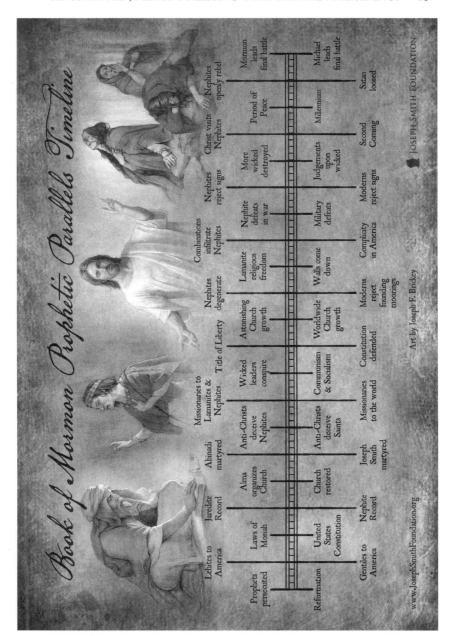

Art by Joseph F. Brickey, www.JosephBrickey.com

The most important Latter-day events, as well as the signs of the times, are foreshadowed in the Book of Mormon in the correct chronological order. This timeline overlays Nephite history with Latter-day prophetic history.

"George Washington's Prayer," Ken Corbett

and Huguenots . . . for their history is well known."[23] For John Taylor and other Latter-day Saints at that time, such history was a basic premise of common thought.

But who recognizes and appreciates the history of the Huguenots today? Now, little more than a century and a half later, in consequence of revisionism, the vast majority of Latter-day Saints have never heard of the Huguenots or the Waldenses—let alone their history and manifold contributions to America and the Restoration of the Gospel! And yet, the Huguenots and Waldenses were responsible, in part, for preserving the foundation of Christianity and liberty in the nations of the world—a contribution Nephi saw in vision. Today, our deconstructed culture seems neither to know, nor to care for this legacy.

Traditionalists endeavor to interpret history through the eyes of God, by means of His Spirit. They seek to understand His mind, and believe that historical interpretation must necessarily be ratified by revelation. Conversely, traditionalists view progressives as deemphasizing revelation—often even rejecting the spiritual realm. Progressives appear to function more as historical chronologists adrift on a sea of scholastic opinion—having no mooring, no anchor,

23   John Taylor, *The Government of God* (Liverpool: S.W. Richards, 1852), 16.

"Let Him Ask of God," Jon McNaughton

and no compass. They find themselves subjected relentlessly to the intellectual winds of change;[24] interpretation is based on one's academic field and individual philosophical models of perception and priority. For progressives, including Arrington, Bitton, and Allen, the measuring rod of academia found Zion's Co-operative Mercantile Institution (ZCMI) more significant than the events surrounding the organization of the Church. ZCMI was also apparently considered far more relevant to humanity than the revelation on the Three Degrees of Glory in section 76 of the Doctrine and Covenants.

Ultimately, the question is one of authority. Are the priorities as recorded in the revelations paramount—or should we look to the scholars and the universities for the final word? Who determines whether the Pilgrims should be considered more important than the Apollo 11 moon landing, or whether the Protestant Reformation should be given preference over WWII?

From the perspective of President Benson, Arrington and his staff of progressive scholars had their priorities severely skewed as

---

24   "That we henceforth be no more children, tossed to and fro, and carried about with every wind of doctrine, by the sleight of men, and cunning craftiness, whereby they lie in wait to deceive." Ephesians 4:14.

a consequence of a fundamental neglect of scripture, indifference to doctrine, and misunderstanding of the unfolding events in the Lord's work of the latter days.

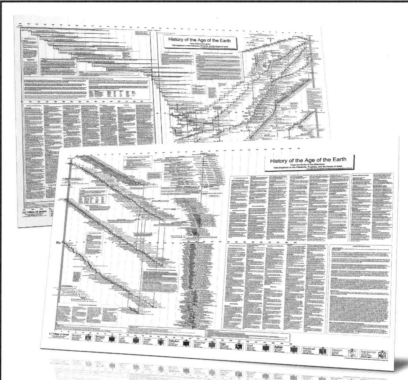

The prophetic events shown to Nephi and highlighted by the Lord in scripture pertain to the House of Israel. The "History of the Age of the Earth: With Emphasis on the Patriarchs, Prophets and the House of Israel" brings together historical and sacred revelations with all the dates for the House of Israel, including documented life spans. In addition to the Biblical record, this timeline includes key figures and nobility through the dark ages and up through the founding of our nation and the Restoration of the Gospel. Even significant astronomical events are noted. This tool brings together people and events visually, along with scriptures and words of prophets—testifying to their importance. (Available for study and purchase at www.JosephSmithFoundation.org.)

7

SEAGULLS COVER-UP
Missing Contemporary Accounts

On April 2, 2020—two days before the 190th Annual General Conference of The Church of Jesus Christ of Latter-day Saints—Wendy Nelson, wife of President Russell M. Nelson, sent a letter to the wives of the General Authorities, calling on the sisters to draw strength from a renowned pioneer miracle: the Miracle of the Gulls:

// The first image that came to my mind even before I got out of bed was Minerva Teichert's painting of the woman praying in fields which have been ravaged by crickets. It is called, The Miracle of the Gulls.

You know that true account. Believers, like you and me, know that the Lord sent numberless seagulls—in the very moment of deepest distress by some, and of deepening faith by others—to devour the crickets and then regurgitate them in the Great Salt Lake. What was the outcome? The lives of some 4,000 pioneers were saved. . . .

As you and I continue to pray—and fast as we are able—the Lord WILL send "seagulls" to devour OUR "crickets" . . .[1]

Wendy Nelson's email refers to the 1848 Miracle of the Gulls, an inspiring narrative passed down from generation to generation from the days of the early pioneers. In Sister Nelson's words: "believers"

---

1   Sarah Jane Weaver, "What Sister Nelson asked the wives of the General Authorities to do amid COVID-19," *Church News*, April 13, 2020, https://www.thechurchnews.com/leaders-and-ministry/2020-04-13/sister-wendy-nelson-letter-general-authority-wives-coronavirus-181120.

know that "the Lord sent numberless seagulls," saving the lives of "some 4,000 pioneers." In a fitting tribute, the California gull was chosen as the state bird of Utah, and the Seagull Monument was subsequently erected on Temple Square and dedicated by President Joseph F. Smith on October 1, 1913. The inscription on that enduring monument reads: "Seagull Monument erected in grateful remembrance of the mercy of God to the Mormon Pioneers." So grateful were the pioneers for the aid rendered by the gulls, that it was "forbidden to shoot, kill or annoy gulls with firearms."[2]

Story Discounts the Miracle

When James Allen and Glen Leonard included the Miracle of the Gulls in *The Story of the Latter-day Saints*[3] in 1976, they chose to give the readers no indication that the gulls were a miracle, or that God had intervened in any way. Instead, the writers weaved innuendo into the language, inferring that to claim the event as a miraculous deliverance was historically unfounded. The only mention of God in *Story's* retelling of this sacred account was the small inclusion of a photo caption explaining that the pioneers began to see—only after some time, perhaps through groupthink—the event as a miracle: "The Saints *soon began* to see this as a sign of divine intervention in their behalf, and the seagull story has been immortalized in music, drama, sculpture, and painting as the great Mormon miracle."[4]

The glaring omission of God from the Miracle of the Gulls account caught the eye of President Ezra Taft Benson and other leaders. The initial critique of *Story,* believed to have been drafted by President Benson's secretary, William Nelson, questioned the shift in recognizing the hand of God, and ". . . the lack of divinity in each episode of Church history described. To give one example, [James B.] Allen and [Glen M.] Leonard mention the coming of the seagulls to swallow the crickets without saying the Lord caused the seagulls to come and eat the crickets."[5] Overall, Arrington noted,

---

2   William Hartley, "Mormons, Crickets, and Gulls: A New Look At An Old Story," *Utah Historical Quarterly* 38, no. 3 (1970): 232.

3   James B. Allen and Glen M. Leonard, *The Story of the Latter-day Saints* (Salt Lake City, Utah: Deseret Book Company, 1976). Hereafter referred to as "Story."

4   Ibid., 250, emphasis added.

5   Leonard J. Arrington Diaries, August 18, 1976; Leonard J. Arrington and

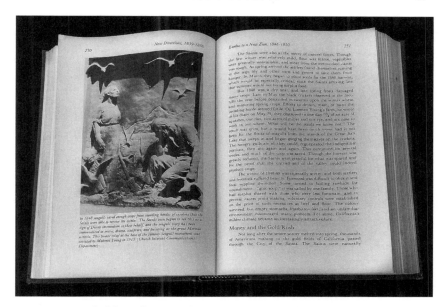

*The arrival of the gulls as retold in the 1976 edition of Story (pictured above)
undermined the providential nature of the miracle.*

the traditionalist leaders and general authorities felt that *Story* "was basically a secular history; did not have enough of the spiritual in this account of our history,"[6] and he recognized that the account of the gulls stood out as a red flag because God had been excised from the history: "[T]he story of the crickets and seagulls [w]as not bringing God into the picture."[7]

William Hartley's Critique

Why did *Story's* authors, James Allen and Glen Leonard, choose to send a message to the Saints that left God missing in action from this celebrated event in Utah history? The journey in discovering that answer begins with a member of Leonard Arrington's History Division staff, William G. Hartley.[8] Two years before joining

Gary James Bergera, *Confessions of a Mormon Historian: The Diaries of Leonard J. Arrington*, 1971-1997, vol. 2 (Salt Lake City: Signature Books, 2018), 223.

6   Ibid., 226.

7   Ibid., 226.

8   William G. Hartley served on Arrington's staff until 1980 when he moved to BYU and joined the Joseph Fielding Smith Institute for Latter-day Saint History, in the midst of the disassembly of Leonard Arrington's team at Church Headquarters. Hartley served as president of the Mormon History Association from 2000-2001

Arrington's staff, Hartley boldly authored an article titled, "Mormons, Crickets, and Gulls: A New Look at an Old Story" for the *Utah Historical Quarterly*. Hartley argued that the traditional account of the Miracle of the Gulls had "assumed legendary characteristics in the folk history of the Rocky Mountain West. . . . the details of the Cricket War of 1848 over the years have been oversimplified, improved upon, and given somewhat legendary characteristics."[9]

Subsequent to the publishing of this article, other scholars have since joined the bandwagon, decrying the Miracle of the Gulls as "over-dramatized"[10]—even mythical. Commenting on the Miracle of the Gulls, Steven C. Harper,[11] a historian for the Church, voiced his own skepticism: "The older a story gets, the more sensational it becomes . . . This is just how stories happen in a folk culture, especially miracle stories."[12] Authors Michael Schelling Durham and Dietrich Dorner expressed their opinion that ". . . the story of the Miracle of the Gulls is now as much legend as fact."[13] Jessie L. Embry and William A. Wilson authored a paper entitled "Folk Ideas of Mormon Pioneers," wherein they disparage the accounts of miracles—including the Miracle of the Gulls—and issue a challenge to their readers:

---

and was awarded the Leonard J. Arrington Award. Hartley co-edited three volumes of the Joseph Smith Papers.

9   William Hartley, "Mormons, Crickets, and Gulls: A New Look At An Old Story," *Utah Historical Quarterly* 38, no. 3 (1970): 225, 238.

10   Trent Toone, "Was the 'Miracle of the Gulls' Exaggerated? LDS Historians Explain," *LDS Living*, July 23, 2018, https://www.ldsliving.com/Was-the-Miracle-of-the-Gulls-Exaggerated-LDS-Historians-Explain/s/88952.

11   Steven C. Harper is an Associate Professor in the Department of Church History and Doctrine at Brigham Young University and a volume editor in the Joseph Smith Papers project. Harper also participated in one of Richard Bushman's summer seminars, mentoring and training the next generation of Latter-day Saint historians. R. Scott Lloyd, "New generation of historians presenting a better view of Mormonism to the world, speaker says," *Deseret News*, June 6, 2015, https://www.deseret.com/2015/6/6/20566192/new-generation-of-historians-presenting-a-better-view-of-mormonism-to-the-world-speaker-says.

12   Trent Toone, "Was the 'Miracle of the Gulls' Exaggerated? LDS Historians Explain," *LDS Living*, July 23, 2018, https://www.ldsliving.com/Was-the-Miracle-of-the-Gulls-Exaggerated-LDS-Historians-Explain/s/88952.

13   Michael Schelling Durham and Dietrich Dorner, *Desert Between the Mountains* (New York: Henry Holt and Company, 1997), 150.

❝ Will they [Mormons] recall the faith-promoting stories they learned in Primary, Sunday school, seminary, and family home evening? Or will they struggle to find out what "really happened"—if that is possible—complete with all the warts? . . .

Most people, Mormons included, are motivated to action, not by what "really happened" in the past but by what they believe happened.[14]

No doubt frustrated by similar insinuations expressed in his own day, President Ezra Taft Benson defended the faithful retelling of our "faith-promoting stories." While addressing BYU students in 1976, he strongly opposed those who suggest that members need to outgrow and forsake childish folklore to discover "what really happened":

❝ . . . there have been and continue to be attempts made to bring this [humanistic emphasis on history] into our own Church history. Again the emphasis is to underplay revelation and God's intervention in significant events . . . . It is a state of mind and spirit characterized by one history buff, who asked: "Do you believe the Church has arrived at a sufficient state of maturity where we can begin to tell our real story?"

Implied in that question is the accusation that the Church has not been telling the truth.

Unfortunately, too many of those who have been intellectually gifted become so imbued with criticism that they become disaffected spiritually.[15]

When it comes to the Miracle of the Gulls, are Sister Nelson and the "believers" she addressed correct in holding to the claim that the "Lord sent numberless seagulls—in the very moment of deepest distress by some, and of deepening faith by others—to devour the crickets and then regurgitate them in the Great Salt Lake," saving

14   Jessie L. Embry and William A. Wilson, "Folk Ideas of Mormon Pioneers," *Dialogue: A Journal of Mormon Thought* 31, no. 3 (1998): 81.

15   Ezra Taft Benson, "God's Hand in Our Nation's History," Brigham Young University Devotional, 1976, https://speeches.byu.edu/talks/ezra-taft-benson/gods-hand-nations-history/.

the lives of the pioneers in response to their faithful, fervent prayers? Or, on the contrary, are we to accept that the progressive historians are correct—that the miraculous portion of the story is mere myth? Can we rigorously test the Miracle of the Gulls, practicing historical scrutiny to see if the traditional account holds up?

The Traditional Story

The traditional narrative of the Miracle of the Gulls is quite simple, as related by Wikipedia:

❝ According to traditional accounts, legions of gulls appeared by 1848 June 9 following fervent prayers by the pioneer farmers. It is said that these birds . . . ate mass quantities of crickets, drank some water, regurgitated, and continued eating more crickets over a two-week period. The pioneers saw the gulls' arrival as a miracle, and the story was recounted from the pulpit by church leaders such as Orson Pratt and George A. Smith . . . The traditional story is that the seagulls annihilated the insects, ensuring the survival of some 4,000 Mormon pioneers who had traveled to Utah. For this reason, Seagull Monument was erected and the California gull is the state bird of Utah.[16]

Does this simple narrative hold up to scholarly, historical scrutiny? Progressives, including Embry and Wilson, are bold to assert that "Historians have examined journals and other contemporary records, and found that *no one* at the time recorded the crickets'[17] arrival as a miracle," providing a basis for their claim that the story only later developed "into a miracle."[18] *LDS Living* echoed this claim in a 2018 article: "Latter-day Saints and their descendants *came to view* these events as divine intervention. . . . The first recorded reference to a miracle came in general conference in September 1853 by apostle Orson Hyde, who said 'the gulls had been agents prepared by the

---

16   "Miracle of the gulls," Wikipedia, August 25, 2020, https://en.wikipedia.org/wiki/Miracle_of_the_gulls.

17   It appears that this is a typo in the original article that has never been corrected. If not, technically this phrase is accurate as uncorrected. No one has ever looked upon the cricket's coming as a miracle—it was the gulls' part of the story that was looked upon as a miracle. If this is not a typo, however, it was very deceptively done by the authors.

18   Jessie L. Embry and William A. Wilson, "Folk Ideas of Mormon Pioneers," *Dialogue: A Journal of Mormon Thought* 31, no. 3 (1998): 93; emphasis added.

hand of providence . . .'"[19] The early Saints, according to these authors, did not initially recognize the coming of the gulls as intervention by God on their behalf—but only later came to that notion through some sort of confused and distorted miscommunication consensus. Only then, according to the critics, did the "legend" emerge, leaving the storytellers to exaggerate details of the gulls' arrival as a dramatic miracle arranged by God.

In short, the progressive narrative claims that those who are willing to "struggle to find out what 'really happened'"[20] will realize that the story told and perpetuated by traditionalist historians and overtrusting members, such as Sister Nelson, is nothing more than myth and folklore.

The space afforded in this volume does not allow for a comprehensive evaluation and discussion of all of the twists and turns accompanying the progressive argument against the Miracle of the Gulls; however, we will tackle one of the most prominent and relevant facets. Seemingly dominant among progressive claims is the bold assertion that: ". . . [N]o one at the time recorded the crickets' arrival as a miracle . . ."[21] This claim underscores the entire validity of the Miracle of the Gulls narrative, and it deserves our attention.

> **PROGRESSIVE CLAIM:** There are no contemporary accounts documenting recognition by the pioneers that the coming of the gulls was a miracle. ". . . [N]o one at the time recorded the crickets' arrival as a miracle . . ."

John Smith's Letter

On June 9, 1848, in the midst of both the difficulties and the deliverance the struggling pioneers were experiencing, John Smith, the presiding leader in the Salt Lake valley, dispatched a letter to Brigham Young and the Quorum of the Twelve Apostles. In his correspondence, he shared the exciting news of the avian rescue unfolding before their eyes:

---

19   Trent Toone, "Was the 'Miracle of the Gulls' Exaggerated? LDS Historians Explain," *LDS Living*, July 23, 2018, https://www.ldsliving.com/Was-the-Miracle-of-the-Gulls-Exaggerated-LDS-Historians-Explain/s/88952.

20   Jessie L. Embry and William A. Wilson, "Folk Ideas of Mormon Pioneers," *Dialogue: A Journal of Mormon Thought* 31, no. 3 (1998): 81.

21   Ibid., 93.

John Smith, Joseph Smith Jr.'s uncle, son of Asael and Mary Duty Smith

‟ . . . there has been a large amount of spring crops put in, and they were doing well till within a few days the crickets have done a considerable damage both to wheat and corn which has discouraged some, but there is plenty left if we can save it for a few days.

The sea gulls have come in large flocks from the Lake and sweep the crickets as they go; **it seems the hand of the Lord in our favor.**[22]

President Smith's dispatch to Brigham Young was penned while the seagulls were in the fields devouring the crickets, demonstrating that recognition of the event as a miracle—the intervention of Divine providence—was not an illusion materializing later—but was a literal, authentic experience witnessed and reported in real time. John Smith's letter is an inconvenient fact ostensibly forgotten by the new history.

---

22   John Smith, Charles C. Rich, and John Young to Brigham Young and the Twelve Apostles, June 9, 1848. Brigham Young office files, 1832-1878 (bulk 1844-1877); General Correspondence, Incoming, 1840-1877; Letters from Church Leaders and Others, 1840- 1877; John Smith, 1847-1849; Charles C. Rich letter; p. 1, Church History Library, https://catalog.churchofjesuschrist.org/assets/c4ce49a0-801f-4c88-bbb2-e1df4c2b40bd/0/0#lds; emphasis added.

The Millennial Star (1848-1849)

Thomas Bullock—who was serving at the time as an assistant to Church Historian and Recorder, Willard Richards—forwarded John Smith's letter on to Levi Richards in England. The first hand account of the miracle was published in the *Millennial Star*, the Latter-day Saint periodical in England, on October 15, 1848. Thus, within only four months after the advent of the seagulls, the story had already made its way *overseas*, published and acknowledged as evidence of "the hand of the Lord in our favor"—faithful evidence of the timely preservation of Latter-day Israel in the wilderness of western America.

However, progressive William Hartley claimed in his 1970 paper: "Likewise unusual is the lack of mention of the 'miracle' in the official Mormon newspaper in England, *the Millennial Star.* . . . Very slight reference to cricket damage plus a passing remark printed in 1849 about the gulls is all that the English Mormons were told about the Cricket War of 1848."[23] Hartley, here again, was not straightforward—nor was he ethical or impartial in portraying all the facts.

Not only did the seagulls come in 1848, but in the spring of 1849, they returned again; only this time their appearance came early enough to curtail serious damage.[24] Although the *Millennial Star* included extensive details about the 1849 version of the miracle of the gulls, Hartley chose to focus only on the 1848 event, leading his readers to believe that the Saints recognized no miraculous intervention in connection with the seagulls. He also neglected to enlighten his readers about the following extensive, miracle-affirming account, published in the *Millennial Star* on December 1,

---

23   William Hartley, "Mormons, Crickets, and Gulls: A New Look At An Old Story," *Utah Historical Quarterly* 38, no. 3 (1970): 234.

24   The reader should note that some progressive articles claim that since seagulls came in 1849, 1855, and in other years, the 1848 appearance cannot be classified as the hand of the Lord intervening on behalf of the pioneers. However, it should be understood that just because an individual is blessed more than once, this does not make each blessing less providential or inspired. Additionally, a rebuttal might include details on how extensive the later appearances of seagulls were. Certainly, "thousands" of seagulls descending, creating "shadows" on the field or "darkening" the heavens, as was described in 1848, is *not* a common occurrence that continues today, leaving us to conclude that contrary to Hartley's claim, the 1848 and 1849 miracles *were* unique.

1849, which recounted the welcome return of the seagulls coming to devour the crickets earlier that year:

> The crickets have not troubled us any this year. Hundreds and thousands of gulls made their appearance early in the Spring, and as soon as the crickets appeared, the gulls made war on them, and they swept them clean, so that there is scarce a cricket to be found in the valley.
>
> **We look upon this as one of the manifestations of the Almighty**, for the mou[n]taineers say that they never found gulls here till the Mormons come.[25] It was truly cheering to see the flocks of these saviors, extending several miles in length, come from the lake early in the morning, and eating crickets all day, then at sun down form in a mass, and wing their way to the lake for a night's rest.
>
> One curiosity about them is, they don't eat the crickets merely to live, but after feeding themselves, they would vomit them up, and go to eating again, and thus continue eating and vomiting throughout the entire day.
>
> It is a matter of astonishment how fast they will pick them up, and a person could form but a poor estimate of the amount destroyed daily by these winged saviors. Suffice it to say, that about three weeks after the gulls made their appearance scarce a cricket could be seen. This is **plainly a miracle** in behalf of this people, **as the sending of the quails in the camp of the Israelites**; and what makes it more manifest is, the fact that, although there were plenty of crickets in the surrounding vallies, where there are no crops, the gulls came by them to the farms, and stayed there till they had cleared them off, although men were at work around them at the time. There has been no damage done by the crickets this season.[26]

The original date of this letter, later reprinted in the *Millennial Star*, was July 16, 1849—not many weeks after the 1849 miracle. The

---

25   This statement evidently means the mountaineers had never witnessed seagulls to the extent experienced in 1848-49—not that seagulls had never been seen along the Wasatch Front.

26   "Correspondence from America," *The Latter-day Saints Millennial Star*, vol. 11, no. 23, December 1, 1849, 366, emphasis added.

*Seagull Monument, dedicated in 1913 by President Joseph F. Smith,
on Temple Square, Salt Lake City, Utah*

publication of the letter in the *Star* overseas in England occurred on
December 1, 1849.

Later in his paper, Hartley went so far as to tell his readers that
"the 'miraculousness' of the event was not clearly recognized by
contemporaries. . . . the *Millennial Star* never told the English Saints
about such a miracle."[27] Hartley's glaring omission of contemporary
account evidence—including John Smith's letter describing the
1848 appearance of the seagulls as the "hand of the Lord," as well
as the subsequent, extensive description of the 1849 reappearance
of the seagulls, both of which appeared in the *Millennial Star*—
demonstrates the egregious and growing issues inherent in the
progressive retelling of our sacred history.

There is no excuse for Hartley's duplicitous deception, nor for its
continued curation and preservation by subsequent 'scholars' until
today. As an example, Hartley's misrepresentation of the *Millennial
Star* accounts was later adopted and perpetuated by others, including

---

27   William Hartley, "Mormons, Crickets, and Gulls: A New Look At An Old
Story," *Utah Historical Quarterly* 38, no. 3 (1970): 238.

the authors of the aforementioned article in *LDS Living*, "Was the "Miracle of the Gulls" Exaggerated? LDS Historians Explain": "The event was not clearly recognized by the LDS faith's First Presidency, its England newspaper, *The Millennial Star*, or those who wrote about the cricket infestation."[28] The article featured William Hartley, Steven Harper, and Casey Paul Griffiths, each represented as official "LDS historians" questioning the miraculous portions of the story.

After due consideration of these facts, it appears incontrovertible that each of these historians is guilty of blatant and inexcusable fraud. Either each is claiming to be an authority on a subject never carefully studied—or, if time was truly taken to evaluate primary sources, the facts are being designedly and deceitfully hidden and misconstrued.

Henry Bigler's Diary Entry

Returning to the question of whether the Saints who were present *at the time* of the cricket infestation believed the coming of the gulls was the intervention of God on their behalf—or just another natural occurrence—the contemporary account of Henry Bigler, to whom the story was related by eyewitnesses less than four months after the miracle, brings additional insight:

 . . . the whole face of earth I am told was literaly [*sic*] covered with large black crickets that seemed to the farmers that they (the crickets) would eat up and comptly [*sic*] destroy their entire crops had it not been for the gulls that came in large flocks and devoured the crickets. I am told that the gulls would feast themselves on the crickets to the full and straight way disgorge them and begin again and thus they did destroy the crickets and save the crops and it was forbidden to shoot or kill a gull and **all looked upon the gulls as a God send**, indeed, **all acknowledge the hand of the Lord was [in] it**, that **He had sent the white gulls** by scores of thousands to save their crops.[29]

---

28   Trent Toone, "Was the 'Miracle of the Gulls' Exaggerated? LDS Historians Explain," *LDS Living*, July 23, 2018, https://www.ldsliving.com/Was-the-Miracle-of-the-Gulls-Exaggerated-LDS-Historians-Explain/s/88952.

29   Henry W. Bigler reminiscences and diaries, 1846-1850, p. 106-107, Church History Library, emphasis added.

According to Bigler's account, "all looked upon the gulls as a God send," "all acknowledge[d] the hand of the Lord was in it," and all believed that "[God] had sent the white gulls by scores of thousands to save their crops." Bigler simply recorded what eyewitnesses undoubtedly communicated to him in the immediate aftermath of the incident with the gulls. It appears that prior to Bigler's letter, but directly following the circumstances involving the gulls, all remaining pioneers believed the occurrence to be miraculous. Perhaps any non-believers—if indeed there were any—had emigrated to California. Bigler also described the great industry present in the Salt Lake Valley, where only a few short months previous there had been desperation and desolation. Faith had been both tested and proven.

Ironically, while Embry and Wilson claimed that "no one at the time" recorded the seagulls' coming as a miracle, they admit that Henry Bigler was told personally by, it would seem, countless eyewitnesses that *the event was* a miracle. Bigler, who had barely arrived in the valley, recorded the story that seemed to be on everyone's lips.

Other Accounts

The following year, Thomas L. Kane, a nonmember friend of the Saints, published "A Discourse Delivered Before the Historical Society of Pennsylvania" in defense of the Latter-day Saints, titled *The Mormon*, in which he described how the hardy and faithful Mormons "prayed and fought, and fought and prayed [against the crickets], but to no purpose," until the seagulls arrived with their long wings "arched in flight 'like an angel's'."[30] Kane mentioned the repeated miracle in 1849, revealing that he was well aware of both incidents, significantly enough to warrant the inclusion of the story in his account just one year subsequent to the 1849 coming of the gulls.

Eyewitnesses also told Orson Hyde of the event, no doubt describing it as a miracle, and leading him to publicly retell the story during a General Conference address five years after the original events transpired:

---

30   Thomas L. Kane, *The Mormons: A Discourse Delivered Before the Historical Society of Pennsylvania* (Philadelphia: King & Baird, 1850), 66-67.

❙❙ ... the crickets came in millions from the mountains, and nearly devoured all that grew; everything that germinated in the shape of food for man was eaten by the insects. But before they had completed the work of destruction, the hand of Providence prepared agents, and sent them to destroy the destroyer; a circumstance that was rare, one that was never known to exist before, and never since to any extent—behold, the gulls came in swarms, and as clouds and eat up the crickets, and checked them in their destructive career; and there was just enough saved to feed the hungry with a scanty morsel.[31]

This conference address was delivered before hundreds, if not thousands, of eyewitnesses to the events described. If those in attendance had been in disagreement, there surely would have been much ado about it.

In summary, a simple investigation reveals multiple contemporary accounts—including the letter from John Smith who recorded the event as representing "the hand of the Lord in our favor," and the journal entry of Henry Bigler who found that "*all* looked upon the gulls as a God send, indeed, all acknowledged the hand of the Lord was in it, that He had sent the white gulls by scores of thousands to save their crops." Affirming the testimonies and records of these faithful pioneers, Church leaders recounted the divine intervention in their public addresses, such as George A. Smith's 1869 discourse depicting the coming of the gulls as having been preceded by prayers from the Saints for God to intervene.[32]

---

31   Orson Hyde, in *Journal of Discourses*, vol. 2 (Liverpool: F. D. Richards, 1855), 114. Discourse given on September 24, 1853.

32   "The brethren contended with them until they were utterly tired out, then calling on the Lord for help were ready to give up the contest, when just at that time there came over from the Salt Lake large flocks of gulls, which destroyed the crickets. They would eat them until they were perfectly gorged, and would then disgorge, vomiting them up, and again go to and eat, and so they continued until the crickets had entirely disappeared, and thus by the blessing of God the colony was saved. I believe the crickets have never been a pest in this vicinity to any serious extent since. This we regard as a special providence of the Almighty.

"The early settlers did not know how to irrigate the crops properly and the result was that their wheat, the first year, was most of it very short, so short that it had to be pulled up by the roots; but singularly enough there was considerable grain in the ear, and they raised enough to encourage them to persevere in their experiments, for their labors were only experiments at that early day and also enabled them to diffuse information on the subject, which proved of general benefit." George A. Smith, in *Journal of Discourses*, vol. 13 (Liverpool: Horace S. Eldredge, 1871), 83-84.

8

SEAGULLS MYTH
Is Our History Invented Folklore?

From the historical record, there can be no question that the 19th-century Saints who experienced the affliction imposed upon them by the marauding crickets recognized the Miracle of the Gulls as a deliverance under the hand of Almighty God. However, while revisionist historians have accused the faithful pioneer Saints of creating a miracle narrative after the fact, it is an interesting twist of irony that today's progressive debunking of the Miracle of the Gulls appears to be the result of scholar 'groupthink.'

Arrington's Sarcastic Parody

When William Hartley published his analysis in 1970, he made several misleading assertions in a thinly veiled attempt to debunk the Miracle of the Gulls by crafting a cunningly written paper. Woven among deliberately placed, derogatory innuendo, Hartley was careful to include portions of contemporaneous accounts—such as John Smith's letter to Brigham Young and Henry Bigler's 1848 report. Without a careful analysis of Hartley's prose, the average reader would likely miss the fact that he omitted the essence of the coincident accounts. On the other hand, by scrutinizing his claims and the research behind his allegations, we can find the basis for debunking Hartley's paper within the paper itself.

Carelessly, when later unobservant historians set out to report on the Miracle of the Gulls, rather than completing their own primary research, they apparently relied upon conjecture relayed from Hartley's research. Names like Embry, Wilson, *LDS Living* (with Harper and Griffith), Gary Bergera, and others, each quoted Hartley as they drew their conclusions from his initial inaccurate circumvention—sometimes asserting their own increasingly exaggerated claims. One such example denies coincident accounts: "Historians have examined journals and other contemporary records and found that no one at the time recorded the crickets' arrival as a miracle."[1] These later claims are recognizably and unmistakably false.[2]

Ironically, when Hartley passed away on April 10, 2018, his obituary recorded one of his favorite quips—that once he departed this mortal world and was "[o]n the other side I'll find out how accurate or inaccurate the histories I wrote really are."[3] Hartley's arguments and subsequent progressive revisionism prompted others unacquainted with the true history to ridicule the traditional version of the Miracle of the Gulls story. On August 4, 1981, Leonard Arrington invented a sarcastic parody revealing an attitude of contempt toward belief in the miracle. He recorded in his diary a mocking celebration of the gulls episode as simply foolish tradition:

" I have learned today the true story of the cricket and seagull episode in Mormon history in 1848. It is well known that birds eat seeds—grain seeds, flower seeds, millet seeds, wheat and so on. The seagulls had been over Salt Lake City for perhaps millennia. At any rate they circled over the fields of grain of the Saints, descended and began to eat the maturing grain, as they still do today. The Saints began to despair that the seagulls were eating

---

1   Jessie L. Embry and William A. Wilson, "Folk Ideas of Mormon Pioneers," *Dialogue: A Journal of Mormon Thought* 31, no. 3 (1998): 93.

2   Even some historians who have expressed doubt as to the miraculous nature of the event have acknowledged, "there are letters and journal entries that show that they [the Saints] thought it was providential. They thought the Lord intervened and sort of turned the tide." Trent Toone, "Was the 'Miracle of the Gulls' Exaggerated? LDS Historians Explain," *LDS Living*, July 23, 2018, https://www.ldsliving.com/ Was-the-Miracle-of-the-Gulls-Exaggerated-LDS-Historians-Explain/s/88952.

While acknowledging the providential belief of the pioneers, progressives still argue over journal accounts that mentioned the crickets, but did not mention the seagulls or specifically attribute the gulls' coming to God—as well as emphasizing that the seagulls eating the crickets was a result of natural instinct. There appears to be a strenuous effort being made by the New Mormon History community to discount the miraculous, and go to extreme lengths to plant seeds of doubt.

3   "Obituary for William G. Hartley," Utah Valley Mortuary, April 16, 2018, https://www.utahvalleyfuneral.com/obituaries/William-Hartley-7/#!/Obituary.

up all their grain. Fearfully, they worried about their future. Nevertheless, they didn't want to shoot the seagulls. They many times sang the song, "Don't Kill the Little Birds." The crickets realized the position the Saints were in and so decided to be a sacrifice for a good purpose. So the crickets came in and lay down, playing dead, which attracted the seagulls away from the grain. The seagulls ate the crickets instead. Thus it was really, in essence, the crickets that saved the Saints' grain crop. This suggests that we ought to put up a new monument on Temple Square to the Mormon cricket.[4]

Our early pioneer forefathers honored these iconic gulls. Now, 133 years later, either in earnest or indifference, Leonard Arrington contemptuously insults what he believes to be superstition on a grand scale in his antithetical parody celebrating the crickets in place of the gulls—a direct inverse of the time-honored, sacred tradition. Those with eyes to see, and ears to hear, know the true meaning behind this reversed, disparaging mimicry.

Leonard Arrington admitted to Elder David B. Haight in 1976, while discussing *Story*, that the primary difference between *Story* and *Essentials in Church History* is not the historical accuracy, but the portrayal of God and providence. After complimenting *Story*, Elder Haight asked Arrington:

❝ You know, not everybody approaches history the same way. . . . For instance, this seems to be approached somewhat differently than Essentials in Church History. I tried to compare what Joseph Fielding Smith said about, let's say, the Haun's Mill Massacre and the Mountain Meadows Massacre, etc., with what is done in this book. As you have gone through the documents in preparation for this book, have you found things that were different than is given in the Essentials of Church History? . . . Joseph Fielding Smith has an approach in which the Lord is responsible for all the things that brought about the growth of the Church and

---

4   Leonard J. Arrington Diaries, August 4, 1981; Leonard J. Arrington and Gary James Bergera, *Confessions of a Mormon Historian: The Diaries of Leonard J. Arrington*, 1971-1997, vol. 3 (Salt Lake City: Signature Books, 2018), 204-205.

the devil is responsible for all things that interfere with that growth. You don't have that approach, do you?[5]

Arrington responded that "basically, the story [was] the same" with a few historical corrections and a greater focus on post-1877 history. However, Arrington observed that Joseph Fielding Smith's interpretation of God's role in history and the interpretation of the progressive historians was *different*. Arrington explained that:

❙❙ Well, when people experienced the influence of the Lord and said so, we have mentioned that, and the devil as well. But there are a wide variety of things that bring about certain developments, economic, political, natural, and so on, and we bring those into the account.[6]

Elder Haight responded to Arrington's answer, "I am glad you do." Ultimately, the primary battleline over which traditionalists and progressives have and will continue to fight, centers on *interpretation* of history. Scholars on both sides can look at the same data and derive very different conclusions—in the end arriving at conflicting perceptions based on their personal worldview. Whether it is the Miracle of the Gulls, Joseph Smith's character, or the Mountain Meadows Massacre, the two clashing worldviews look at the same events and return with divergent interpretations.

Arrington & Benson Spar over God in History

Hartley's 'debunking' of the Miracle of the Gulls—a continuance of the progressive New Mormon History's trend to exclude God from history—was fuel for the fire in the ongoing heated confrontation between Leonard Arrington and Ezra Taft Benson, as well as other traditionalist leaders over the substance of *Story*. President Benson was adamant in his feelings, and correct in his assessment, that Arrington's liberal history department was cutting God from history. Arrington retaliated by claiming that their history did nothing of the sort—that from his perspective, God was given His proper place. Arrington's diary and the contemporaneous talks delivered by

---

5   Leonard J. Arrington Diaries, August 27, 1976; Ibid., 2:224.
6   Ibid.

President Benson during this era of conflict appear to reveal that both 'sides'—the traditionalists and the progressives—were talking past one another because they held antithetical understandings of God and the spiritual realm. Their understanding of who God is, how He acts, what constitutes a miracle, and the role and reality of Lucifer— the adversary of truth—were vastly different, even diametrically opposed. This atmosphere of miscommunication fostered and led to failed attempts in mutual understanding. Arrington expressed his true feelings on these matters in the privacy of his diary, where they would remain concealed for nearly four decades before being disclosed to the public.

Arrington continued to advocate for the New Mormon History and to debate the legitimacy of their new narrative in his conversations with general authorities, including Elder Boyd K. Packer. One November night in 1977, Arrington and his wife broke away from the battlefield to attend a dinner and program hosted by Harold Kline Beecher and his wife, Margaret. In attendance was Melvin Ballard, and his son, M. Russell Ballard, a future member of the Quorum of the Twelve Apostles. At this time, however, the younger Elder Ballard was newly called as a member of the Quorum of the Seventy. After dinner, Arrington recorded that Elder Ballard arose and shared an experience from his mission to Toronto, Canada in the early 1970s. Arrington recorded the details of the account in his journal the next day; but his entry made it clear that he disagreed with President Ballard's sentiments that "Satan is real":

// Brother [M. Russell] Ballard [Jr.] began by reading from Richard Evans's history of the [LDS] Church in England, the episode in which Heber C. Kimball and colleagues experienced the devil before they began their extensive baptisms in Preston. He then said that this had always seemed to him like something that happened in the early church and was not happening in the church today. But his experience in Toronto had convinced him that it could happen today just as much. The more successful our missionary activities, the more opposition is presented by Satan. When we are contented with low baptisms and our activity is

desultory Satan is not worried. But when we are making great success the influence of Satan is present.[7]

Arrington, an avowed skeptic of attributing adversity to "the devil," preferred instead to downplay the supernatural with explanations that focused on "certain developments, economic, political, natural, and so on."[8] As Arrington recorded what he remembered of Elder Ballard's comments, it was clear that Arrington wasn't buying the "influence of Satan" in the interpretation of the story.

Elder Ballard went on to describe how the number of baptisms had been increasing in Toronto, "attract[ing] Satan's opposition." He described the actions of one sister, in particular, who was struggling with her testimony and began to act strangely while traveling with others to the temple. Her husband, the branch president, the missionaries, and others, administered to her without success. Elder Ballard was then summoned. His first thought was, "Here is a mental case;" but a few days later, he was persuaded to travel to her home:

As he neared the home she yelled out, "Don't let that man in, don't let that man in!"

When he reached her he saw a face that was contorted in such a way that she was unrecognizable. She spoke with a completely different voice than her regular voice, a deep voice. She spoke in a different manner than she had ever been known previously to these attacks. He asked the stake president to administer to her again, which he did, and they could feel Satan leave her but remain in the room. It was obvious to all of them that Satan was still present. And within a few minutes he was back in her body. Brother Ballard then for the first time felt very certain that this was indeed Satan and not a mental problem. He realized also that he was the ultimate Church authority in the region . . . Brother Ballard gave her a blessing that he says went on for twenty or thirty minutes, and so evident was it that Satan was there that he carried on a dialogue with Satan rebuking him, and through the woman's body and voice he [Satan] countered

---

7   Leonard J. Arrington Diaries, November 11, 1977; Ibid., 2:428; brackets in original.

8   Leonard J. Arrington Diaries, August 27, 1976; Ibid., 2:224.

with threats, with strong statements, with vile and sarcastic statements. But he [Ballard] kept insisting on the authority of the Priesthood and of Jesus Christ and ultimately was able to drive out Satan not only from the body of the woman but from the room completely. After that long blessing the woman, completely exhausted, returned to her normal self-voice, mean [mien], appearance, and so on, and she has had no reocurrence since that time.[9]

One can only imagine Arrington's thoughts as he listened to Elder Ballard relate his experience. The next day, he recorded in his diary the incredulous realization that "Elder Ballard seems to be completely convinced that Satan is real, that he appears where there is weakness and where his influence is needed to counteract the progress of the Church and the faith where it is taking place." A bemused Arrington noted what he perceived as the cognitive dissonance his traditionalist colleague faced, writing that from the outside, Elder Ballard appeared as a "perfectly normal, intelligent and rational person," and yet he believed in a devil. "Elder Ballard seemed to be very sincere and very serious," Arrington decided— though he was clearly not convinced.[10]

For traditionalists, this difference in worldviews seems reminiscent of Nephi's prophecy of the last days—that there would be "others he [the devil] flattereth away, and telleth them there is no hell; and he saith unto them: I am no devil, for there is none."[11] Mormon also recorded that prior to the coming of Christ to the Nephites, and preceding the great Nephite destruction, there was a movement among some of the "believing" members advancing the precept that it was not *"reasonable"* to trust in the prophecies and "great and marvelous works" which had been foretold. These individuals "began

---

9   Leonard J. Arrington Diaries, November 11, 1977; Ibid., 2:429; brackets in original.

10   Ibid., 429-430.

11   Full context and reference of prophecy as found in 2 Nephi 28:20-26: "For behold, at that day shall he rage in the hearts of the children of men, and stir them up to anger against that which is good. And others will he pacify, and lull them away into carnal security, that they will say: All is well in Zion; yea, Zion prospereth, all is well—and thus the devil cheateth their souls, and leadeth them away carefully down to hell. And behold, others he flattereth away, and telleth them there is no hell; and he saith unto them: I am no devil, for there is none . . ."

to depend upon their own strength and upon their own wisdom," voicing the declaration that the "tradition[s]" handed down by the forefathers were "wicked," and instrumental in "keep[ing the people] in ignorance," binding them down as "servants" to those who taught revelation and doctrine. During that time of progressive conflict, only the "most believing part" of the Nephites and Lamanites resisted this attack on their righteous traditions and the 'unreasonable' miracles taught by the fathers.[12]

Does it Matter?

In the midst of this 'tumult of opinions,' one is led to ask, *Does it really matter? Does it matter whether the coming of the gulls was a miracle or mere naturalistic chance? Does it matter whether our history is interpreted by progressives or by traditionalists? Are we wasting time debating minor issues?* For answers, a survey of the enduring or changing faith of the children, the grandchildren, and the great-grandchildren of those who were fed progressive—or traditionalist—history is needful. *What are the fruits?*

Good, honest, and faithful parents throughout the Church are experiencing an unprecedented abandonment of the faith by their children and grandchildren, who have grown up on a diet of New Mormon History. The hearts of fathers and mothers are breaking, much like the righteous Lamanite parents who experienced "much sorrow" over the "wickedness of the rising generation." These ancient children were being led away by the 'revisionist'-at-the-time "flattering words" and "lyings" of the Zoramites.[13]

For today's traditionalists, President Benson dedicated his life to defending the historic faithful position, battling like a modern Captain Moroni the ceaseless onslaught of progressive ideology in politics, in revisionist history—in a society untethered from its traditional moorings. Sadly, as is so often the case in the Book of Mormon, the rising generation—including one of President Benson's own grandchildren—was swept away by the allure of progressive ideology. While grandfather Ezra served as President of the Church, his disaffected grandson, Steve Benson, requested his name be removed from the Church, and publicly voiced his

12   See Helaman 16; emphasis added.

13   3 Nephi 1:29.

opposition to the Church and its accompanying teachings. Steve has since expressed his contempt for religion in general, stating that, "If, as the true believers claim, the word 'gospel' means good news, then the good news for me is that there is no gospel, other than what I can define for myself, by observation and conscience." Not willing to let his disbelief lay dormant, the younger Benson addressed a body of fellow anti-religionists at the 22nd annual Freedom From Religion Foundation in 1999, where he heralded his anathema: "As a freethinking human being, I have come not to favor or fear religion, but to face and fight it as an impediment to civilized advancement."[14]

The now faithless Benson began moving on a path away from God by fully embracing the progressive ideology and interpretations of Latter-day Saint history, believing that "the church has doctored its past" and claiming that:

> **"** ... [Joseph] Smith was convicted in court for being a money-digging charlatan, was accused by his followers of swindling their cash in a clumsy bank fraud scheme, and was exposed by a group of skeptics that tricked him into 'translating' a set of supposedly ancient brass plates that had actually been manufactured in a local blacksmith's shop.[15]

> Steve Benson continued to falsely assert that Joseph " ... was both a believer in astrology and a dabbler in the occult, and what you have is a somewhat different picture from the one the church paints of its inventor."[16]

In 2012, Steve decried his ongoing frustration with what he alleged was "propaganda" built out of the Miracle of the Gulls account, claiming Leonard Arrington's old friend and colleague, William Hartley as his authority:

---

14   Steve Benson, "Latter-Day Saint To Latter-Day Ain't," Freethought Today, December 1999, https://web.archive.org/web/20101231142607/https://ffrf.org/legacy/fttoday/1999/December99/benson.html.

15   Ibid.

16   Steve Benson, "Good-bye to God: Editorial Cartoonist's Journey From Jesus to Journalism-- and Beyond," LDS-Mormon.com, http://www.lds-mormon.com/benson2.shtml.

❝ Gullible on the Gulls: Another Typically Bird-Brained Distortion by the Mormon Church of What Really Happened with Those Crickets . . .

Despite ceaseless propaganda efforts by the Mormon Church to claim otherwise, the so-called "Miracle of the Gulls" was actually not an all-that-unusual (and certaintly [sic] not at all miraculous) event. To the contrary, it was a natural phenomenon that predictably took flight (so to speak) as a Mormon wonder tale that has over time been hyped up to a myth of, well, Biblically-baloney proportions.

Indeed, for generations of brainwashed believers, this sensationalized account has been used by the LDS Church for its own purposes to create and perpetuate a false, fablized, go-to story of supposed faith-based "specialness" for Mormons earnestly seeking justification of their overblown sense of God-chosen superiority (truth be damned).

It's time for the faithful Mormon sheep to wake up, rise from their feathered pillows and smell the coffee instead of drinking the Kool-Aid.

Below is a comprehensive assessemnt [sic] of what actually took place in 1848 in the Salt Lake Valley between the birds and the bugs. Authored by William Hartley, it is entitled "Mormons, Crickets, and Gulls: A New Look at an Old Story" (published in "The New Mormon History," D. Michael Quinn, ed. [Salt Lake City, Utah: Signature Books, 1992], pp. 137-51. with footnotes):[17]

How many of our youth have been led to believe—like Steve Benson, who cultivated the seeds of doubt sown by 'broad-minded' inaccuracy—that our past is filled with myth and distorted historical fabrication? How many minds has the revisionism of men like Hartley and Arrington swayed? During the Lord's mortal sojourn, He warned His disciples, "Ye shall know them by their fruits. Do men gather grapes of thorns, or figs of thistles? . . . A good tree cannot bring forth evil fruit, neither can a corrupt tree bring forth good fruit."[18] What is the fruit of New Mormon History?

---

17   Steve Benson, "Gull-ible Mormons swallow the fable of the crickets and the gulls," *ExMormon.org,* https://www.exmormon.org/phorum/read.php?2,1810674.

18   3 Nephi 14:16, 18.

9

A Newly Concocted, Not-So-Honorable Joseph Smith

During President Ezra Taft Benson and Leonard Arrington's spar in the First Presidency Conference Room on September 21, 1976, President Benson voiced his deeply held concern that *The Story of the Latter-day Saints*[1] "tended to degrade or demean Joseph Smith."[2]

Traditional history had portrayed the Smith family as "honest and industrious, pious and benevolent."[3] For example, President George Q. Cannon's 1886 biography[4] portrayed the Smith family as "wast[ing] no time in useless repining," but diligently working "to maintain their honest name, to live in happiness, and to devote some hours of each week to the rudimentary education of the younger children."[5] Joseph Smith modeled Christian honor and industry, which, according to Elder Cannon, he did by:

1 James B. Allen and Glen M. Leonard, *The Story of the Latter-day Saints* (Salt Lake City, Utah: Deseret Book Company, 1976). Hereafter referred to as "*Story.*"

2 Leonard J. Arrington Diaries, September 21, 1976; Leonard J. Arrington and Gary James Bergera, *Confessions of a Mormon Historian: The Diaries of Leonard J. Arrington, 1971-1997,* vol. 2 (Salt Lake City: Signature Books, 2018), 238.

3 George Q. Cannon, *The Life of Joseph Smith* (Salt Lake City, Utah: Salt Lake City Juvenile Instructor Office, 1888), 32.

4 Recommended by Ezra Taft Benson in 1976, "No writer can ever accurately portray a prophet of God if he or she does not believe in prophecy. They cannot succeed in writing what they do not have in personal faith. That is why the best biography on Joseph Smith to date was one done by one who knew him and who served the Church as an apostle and member of the First Presidency. I refer to George Q. Cannon's inspiring work, *The Life of Joseph Smith.*" Ezra Taft Benson, "God's Hand in Our Nation's History," Brigham Young University Devotional, 1976, https://speeches.byu.edu/talks/ezra-taft-benson/gods-hand-nations-history/.

5 George Q. Cannon, *The Life of Joseph Smith* (Salt Lake City, Utah: Salt Lake City Juvenile Instructor Office, 1888), 34.

❙❙ ... working with his hands to aid in the family maintenance, while his mind was busy with eternal truths. ... heroism in the honest, uncomplaining home-toil of youth: ... that heroism is doubly beautiful in the life of Joseph, who knew already his destiny, divinely ordained. ...

No husbandman of all that neighborhood was more industrious than he; and, except for the hatred bred against him by false teachers and their followers, no one would have had a better reputation.[6]

Conversely, Arrington and James B. Allen criticized George Q. Cannon's biography in 1969, claiming that it "embellish[ed] the narrative with his own interpretations and dramatic style."[7]

During the mid-1900s, subtle contradictions to this picture of honor and integrity began to infiltrate Latter-day Saint publications. *Story* acknowledged the hard-working habits of the Smith family, as well as the Christian parenting practices of Joseph Smith Sr. and Lucy Mack Smith. "Under the tutelage of their father, the family studied the scriptures together and were led by him in family prayer. No pains were spared, the Prophet recalled later, in instructing him in the principles of Christianity."[8]

However, *Story* also implied that Joseph Smith was initially unwilling to "open himself" to God's will:

❙❙ Not until he was determined and ready to open himself to the mind and will of God—to allow divine inspiration to help mold his character and destiny—would young Joseph Smith become different from what he was. By 1820 he was ready.[9]

Chapter 2 took a darker turn, however, as the new narrative referred to Joseph Smith as a "teenage boy attracted to the wealth of the world—even after his remarkable spiritual manifestations."[10] The Prophet was portrayed in *Story*, during his travel to the Hill

---

6   Ibid., 46.

7   Leonard J. Arrington and James B. Allen, "Mormon Origins in New York: An Introductory Analysis," *BYU Studies* 9, no. 3 (Spring 1969): 12.

8   James B. Allen and Glen M. Leonard, *The Story of the Latter-day Saints* (Salt Lake City, Utah: Deseret Book Company, 1976), 21.

9   Ibid., 22.

10   Ibid., 33.

Cumorah, as "obsess[ed]" with "thoughts of potential wealth . . . Already the young man was thinking contrary to instructions."[11]

Succeeding pages wove in claims that, until this point, had been largely regarded by faithful historians as nothing more than anti-Mormon propaganda. *Story* now gave those disparaging ideas credence:

> // One of the curious sidelines with which he [Joseph Smith] became involved was seeking for buried treasure. A mild craze of this activity excited the farmers of New York in the 1820's, based partly on superstitious reliance on folk magic, partly on belief in legend and folklore of buried Indian treasure and hidden Spanish pirate hoard. . . . It was not unusual to find men and boys spending time following tales of buried wealth, and apparently some of the Smith family, including Joseph, became involved for a time. In a way, it might be said that this was part of Joseph's rude awakening to reality. Already he had been chastened for thinking of the gold plates as a source of income, and it is not improbable that the economic privation he knew could lead him to less sacrilegious schemes for acquiring wealth.[12]

While Allen and Leonard quietly acknowledged that they did not know "the original source of such rumors nor whether they had any basis in fact," the authors proceeded to portray Joseph as a man who had "a reputation for possessing certain psychic powers to locate buried treasure."[13] The Smith family, *Story* alleged, were "following tales of buried wealth."[14]

Story was likely the first publication ever released under the auspices and sanction of the Church promoting the idea of Joseph Smith's involvement in magic and treasure digging. This progressive avowal stood in stark contrast to the Church's official, long-standing narrative upheld by all of the presidents of the Church since the Prophet's martyrdom in 1844. In 1882, Joseph Smith's nephew, President Joseph F. Smith strongly denounced comparable slanders as mere lies calculated to tarnish the Prophet:

---

11   Ibid., 33.
12   Ibid., 35-36.
13   Ibid., 36.
14   Ibid., 35.

⁄⁄ He was accused of nearly everything that was vile, by his enemies, who, as is well known by the Latter-day Saints, were generally entirely ignorant of his true character and mission. . . . He was called "a money digger," and many other contemptuous things. If you will look at his history, and at the character of his parents, and surroundings, and consider the object of his life, you can discover how much consistency there was in the charges brought against him. All this was done to injure him. He was neither old nor "a money digger," nor an impostor, nor in any manner deserving of the epithets that they applied to him.[15]

President Joseph F. Smith's testimony is substantially supported by historical data and verifiable facts. Every contemporary account accusing Joseph of a treasure digging career comes from an apostate member or anti-Mormon antagonist fixed on destroying the credibility of the Church.[16] For over 190 years, the dominant narrative of the Church declared that Joseph Smith was *not* involved in a money-digging vocation and that he never dabbled in magic. While mortal, he lived a life above reproach, approaching a perfection and purity exceeding any prophet ever to live, excepting the Son of God—the Savior of the world—Himself.

In 1976, for the first time, an official publication of the Church would publicize a revision to the long-held narrative of its history. The title page to *Story* declared, "Published in Collaboration with the Historical Department of The Church of Jesus Christ of Latter-day Saints." The foreword explained that "officials of the Church" recommended the volume, and "with the approval of the First Presidency, we asked two of our finest historians, James B. Allen and Glen M. Leonard, to undertake the task of preparing this history." Was Church headquarters behind the promotion of this new

---

15   Joseph F. Smith, "Greatness of the Work Inaugurated and Accomplished By the Prophet Joseph Smith," in *Journal of Discourses*, vol. 24 (Liverpool, 1884), 13; Joseph F. Smith, *Gospel Doctrine* (Salt Lake City, Utah: Deseret Book, 1975), 482-483.

16   L. Hannah Stoddard and James F. Stoddard III, *Seer Stone v. Urim & Thummim: Book of Mormon Translation on Trial* (Joseph Smith Foundation, 2019), 96-98, 100-102, 120-123, 192-214; Joseph Fielding Smith, *Doctrines of Salvation, vol. 3* (Salt Lake City, Utah: Bookcraft, 1956), 225-226; Joseph Fielding McConkie and Craig J. Ostler, "The Process of Translating the Book of Mormon," *Revelations of the Restoration: A Commentary on the Doctrine and Covenants and Other Modern Revelations* (Salt Lake City, UT: Deseret Book, 2000), 89-98.

narrative, with the accompanying confusion and faith crisis it must certainly cause among the members?

Treasure Digging

When reviewing the arguments and historical sources relied upon by progressives in the new portrayal of Joseph Smith, logical questions are necessarily raised concerning the veracity and authenticity of those sources. Moreover, it turns out that some of the documents are likely fraudulent.

On page 41 in the second edition of *Story*, Allen and Leonard apparently attempt to shore up extremely weak evidence explaining that when Joseph Smith worked for Josiah Stowell,[17] "Official articles of agreement were drawn up, and the Smiths were to share in the profits."[18] Years later, in *Rough Stone Rolling*, Richard Bushman would also draw on the "articles of agreement" document to support the idea that Joseph Smith and his father took shares in a treasure-hunting enterprise:

 A set of "Articles of Agreement," dated November 1, 1825 [though published only much later], indicated that Joseph and his father were to receive two-elevenths of the ore in the mine or "the coined money and bars or ingots of Gold or Silver" reputed to lie hidden underground.[19]

---

17   In 1825, Joseph was employed as a "common labourer" by Josiah Stowell, who required him to work with other men digging and searching for an old Spanish mine. Stowell believed the legends of Spanish treasure circulating about the area, and had begun digging for the mine before Joseph was hired. In the end, Joseph finally succeeded in convincing Stowell to cease the foolish venture. Joseph Smith himself repudiated claims that he was involved in treasure digging:

"[In October 1825] I hired with an old Gentleman, by name of Josiah Stoal [*sic*] who lived in Chenango County, State of New York. He had heard something of a silver mine having been opened by the Spaniards in Harmony, Susquahanah [*sic*] County, State of Pensylvania [*sic*], and had previous to my hiring with him been digging in order if possible to discover the mine. After I went to live with him he took me among the rest of his hands to dig for the silver mine, at which I continued to work for nearly a month without success in our undertaking, and finally I prevailed with the old gentleman to cease digging after it. Hence arose the very prevalent story of my having been a money digger." Joseph Smith, History, circa June 1839–circa 1841 [Draft 2], p. 7-8, The Joseph Smith Papers.

18   James B. Allen and Glen M. Leonard, *The Story of the Latter-day Saints* (Salt Lake City, Utah: Deseret Book Company, 1992), 41.

19   Richard L. Bushman, *Joseph Smith: Rough Stone Rolling* (New York: Vintage Books, 2006), 48.

Amusingly, the "agreement" mentioned in *Story*, and to which Richard Bushman confidently referred, was not based on authenticated documents. Present scholarship affords no provenance for this alleged contract, as corroborated in the Joseph Smith Papers historical introduction to the document:

// This document does not appear among this volume's featured texts because it cannot be authenticated. No manuscript of the contract exists, and it is known only through its publication in Utah's then avowedly anti-Mormon *Salt Lake Daily Tribune* [April 23, 1880], fifty-five years after it was purportedly written and two thousand miles distant. Even copies of the 20 March 1880 issue of the *Susquehanna Journal*, where it reportedly first appeared in print, cannot be located.

... there is no credible evidence that JS participated in digging for buried treasure in Pennsylvania before 1825.[20]

In other words, the document that allegedly 'proved' Joseph Smith's interest in money digging does not exist. An anti-Mormon newspaper published an account fifty-five years *after* the original events—long after any eyewitness participants could confirm or deny the incident—and even the first reported appearance, in 1880, cannot be verified. And yet this "evidence" was touted in *Rough Stone Rolling* and in *Story*. Why would Richard Bushman, James Allen, and Glen Leonard use a non-authenticated source? Similar concerns can be detailed with the other so-called 'sources.'

In 1976, President Benson and other leaders succeeded in blocking any republication of *Story*. However, in 1986, a second printing was approved. President Benson reportedly opposed the republication as President of the Church;[21] but he was ostensibly

---

20   Joseph Smith Papers, "Appendix 1: Agreement of Josiah Stowell and Others, 1 November 1825," Historical Introduction, https://www.josephsmithpapers.org/paper-summary/appendix-1-agreement-of-josiah-stowell-and-others-1-november-1825/1#historical-intro.

21   According to the description of the Marvin S. Hill papers located at the University of Utah libraries, there are files documenting "Benson's critique of the 'New Mormon' history, and his opposition to the re-publication of Allen and Leonard's 'The Story of the Latter-day Saints.'" "Marvin S. Hill papers, 1788-2006," Archives West, http://archiveswest.orbiscascade.org/ark:/80444/xv96926; due to inability to access the archives as a result of the COVID-19 restrictions

Articles of Agreement published in The Daily Tribune, April 23, 1880

overruled, and *The Story of the Latter-day Saints*, Second Edition was published in 1992.

The second edition claimed that Joseph Smith dabbled in "youthful experiments with treasure-seeking," and even professed in 1826 "that he had a stone through which he once looked for treasure and lost articles." Joseph's father is depicted as expressing his 'mortification' that the power of God had been "used [by the young Joseph Smith] only in search of filthy lucre."

Traditionalist believers had maintained that the power of God cannot be used for satanic purposes, whereas the new progressive narrative portrayed the Prophet Joseph Smith as using the power of God, or conversely the power of the devil, for "filthy lucre." *Story* explained that Joseph Smith Sr. hoped that one day "young Joseph would know more clearly the will of God concerning him." Instead of depicting a noble youth, *Story* described Joseph as a less-than-ordinary boy who "gradually transcended his youthful involvement with treasure hunters."[22]

---

throughout 2020, the authors will include the documentation in a subsequent printing of this volume.

22   James B. Allen and Glen M. Leonard, *The Story of the Latter-day Saints* (Salt Lake City, Utah: Deseret Book Company, 1992), 41–42. Allen and Leonard's statements are based on the claims of an anti-Mormon, William D. Purple, who wrote more than five decades after the alleged events. Purple's claims are extremely questionable and are not based in any contemporary historical records or verifiable documentation. For a debunking of the accusations that Joseph Smith was involved in magic and treasure digging, as relates to the 1826 trial, visit www.JosephSmithFoundation.org.

Who Was Joseph Smith?

According to *Story*'s authors James Allen and Glen Leonard, Joseph Smith was a weak man. Both editions speak of the Prophet's alleged "business failures," arguing that Latter-day Saints should "separate his role as prophet and religious leader from his activities in the temporal world."[23] Richard Bushman would later magnify this roguish portrayal of Joseph Smith in *Rough Stone Rolling*, wherein he portrayed the Prophet Joseph as weak in judgment, a purveyor of foolish financial advice, and offering flawed counsel regarding so-called "temporal" affairs.[24] *Story* simply argued that focusing on the Prophet's flaws and sinful tendencies allows us to "comprehend what makes a prophet." The underlying point of this progressive view is that a great prophet is not necessarily a great man:

// Perhaps it is only by understanding his [Joseph Smith's] humanness that the reader of Latter-day Saint history can comprehend what makes a prophet. Though imperfect, Joseph Smith was striving toward perfection. When he made mistakes or sometimes succumbed to temptation he took seriously the scriptural promise of God's forgiveness if he would overcome his weaknesses through prayer and effort. The Prophet exhibited such boundless faith in Christ's promise that even with, or in spite of, his weaknesses,

---

23   James B. Allen and Glen M. Leonard, *The Story of the Latter-day Saints* (Salt Lake City, Utah: Deseret Book Company, 1976), 114; James B. Allen and Glen M. Leonard, *The Story of the Latter-day Saints*, 2nd ed. (Salt Lake City, Utah: Deseret Book Company, 1992), 123.

24   Note the contrast with the testimony of those who knew the Prophet. Jesse W. Crosby, "The Prophet had great ability as a financier; and had his enemies left him, he would have become one of the wealthiest men in America. Everything his hand touched seemed to prosper. His fields were always in good condition and yielded well. When people came to see him--and he had many visitors--their teams were fed the best of hay and his barn was full. No other orchard had as fine fruit as did his. If an inferior cow was by any means shoved on him, it would be but a short time before she became a first-class milker. Many men sought his advice when in financial difficulty, and none failed to profit by it if they followed the counsel he gave.

A period of great prosperity for him would seem to induce a raid upon him. One trial after another would be launched upon him, until he would be left penniless and perhaps in debt." *Stories from notebook of Martha Cox, grandmother of Fern Cox Anderson*, p. 1, Church History Library, https://catalog.churchofjesuschrist.org/assets?id=51118bdd-bd9b-495f-8374-ad7aae3e5ae8&crate=0&index=0.

he could apparently draw closer to the Divine than others and become an instrument in restoring the gospel.[25]

Conversely, traditionalists declare that the Prophet Joseph Smith did not merely strive for perfection, but that he achieved a degree of holiness and honor greater than any other man, except the Son of God. He was great, not in spite of his weaknesses, but because of his inherent righteousness—a trait he manifested in his daily life as much or more than any other follower of Jesus Christ in history. While it is true that no man in history was entirely sinless, true traditionalists accept the statements made by numerous Presidents of the Church—and by those who knew him best, including Eliza R. Snow and others—that Joseph Smith stands next to Jesus Christ in greatness, and more importantly, in purity and holiness. The following is a *very small* sample of the many declarations that speak to this fact:

// Brigham Young

I do not think that a man lives on the earth that knew him any better than I did; and I am bold to say that, Jesus Christ excepted, no better man ever lived or does live upon this earth. I am his witness. He was persecuted for the same reason that any other righteous person has been or is persecuted at the present day.[26]

John Taylor:

[Joseph and Hyrum Smith] those two, the best of Adam's race.[27]

Wilford Woodruff:

There is not so great a man as Joseph standing in this generation.... His mind, like Enoch's, expands as eternity, and only God can comprehend his soul.[28]

---

25   James B. Allen and Glen M. Leonard, *The Story of the Latter-day Saints* (Salt Lake City, Utah: Deseret Book Company, 1976), 31-32.

26   Brigham Young, "A Knowledge of God Obtained Only Through Obedience to the Principles of Truth," *Journal of Discourses*, vol. 9 (Salt Lake City, 1974), 332. Discourse given on August 3, 1862.

27   "Poetry," *Times and Seasons* 6, no. 14 (August 1, 1845): 991.

28   Wilford Woodruff, Journal History of The Church of Jesus Christ

... no greater prophet than Joseph Smith ever lived on the face of the earth save Jesus Christ.[29]

I look upon Joseph Smith as the greatest prophet that ever breathed the breath of life, excepting Jesus Christ.[30]

Lorenzo Snow:

There never was a man that possessed a higher degree of integrity and more devotedness to the interest of mankind than the Prophet Joseph Smith.[31]

Joseph F. Smith

... Joseph Smith is held in reverence, his name is honored; tens of thousands of people thank God in their hearts, and from the depths of their souls, for the knowledge the Lord has restored to the earth through him, and therefore they speak well of him and bear testimony of his worth.[32]

Heber J. Grant

Those who know him, those who know his teachings, know his life was pure and that his teachings were in very deed God's law.[33]

George Albert Smith

There have been some who have belittled him, but I would like to say that those who have done so will be forgotten and their remains will go back to mother earth, if they have not already gone, and the odor of their infamy will never die, while the glory and honor and majesty and courage and fidelity manifested by

of Latter-day Saints, April 9, 1837, Church History Library, https:// catalog.churchofjesuschrist.org/assets?id=d87cf687-399a-497c-889c-af5de8ea18ca&crate=0&index=48.

29   Wilford Woodruff, "Organization of the First Presidency—Responsibility of the Saints, Etc.," *Journal of Discourses*, vol. 21 (Salt Lake City, 1881), 317. Discourse given on October 10, 1880.

30   Wilford Woodruff, *The Deseret Weekly*, vol. 38, March 23, 1889, 389.

31   Lorenzo Snow, *Conference Report*, April 1898, 64.

32   Joseph F. Smith, *Gospel Doctrine* (Salt Lake City: Deseret Book Company, 1975), 481.

33   Heber J. Grant, *Conference Report*, April 1943, 8.

the Prophet Joseph Smith will attach to his name forever. So we have no apologies to make.[34]

David O. McKay

Joseph Smith had "the best blood of this country . . . "[35]

Great men have the ability to see clearly into the heart of things. They discern truth. They think independently. They act nobly. They influence strong men to follow them. Small men sneer at them, ridicule them, persecute them, but the critics die and are forgotten, and the great man lives on forever.

Some of Joseph Smith's contemporaries sneered at him; others admired him; his followers revered him.[36]

Eliza R. Snow

. . . [N]ever, since the Son of God was slain

Has blood so noble, flow'd from human vein

. . . But TWO [Joseph and Hyrum], so wise, so virtuous, great and good,

Before on earth, at once, have never stood

Since the creation[37]

Daniel D. McArthur

To me, Joseph Smith seemed to possess more power and force of character than any ordinary man. I would look upon him when he was with hundreds of other men, and he would appear greater than ever.[38]

---

34   George Albert Smith, *Conference Report*, April 1946, 181-182.

35   David O. McKay, *Conference Report*, October 1931, 12.

36   David O. McKay, *Pathways to Happiness* (Salt Lake City: UT: Bookcraft, 1957), 284-285.

37   Eliza R. Snow, "The Assassination of Gen'ls Joseph Smith and Hyrum Smith. First Presidents of the Church of Latter Day Saints; Who Were Massacred by a Mob in Carthage, Hancock County, Ill, on the 27th of June, 1844," *Times and Seasons* 5 (July 1, 1844): 575.

38   Daniel D. McArthur, "Recollections of the Prophet Joseph Smith," *Juvenile Instructor* 27 (February 15, 1892): 128-129.

Peter Hardeman Burnett (non-member)

. . . [Joseph Smith] was much more than an ordinary man. He possessed the most indomitable perseverance, was a good judge of men, and deemed himself born to command, and he did command. . . . his manner was so earnest, and apparently so candid, that you could not but be interested.[39]

Jesse N. Smith

I first saw the Prophet in Kirtland, though I was then but a child. The Prophet was incomparably the most God-like man I ever saw. I know that by nature he was incapable of lying and deceitfulness, possessing the greatest kindness and nobility of character. I felt when in his presence that he could read me through and through. I know he was all that he claimed to be.[40]

One testimony came from the Prophet's brother, a man to whom Joseph looked upon as a dear friend—a man who knew Joseph in his intimate moments and who would mingle his blood in the martyrs' testimony. Hyrum Smith shared his testimony through word and deed as to where Joseph stood in his role as Prophet: ". . . Joseph has the spirit and power of all the Prophets."[41]

The authors of this work express their sure witness that the Prophet Joseph Smith represents the latter-day consummation and culmination of every prophet who lived on this Earth. He held the spiritual gifts, keys, and power of Adam, Enoch, Melchizedek, Noah, Abraham, Isaac, Jacob, Joseph, Isaiah, Jeremiah, Elijah, Elisha, John the Baptist, Peter, James, John, and numerous others. Not only did the aforementioned prophets' lives and works foreshadow that of the Lord Jesus Christ—these holy men also, in like manner, presented a type and shadow of Joseph Smith's character and ensuing work during their own mortal ministries.

---

39   Peter Hardeman Burnett, *Recollections and Opinions of an Old Pioneer* (New York: D. Appleton and Company, 1880), 67.

40   Jesse N. Smith, "Recollections of the Prophet Joseph Smith," *Juvenile Instructor* 27 (January 1, 1892): 23-24.

41   Full statement: "There were prophets before Adam, and Joseph has the spirit and power of all the Prophets." Joseph Smith, History, 1838-1856, volume E-1, April 28, 1844, p. 2025, The Joseph Smith Papers.

10

True Scholarship Cracks
the Faith Crisis

Will an honorable Joseph Smith hold up to scholarly historical scrutiny? Traditionalists concur with the preceding witnesses of Joseph Smith, and they believe that *true* history substantiates and vindicates the greatness of the Prophet. They are not afraid of controversial episodes, but rather embrace intense scholarly research and welcome an open discussion and investigation into all historical sources. Furthermore, traditionalists know that subjecting the data and the facts to the rigor of *true* scholarship has affirmed, and will continue to reveal, the Prophet Joseph Smith as the man of honor and integrity whom his defenders have upheld.

At the same time Arrington and his progressive-historian colleagues were working to rewrite the character of the Prophet Joseph Smith, another scholar was studying Joseph just as intently, yet deriving completely different conclusions. Truman G. Madsen[1] knew Arrington, and even served as chairman of an organization known as the "Mormon Origins in New York," of which Arrington, Richard Bushman, and James Allen were members.[2] Madsen was every bit as credentialed as Arrington—holding a Ph.D. from Harvard University—but in contrast to Arrington's college experience, "[t]he

---

1   Truman Madsen noted, "I was named after Truman O. Angell, architect of the Salt Lake Temple, and Grant after my maternal grandfather, Heber J. Grant." "Timeline," Truman G. Madsen, http://trumanmadsen.com/new/?page_id=53.

Since Heber J. Grant's mother, Rachel Ivins Grant, was sealed to the Prophet Joseph Smith as a plural wife, Truman always considered himself a descendant of the Prophet.

2   "Mormon Origins in New York" was founded in 1967. This interesting story will be discussed in more detail in *Rough Stone Rolling Debunked*.

revelations of Joseph Smith were an anchor for Truman during his philosophy studies at Harvard."[3] Madsen "read about the Prophet Joseph Smith every day for at least thirty minutes," though when preparing for lectures he "studied long periods, sometimes long days." Madsen helped fund Andrew F. Ehat's *The Words of Joseph Smith*, he funded and edited *The Concordance of the Doctrinal Statements of Joseph Smith,* and he presented the famous 1978 Education Week "Joseph Smith lectures." All of this activity was taking place at the very same time Madsen's historian colleagues, Arrington and Bushman,[4] were pushing their new, progressive version of the Prophet.

While Arrington and Bushman promoted a flawed prophet, exposing supposed hidden blemishes, Madsen's research of the Prophet Joseph Smith gave him an entirely different perspective:

> *"It's the character of Joseph Smith that's being assaulted and vilified," Truman noted. "You go on the web, you're going to find every kind of vicious statement about how rotten a man he was. These [the Quorum of the Twelve of Joseph Smith's day] are people who knew him daily and intimately and in [the] most sacred circumstances, and they leave no question that his life was noble and true and that, in my way of summing it up, he went through the veil without spot and blameless. I not only have a testimony that he was a prophet, I have a testimony of his character, which then gives me confidence in everything else he did and everything else he said."[5]*

Why did Madsen come to an opposite conclusion of that deduced by Bushman? What was the fruit of Madsen's scholarship? In his biography, *The Truman G. Madsen Story*, documented letters are found from members whose lives were forever changed by Madsen's research on Joseph Smith. One letter from a young man in Australia particularly touched him:

---

3   Barnard N. Madsen, *The Truman G. Madsen Story: A Life of Study and Faith* (Salt Lake City: Deseret Book, 2016), 369.

4   See chapter "Backtracking on the New Sesquicentennial History."

5   Barnard N. Madsen, *The Truman G. Madsen Story: A Life of Study and Faith* (Salt Lake City: Deseret Book, 2016), 373; brackets in original.

❝ Dear Bro Madsen,

Some 16 years ago, when I was about 15 I received a phone call from my home teaching companion to go home teaching. At the time I was trying to find ways of not having to go but ended up not having a good enough excuse in time. As it ended up I was in the car 15 minutes later heading to see our families. Playing in the car was a talk tape by a man named Truman G. Madsen talking about the Prophet Joseph Smith. I started to listen to the tape and was soon engrossed in it. At the end of the home teaching visit I asked my companion if I could borrow the tape. He allowed me to borrow all 4 tapes. I spent the next three months listening to them every day. It was a very powerful time in my life. I was the only member of the church at my school and was the only active teacher in the Aaronic Priesthood in my ward. Listening to those tapes provided an environment for me to gain a testimony of the Prophet Joseph Smith. I can still remember one day listening to you talk about Carthage and feeling the Spirit testify strongly that Joseph died a Prophet of the Lord. . . .

Being a teenager and not having strength in numbers around me in a gospel sense, it was great to have you teach me of the Prophet Joseph. In short, those tapes gave me, a young man in Geelong, Australia, a turning point that solidified my desire to serve a mission and to marry in the temple. . . .

There is no doubt in my mind that one day when all is said and done and the work is finished, that Joseph will come up to you, put his big arm around you, and say, "Thanks Truman, for making my name known for good."

May you and your family be blessed for your love of the Lord and the Prophet.[6]

Madsen was professionally credentialed. He held a doctorate from Harvard University and spent countless hours pouring through original documents. He studied the same material and source documents as his progressive contemporaries, but the data led him

---

6   Ibid., 378-379.

to draw the conclusion that Joseph Smith was a man of character and honor—and he testified of those findings.

Why did Richard Bushman arrive at one conclusion and Truman Madsen a diametrically opposed, alternate determination? They were looking at essentially the same data, at the same time, with similar credentials.

'Humanizing' Joseph Smith

Progressive history too often tends to interpret the greatness of men and women in history through the biographer's or the historian's own personal lens. This lens is shaped by the lifestyle and the moral character of contemporary culture, and accentuates—or more often manufactures—the imperfections that allow for a portrayal depicting heroes as weak or 'just like us.' As a result, progressives look dubiously upon men and women of exceptional righteousness and holiness as 'unrealistic' icons—myths built up only within the minds of 'uneducated' people.

On the other hand, traditionalists maintain without reservation that Joseph Smith is *not* 'just like us'—a tether affirmed in his own declaration: "A disposition to commit [any great or malignant sins] . . . was *never* in my nature,"[7] and "I never did harm any man since I have been born in the world . . . I never think evil nor think any thing to the harm of my fellow man—& when I am called at the trump & weighed in the balance you will know me then . . ."[8] In truth, Joseph Smith "lived great, and he died great in the eyes of God . . ."[9] Greatness was not only possible, but was realized in the public and private life of the Prophet. His mind was pure, and his hands were clean. He lived a life of honor. "Would to God, brethren, I could tell you who I am!" he told the Saints. "Would to God I could tell you what I know! But you would call it blasphemy, and there are men upon this stand [Quorum of the Twelve and other leaders] who would want to take my life."[10] One either has to take

---

7   Joseph Smith History 1:28, emphasis added.

8   Joseph Smith, Minutes and Discourses, 6–9 April 1844, as Reported by Thomas Bullock, p. 22, The Joseph Smith Papers.

9   Doctrine and Covenants (1844 edition), p. 444, The Joseph Smith Papers. Currently Doctrine and Covenants 135:3.

10   Orson F. Whitney, *Life of Heber C. Kimball* (Juvenile Instructor Office, 1888), 333.

these statements from the Prophet Joseph seriously, or conclude that he suffered from an extreme case of delusions of grandeur. Either he was who he claimed to be, or he was the most arrogant of men. Either the Prophet's character and degree of perfection was and is incomprehensible to the Saints, and will not be revealed until the Judgement,[11] or he was the arch deceiver. Some of us can bear witness from literal personal experience that the Prophet Joseph was in very deed everything, and more, than he claimed to be.

President Benson Takes a Stand

Clearly a traditionalist in ideology, President Ezra Taft Benson condemned the defamation of righteous men and women throughout history—especially those involved with the history of the Restoration and the founding of America—when he addressed the BYU student body in 1976:

---

11   "You don't know me— you never knew my heart; no man knows my history; I cannot tell it— I shall never undertake it. . . . I never did harm any man since I was born into the world. My voice is always for peace. I cannot lie down until all my work is finished. I never think any evil, nor do any thing to the harm of my fellow man. When I am called by the trump of the Archangel, and weighed in the Balance, you will all know me then. I add no more. God bless you all." Joseph Smith, History, 1838–1856, volume E-1, April 7, 1844, p. 1979, The Joseph Smith Papers.

Mary Elizabeth Rollins Lightner recorded the Prophet Joseph Smith telling her,"'They say I am a fallen Prophet, but I am more in favor with my God this day than ever before in my life. They little know who I am, and I dare not tell. They will not know who I am until they see me at the bar of God.'

". . . I [Mary Elizabeth Rollins] said, 'Brother Joseph, how do you know you yourself will be saved?' He replied, 'I know I will. I have the oath of God on it and God cannot lie.' He said John the Revelator was caught up to the third heaven, but I know one who was caught up to the seventh heaven and saw and heard things not lawful for me to utter." Diary of Mary Elizabeth Rollins Lightner, 1936; Mary Elizabeth Rollins Lightner family collection, 1833-1973; Diary of Mary Elizabeth Rollins Lightner, 1936; p. 3, Church History Library, https://catalog.churchofjesuschrist.org/assets?id=1887fff0-c725-4c48-b685-9375da0724ef&crate=0&index=4.

"People little know who I am when they talk to me, and they never will know until they see me weighed in the balance in the Kingdom of God. Then they will know who I am, and see me as I am. I dare not tell them and they do not know me." Remarks by Mary F. Lightner at Brigham Young University, April 14, 1905; Mary Elizabeth Rollins Lightner family collection, 1833-1973; Mary Elizabeth Rollins Lightner writings and remarks, 1902, 1905; p. 5, Church History Library, https://catalog.churchofjesuschrist.org/assets?id=cef69c4d-9631-4033-8f25-9f097f63bdb3&crate=0&index=12.

▟▟ I know the philosophy behind this practice—"to tell it as it is."
All too often those who subscribe to this philosophy are not
hampered by too many facts. When will we awaken to the fact
that the defamation of our dead heroes only serves to undermine
faith in the principles for which they stood, and the institutions
which they established? Some have termed this practice as
"historical realism" or moderately call it "debunking." I call
it slander and defamation. I repeat, those who are guilty of it
in their writing or teaching will answer to a higher tribunal.[12]

True traditionalists do not fear examining and exposing genuine
flaws and weaknesses in historic characters. They do, however,
recognize that true heroes always, and without exception,
exemplify authentic goodness and honor—whereas antiheroes are
conversely a 'counterfeit.'

According to President Benson, the true source of the progressive
attempt to 'debunk' the virtue of righteous men and women is a
strategy, well-meaning or not, to "undermine faith in the principles
for which they stood . . ."[13]

In truth, the revisionist elements within *The Story of the Latter-
day Saints* were mild compared to the progressive Latter-day Saint
narrative being published today—nearly a half century distant from
President Benson's controversy with Arrington. This great shift is
clearly evident, as Greg Prince commented during a 2018 interview
with John Dehlin on a Mormon Stories podcast:

▟▟ . . . if you read *Story of the Latter-day Saints* now, having read
things that have been published in the intervening decades,
you just have to smile and ask "What was the fuss?" because it
is such a mild, non-confrontational, non-threatening book by
today's standards, and yet at the time that it was published, it
threatened the daylights out of these people.[14]

---

12   Ezra Taft Benson, "God's Hand in Our Nation's History," Brigham Young
University Devotional, 1976, https://speeches.byu.edu/talks/ezra-taft-benson/
gods-hand-nations-history/.

13   Ibid.

14   Mormon Stories Podcast, "Mormon Stories #889: Greg Prince - Leonard
Arrington and the Writing of Mormon History Pt. 1," Mar 26, 2018, video,
01:11:22, https://youtu.be/iIKK-RmtiSs?t=4282.

President Benson was one of "these people." One can only imagine his feelings as he perused *Story;* yet there can be no doubt about his final assessment. For President Benson, it was imperative that this false history never be promoted—least of all by the Church—and he was determined to stop the printing of this book. Lavina Fielding Anderson wrote in *Dialogue:*

▌▌ *The Story of the Latter-day Saints*, by James B. Allen and Glen Leonard, is published [in 1976]. It sells out within a few months but is not reprinted because some general authorities are offended at its approach. A second printing eventually appears in 1986, and a new edition is published in 1993. . . .

. . . Elder Ezra Taft Benson defines "historical realism" as "slander and defamation," . . . He also warns them [CES personnel] not to buy the books or subscribe to the periodicals of "known apostates, or other liberal sources" or have such works on office or personal bookshelves.[15]

The modified second edition of *Story* included a disclaimer at the beginning, noting, "This work is not an official publication of the Church of Jesus Christ of Latter-day Saints. The views expressed herein are the responsibility of the authors and do not necessarily represent the position of the Church or of Deseret Book Company."[16] This was a far cry from the original 1976 title page which read, "Published in Collaboration with the Historical Department of The Church of Jesus Christ of Latter-day Saints" and the original foreword which included, "with the approval of the First Presidency, we asked two of our finest historians, James B. Allen and Glen M. Leonard, to undertake the task of preparing this history."

For traditionalists, President Benson was a hero, pushing back the tide of false historical interpretation. For progressives, President Benson stood as a formidable boulder squarely in the path of "real history" and liberal enlightenment—a hiss and a byword, a 'black hat' among leaders who otherwise might be open to the progressive

---

15   Lavina Fielding Anderson, "The LDS Intellectual Community and Church Leadership: A Contemporary Chronology," *Dialogue: A Journal of Mormon Thought* 26, no. 1 (Spring 1993): 10.

16   James B. Allen and Glen M. Leonard, *The Story of the Latter-day Saints*, 2nd ed. (Salt Lake City, Utah: Deseret Book Company, 1992), iv.

ideology. In the broad-minded paradigm, he was an 'old fogey,' setting the Church backward several decades.

Now, more than a quarter of a century from President Benson's death, Church members are witnessing a resurgence of the money-digging Joseph Smith, a notion heavily promoted both by uninformed members and anti-members alike that has contributed to an overwhelming crisis of faith for ever-growing numbers. After all, what faithful member of the Church would place confidence in a treasure-seeking, occultic, arrogant playboy—a philanderer who had a greed for wealth and followed after the lure of buried treasure instead of following the Lord's call with his heart and soul? Certainly, no good Christian can accept a corrupt, devilish man as the Lord's prophet—a man "from whom nobody would want to buy a used car, much less receive a plan of salvation."[17]

Dehlin Capitalizes From the Progressive 'Joseph Smith'

John Dehlin, a former member and likely the leading antagonist of the Church, recognized the power of this argument. In 2005, he founded Mormon Stories—a podcast series designed to support "Mormons who are transitioning away from either orthodox Mormonism, or from Mormonism altogether."[18] In 2019, Mormon Stories launched a billboard along I-15 advertising: "Was Joseph Smith a treasure digger?" On May 6, 2019, Dehlin announced in seeming delight that during the billboard campaign, of which the treasure digging signboard was a principal placard, they received "a 10-15% increase in new visitors" to their website.[19]

In addition to their billboard campaign, Mormon Stories published a series of essays promoting the revisionist history, now accepted by most Latter-day Saint academics. Nearly 7,000 views later, the Facebook reaction to the "Folk Magic/Treasure Digging" essay is representative of the reaction of most members in general. "Informative and disturbing," read one comment. "This is the first I

---

17   Daniel Peterson, "Defending the Faith: Were Smiths workers or slackers?" *Deseret News*, May 26, 2011, https://www.deseret.com/2011/5/26/20372831/defending-the-faith-were-smiths-workers-or-slackers.

18   "About," Mormon Stories, https://www.mormonstories.org/about/.

19   John Dehlin, "Mormon Stories Truth Claims Billboard Campaign (Completed!)" Mormon Stories, May 6, 2019, https://www.mormonstories.org/billboard/.

have heard that Joseph also used the stone in his hat to dig for treasure. . . . it's so preposterous!" another woman commented. She received the response, "So many LDS people are in that boat with you. But now you know. . . . it is terrible for the church to lie to its membership."[20] Another listener exclaimed, "Trickery at its finest. Wow."

On Dehlin's Youtube version, heart-breaking stories of shattered faith abounded in reaction to the Mormon Stories essay linking Joseph

Billboard sponsored by Mormon Stories, Idaho Falls, Idaho, September 2020

Smith to money digging and magic, peppering the comments section below the video:

❝ John, I will forever be in your debt. Your work has helped me realize that I'm not alone, and that there is hope. I've served 17 years in prison, because I was addicted to drugs, and while there I turned my life around, giving full credit to the church. Now I see things differently.[21]

. . . maybe with the billboards and the obvious character that John Dehlin possesses and illuminates with every podcast/YouTube program more [Mormons] may begin to wonder who's really telling the truth and who's hiding it with every fiber of their beings.[22]

---

20   Mormon Stories Podcast, "Joseph Smith's Involvement in Folk Magic and Treasure Digging," Facebook video, https://www.facebook.com/watch/live/?v=393725884720879&ref=watch_permalink. Note that the latter response was later deleted either by the admins of the page or the original poster.

21   Mormon Stories Podcast, "Joseph Smith's Involvement in Folk Magic and Treasure Digging," YouTube video, February 27, 2019, https://www.youtube.com/watch?v=egxsmp4_Dv0.

22   Ibid.

... the Lds church [h]as actively hidden/distorted/lied about its own history so much that it is completely immoral to proselyte to people under those conditions. I was a member for years before realizing I was completely lied to. I am not referring to spiritual theology. I was lied to about factual history of the church. Years of my life and tens of thousands of dollars based on a lie."[23]

There are hundreds of other stories, both recorded and unexpressed. As one commenter on Dehlin's video asked: "Why would you want to stay in the church after knowing the truth?"[24]

From our own intense study of the relevant historical documents, we have uncovered absolutely *no credible evidence* that Joseph Smith ever had a career in money digging or was ever involved in magic. We adamantly and confidently refute such claims. This crisis of faith occurring for so many thousands of members is tragically unnecessary.

Yet in spite of the lack of credible evidence, progressive New Mormon Historians continue to promote the unfounded myth of Joseph Smith's treasure hunting activities as documented and credible fact. Those involved with the Joseph Smith Papers wrote in the introduction to Volume 1:

/ / Harboring the perpetual hope of the poor for quick riches, Joseph Smith Sr. searched for lost treasure, often with the help of Joseph Jr. Like many of their neighbors, the family combined the use of divining rods and seer stones with conventional forms of Christian worship. In his early twenties, Joseph Jr. had to extricate himself from the local band of treasure seekers before he could focus on his calling to translate the Book of Mormon.[25]

Whether the voice promoting the money-digging adaptation of Joseph Smith is coming from a disaffected member or a prominent Latter-day Saint historian, the effect is the same: members experience a wrenching feeling of betrayal.

---

23 Ibid.

24 Ibid.

25 Dean C. Jessee, Ronald K. Esplin and Richard Lyman Bushman, general eds., *The Joseph Smith Papers, Journals, Vol. 1: 1832-1839* (Salt Lake City, UT: The Church Historian's Press, 2008), xix.

In truth, the faith crisis erupting before our eyes in the 21st-century can trace its origins to seeds planted decades earlier. In the 1970s, Leonard Arrington and his New Mormon Historians were doing their best to introduce the progressive narrative at Church headquarters. A few years after the *Story* episode, controversy again surfaced when Richard Bushman submitted his manuscript for the first volume of a new Church history series, originally intended for release in conjunction with the sesquicentennial celebration of the founding of the Church. Bushman's volume, later published as *Joseph Smith & the Beginnings of Mormonism,* was far more progressive than the earlier *Story* in its promotion of Joseph Smith as the "lazy son of a money digger"[26] who "searched for treasure with the help of his family."[27] It also declared that the Smith family could not "distinguish true religion from superstition,"[28] and articulated that the Prophet had to eventually "extricate himself from the schemes of the Palmyra magicians and money diggers."[29] Lucy Mack Smith, the mother of the Prophet, was portrayed as "proud"[30] and "sensed acutely the 'attention and respect which are ever shown to those who live in fine circumstances.'"[31] Mother Smith was also characterized as "belligerent,"[32] "capable of anger,"[33] and having a "high-strung" temper.[34] Bushman appropriately dedicated his new progressive volume "To Leonard Arrington."[35]

Many progressive historians justified themselves in the writing of this new narrative, believing that it was their contribution to 'scholarly' history. While traditionalist history had been written primarily by men without academic degrees, these 'cutting edge' credentialed historians were eager to introduce the philosophies

---

26 Richard L. Bushman, *Joseph Smith and the Beginnings of Mormonism* (Urbana and Chicago: University of Illinois Press, 1984), 127.

27 Ibid., 73.

28 Ibid., 72.

29 Ibid., 7.

30 Ibid., 10-11.

31 Ibid., 11.

32 Ibid., 10.

33 Ibid.

34 Ibid., 11, 36.

35 Ibid., dedication.

they had picked up in academia into their Latter-day Saint writings and teachings. In the first edition of *Story*, the authors explained this trend and legitimized their new narrative by suggesting it was written with a more "scholarly tone":

❝ Very early in Church history, writers began taking sides as critics or defenders of Joseph Smith and Mormonism, and only more recently have histories taken a more religiously neutral and scholarly tone. Historians now are trying to understand and assess the historical evidence used by both detractors and defenders.[36]

In other words, this new trend among historians holds that the early writers of Church history—men including Wilford Woodruff, George A. Smith, and Joseph Fielding Smith—had written a shamefully biased history to defend what they believed to be the Gospel of Jesus Christ, to defend the character of the Prophet Joseph Smith, and to defend their own biases. In progressive eyes, defending the Gospel of Jesus Christ as Joseph Smith taught it was resorting to polemics and could have no place among 'scholarly' histories. The historians must remain 'neutral,' and more tolerant and understanding of antagonists and Joseph's detractors. *Story* referred readers to Fawn Brodie—who christened herself the "female Judas Iscariot"[37]—for a "discussion of specific issues."[38] Was this scholarship? Or merely revisionism cloaked under a thinly veiled spectre of "neutrality"?

As the debate over *Story* and other works intensified, division arose among Church leaders. Some were for, others against, but most chose to quietly pull back in an attempt to remain neutral.

---

36   James B. Allen and Glen M. Leonard, *The Story of the Latter-day Saints* (Salt Lake City, Utah: Deseret Book Company, 1976), 661.

37   Newell G. Bringhurst, *Fawn McKay Brodie: A Biographer's Life* (Norman, University of Oklahoma Press, 1999), 243.

38   James B. Allen and Glen M. Leonard, *The Story of the Latter-day Saints* (Salt Lake City, Utah: Deseret Book Company, 1976), 661.

11

THE ULTIMATE SHOWDOWN
BETWEEN TWO BOYS FROM IDAHO

After the anxious meeting with the First Presidency, and Elders Ezra Taft Benson, Mark E. Petersen, Bruce R. McConkie, and Howard W. Hunter, on September 21, 1976, Leonard Arrington left feeling unfairly judged and "very much shaken":[1]

// If we were to go as far as to write primarily for young people in a faith-promoting manner there are dozens of persons who would be a far better Church Historian than I. I began to doubt whether I was the right person to have this assignment and I began to consider seriously whether to offer my resignation and whether to consider seriously other employment.[2]

As previously noted, President Benson later reportedly asked that *The Story of the Latter-day Saints*[3] "be shredded."[4] His strong feelings regarding the book appear in a personal letter, which made its way, unintentionally, into the hands of Arrington sometime later:

---

1   Leonard J. Arrington Diaries, October 22, 1976: Leonard J. Arrington and Gary James Bergera, *Confessions of a Mormon Historian: The Diaries of Leonard J. Arrington*, 1971-1997, vol. 2 (Salt Lake City: Signature Books, 2018), 270.

2   Ibid.

3   James B. Allen and Glen M. Leonard, *The Story of the Latter-day Saints* (Salt Lake City, Utah: Deseret Book Company, 1976). Hereafter referred to as "*Story*."

4   Richard Stephen Marshall, "'The New Mormon History': A Senior Honors Project Summary," May 1, 1977, Department of History, University of Utah Special Collections, Marriott Library, University of Utah, 38; photocopy in our possession.

❝❝ Haybron Adams took me to his office and sa[i]d, "I would like to show you a letter which somehow came into my hands." It was a xerox of a letter from Ezra Taft Benson to a Brother Huerder (I think) [Buerger].[5] The letter was dated, I think, June 23, 1978. Based on the response one supposes that this "Brother Huerder" [Buerger] had written Brother Benson about Story of the Latter-day Saints and about the article in Dialogue two or three years ago by Duane Jeffrey on "Seers, Servants, and Evolution." At any rate, Brother Benson replied rather tersely, essentially as follows: "In reply to your question about Story of the Latter-day Saints, let me say that it will never be republished."[6]

It is certain, even from the few remaining fragments of evidence still extant, that surveillance, undercover operations, and duplicity were all part of this head-to-head confrontation between two former farm boys from Idaho. The stakes were high on both sides. Each believed they were battling for the heart and soul, the very survival, of the Restoration. These two men who found themselves struggling in this war over Latter-day Saint history—Dr. Leonard Arrington and President Ezra Taft Benson—clearly held opposing views about spirituality and interpretation of history; yet remarkably, they shared some striking similarities in background and interests.

Leonard Arrington was born the third of eleven children in Twin Falls, Idaho. Ezra Taft Benson was born on his family's farm in Whitney, Idaho, the eldest of eleven. Leonard chose to study agricultural science in college, and later switched to agricultural economics. Ezra, eager to be abreast of the latest state-of-the-art farming techniques, received his master's degree in agricultural economics in 1927 from Iowa State University. Additionally, Ezra began his college studies at Utah State Agricultural College (USAC, now Utah State University), the same university where Leonard would later serve as a professor and the institution to whom he would eventually donate his research and personal papers. Both Ezra and Leonard retained a passion for agriculture and economics throughout

---

5   Bracketed text added by Gary J. Bergera in *Confessions of a Mormon Historian: The Diaries of Leonard J. Arrington, 1971-1997.*

6   Leonard J. Arrington Diaries, August 15, 1978; Leonard J. Arrington and Gary James Bergera, *Confessions of a Mormon Historian: The Diaries of Leonard J. Arrington, 1971-1997,* vol. 2 (Salt Lake City: Signature Books, 2018), 591-592; brackets in original.

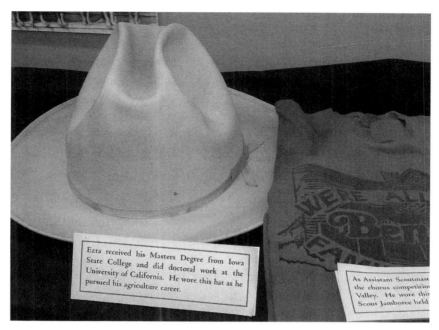

Ezra Taft Benson's hat and shirt by Ben P L under CC BY-SA 2.0

their lives, with Ezra serving farmers throughout the nation as a member of President Dwight D. Eisenhower's presidential cabinet.

Leonard was known for his friendly, outgoing, amiable personality. His Christmas card list included the addresses of 5,000 friends.[7] Ezra was likewise known as an attentive, engaging, and warmhearted friend who was even voted 'Most Popular Man' at BYU in 1926.[8]

Culturally, they came from very similar backgrounds, and yet they perceived the world—and more particularly the Church and the Gospel—in polar opposite ways.

Upon his graduation from high school, Leonard was determined to attend college. His father, Noah Arrington, encouraged him to serve a mission for the Church, and offered to make the necessary sacrifices for him to go, despite the added hardship that would be

---

7   Kristen Moulton, "Diary of Famed Mormon Historian Reveals More of the Man," *The Salt Lake Tribune*, September 24, 2010, https://archive.sltrib.com/article.php?id=50275670&itype=cmsid.

8   "The Life and Ministry of Ezra Taft Benson," The Church of Jesus Christ of Latter-day Saints, https://www.churchofjesuschrist.org/study/manual/teachings-of-presidents-of-the-church-ezra-taft-benson/the-life-and-ministry-of-ezra-taft-benson?lang=eng.

imposed relating to the financial difficulties of the Great Depression.[9] Having no interest himself in serving a mission, Leonard declined, announcing instead his decision to attend the University of Idaho.

While Leonard declined his father's request that he serve a mission, Ezra and his family made great sacrifices to fulfill the call to serve. When Ezra was twelve years old, his father, George, was called on a mission. His sister, Margaret, remembered that young Ezra "did the work of a man, though he was only a boy. He took the place of his father for nearly two years."[10] Ezra himself later commented:

> I suppose some in the world might say that his acceptance of that call was proof he did not really love his family. To leave seven children and an expectant wife at home alone for two years, how could that be true love?
>
> But my father knew a greater vision of love. He knew that "all things shall work together for good to them that love God" (Romans 8:28). He knew that the best thing he could do for his family was to obey God.
>
> While we missed him greatly during those years, and while his absence brought many challenges to our family, his acceptance proved to be a gift of charity. Father went on his mission, leaving Mother at home with seven children. (The eighth was born four months after he arrived in the field). But there came into that home a spirit of missionary work that never left it. It was not without some sacrifice. Father had to sell our old dry farm in order to finance his mission. He had to move a married couple into part of our home to take care of the row crops, and he left his sons and wife the responsibility for the hay land, the pasture land, and a small herd of dairy cows. . . .
>
> Later the family grew to eleven children—seven sons and four daughters. All seven sons filled missions, some of them two or three missions. Later, two daughters and their husbands filled full-time missions. The two other sisters, both widows—one

---

9   Leonard J. Arrington and Gary James Bergera, *Confessions of a Mormon Historian: The Diaries of Leonard J. Arrington*, 1971-1997, vol. 1 (Salt Lake City: Signature Books, 2018), 18.

10   Margaret Benson Keller, in Sheri L. Dew, *Ezra Taft Benson: A Biography* (Salt Lake City, Utah: Deseret Book Company, 1987), 34.

Ezra with his mother, Sarah, and siblings around the time of his father's mission

the mother of eight and the other the mother of ten—served as missionary companions in Birmingham, England.

It is a legacy that still continues to bless the Benson family even into the third and fourth generations. Was not this truly a gift of love?[11]

Ezra fulfilled his own call to serve for two years in England when he was 19 years old, in the midst of intense anti-Mormon opposition, and in less-than-desirable living conditions. Elder Benson's companion, Elder Palmer, remembered:

There was a bed and a narrow cot. . . . Elder Benson and I slept on the bed. The springs at the best were stretched and old; with the weight of two men, we slept with sunken springs almost to the bare floor. . . . Elder Benson [and I] . . . called this situation home for better than the whole next year.[12]

Elder Benson's mother wrote him a letter during his time in the field, counseling him to: "Be prayerful, Ezra T., and do not fail to keep

11   Ezra Taft Benson, "Godly Characteristics of the Master," General Conference, October 1986, https://www.churchofjesuschrist.org/study/general-conference/1986/10/godly-characteristics-of-the-master?lang=eng.

12   Sheri L. Dew, *Ezra Taft Benson: A Biography* (Salt Lake City, Utah: Deseret Book Company, 1987), 52.

Ezra seated far right of the front row during his mission to England in 1922; David O. McKay (seated middle front row) was his mission president

the commandments of the Lord and trust in him at all times and he cannot help blessing you to fill an honorable mission."[13] In spite of the difficulties he faced, Elder Benson maintained his cheerfulness and determination. Many years later in life, he would remark, "I've never had a real test of my faith, because I've always felt that regardless of the seriousness of conditions, the Lord was on our side."[14]

Upon returning home from his mission, Ezra began pursuing his college education. It is interesting to note the differences in how Ezra and Leonard confronted the conflict between Darwinian Evolution and the faith of their fathers during their university years—as well as the drastic contrast in outcomes.[15] While Leonard, early on, abandoned his belief in Creation, Ezra used his educational experiences to strengthen and support the facts, which fortified his faith:

// At the time [of Ezra Taft Benson's study at BYU's summer school] attorneys William Jennings Bryan and Clarence Darrow were arguing the case of evolution in the Scopes "monkey trial"

---

13   Ibid., 53.

14   Ibid., 51.

15   Details can be found in *Faith Crisis, Volume 1*, Chapter 9, "Arrington's Faith Crisis in College."

in the South, and this prompted open debate on science versus religion, which Ezra absorbed with interest. He strongly opposed Darwin's theory of species development and took that stand in his debate.[16]

Now, in 1976, these two Idaho farm boys from large and faithful Latter-day Saint homes, each having chosen diverging life paths upon which to tread, now faced each other directly—head-to-head—over how to interpret, write, and promote the history of their faith. How should The Church of Jesus Christ of Latter-day Saints, to which they both belonged, move forward?

Arrington's Response

The day after his meeting with the First Presidency (Spencer W. Kimball, N. Eldon Tanner, and Marion G. Romney), President Ezra Taft Benson, and Elders Mark E. Petersen, Howard W. Hunter, and Bruce R. McConkie, of The Quorum of the Twelve Apostles, Leonard Arrington sat down with James Allen and Davis Bitton to bemoan the situation and to consider the ongoing game plan:

 Elders Benson and Petersen will never accept books written by us, given our understanding of history. They want the glorious stories of the Restoration, unsullied by discussions of practical problems and controversial evidence. They want Prophets without warts, revelation direct from on high in pure vessels. They want faith promoting stories and moral homilies. They feel strongly and will vigorously oppose all our books, written as we understand history.

. . . we shall have to be more careful in what we write and say and publish, and be more careful to consult, ask advice and get suggestions. . . .

I shall have to take full responsibility for all that we do, and I shall have to be more careful, more cautious. I shall be watched like a hawk. I'm still ebullient, still optimistic, still determined to do what we must do. But we shall have to give on some little

---

16   Sheri L. Dew, *Ezra Taft Benson: A Biography* (Salt Lake City, Utah: Deseret Book Company, 1987), 81.

things to preserve our status as screeners of our own materials. Some of the younger historians will think I'm losing some integrity, but that's part of the price we shall have to pay, and I hope you brethren, at least, can continue to be as supportive and helpful as you have been. The Lord is with us yet![17]

It is apparent that both sides in this controversy over Church history believed the Lord was on their side. Traditional wisdom records Abraham Lincoln once humbly observing, "Sir, my concern is not whether God is on our side; my greatest concern is to be on God's side, for God is always right."[18] Or, as a line from the movie *Cromwell* reminds us, "It's an odd thing. . . . Every man who wages war believes God is on his side. I'll warrant God should often wonder who is on His."[19]

Arrington, however, maintained his confidence. During October 1976, "a friend" informed him that George W. Pace, a member of the BYU religion faculty, had been "strongly opposed" to his appointment as Church Historian. Pace was in close communication with President Benson's assistant, William Nelson, and disapproved of *Story*. Arrington, however, took no notice. Pace was a "Holy Ghoster," a title assigned to persons who, Arrington wrote, were "disgusted by attempts to intellectualize the gospel and our history . . . ." Progressives, like Arrington, misinterpreted traditionalist reliance upon revelation and spiritual experience as "attempt[ing] to motivate students by tears rather than by logic or evidence."[20] To Arrington's understanding, revelation did not include the mind and the heart—but only emotion. However, the Lord has clarified that the Spirit of God should impact both the mind and the heart, and that each is essential to true understanding.[21] Revelation and emotion are not synonymous, neither are they interchangeable.

---

17   Leonard J. Arrington Diaries, September 22, 1976; Leonard J. Arrington and Gary James Bergera, *Confessions of a Mormon Historian: The Diaries of Leonard J. Arrington*, 1971-1997, vol. 2 (Salt Lake City: Signature Books, 2018), 241.

18   "The Light of Life," *Manford's New Monthly Magazine* 30 (August, 1886): 495.

19   Ken Hughes, dir., *Cromwell* (Columbia Pictures, 1970), DVD.

20   Leonard J. Arrington Diaries, October 22, 1976; Leonard J. Arrington and Gary James Bergera, *Confessions of a Mormon Historian: The Diaries of Leonard J. Arrington*, 1971-1997, vol. 2 (Salt Lake City: Signature Books, 2018), 273.

21   For additional discussion, see the article "Music: The Forgotten Language of the Heart," Joseph Smith Foundation, https://josephsmithfoundation.org/papers/music-the-forgotten-language-of-the-heart/.

Losing Patience with President Benson

On Thursday, September 23, 1976, Arrington's telephone rang again. Upon answering, he heard the voice of Ernest Wilkinson, former president of BYU-Provo. Arrington had asked Wilkinson to put in a few good words for him to President Benson, and Wilkinson was reporting back. During their conversation, President Benson had expressed his disappointment to Wilkinson over the "secular" re-interpretation of Latter-day Saint history promoted in Allen and Leonard's book. Wilkinson recorded in his diary President Benson's fear that, "in their attempt to satisfy and ingratiate themselves with historians, they have neglected the future destiny of young people in the Church."[22] A frustrated Arrington, who was quickly "losing confidence in the fairness and wisdom"[23] of Ezra Taft Benson, disagreed.

The loss of trust in President Benson's "fairness and wisdom" was no doubt due to misunderstanding and miscommunication, as well as the soberness with which President Benson approached his stewardship; President Benson had been long known for his uncommon compassion and discipleship. According to *Ezra Taft Benson: A Biography*:

> Elder Benson's schedule during the first half of 1973 would have been grueling for a man half his age, let alone someone nearly seventy-four. . . . But [he was] not too busy, evidently, to leave a personal touch as he traveled. One Stake president, later named a General Authority, related the impact Elder Benson had on him: "I am amazed at your attention to the needs of people. I first noticed it . . . when I was a stake president and you dedicated our new stake center. When you left I felt I was the most important person in your life.[24]

---

22   Ernest L. Wilkinson Diary, September 22, 1976. Brigham Young University, Harold B. Lee Library, L. Tom Perry Special Collections, Ernest Wilkinson Papers, UA 1000, Box 105, Fd. 4.

23   Leonard J. Arrington Diaries, October 22, 1976; Leonard J. Arrington and Gary James Bergera, *Confessions of a Mormon Historian: The Diaries of Leonard J. Arrington, 1971-1997*, vol. 2 (Salt Lake City: Signature Books, 2018), 273.

24   Sheri L. Dew, *Ezra Taft Benson: A Biography* (Salt Lake City, Utah: Deseret Book Company, 1987), 423.

Sheri Dew, President Benson's biographer, also related that a few years after the skirmish over *Story,* President Benson was visiting Athens when he learned of a member who:

// ... despite intense pressure to do so, had refused to renounce his membership. As a result, this man's business had been boycotted, his children were not permitted to attend school, and he had subsequently become inactive. President Benson drove across Athens (though he had only four hours in the Greek capital) to visit the man, who was shocked when the General Authority knocked at his door. An assistant traveling with President Benson recalled the scene: "President Benson wanted to hear this man's story from his own lips. The President was very moved by what he heard. Before we left President Benson pulled this man to him and said, 'God bless you, my brother. I want you to know our prayers are with you.' The man had tears in his eyes. . . . Several months later the district president from Athens visited Salt Lake City and told us something miraculous had happened. The restrictions had been lifted, the children allowed to return to school and the man was back at church. President Benson gave that brother who'd been discouraged and downtrodden the courage to come back."[25]

President Benson's differences with Arrington's history division were not rooted in prejudice or animosity, but rather with the question that drove every decision in his life: "What is best for the kingdom?" Future President of the Church, Russell M. Nelson, explained:

// In any consideration, even if it was not his opinion, President Benson measured a situation against only one standard—What's best for the kingdom? If it meant a wrinkle might have to be folded in a way he wouldn't have done it, so be it. He wanted only what was best for the kingdom. He *listened* to counsel.[26]

President Benson would doubtless have been open to dialogue and resolution; but Arrington did not appear interested in reconciling the gulf between their particular estranged worldviews. Arrington

25　Ibid., 435-436.
26　Ibid., 430.

and his colleagues determined to overlook President Benson's criticism and push through with *Story,* concluding that it was time to employ "greater extremes in skirting around those two brethren and those who support them."[27]

Thus far, Deseret Book had sold more than 15,000 copies of the book, and was still advertising the new progressive narrative through brochures, as well as radio and TV advertisements. A positive review by Scott Kenney was published in the *BYU Today* alumni magazine. George Ellsworth published another complimentary review in *BYU Studies,* and there were some members of the Quorum of the Twelve who privately expressed their support to Arrington, creating a sense of validation which left him feeling "completely confident of what I am doing."[28]

"[T]he Church of the future will be grateful for what we do," Arrington prophesied on November 2, 1976. "[W]e must do it even by fighting the bureaucracy, and we must expect to lose many of our fights with officialdom, and expect heavy criticism. But in the interest of the Church, in the interest of the Lord, we should persevere."[29]

During the fall of 1976, Arrington instructed his staff that they needed to be "more careful" because "some of the Brethren don't favor the kind of history we write." It will "take a generation to educate the Church to historical trends,"[30] he surmised. Such a reconstruction would require time and patience, Arrington knew. In light of mounting opposition from Ezra Taft Benson, Mark E. Petersen, and other leaders, Arrington and his colleagues resolved to adopt a more obscured, more guarded, covert strategy.

Covert Methods

It seems clear that there was some discussion between members of the First Presidency and the Quorum of the Twelve as to how works such as *The Story of the Latter-day Saints* should receive approval for publication. A few months after the initial firestorm

---

27   Leonard J. Arrington Diaries, October 22, 1976; Leonard J. Arrington and Gary James Bergera, *Confessions of a Mormon Historian: The Diaries of Leonard J. Arrington* 1971-1997, vol. 2 (Salt Lake City: Signature Books, 2018), 273.

28   Ibid., 272.

29   Leonard J. Arrington Diaries, November 2, 1976; Ibid., 291.

30   Leonard J. Arrington Diaries, September 23, 1976; Ibid., 243, footnote 46.

surrounding *Story,* Arrington submitted a copy of his diary record to Elders Delbert L. Stapley and Howard W. Hunter to explain his decision to bypass the submission of *Story* for review by Correlation before printing. To justify his decision, Arrington explained that he had been instructed by the now-deceased President Harold B. Lee not to screen his works through Correlation, but instead through Arrington's own "screening committee of professional historians." As evidence, he submitted an entry which he claimed was from his diary. However, the account Arrington submitted was entirely *different* from the original; he had altered the account to "strengthe[n] his case." Arrington's biographer, Greg Prince, explained:

// As a follow-up to the September meeting with the First Presidency, Stapley and Hunter, the Historical Department's advisors, asked that Leonard document the background of *Story.* In a lengthy written response, he justified the division's special exception on the basis of a conversation—not a document—with Church president Harold B. Lee in August 1973. He prefaced the report by writing, "Let me copy from my own diary record the consequent conversation" . . .

But there was a problem with that account: It did not square with Leonard's actual diary entry for that date . . .

Perhaps Lee had discussed a Correlation Committee decision with Leonard, but the diary entry that recounts that conversation does not substantiate such a discussion. It appears that Leonard took literary license with the diary entry in writing to the two apostles in 1976, clearly for the purpose of strengthening his case that his division should be exempted from Correlation.[31]

Prince's depiction of the incident far understates the true depth of Arrington's deception. A comparison below reveals that nearly the entire entry submitted by Arrington had been fabricated.

Arrington deleted three paragraphs from the original entry detailing controversies with publications by Ezra Taft Benson and Alvin R. Dyer, in addition to the strikethrough sections below. The

---

31   Gregory A. Prince, *Leonard Arrington and the Writing of Mormon History* (Salt Lake City, UT: Tanner Trust Fund and J. Willard Marriott Library, 2016), 297-298.

modifications added for the entry submitted to the advisors, which were not included in the original, are set in italics under the "Diary Entry Submitted to Advisors" column:

Original Diary Entry	Diary Entry Submitted to Advisors
He [Lee] began talking about the problem of having committees read books by Church authorities. [Deleted paragraphs] ~~I thought it a good omen that President Lee would~~ speak so frankly ~~and informally with me~~ about such matters.[32]	President Lee *then* began talking about the problem of having committees read books by *General* Authorities. *He then told me some experiences, which I regard as confidential and am therefore not recording. I was somewhat surprised that he would* speak *to me* so frankly about *these* matters. *President Lee then talked to me about the histories we were writing. He expressed the feeling that I should establish a screening committee of professional historians who were loyal to the Church, and that this committee should help assure that our books were accurate and readable. He did not believe, he said, that the Correlation Committee was equipped to evaluate our history books. He thought this should be done by professionally trained historians.*[33]

Around this time, concerns were also being raised regarding progressive proselytizing in relation to liberal-leaning professors advocating socialistic practices as viable alternatives to free markets in BYU coursework. Additional concerns had trickled up to general authorities as a result of apprehensions respecting staff members in

---

32   Leonard J. Arrington Diaries, August 9, 1973; Leonard J. Arrington and Gary James Bergera, *Confessions of a Mormon Historian: The Diaries of Leonard J. Arrington, 1971-1997*, vol. 1 (Salt Lake City: Signature Books, 2018), 571-572.

33   Gregory A. Prince, *Leonard Arrington and the Writing of Mormon History* (Salt Lake City, UT: Tanner Trust Fund and J. Willard Marriott Library, 2016), 297.

the Political Science and History departments at BYU who were "becoming too tolerant of socialism."[34] Arrington recorded in his diary on April 11, 1977:

❝ Last Thursday morning a special meeting was held at BYU with all of the staff members in Political Science and History in attendance. The meeting was convened by Dallin Oaks, Bob Thomas, and Jeff Holland. Apparently those three had met a few days previously with Boyd Packer, Gordon Hinckley, and Tom Monson and they had been told that General Authorities have made criticisms of certain actions of members of the two faculties during the past few months.[35] The General Authorities expressed their concern and wished to have this meeting held in order to help the staff members realize the importance of discretion in their activity as professors. Reasons for discontent with the behavior of staff members is based on five episodes[36] ... The meeting was friendly and the purpose was simply to call

---

34   Leonard J. Arrington Diaries, April 11, 1977; Leonard J. Arrington and Gary James Bergera, *Confessions of a Mormon Historian: The Diaries of Leonard J. Arrington*, 1971-1997, vol. 2 (Salt Lake City: Signature Books, 2018), 364, footnote 53.

35   Gary Bergera's footnote in *Confessions of a Mormon Historian* explains, "Ezra Taft Benson thought BYU was becoming too tolerant of socialism. Oak's response was to advise some of the faculty to be cautious about how they approached the school's 'silent contest of extremists of the right wing.' Bergera and Priddis, Brigham Young University, 221-26." Ibid. See also, Gary James Bergera and Ronald Priddis, *Brigham Young University: A House of Faith* (Salt Lake City: Signature Books, 1985), 221-226.

36   Arrington elaborated on the "five episodes" saying: "Frank Fox and Revolutionary heroes. *(Footnote #54 by Bergera: "Fox had delivered a lecture on George Washington that Benson believed did not venerate the country's founder enough.")* Jim and Glen book [*The Story of the Latter-day Saints*]. Ray Hillam and spy episode. *(Footnote #55 by Bergera: "Hillam was talking about how former BYU President Ernest Wilkinson had gone about determining the faculty's political leanings by having students inform on them. Bergera, '1966 BYU Student Spy Ring.'")* Marvin Hill review of BYU history. *(Footnote #56 by Bergera: "Hill wrote a critical review of the one-volume BYU history authored by Wilkinson and Skousen. The review was published in BYU Studies in the autumn 1976 issue.")* BYU professor invites Mormon Communist to speak to his classes *(Footnote #57 by Bergera: "In March two BYU professors had invited Wayne Holley, a BYU alumnus and leader of the Utah Communist party, to address their political science classes. Bergera and Priddis, Brigham Young University, 222-23.")* and then he [the Communist] advertises it to get legitimacy in Salt Lake High School." Leonard J. Arrington Diaries, April 11, 1977; Leonard J. Arrington and Gary James Bergera, *Confessions of a Mormon Historian: The Diaries of Leonard J. Arrington*, 1971-1997, vol. 2 (Salt Lake City: Signature Books, 2018), 364; brackets in original.

to their attention the importance of being discreet and wise in what they did.[37]

The tension between the traditionalists and progressives over the writing of Latter-day Saint history seemed to surface in the political realm as well—with strong feelings on both sides, threatening at times to reveal the disunity that occurred among prominent members and leaders behind closed doors. On October 28, 1976, Arrington recorded in his diary a politically-charged incident occurring at BYU just a few days previous:

> **❝** ... BYU had offered each of the major parties an opportunity to speak to the BYU student body, and yesterday Ronald Reagan was there to discuss Republicanism. He had a large audience. Persons thought his talk was fine and appropriate and well done. Apparently the student who gave the closing prayer, however, revolted many people—some of those who mentioned it to me said they felt like vomiting because he prayed that "we all might leave those parties and commitments which are foreign to thee and join the party which we know represents Thy wishes" and went on in this vein.
>
> Observers said that Reagan was given three standing applauses and in each instance Elder [Ezra Taft] Benson who was present representing the Church led in the standing applause. They reported that in each instance Dallin Oaks who was seated right next to him remained seated. This certainly required courage for him to do that.[38]

Arrington rightfully appreciated the courage characterized by his leaders in standing (or sitting) for their convictions—a sentiment traditionalists share. Arrington's previous entry also fell along a political vein, recording his reminiscences of casting his first vote for a President of the United States—a vote given to Franklin D. Roosevelt. Arrington was fully aware that President Heber J. Grant and other Church leaders had vehemently opposed Roosevelt's

---

37 Ibid., 364.
38 Leonard J. Arrington Diaries, October 28, 1976; Ibid., 280; brackets in original.

election;[39] but Arrington disagreed, expressing that "my first vote in a presidential election was for Roosevelt. And I was proud of it and have never regretted it."[40] While he "tended to vote for the man rather than the party or its platform," Arrington's presidential voting choices from 1948-1972[41] reveal that he favored and voted primarily for Democratic candidates. In 1964, he voted for Lyndon B. Johnson over Barry M. Goldwater, because he considered "Goldwater to be a die-hard dogmatic conservative—too conservative to look after the best interests of the nation." Arrington considered himself an "Independent" who was "apolitical in public stance"; but privately, he clearly leaned towards liberal and progressive policies. In 1972, he described himself in a letter as a "liberal" to his son, Carl.[42] Arrington also identified himself as a follower of John Maynard

---

39   The American people elected Roosevelt as President of the United States for an unprecedented four consecutive terms, from 1933–1945. Upon his death in office, President J. Reuben Clark Jr. lamented: "The Lord gave the people of the United States four elections in order to get rid of him, but they failed to do so in these four elections, so He held an election of His own and cast one vote, and then took him away." Michael Kent Winder, *Presidents and Prophets: The Story of America's Presidents and the LDS Church* (Covenant Communications, 2007), 248.

Nevertheless, before that would happen, the Saints rejected the counsel and advice of the Church's First Presidency, and Roosevelt carried Utah in all four elections:

"In 1936, Roosevelt won every state in the Union except Maine and Vermont. As convincing as the victory was nationally, it was even more so in Utah, where FDR had over 69 percent of the vote. Determined that Utah should not support FDR's bid for a third term in 1940, the General Authorities once again drafted a joint anti-Roosevelt statement but settled on issuing a less dramatic unsigned editorial. . . . In 1940, Utah was one of the strongest pro-Roosevelt states, giving him over 62 percent of the vote and opponent Wendell Willkie under 38 percent. When the pro-FDR tallies came in on election night in Utah, President Grant saw the total and was 'dumbfounded.'" Ibid, 251.

As President of the Church, President Grant recorded in his journal that he was deeply concerned that about half of the Latter-day Saints almost worshipped Roosevelt and his policies. He regarded Roosevelt's neo-socialism as "one of the most serious conditions that has confronted me since I became President of the Church." Ibid, 251.

40   Leonard J. Arrington Diaries, October 27, 1976; Leonard J. Arrington and Gary James Bergera, *Confessions of a Mormon Historian: The Diaries of Leonard J. Arrington, 1971-1997*, vol. 2 (Salt Lake City: Signature Books, 2018), 277.

41   1948 — Dewey (R); 1952 — Stevenson (D); 1956 — Stevenson (D); 1960 — Kennedy (D); 1964 — Johnson (D); 1968 — Humphrey (D); 1972 — Nixon (R).

42   "I suppose a lot of 'intellectuals' might have been pleased that an academic person who was a 'liberal' received the appointment." Gregory A. Prince, *Leonard Arrington and the Writing of Mormon History* (Salt Lake City, UT: Tanner Trust Fund, and J. Willard Marriott Library, 2016), 160.

Keynes' socialistic economic ideals. In this matter, he clashed again with the Constitutionalist defender, Ezra Taft Benson.[43]

Progressives Adopt Pseudonyms

On July 16, 1977, Arrington expressed frustration with what he referred to as his struggle in opposing "anti-intellectualism."[44] Books and papers by progressive authors were being declined for publication by the Church. According to Arrington, Ezra Taft Benson and Mark E. Petersen had succeeded in placing the founder of *Dialogue,* Eugene England, on a "blacklist," blocking his books from being published by Deseret Book, BYU Press, or Bookcraft. Carol Lynn Pearson had been on the blacklist for a time due to her feminist activity, and James Allen was now blacklisted for his *The Story of the Latter-day*

---

43   See *Faith Crisis, Volume 1,* chapter 13, "William Godbe: Spiritualism, Socialism, Economics." For traditionalists, John Keynes' philosophies, despite their widespread acceptance and resurgence during recent years, stand in direct opposition to principles espoused within the Gospel of Jesus Christ. Expounding on the dangers of liberal education during a General Conference address in October 1970, President Ezra Taft Benson identified Keynes as one of five specific antichrists in our day:

> "As a watchman on the tower, I feel to warn you that one of the chief means of misleading our youth and destroying the family unit is our educational institutions. President Joseph F. Smith referred to false educational ideas as one of the three threatening dangers among our Church members. There is more than one reason why the Church is advising our youth to attend colleges close to their homes where institutes of religion are available. It gives the parents the opportunity to stay close to their children; and if they have become alert and informed as President McKay admonished us last year, these parents can help expose some of the deceptions of men like Sigmund Freud, Charles Darwin, John Dewey, Karl Marx, John Keynes, and others. Today there are much worse things that can happen to a child than not getting a full college education. In fact, some of the worst things have happened to our children while attending colleges led by administrators who wink at subversion and amorality." Ezra Taft Benson, "A Plea to Strengthen Our Families," *Conference Report,* October 1970, 22.

44   "We seem to be going through a period of anti-intellectualism. On the one hand, BYU, Ricks, SUU and U of U, and other Mormon or semi-Mormon institutions, are graduating bright young Mormon intellectuals in increasing numbers. On the other hand, they are finding it more and more difficult to merge their talent and ability with the Church and its program. [People such as] Lowell Bennion. Gene England, despite his devotion to the Church and the Gospel, his sincerity, and his desire to please, is not permitted to publish. Deseret Book will not handle his books, BYU Press will not publish his work, nor will Bookcraft. Just because he was a founding editor of Dialogue. And those who insist on his name [being] on the blacklist are Elder Benson and Elder Petersen." Leonard J. Arrington Diaries, July 16, 1977; Leonard J. Arrington and Gary James Bergera, *Confessions of a Mormon Historian: The Diaries of Leonard J. Arrington, 1971-1997,* vol. 2 (Salt Lake City: Signature Books, 2018), 390-391.

Saints. Even Arrington, while serving as Church Historian, was unable to have his books published by the Church "without specific clearance by the Quorum of the Twelve." Scott G. Kenney (publisher of *Sunstone*), Claudia L. Bushman (co-founder of *Exponent II*), and others, were also not approved—and Arrington knew it was time to resort to more 'discreet' methods:

> // It is now necessary for Mormon intellectuals to publish under pseudonyms. I will not reveal here the pseudonyms being used, but there are several who use them, and thus far they are "getting away with it."[45]

For the moment, traditional voices seemed to be successfully paddling against the tide of progressive encroachment. But this cold war was far from over.

---

45   Ibid., 391.

12

A Boy's Paper Finds Its Way Into Hands of the Brethren

The controversy surrounding *The Story of the Latter-day Saints* seemed to be settling when yet "another land mine"[1] exploded in the path of the New Mormon History movement. This blowup originated from the most unexpected of sources—a young, inexperienced, undergraduate student—Richard Marshall.

In May of 1977, returned-missionary Richard Marshall wrote a senior honors thesis for his University of Utah bachelor's degree, which he titled "The New Mormon History." In his paper, Marshall traced the motivations and chronology of the New Mormon History, the influence and ascension of progressive historians within the Church, the founding of both *Dialogue* and the *Mormon History Association*, and events surrounding Arrington's department at Church Headquarters. In short, Marshall's thesis laid out in celebratory language the premeditated—and successful—progressive shift within the Church with an articulation which proved to be far too clear, transparent, and straightforward.

What led up to this scholastic land mine? Unfortunately for the as-yet-cloaked revisionist historians and intellectuals, Marshall was an eager, naive undergrad, unschooled in the stratagem of the upper echelon of this secretive movement when he set out to develop his seemingly innocuous and unassuming paper. The trouble was, his thesis and style were altogether too honest, too upfront, and too unambiguous in dealing with the New Mormon History agenda—information that in the 'wrong' hands could prove volatile.

---

1   Leonard J. Arrington, *Adventures of a Church Historian* (University of Illinois Press, 1998), 154.

Conflict with President Benson

Right out of the gate, Richard Marshall acknowledged that "Mormon scholars have generally had difficulty being accepted by the mainstream Mormon community." And why? The members were "largely conservative and middle class . . . largely ignorant," and believed in a version of history that progressives rejected based on the notion that the narrative had "been distorted and mythologized in order for it to conform to twentieth-century society." Marshall further explained: "[T]hese myths are made and perpetuated by General Authorities who teach the things they have learned in Sunday School."[2]

Moreover, Marshall revealed a certain disdain for advocates of the traditional narrative—particularly for one specific ecclesiastical leader whom the New Mormon Historians feared as a genuine threat to their endeavors: once again, President Ezra Taft Benson. During an interview with Eugene England (co-founder of *Dialogue*), England revealed to Marshall "that many of his colleagues at the LDS Institute of Religion at the University of Utah were 'disturbed' by Benson's talk [The Gospel Teacher and His Message[3]]." Max Parkin, an instructor for the Institute of Religion at the University of Utah, remarked that "many of the instructors 'closed their ears and refused to listen' to Benson's talk."[4]

At the time, President Benson held the office of President of the Quorum of the Twelve, placing him next in line as the likely successor to the office of President of the Church—a possibility the rank-and-file progressive historians dreaded. Marshall candidly related the summation from his discussions with Arrington and others:

---

2   Richard Stephen Marshall, "'The New Mormon History': A Senior Honors Project Summary," May 1, 1977, Department of History, University of Utah Special Collections, Marriott Library, University of Utah, 82; photocopy in our possession.

3   The Gospel Teacher and His Message was given by Ezra Taft Benson as an indirect response to *The Story of the Latter-day Saints,* and was built upon his previous address at BYU, *God's Hand in Our Nation's History.*

4   Richard Stephen Marshall, "'The New Mormon History': A Senior Honors Project Summary," May 1, 1977, Department of History, University of Utah Special Collections, Marriott Library, University of Utah, 39; photocopy in our possession.

THE NEW MORMON HISTORY

by

Richard Stephen Marshall

A Senior Honors Project Summary submitted to the
faculty of the University of Utah in partial fulfillment of the requirements of the

Honors Degree of Bachelor of Arts

History

UNIVERSITY OF UTAH

May 1, 1977

Richard Marshall's thesis, "The New Mormon History" 1977

❛❛ This conflict is underscored by the distinct possibility that Elder[5] Benson will become the thirteenth president of the Church in the event of the death of Spencer W. Kimball. That could turn out to be an unlucky number indeed for LDS historians who want to publish objective New History.[6]

Marshall's thesis underscored without exaggeration the conflict between President Benson and the champions of New Mormon History. Arrington himself cringed at President Benson's almost certain future appointment as President of the Church, and verbalized his frustration in his diary on September 6, 1976:

❛❛ It is clear that President Benson will not stand for our 'real' history. And since he is next in line, and president of the Twelve, we are in a powerless position, and no one wishes to consider our own rationale.[7]

---

5   Marshall uses the term "Elder" for President Benson which is appropriate, but at this time, Ezra Taft Benson was President of the Quorum of the Twelve Apostles.

6   Richard Stephen Marshall, "'The New Mormon History': A Senior Honors Project Summary," May 1, 1977, Department of History, University of Utah Special Collections, Marriott Library, University of Utah, 39; photocopy in our possession.

7   Leonard J. Arrington Diaries, September 6, 1976; Leonard J. Arrington and

In the minds of Arrington and his New History evangelists, the issue was what they perceived as 'real' history. A serious disconnect existed in influential Church circles in 1976—a disconnect which continues to this day among historians, among Church leaders, and among members who have an awareness of the issues. What exactly is 'real' history? Is 'real' history naturalistic—without God in the picture? Does 'real' history require advanced degrees in order to be written or understood? Or is Arrington's version of 'real' history a supplantation of 'true' history as is contained in the pages of the Book of Mormon, the Book of Abraham, and the Book of Moses? This was—and still is—the conflict dividing progressives and traditionalists. Arrington saw traditionalist leaders as obstacles in the promotion of an 'accurate' portrayal of the Church's history:

❝ . . . Benson and his allies succeeded in delaying a second printing [of *The Story of the Latter-day Saints*] until 1986, four years after the History Division had been disbanded and moved to BYU. And Leonard's tactical victory was more than offset by his strategic defeat, for the *Story* episode marked a permanent downturn in the fortunes of the History Division.[8]

Later, James Allen would comment about the resistance extended by the traditionalist camp: "The new and open approach to history threatened their long-held conservative values because it implied changing fundamental principles, which was uncomfortable."[9]

To this day, Ezra Taft Benson still holds his designation as the chief opponent of New Mormon History. Throughout the intensity of this tug-of-war with Arrington, he refused to compromise, and many progressives still harbor conflicted feelings for his unwavering stand in promoting a faithful approach, as opposed to an intellectual, humanistic attitude toward history. While others in his circles were hesitant or unsure of the best course of action with respect to the

---

Gary James Bergera, *Confessions of a Mormon Historian: The Diaries of Leonard J. Arrington, 1971-1997,* vol. 2, (Salt Lake City: Signature Books, 2018), 226.

8   Gregory A. Prince, *Leonard Arrington and the Writing of Mormon History* (Salt Lake City, UT: Tanner Trust Fund and J. Willard Marriott Library, 2016), 291.

9   A review by James B. Allen, "Gregory A. Prince. Leonard Arrington and the Writing of Mormon History," *BYU Studies Quarterly* 57, no. 2 (2018): 183-184, footnote 1.

swift current of transformation in Restoration history, President Benson stood firm and resolute. Greg Prince, Arrington's biographer, observed: "While Benson had powerful allies in his campaign—most notably Mark Petersen and Boyd Packer—he was its undisputed leader."[10] Subsequent to the controversy over *The Story of the Latter-day Saints,* President Benson launched an offensive against the progressive Historical Department led by Arrington. Prince charged Benson with fostering a "campaign to eliminate 'humanistic emphasis on history' from the department—a campaign that, in the short term, he won."[11] Would this be a short-term victory, or would the effect continue to ripple forward?

Fawn Brodie's *No Man Knows My History*

Richard Marshall candidly noted that Fawn Brodie's biography of Joseph Smith, *No Man Knows My History,* had broken down the barriers and paved the way for New Mormon History:

❞ ... Flanders and Hansen point to the publication of Fawn McKay Brodie's No Man Knows My History as an event of great significance in the history of the New Mormon History.... Robert Flanders calls the book "a landmark ... a transitional work," linking both the Old and the New Histories. He adds that a "new era dawned with her book. All subsequent serious studies of early Mormonism have necessarily had Brodie as a reference point."[12]

Terryl L. Givens, whose voice is among the current progressive elite, would later confirm that: "Robert Flanders considered Brodie's book a 'landmark' which influenced all subsequent history ...."[13]

Fawn McKay Brodie, a niece of President David O. McKay and granddaughter of former BYU President George H. Brimhall, was a

---

10   Gregory A. Prince, *Leonard Arrington and the Writing of Mormon History* (Salt Lake City, UT: Tanner Trust Fund and J. Willard Marriott Library, 2016), 281.

11   Ibid., 280.

12   Richard Stephen Marshall, "'The New Mormon History': A Senior Honors Project Summary," May 1, 1977, Department of History, University of Utah Special Collections, Marriott Library, University of Utah, 24; photocopy in our possession.

13   Terryl L. Givens, *People of Paradox: A History of Mormon Culture* (Oxford University Press, 2007) 379, footnote 71.

unique insider in this complex struggle as she renounced the faith of her fathers. During Brimhall's service as president of BYU, President Joseph F. Smith dismissed three of the university's professors for feverishly advocating Darwinian Evolution, Biblical Criticism, and a progressive interpretation of Latter-day Saint history.[14] Brodie grew up in a conflicted family with a father devotedly engaged in Church service, serving as stake president, mission president of the Swiss Austrian Mission, and as an assistant to the Quorum of the Twelve. Her mother, conversely, was a "quiet heretic."[15]

Born and raised in the Church, Brodie began to doubt her faith and tradition as she found herself engulfed in an environment of doubt and skepticism—a breach brought on by the separation from her family while studying for her bachelor's degree at the University of Utah. The growing concerns surrounding the historicity of the Book of Mormon further eroded her faith while she was entirely removed from her homelife in pursuit of a master's degree at the University of Chicago. Soon thereafter, she celebrated her release from all things 'Mormon':

// "It was like taking a hot coat off in the summertime." The sense of liberation I had at the University of Chicago was exhilarating. I felt very quickly that I could not go back to the old life, and I never did.[16]

Brodie considered *herself* a heretic—following in the vein of her mother. Her maternal grandfather, George H. Brimhall—while serving as the president of BYU—"brought in people like G. Stanley Hall and John Dewey as lecturers, and philosophers and psychologists who were fascinated by the Mormon scene."[17] Brimhall

---

14   "13) 3 BYU PROFESSORS: Why did President Joseph F. Smith dismiss three professors from Brigham Young University for teaching organic evolution?" Joseph Smith Foundation FAQS, https://josephsmithfoundation.org/faqs/science/13-3-byu-professors-why-did-president-joseph-f-smith-dismiss-three-professors-from-brigham-young-university-for-teaching-organic-evolution/; Boyd K. Packer, "The Snow-White Birds," Brigham Young University Conference, August 29, 1995, https://speeches.byu.edu/talks/boyd-k-packer/snow-white-birds/.

15   Newell G. Bringhurst, *Fawn McKay Brodie: A Biographer's Life* (Norman, University of Oklahoma Press, 1999), 20.

16   Shirley E. Stephenson and Fawn M. Brodie, "Fawn McKay Brodie: An Oral History Interview" *Dialogue: A Journal of Mormon Thought* 14, no. 2 (Summer 1981): 100.

17   "Fawn Brodie - author of 'No Man Knows My History'," The Salamander

Joseph F. Smith dismissed three BYU professors for advancing Darwinian Evolution and Biblical Criticism

George H. Brimhall, BYU President 1904-1921

would foster a climate of conflicted leadership at BYU, attempting to placate both his liberal faculty and the conservative leaders of the Church. For reasons not fully known, but presumably abetted by irreconcilable conflict, Brimhall would later take his own life with a hunting rifle.

Brimhall's children evidently harbored doubts stemming from their home life and the burgeoning liberal environment at BYU. These same doubts had a strong influence on Fawn Brodie's mother, Fawn Brimhall, whom the younger Fawn felt a closeness to through her own developing attitude toward the Church. Both mother and daughter were intrigued by the philosophies of academia before finally following the path of those espousing liberal far-left agendas. Fawn Brimhall would remain a closet disbeliever even while following her general authority husband in his Church service, until she eventually succeeded in taking her own life after several failed attempts.

Fawn Brodie's uncle, Dean Brimhall, was also a closet disbeliever while working as a BYU professor and in many other capacities.

Society, http://www.salamandersociety.com/interviews/fawnbrodie/.

Brodie's early doubts must certainly have been fostered and cultivated while living with her "heretic" uncle Dean and attending the University of Utah. When Brodie was only 24, being an erudite, budding writer, she made up her mind to write a biography of Joseph Smith:

" ... in the summer of 1943 Brodie visited Salt Lake City to do research and to consult with her family. . . .

> While in Salt Lake City, Fawn visited the Mormon Church Library-Archives, where she found access to research materials highly restricted. She gained access only by being "introduced about the place as Brother Mckay's daughter," an artifice, she confessed, that made her feel "guilty as hell." Nevertheless she pursued the research, being very discreet in not asking for anything remotely anti-Mormon and spending most of her time going through two early Mormon newspapers published in Nauvoo.[18]

Brodie published her divisive biography, *No Man Knows My History,* in 1945, theorizing that the Prophet Joseph was a good-humored, indolent, personable, but unsuccessful treasure seeker who conceived of and developed the notion of golden plates and a religious novel—the Book of Mormon—to disentangle himself from his own, as well as his family's, financial disgrace. Brodie's initial drafts were darker than the finished product, as she received feedback suggesting that she adapt her presentation to come across as more 'objective.' In addition to her self-proclaimed liberalism and heresy, she would later reportedly refer to herself as the "leading female Judas Iscariot [within Mormondom]."[19] Mormon apologist, Louis C. Midgley, said she "forged a reputation as a controversial psychohistorian."[20] As viewed by traditionalists, the title 'Jezebel' might have been more fitting.

Following the release of her book, George Albert Smith, a grandson and namesake of Joseph Smith's cousin, George A. Smith, arose in General Conference to not-so-delicately renounce the work of Brodie and others moving in the same direction:

---

18   Newell G. Bringhurst, *Fawn McKay Brodie: A Biographer's Life* (Norman, University of Oklahoma Press, 1999), 84.

19   Ibid., 243.

20   Louis Midgley, "The Legend of Legacy of Fawn Brodie," *Review of Books on the Book of Mormon 1989–2011* 13, no. 1 (2001): 21.

❝ There have been some who have belittled him, but I would like to say that those who have done so will be forgotten and their remains will go back to mother earth, if they have not already gone, and the odor of their infamy will never die, while the glory and honor and majesty and courage and fidelity manifested by the Prophet Joseph Smith will attach to his name forever. So we have no apologies to make.[21]

Fawn Brodie's work left an indelible impact on many Latter-day Saint scholars and authors. While Leonard Arrington disagreed with some of Brodie's conclusions, he complimented her book for pressing the boundaries and forcing "a new approach to Church history which is more honest, more realistic, and prepares the conditions for what we are now doing in the Historical Department."[22]

Brodie's biography of Joseph Smith altered the lens through which many Latter-day Saint members and scholars began, and continue to view Joseph Smith and the Restoration of the Gospel. Stewart L. Udall, U.S. Secretary of the Interior from 1961 to 1969, under presidents John F. Kennedy and Lyndon B. Johnson, thanked Brodie "for helping to liberate him from Mormon dogma through *No Man Knows My History . . .*"[23] Like Brodie, Udall descended from multi-generational Latter-day Saint pioneer stock and was born into a "religious family, a strong family."[24] Udall abandoned the faith of his youth after returning from a mission and finishing

> *Brodie's biography altered the lens through which Latter-day Saints began to view Joseph Smith*

---

21   George Albert Smith, *Conference Report* (April 7, 1946) 181-182.

22   Leonard J. Arrington Diaries, October 25, 1972; Leonard J. Arrington and Gary James Bergera, *Confessions of a Mormon Historian: The Diaries of Leonard J. Arrington*, 1971-1997, vol. 1 (Salt Lake City: Signature Books, 2018), 323.

23   Newell G. Bringhurst, *Fawn McKay Brodie: A Biographer's Life* (Norman, University of Oklahoma Press, 1999), 188.

24   Stewart L. Udall, "Stewart L. Udall," in *Leaving the Fold: Candid Conversations with Inactive Mormons*, ed. by James W. Ure (Salt Lake City: Signature Books, 1999), 68.

his college education. Broadly influenced by Sterling McMurrin and Lowell Bennion—both members of the Swearing Elders—Udall would call the former, a "dear frien[d] for life."[25] Akin to Arrington, Udall gravitated toward Franklin D. Roosevelt's liberal policies and political affiliation—factors marking other distinguishable differences between progressive and traditionalist interpretation of historical events. Udall noted that his Democratic affiliation and liberal mindset were instrumental in his becoming inactive in the Church.[26]

Many felt the wide-ranging effects of *No Man Knows My History*, including Brodie's biographer, Newell G. Bringhurst, who observed Brodie's impact on the 'scholarly' approach to Restoration history:

// Her portrait of Mormonism's founder in *No Man Knows My History* helped set the agenda for the so-called new Mormon history, particularly as it involved studies of Mormon origins and developments within the early Latter-day Saint movement. "In many ways it was a seminal study that served as a transition point" between "the old and the New Mormon history," Mormon studies scholar Roger D. Launius noted, with "the 'old' generally viewed as polemical[27] while the 'new' was considered less concerned with questions of religious truth and more interested in understanding why events unfolded the way they did." Launius concluded that "it is a measure of the success of [Brodie's] biography of Smith that it is still considered fifty years later the standard work on the subject and the starting point for all analyses of Mormonism."[28]

Bringhurst was accurate in his assessment that progressive Mormonism had a new "standard work" and foundational "starting point." Marshall's 1977 paper noted that Brodie's work had paved the way for a new, progressive Latter-day Saint history. He quoted

---

25   Ibid., 69.

26   Ibid., 69-70.

27   Polemical is defined as "arguing very strongly for or against a belief or opinion," "Polemical," Collins Dictionary, https://www.collinsdictionary.com/us/dictionary/english/polemical. Polemical is also defined as "(of a piece of writing or a speech) strongly attacking or defending a particular opinion, person, idea, or set of beliefs:" "Polemical," Cambridge Dictionary, https://dictionary.cambridge.org/us/dictionary/english/polemical.

28   Newell G. Bringhurst, *Fawn McKay Brodie: A Biographer's Life* (Norman, University of Oklahoma Press, 1999), 266.

Klaus J. Hansen's comment that his own work, *Quest for Empire*, was not as controversial because:

❰❰ . . . Fawn Brodie's excessively maligned biography of Joseph Smith may well have preempted most of the shock value of the secular approach for Mormons. What might have been cause for excommunication in 1945, was, in 1967, merely occasion for the privately expressed if stinging rebuke by a General Authority . . .[29]

Clearly, Mormonism was moving in an entirely divergent direction from its origins. For the growing nucleus of progressive influence, these were positive signs of change worthy of celebration. Marshall also noted the formation of *Dialogue*, a progressive publication founded in 1966, and its influence on BYU—specifically its academic journal, *BYU Studies Quarterly*:

❰❰ Brigham Young University Studies was founded in 1959 and caused a stir with the publication of its first issue, as this writer understands it, because of the article by Leonard Arrington, "An Economic Interpretation of the Word of Wisdom." The periodical obviously succumbed to pressure from above and did not publish anything for a year. Then it reappeared in 1961 with an entirely new board of editors. In recent years BYU Studies has tended toward the kind of objectivity characterized by Dialogue. James Clayton notes that it was predicted that one of the things Dialogue would do would be to drive BYU Studies to the left, which it appears has happened.[30]

Marshall certainly did not consider himself a traditionalist, but his exuberance and enthusiasm for the success of the progressive movement—and his own attempt to celebrate their pursuits and accomplishments—led him to produce a paper that, for the progressive scholars he spoke about, was just a little too honest. In his paper, Marshall even quoted Arrington's likely-not-to-be-

---

29   Richard Stephen Marshall, "'The New Mormon History': A Senior Honors Project Summary," May 1, 1977, Department of History, University of Utah Special Collections, Marriott Library, University of Utah, 24; photocopy in our possession.

30   Ibid., 26; photocopy in our possession; emphasis in original.

repeated warning, "to call this [our] type of history a 'New History' 'gets us into trouble with the General Authorities.'"[31] Still, Marshall included Arrington's acknowledgement that there had been some "conflict between leaders and historians" in what he called a "conflict between the secular and the spiritual,"[32] although Arrington "tried to downplay any conflict between scholars and the General Authorities."[33] Marshall attributed their anxious comments as merely a reflection of "their situation"—as employees of the Church—which "undoubtedly does not allow them to be critical to any great degree."[34]

While seeking candidates to interview for his thesis paper, Marshall approached one scholar who wished to remain anonymous. His response to Marshall was: "You say you've talked to Arrington, Parkin and Durham? Well, take the exact opposite view from them and put me down for that. . . . I've already gotten too much criticism for my views. I don't want to get any more than I have to." Marshall noted that the man seemed "almost bitter as he spoke." The conflict over Latter-day Saint history was clearly a war that was exhausting recruited players on both sides. Marshall's interviewee seemed discouraged, lamenting that "[v]irtually all LDS historians agree with Arrington and Durham."[35] Was this an indication that the traditionalists were losing the war?

> *"You say you've talked to Arrington, Parkin and Durham? Well, take the exact opposite view from them and put me down for that."*

Thesis in the Hands of the Brethren

After Richard Marshall finished his thesis, copies began circulating among prominent individuals, including the general authorities,

---

31   Ibid., 13; photocopy in our possession.

32   Ibid., 31.

33   Ibid., 82.

34   Ibid., 83.

35   Ibid., 85.

causing panic to set in among Leonard Arrington and his team. Marshall had "also interviewed Mark E. Petersen, who, turning the tables, interviewed *him* and wanted a copy of the paper. The student provided him a copy; Petersen provided copies to the Twelve."[36]

Greg Prince noted the increasing apprehension and gathering storm clouds resulting from the paper's forthright conclusions:

ʻʻ ... Marshall's paper was not helpful to a division struggling to position itself as being—or at least appearing—more orthodox....

Three months after Homer Durham's arrival and Marshall's paper, Leonard noted his disappointment—not so much with where the History Division was heading, but how, including the creation by the Quorum of the Twelve of a sub-committee to "look into the affairs of the Historical Department. And by that he meant only the History Division of the department. This sub-committee consisted of Elder Petersen, Elder Hinckley, and Elder Packer," two of them being openly hostile to the division.[37]

There were consequences, and on December 8, 1977, Arrington met with Elder Durham to discuss new changes occurring within the department:

ʻʻ He wanted to tell me three things. First, that our division was very suspect, had very little standing with "the Brethren," and he was trying to "save" us by keeping a tight rein on us. Our freewheeling style of operation, without strict control from above, would have to be curbed. . . . we must cut down on our writing . . . approve in advance every research project, every assignment to every staff member, every article. In short, he wants to be the Church Historian, I am to be a supervisor of the History Division.[38]

---

36 Leonard J. Arrington, *Adventures of a Church Historian* (University of Illinois Press, 1998), 154; emphasis in original.

37 Gregory A. Prince, *Leonard Arrington and the Writing of Mormon History* (Salt Lake City, UT: Tanner Trust Fund and J. Willard Marriott Library, 2016), 300.

38 Leonard J. Arrington Diaries, December 8, 1977; Leonard J. Arrington and Gary James Bergera, *Confessions of a Mormon Historian: The Diaries of Leonard J. Arrington*, 1971-1997, vol. 2 (Salt Lake City: Signature Books, 2018), 440.

Elder Durham also increased departmental monitoring, including his request that Arrington provide "a detailed report on what each staff member is working on . . . a note on every change in assignment or new assignment."[39] Arrington felt betrayed. He had understood Elder Durham to be a man who shared similar progressive ideals; but now Durham seemed to be playing a game to win favor with the general authorities. Arrington lamented, "I suppose I am most hurt by Elder Durham displaying a complete lack of confidence in my handling of this and other matters. Where is the brotherly encouragement? Where is the appreciation? Why the suspicion, the distrust?"[40] Arrington seemed to feel that when the pressure came on, he was thrown under the bus. He finished his entry with, ". . . the entire interview was a vote of no confidence."[41]

Years later, Arrington lashed out in frustration, feeling that Marshall had chosen specific statements from his interview "out of context," making Arrington appear "heretical and disloyal."[42] However, Greg Prince observed that Arrington:

" . . . overplayed both his role and Marshall's motives. Marshall . . . quoted him only twice, and then in an appropriate context. . . .

Nothing that Leonard was quoted as saying would have been problematic even to the conservative apostles who took issue with him on other matters.[43]

Regardless, the damage had been done, and in Arrington's mind, Marshall had been carelessly—although inadvertently—involved in stirring the pot.

---

39 Ibid., 440.

40 Ibid., 441.

41 Ibid., 441.

42 Gregory A. Prince, *Leonard Arrington and the Writing of Mormon History* (Salt Lake City, UT: Tanner Trust Fund and J. Willard Marriott Library, 2016), 298.

43 Ibid., 299.

13

CHANGING THE CHURCH TO FIT IN
WITH THE WORLD

The true problem Richard Marshall's thesis posed for the progressive movement was that it prematurely unmasked the underlying and long-sought-for transformation within the scholarly community and the Latter-day Saint membership at large. Greg Prince noted in the Arrington biography that Church members were increasingly modifying their long-held stance:

" ... Marshall did point out what should have been obvious then—and is obvious now—which is doubtless why Leonard, connecting the dots of the subsequent dismantling of the History Division, saw the Marshall paper as a significant next step on the slippery slope. "That the Mormon Church has gone through a type of 'naturalistic humanism' is evidenced by the treatment its history has been receiving in recent years by scholars both within and without the Church, as well as in the many doctrinal, political and social changes which the Church has undergone since its organization."

In other words, with or without the work of Leonard Arrington and his colleagues in the History Division, Mormon historiography had shifted . . .[1]

---

1   Gregory A. Prince, *Leonard Arrington and the Writing of Mormon History* (Salt Lake City, UT: Tanner Trust Fund and J. Willard Marriott Library, 2016), 299.

Slouching Toward Cumorah?

Some saw these changes as evidence of greater rational thought and reasoning—'progress' from uneducated roots to greater sophistication and enlightenment. Traditionalists saw these changes as a threat to the inspired, solid foundation laid by Joseph Smith and other righteous leaders. President Boyd K. Packer would later plead with leaders for a course correction during a Regional Representatives Seminar in 1990:

❝ In recent years I have felt, and I think I am not alone, that we were losing the ability to correct the course of the Church. You cannot appreciate how deeply I feel about the importance of this present opportunity unless you know the regard, the reverence, I have for the Book of Mormon and how seriously I have taken the warnings of the prophets, particularly Alma and Helaman.

Both Alma and Helaman told of the church in their day. They warned about fast growth, the desire to be accepted by the world, to be popular, and particularly they warned about prosperity. Each time those conditions existed in combination, the Church drifted off course. All of those conditions are present in the Church today.[2]

In addition to President Packer's earnest warning of dangers existing within the Church, President Joseph F. Smith also gave a highly-publicized admonition concerning hidden threats within:

❝ There are at least three dangers that threaten the Church within, and *the authorities need to awaken* to the fact that the people should be warned unceasingly against them. As I see these, they are: 1. Flattery of prominent men in the world, 2. False educational ideas and 3. Sexual impurity.[3]

President Packer and President Joseph F. Smith feared that the desire to seek for, and allow, secular and progressive influences to shift the thinking of the leaders as well as the members toward a

---

2   Boyd K. Packer, "Let Them Govern Themselves," Regional Representatives Seminar, March 30, 1990; Boyd K. Packer, "Let Them Govern Themselves," *Sunstone* 14 (October 1990): 30.

3   Joseph F. Smith, "Three Threatening Dangers," *Improvement Era*, March 1914, 476–477; emphasis added.

broader acceptance of the intellectual world, would lead the Latter-day Saints down a road previously trodden by the Nephite Saints in the Book of Mormon. President Packer expounded on the dangers of accepting worldly influences:

❝ Helaman repeatedly warned, I think four times he used these words, that the fatal drift of the church could occur "in the space of not many years." In one instance it took only six years. (See Helaman 6:32, 7:6, 11:26)

The revelations tell us that there are limits to what mankind will be allowed to do. When those limits are reached, then comes destruction. And, the patience of the Lord with all of us who are *in leadership positions*, is not without limits.[4]

Boyd K. Packer, 1976

While President Packer saw danger in drifting away from traditional doctrines and standards, the progressives saw the change in an entirely different light. Marshall began his thesis celebration of the New Mormon History with a quote by Klaus J. Hansen:[5] "Mormonism in 1974 differs fundamentally from the Mormonism of 1890 . . . ."[6] Marshall went on to say that, "Many would attribute the changes the Church has undergone

---

4   Boyd K. Packer, "Let Them Govern Themselves," Regional Representatives Seminar, March 30, 1990; Boyd K. Packer, "Let Them Govern Themselves," *Sunstone* 14 (October 1990): 30; emphasis added.

5   Professor emeritus, Queen's University, Kingston, Canada.

6   Richard Stephen Marshall, "'The New Mormon History': A Senior Honors Project Summary," May 1, 1977, Department of History, University of Utah Special Collections, Marriott Library, University of Utah, 1; photocopy in our possession.

since its organization in 1830 to the influence of contemporary secular forces."[7] Marshall pointed out that the Church had become more popular with the general society when it gave up certain doctrines, such as plural marriage, consecration, and other politically-charged 'tenets.' To validate his claim, Marshall cited Christopher Lasch's commentary in the *New York Review of Books*:

" It is not as a *religious* force that Mormonism now makes itself felt. It makes itself felt precisely in the degree to which the Mormon influence has ceased to be distinguishable from any other vested influence. As long as the Mormons were different from their neighbors, their neighbors hounded them mercilessly. Only when they gave up the chief distinguishing features of their faith did the Latter-day Saints establish themselves as a fixture of the eccliastical [*sic*] scene, another tolerated minority.[8]

Building on the perspective that the progressive movement was an advocate for change, Marshall elaborated on Lasch's comment:

" Most members of the Church today are unaware that the Church has changed in the last one hundred years, that it has given up any distinguishing features, or that it has adapted itself to American society, a thing abhorrent to the early leaders of the Church. Hansen notes in this regard, "Social change can sometimes be rationalized most effectively under the pretense that it isn't going on."[9]

Marshall believed that the progressives were inducting a "secularization" of the narrative within the Church, and had successfully convinced the general membership to "rationaliz[e]" revisions that were "adjusting the Church to fit within contemporary

---

7   Ibid.

8   Christopher Lasch, "Burned Over Utopia," The New York Review of Books, January 26, 1967, https://www.nybooks.com/articles/1967/01/26/burned-over-utopia/; emphasis in original. Note: Marshall's quotation of Lasch in his thesis contained some minor typos and differences in the wording. For the purpose of this book, we have quoted the original, correct quotation from Lasch's 1967 article for the sake of accuracy.

9   Richard Stephen Marshall, "'The New Mormon History': A Senior Honors Project Summary," May 1, 1977, Department of History, University of Utah Special Collections, Marriott Library, University of Utah, 3; photocopy in our possession.

society"[10] as though they constituted further revelation from God. Marshall quoted Dr. Asael C. Lambert as observing that "one of the effects of secularism has been to produce a brand of Mormons which he calls 'realists' or 'variant Mormons.'"[11] One trend Lambert noted was that the "size of the Mormon family steadily decrease[s], and many of them have themselves limited the number of their own children . . ."[12]

Progressive historian Matthew Bowman would later author *The Mormon People*, dedicated to Richard Bushman, which notes that the entire culture of America was veering away from the principles of its foundation at the same time the progressive movement was similarly influencing the Latter-day Saints. American sociologist, Armand L. Mauss, recognized that Bowman's book:

> . . . has an important original argument . . . namely that the Church was strongly influenced by the Progressive movement so prominent in its American surroundings during the first half of that century. . . . Many earlier scholars have recognized the assimilation or "Americanization" of Mormons that occurred during this period, but Bowman points to Progressivism as the main inspiration for that assimilation . . . .

> The chapter includes brief forays into the significance of independent cultural developments among Mormon intellectuals and artists of recent decades, including the "new Mormon history" introduced by Leonard J. Arrington at the Church's own historical department, the Mormon History Association, Book of Mormon scholarship, the Foundation for Ancient Research and Mormon Studies (FARMS), and the publication of *Dialogue* and *Sunstone*. The author acknowledges resistance from Church leadership to some of these developments, and this resistance eventually expressed itself in some highly publicized excommunications during the 1990s.[13]

---

10   Ibid., 8.

11   Ibid., 8.

12   Ibid., 9.

13   Armand L. Mauss, "The Mormon People: The Making of an American Faith," *BYU Studies Quarterly* 52, no. 3 (2013): 164-167.

There is little debate among scholars as to whether or not 'Mormonism' is changing—drifting toward the left. For traditionalists and conservatives these changes are viewed as a departure—as harmful and straying from foundational moorings. Many view the prophetic Nephite warnings as a voice from the dust pleading that we should not follow the same road traveled to Cumorah at least twice previously.

Max Parkin Remembers Marshall

One of the scholars whom Richard Marshall spoke with was Max H. Parkin, who would later serve as the editor for *The Joseph Smith Papers, Documents, Vol. 4,* and *The Joseph Smith Papers, Documents, Vol. 5.* Parkin taught for the Church Educational System (CES) and worked as a researcher in the Museum of Church History and Art. During an interview with Alexander L. Baugh in 2015, Parkin recalled and commented on the decades-old controversy surrounding Marshall's thesis paper. Parkin disagreed with President Benson's assessment of *The Story of the Latter-day Saints,* and it was he who shared with Marshall that "many of the instructors 'closed their ears and refused to listen' to Benson's talk."[14] He also later remembered that after President Benson spoke, his son Kevin Parkin whispered the somber question: "Dad, now what are you going to do?"[15]

> *"many . . . closed their ears and refused to listen" to President Benson's talk*

Marshall also documented Parkin's opinion of Fawn Brodie's biography, *No Man Knows My History*:

---

14   Richard Stephen Marshall, "'The New Mormon History': A Senior Honors Project Summary," May 1, 1977, Department of History, University of Utah Special Collections, Marriott Library, University of Utah, 39; photocopy in our possession.

15   Alexander L. Baugh and Max H. Parkin interview, from the book *Conversations with Mormon Historians* (Provo: Brigham Young University, Religious Studies Center, 2015).

❦❦ Max Parkin initially intended to do his master's thesis on Brodie's work, in an attempt to show that she had misinterpreted and misquoted her sources. It soon became evident to him, however, that she was correct in her use of original sources. Parkin abandoned his thesis because "I didn't want my name attached to a thesis which vindicated Fawn Brodie.[16]

Parkin later admitted that he was disappointed that Joseph Fielding Smith "didn't take Mrs. Brodie seriously, nor any of her more accusing disclosures about the Prophet Joseph Smith."[17]

When Marshall's thesis paper was finished, it caused some issues for Max Parkin's career:

❦❦ After the student finished his senior paper, unfortunately it got into the hands of Jerald and Sandra Tanner, anti-Mormon publishers, who printed it. When the members of the Church Board of Education (that is, the First Presidency and Twelve) read the Tanner publication, as Brother Christensen later told me they had, my job was on the line. Eventually, to resolve the issue and to get me away from the fishbowl of the Salt Lake Institute, I was offered a position to teach at BYU. This was a great relief, but again, my wife did not want to move, so Brother Christensen, as administrator, suggested that a letter of apology from me to the Brethren might suffice, which it did.[18]

---

16   Richard Stephen Marshall, "'The New Mormon History': A Senior Honors Project Summary," May 1, 1977, Department of History, University of Utah Special Collections, Marriott Library, University of Utah, 25; photocopy in our possession.

17   Alexander L. Baugh and Max H. Parkin interview, from the book *Conversations with Mormon Historians* (Provo: Brigham Young University, Religious Studies Center, 2015).

In another interview, Max Parkin "described his own initial crisis of faith as a result of reading Fawn Brodie's *No Man Knows My History*, but explained that doing his own research had allowed him to come 'out of the struggle with a greater understanding of Joseph Smith and with tougher spiritual convictions.'" Craig L. Foster, "Conversations with Mormon Historians," *Interpreter: A Journal of Latter-day Saint Faith and Scholarship* 19 (2016): 401.

Parkin shared with Alexander Baugh, "Though still anchored in faith, I went through a spiritual struggle with what I found in examining Mrs. Brodie's sources and was left without anyone else to discuss them with meaningfully. Consequently, because of two growing concerns, I concluded not to finish the thesis." Alexander L. Baugh and Max H. Parkin interview, from the book *Conversations with Mormon Historians* (Provo: Brigham Young University, Religious Studies Center, 2015).

18   Ibid.

Parkin explained in his 2015 interview with Alexander Baugh that while he (Parkin) considers himself a "conservative, theologically" he is a "moderate to progressive in reporting history." Parkin had originally pursued a career in aviation, working with the United States Armed Forces and Western Airlines. However, in the 1950s, T. Edgar Lyon—a member of the Swearing Elders and colleague of Leonard Arrington—inspired Parkin to switch his direction toward Latter-day Saint history. Parkin commended Richard Bushman as one of his "excellent graduate teachers." He additionally proposed the works of Richard Bushman, Leonard Arrington, James Allen, Davis Bitton, Dean Jessee, and Donna Hill as "faithful works" of Latter-day Saint history.[19]

Parkin mentioned that he was "impressed" by Arrington, and from him "learned important things about how our history was written that we previously had not known." Parkin was one of many historians whom Arrington mentored, providing "guidance and leadership" and explaining that Arrington "helped me in my dissertation research." Arrington chose Parkin as one of the authors of his proposed sesquicentennial history and Parkin, in turn, shared disapproval of the "mistrust" expressed by some of the General Authorities toward Arrington and New Mormon History.[20] For both of these scholars, the New Mormon History held the key to correctly interpreting Latter-day Saint history.

> *"Mormon history has already been largely re-written in my lifetime"*

As with others, Parkin experienced a welcome change in fortunes for himself and other New Mormon History scholars when in 2000, Richard Bushman invited him to participate in the Joseph Smith Papers Project:

// Meanwhile, in August 2000, while on my Kirtland research mission in Salt Lake, Richard L. Bushman invited me to join him, Dean Jessee, and others to work on the Joseph Smith

---

19　Ibid.
20　Ibid.

Papers Project. . . . Ron Esplin succeeded Leonard Arrington as director of the Joseph Fielding Smith Institute of Latter-day Saint History at BYU, the institutional custodian of the Joseph Smith Papers Project at the time, and Dr. Esplin would serve as the Papers Project's managing director.[21]

Parkin saw Arrington as a "significant action hero" in laying the foundation for the Joseph Smith Papers Project, along with many other projects Arrington's students and colleagues continue to pursue today. He joined in celebration that "the vision and hope held by Dean Jessee and Leonard Arrington, [is] now being realized!"[22]

Mormonism—One Truth Among Many?

Richard Marshall's controversially-revealing thesis explored the breadth and depth of the development of New Mormon History, including the inner workings and the scheme of tight-lipped scholarship that had grown up around it. One of the progressive tenets he tackled was the growing angst among Latter-day Saint scholars over the claim that Mormonism was the only true and living faith—a notion these moderns felt the Church and its membership should dismiss as egocentric rhetoric.

In 1966, Philip A. M. Taylor authored a paper entitled, "The Life of Brigham Young—A Biography Which Will Not be Written" for publication in *Dialogue,* wherein he observed a change that had already begun to take hold among the scholars:

/ / Mormon history has already been largely re-written in my lifetime. Scholars are no longer obsessed by the question of the validity of Mormon theology or the authenticity of Joseph Smith's claims. They are far more willing than half a century ago to accept Mormonism as one historical faith among others and to study its effects.[23]

---

21   Ibid.

22   Ibid.

23   Philip A. M. Taylor, "The Life of Brigham Young: A Biography Which Will Not Be Written," *Dialogue: A Journal of Mormon Thought* 1, no. 3 (Autumn, 1966): 110; Richard Stephen Marshall, "'The New Mormon History': A Senior Honors Project Summary," May 1, 1977, Department of History, University of Utah Special Collections, Marriott Library, University of Utah, 39-40; photocopy in our possession.

Despite the reticence of some members to accept the Church's long-standing tenet, the conviction that the Restoration and subsequent ecclesiastical organization established by the Prophet Joseph Smith as "the only true and living church" comes from a revelation given to the Prophet Joseph Smith on November 1, 1831, proclaiming that:

❧❧ . . . those to whom these commandments were given, might have power to lay the foundation of this church, and to bring it forth out of obscurity and out of darkness, the only true and living church upon the face of the whole earth, with which I, the Lord, am well pleased, speaking unto the church collectively and not individually—

For I the Lord cannot look upon sin with the least degree of allowance;[24]

The traditional narrative boldly asserts that throughout the history of the Earth, prophets appointed by God held keys and power which enabled their central roles in officiating the Kingdom of God. All of these preeminent prophets came *in person* to deliver up to the Prophet Joseph Smith the keys that they personally held in their respective dispensational periods.[25] The Prophet Joseph, as head of the last and greatest of all dispensations[26] and the foretold restorer of all things,

---

24   Doctrine & Covenants 1:30-31.

25   President Joseph Fielding Smith taught, "It was not sufficient that John the Baptist came with the keys of the Aaronic Priesthood, and Peter, James, and John with the keys of the Melchizedek Priesthood, by virtue of which the Church was organized, but there had to be an opening of the heavens and a restoration of keys held by all the prophets who have headed dispensations from the days of Adam down to the days of Peter, James, and John. These prophets came in their turn and each bestowed the authority which he held. . . .

"All the keys of all dispensations had to be brought in order to fulfil [*sic*] the words of the prophets and the purposes of the Lord in bringing to pass a complete restoration of all things. Therefore the father of the human family, the first man on the earth, Adam, had to come, and he came with his power. Moses came, and others. All who had keys came and bestowed their authorities. . . . We have not the dates when some of these authorities were made manifest, but the Prophet Joseph Smith in writing to the Saints in Nauvoo in regard to the salvation of the dead declared, as we have it recorded in Section 128 of the Doctrine and Covenants [verses 17–21], that all these prophets came with their keys in the dispensation in which we live." "The Keys of the Priesthood Restored," *Utah Genealogical and Historical Magazine*, July 1936, 98, 101.

26   President Heber C. Kimball taught, "Are the keys here? Yes, the very keys that our Father placed upon His Son Jesus; and He placed that authority upon Peter and his associates; and they have been restored again to this earth through the

required of those prophets the keys and power held and preserved by them as heads of their respective stewardships. In order to perform his mission—the Marvelous Work and Wonder foretold by *all* the holy prophets since the world began—the Prophet needed all former keys and authority. The Prophet was entitled to these blessings because of his personal righteousness, his foreordained mission, and the genealogical bloodline through which he descended.[27] Thus, the torch was being passed on to the rightful heir, requiring the bestowal of the necessary keys, the authority, and the mantle to carry on the mission of the Latter-day Servant during the final, winding up scene.

Before the Prophet Joseph Smith died in the tragic events of June 27, 1844, he delegated authority and keys to the Twelve with the simple, straightforward commission: build the Kingdom by carrying on the work of God that he, the Servant of God, had laid out.[28] Brigham Young recalled:

---

ministration of the Prophet Joseph. It is written that the first shall be last, and the last first. This is the last kingdom, and the Lord will make it first; for it has got to raise up, and establish, and confer power upon every one of those kingdoms that have been. That is what we have got to do. Why do you not realize this? You could, if you lived your religion and called upon God by day and by night." Heber C. Kimball, "The Latter-Day Kingdom—Men not to Be Governed By Their Wives—Love to God Manifested By Love to His Servants," in *Journal of Discourses*, vol. 5 (Liverpool: Asa Calkin, 1858), 28. Discourse given on July 12, 1857.

27   L. Hannah Stoddard and James F. Stoddard III, *Hidden Bloodlines: The Grail & the Lost Tribes in the Lands of the North* (Salem: Joseph Smith Foundation, 2017), DVD.

28   "All that President Young or myself, or any member of the quorum need have done in the matter was to have referred to the last instructions at the last meeting we had with the Prophet Joseph before starting on our mission [to the eastern states]. I have alluded to that meeting many times in my life.

"The Prophet Joseph, I am now satisfied, had a thorough presentiment that that was the last meeting we would hold together here in the flesh. We had had our endowments; we had had all the blessings sealed upon our heads that were ever given to the apostles or prophets on the face of the earth. On that occasion the Prophet Joseph rose up and said to us: 'Brethren, I have desired to live to see this temple built. I shall never live to see it, but you will. I have sealed upon your heads all the keys of the kingdom of God. I have sealed upon you every key, power, principle that the God of heaven has revealed to me. Now, no matter where I may go or what I may do, the kingdom rests upon you.'

"Now, don't you wonder why we, as apostles, could not have understood that the prophet of God was going to be taken away from us? But we did not understand it. The apostles in the days of Jesus Christ could not understand what the Savior meant when he told them 'I am going away; if I do not go away the Comforter will not come.' Neither did we understand what Joseph meant. 'But,' he said, after having done this, 'ye apostles of the Lamb of God, my brethren, upon your shoulders

// I said to Brother Joseph, the spring before he was killed, "You are laying out work for twenty years." He replied, "You have as yet scarcely begun to work; but I will set you enough to last you during your lives, for I am going to rest." All I [Brigham] can do or ask now is to do the work, so that it will be right and acceptable to him when he comes here again.[29]

In the Lord's preface to the Doctrine and Covenants, the Lord explained that he had endowed Joseph Smith with the authority, revelations, and commandments to bring forth the Restoration, a latter portion of this Marvelous Work and Wonder being the establishment of "the only true and living church."[30]

On the day the Church was organized, the Lord gave a revelation to stand as the charter of the Church, commanding the members and leaders—both present and future—to "give heed unto all his [Joseph

"Aaronic Priesthood Restoration," Ken Corbett

this kingdom rests; now you have got to round up your shoulders and bear off the kingdom.' And he also made this very strange remark, 'If you do not do it you will be damned.'" Wilford Woodruff, "The Keys of the Kingdom," *The Latter-day Saints Millennial Star*, vol. 51, no. 35, September 2, 1889, 546.

29   Brigham Young, "Testimony of the Spirit—Revelation Given According to Requirements—Spiritual Warfare and Conquest, Etc.," in *Journal of Discourses*, vol. 5 (Liverpool: Asa Calkin, 1858), 331. Discourse given on October 7, 1857.

30   Doctrine and Covenants 1:30.

Smith's] words and commandments which he shall give unto you," promising that if the counsel was followed, "the gates of hell shall not prevail against you; yea, and the Lord God will disperse the powers of darkness from before you, and cause the heavens to shake for your good, and his name's glory."[31]

The institution Joseph Smith restored, using the keys and authority given to him by God, was both true and living. While no leader or member of the Church is perfect or inerrant, to the degree the teachings and revelations of Joseph Smith are followed, we have the divine promise that we will continue to experience success in our efforts.

Traditionalists, while allowing that all faiths have truth and goodness ensconced in their precepts, hold to the fundamental doctrine revealed by the Lord that the organization established by Joseph Smith is the only faith on the Earth possessing priesthood authority and keys from God. The Church and its members may be flawed—even, at times, disconcertingly flawed—but the foundation is authorized. We can fully rely on the revelations of the Prophet Joseph Smith as representing the word of God without error—a testimony repeatedly affirmed by the Prophet who testified: "there is no error in the revelations which I have taught." As Gordon B. Hinckley iterated during a Christmas devotional on December 7, 2003: "I look to [Joseph Smith]. I love him. I seek to follow him. I read his words, and they become the standards to be observed in guiding this great Church as it moves forward in fulfilling its eternal destiny."[32]

A growing number of progressive members and scholars, however, take issue with the traditionalist conviction of the 'one true faith.' Philip Taylor reputed in 1966 that Latter-day Saint scholars were rewriting Latter-day Saint history to avoid defending the Restoration, the Prophet Joseph Smith, and "the validity of Mormon theology or the authenticity of Joseph Smith's claims."[33]

Today, in the 21st-century, we are witnessing a growing renunciation of the 'one true faith' claim among Millennials and other progressive Mormons. In 2012, progressive Latter-day Saint author and professor

---

31   Doctrine and Covenants 21:6.

32   Gordon B. Hinckley, First Presidency Christmas Devotional, December 7, 2003, The Church of Jesus Christ of Latter-day Saints.

33   Phillip A. M. Taylor, "The Life of Brigham Young—A Biography Which Will Not be Written," *Dialogue: A Journal of Mormon Thought* 1, no. 3 (Fall 1966), 110.

Joanna Brooks blogged about a young woman who wrote to share her perplexity: "I'm a 19 year old progressive Mormon woman, and I'm so frustrated at church. . . . I'm not particularly invested in the whole Mormonism-is-the-one-true-way approach, and I feel like the more I learn and see, the more I find paradox and confusion in everything around me."[34]

Before Steve Otteson,[35] a disaffected member who struggled with the one true faith doctrine, was excommunicated from the Church, he spelled out progressivism:

// So why do progressive Mormons try to stay if they don't think the LDS church is true? First of all, they reject the black and white thinking of the "all or nothing" proposition. In their eyes, the LDS church isn't the one true church, but then there **is** no one true church. They see both good and bad in the church, just like any church. Progressive Mormons usually have friends and family that they love who believe in the church, and they want to stay close to them. They might enjoy serving other members of their ward. Perhaps they hope they can help others become more open-minded, so that the black and white thinking can begin to change.[36]

In a 2015 op-ed in the *Salt Lake Tribune*, Julienna Viegas-Haws noted, "A growing number of members of The Church of Jesus Christ

---

34   "I'm a 19 year old progressive Mormon woman, and I'm so frustrated at church. Help?" Ask Mormon Girl, April 23, 2012, https://askmormongirl. wordpress.com/2012/04/23/im-a-19-year-old-progressive-mormon-woman-and-im-so-frustrated-at-church-help/.

35   In 2017, Steve Otteson announced he joined the Community of Christ because "Community of Christ doesn't claim to be **the one** true church. Instead they say they strive to be a true church. They are what I wish the LDS church would someday evolve into, but at my age I'm not willing to wait around for the LDS church to change. Community of Christ (and I) acknowledge it isn't the only path to spirituality, but it works for me so I'm thrilled to have joined them. . . . The woman who confirmed me is like another grandma to me, and the one in the glasses who helped her is a Seventy." Steve Otteson, "Joining Community of Christ," Indie Mormon, November 15, 2017, http://indiemormon.com/2017/11/15/joining-community-of-christ/; emphasis in original.

36   Steve Otteson, "Why I Stay Away," Indie Mormon, October 2, 2015, http://indiemormon.com/2015/10/02/Julienna Viegas-Haws, "Op-ed: What do progressive Mormons want? A dialogue about change," *The Salt Lake Tribune*, August 7, 2015, https://www.sltrib.com/opinion/commentary/2015/08/07/op-ed-what-do-progressive-mormons-want-a-dialogue-about-change/.why-i-stay-away/.

of Latter-day Saints consider themselves 'progressive Mormons.'" According to her "loos[e]" definition, she described "progressive Mormons as those who are less likely than traditional Mormons to believe in . . . the LDS Church's unique restoration claims[,] literal interpretations of scripture . . ."[37]

In their own words, most progressives feel that the Gospel of Jesus Christ as restored by Joseph Smith includes inspired principles within its theology, but that it ranks as only *one among many* faiths and philosophies manifesting a touch of divine influence. For progressives, the Prophet Joseph Smith was a great thinker—inspired even; but to tout the one-and-only truth dogma is perceived as arrogant—even parochial. Moreover, the presumption exists that many

---

Are Joseph Smith's revelations merely a cultural product of his time?

---

of Joseph Smith's revelations are merely products of his time. Scholars evaluate his teachings, sorting out his statements they consider relevant today—and casting aside those they deem old-fashioned, prejudiced, chauvinistic, and unsophisticated.

Leonard Arrington fully embraced this new liberal progressive position, as evidenced by a conversation with Fred Buchanan while visiting Arrington in 1970. Buchanan was struggling through a crisis of faith, but Arrington advised that there was "more than one way to be a Mormon":

// When I returned to Utah in 1970 after seven years in Ohio seeking a Ph.D. in education, I seemed to be slipping in the direction of making an "either/or" decision about my relationship to the Church. During a visit to Logan, I sought out Leonard Arrington. Between general conference sessions, we had a long talk about my doubts and my future relationship to the Church. It was at that time that Leonard calmed some of my fears by suggesting that there was more than one way to be a

---

37   Julienna Viegas-Haws, "Op-ed: What do progressive Mormons want? A dialogue about change," *The Salt Lake Tribune*, August 7, 2015, https://www.sltrib.com/opinion/commentary/2015/08/07/op-ed-what-do-progressive-mormons-want-a-dialogue-about-change/.

Mormon. He suggested that in reality there was considerable variety of perspectives within the fold; and in his homespun way, he illustrated the diversity among the Mormons by saying that there were some who wore temple garments all the time; some who wore them on weekends; some only during the day, and some on special occasions only.[38]

Genevieve Draper spoke of Arrington's spiritual reasoning in a Utah State University paper entitled, "Knowing the Man in History":

▮▮ In 1936 Arrington recorded a change in his spiritual attitude, a change of tolerance. Though previous to his experiences in college he had believed only his church right, "Now I realize there is good and bad, but mostly good, in all of them."[39]

Arrington's friend, Carol Lynn Pearson, an acclaimed poet and author, wrote several films for the Brigham Young University Motion Picture Studio. Pearson authored the musical *My Turn on Earth,* a widely popular production premiering in 1977 and redistributed worldwide by Deseret Book in 2008. However, most are not aware that in the midst of her influence, Pearson expressed to Arrington her frustration with the one true Gospel claim: "Things which 'bug' her include our claiming to be the only true church, when she believes that there are other churches that have as valid a claim as we."[40] According to his biography, Arrington shared Pearson's viewpoint:

▮▮ The testimony that Leonard bore was inclusive, and not exclusive. That is, while he pledged allegiance to the Mormon Church and witnessed that he saw God's presence within it, he was comfortable with the truth claims of believers within other religious traditions . . . Feminist and poet Carol Lynn Pearson later queried him regarding the Mormon Church's exclusivist

---

38   "In Memoriam, Leonard J. Arrington," *Journal of Mormon History* 25, no. 1 (February 15, 1999), 26-27.

39   Genevieve Draper, "Knowing the Man in History," (2010), Arrington Student Writing Award Winners, Paper 4, 2, https://digitalcommons.usu.edu/cgi/viewcontent.cgi?article=1005&context=arrington_stwriting.

40   Leonard J. Arrington Diaries, February 12, 1979; Leonard J. Arrington and Gary James Bergera, *Confessions of a Mormon Historian: The Diaries of Leonard J. Arrington*, 1971-1997, vol. 2 (Salt Lake City: Signature Books, 2018), 720.

claims. "I asked Leonard if he could ever foresee a day when the Brethren would ever, *ever* modify the stand of being the only true Church and just say we're a darn good Church. He said— seriously—that he thought maybe in twenty years they might be ready for that. I expressed my surprise, and he said that the young people today are not buying everything they're told."[41]

And therein lies the rub—progressives presuppose that the Church's doctrine is inherently exclusive; yet the Prophet Joseph Smith taught in word and deed that the Gospel is *inclusive*. Some are surprised by the assertions vocalized in a speech the Prophet gave to a predominantly non-member audience in Washington, D.C.:

> **❝** . . . [The Prophet Joseph] closed by referring to the Mormon Bible [Book of Mormon], which he said, contained nothing inconsistent or conflicting with the Christian Bible, and he again repeated that all who would follow the precepts of the Bible, whether Mormon or not, would assuredly be saved.[42]

One recorder of the Prophet's speech noted the humility in the address, confessing that, "His religion appears to be the religion of meekness, lowliness and mild persuasion."[43] With the Prophet Joseph there was no arrogance of being 'the only kid on the block,' but he also insisted upon the essential requirement of authority.

The Prophet Joseph was repeatedly clear; the Church established by God through His servant exclusively holds divine keys and authority—and so long as, or to the extent that, the Church remains moored to the revelations and teachings contained in the standard works—it can be considered Christ's Church. The Lord proclaimed during His appearance to the Nephites:

---

41   Gregory A. Prince, *Leonard Arrington and the Writing of Mormon History* (Salt Lake City, UT: Tanner Trust Fund, and J. Willard Marriott Library, 2016), 121.

42   Joseph Smith, History, 1838–1856, volume C-1, February 6, 1840, p. 1015, The Joseph Smith Papers.

43   Joseph Smith, Discourse, February 5, 1840, p. 3, The Joseph Smith Papers.

❧❧ ... if it [the Church] be called in my name then it is my church, if it so be that [it is] built upon my gospel.

... And if it so be that the Church is built upon my gospel then will the Father show forth his own works in it.

But if it be not built upon my gospel, and is built upon the works of men ... by and by the end cometh, and they are hewn down and cast into the fire ...[44]

For the Lord Jesus Christ and the Prophet Joseph Smith there was no arrogance in being 'the one and only true Church.' Any good man or woman would eventually be saved if he or she lived in accordance with the truths taught in the Bible. The Church—then as now—although having divine authority, was only as true as the lives of each member reflected the works of the Father. It is the duty of each member today to live entirely worthy, making it possible for the Restored Church to represent Christ's true and living Church. In effect, each member is on trial—on their own personal journey of choice and accountability—as they help define whose church this is. Which direction will we take?

An increasing number of progressive members view with envy the new, liberated-from-archaic-tradition direction taken by our ecclesiastical cousins who remained behind in Nauvoo and elsewhere. Abandoning the one-true-gospel position was a revisionist path leading to a broader, less peculiar acceptance—a path taken by the Reorganized Church of Jesus Christ of Latter-day Saints (RLDS), now known as the Community of Christ:[45]

---

44   3 Nephi 27:8, 10-11.

45   For nearly 137 years, fierce debate had raged over the contentious issue of who was the Prophet Joseph Smith's rightful successor. The Church of Jesus Christ of Latter-day Saints claimed Brigham Young and the Quorum of the Twelve Apostles jointly held that role; but others disagreed. Founded originally with the support of Joseph Smith III and Emma Smith Bidamon, The Reorganized Church of Jesus Christ of Latter Day Saints (RLDS), known today as the Community of Christ, upheld Joseph's son, Joseph Smith III, as the true successor. Emma's other sons, Frederick, Alexander, and David Smith became zealous defenders of the Reorganized Church, expressing extreme antagonism toward the "Brighamites." During the last century, the Reorganized Church of Jesus Christ has increasingly embraced progressive viewpoints and stances. After renouncing plural marriage, the Book of Abraham, Joseph Smith's teachings on women and the priesthood, baptisms for the dead, and other aspects of the Restoration, the RLDS Church distanced itself from the Prophet Joseph Smith; and in 2001, the RLDS voted to

Joseph Smith III, son of Joseph Smith and Emma Smith Bidamon was President of the RLDS (now Community of Christ) for 54 years.

" In contrast, Community of Christ has de-emphasized its traditional tenet that it is the one true church and has adopted a viewpoint that all faith traditions can offer a pathway to spiritual enlightenment. Barbara McFarlane Higdon has called Community of Christ a "unique member of the body of Christ, the universal community of believers." Higdon also suggests that prior claims that the church had been "restored" were tantamount to idolatry. Community of Christ has therefore moved towards ecumenism and inter-faith dialogue. Nevertheless, Community of

---

change its name to the "Community of Christ." Some saw this change as a "move back toward Protestantism," and a signal of a "willingness to evolve when it comes to social issues," as "liberal Mormons find refuge in the Community of Christ." Garnet Henderson, "Dissatisfied Liberal Mormons Find Refuge in the Community of Christ," *The Guardian*, October 1, 2015, https://www.theguardian.com/us-news/2015/oct/01/women-lgbt-mormons-community-of-christ.

Historian Ken Mulliken called this move "historical amnesia" as the RLDS "abandoned their past and created a new organization that was focused on social interaction (Community) and shared mission (Christ)." Kenneth Robert Mulliken, "Historical Amnesia: Corporate Identity and Collective Memory in the Reorganized Church of Jesus Christ of Latter Day Saints, 1915-2001" PhD diss., University of Missouri, Kansas City, 2011, https://citeseerx.ist.psu.edu/viewdoc/download?doi=10.1.1.462.6719&rep=rep1&type=pdf.

Christ "steadfastly affirms the primacy of continuing revelation instead of creedal rigidity."[46]

While Joseph Smith taught that scripture was divine revelation, the Community of Christ version of the Doctrine and Covenants Section 163 reads: "Scripture has been written and shaped by human authors through experiences of revelation and ongoing inspiration of the Holy Spirit in the midst of time and culture."[47] In other words, scripture is not the revealed word of God, but inspiration mixed with culture and other parochial prejudices. The Community of Christ supported a male-only priesthood until 1984, when women won the bid to hold priesthood authority and began to receive ordination. Originally excluded, practicing members of the LGBT community were allowed priesthood ordinations commencing throughout 2012-2014. In contrast with the 'Salt Lake City-based' Church of Jesus Christ, the Community of Christ 'temples' do not require recommends or worthiness interviews to enter, and are open to the public. Although they initially accepted the doctrine of baptism for the dead, they now renounce such teachings.

Observing the progressive shift in the history and doctrine within the fellowship of the Community of Christ, some understand that progressive Latter-day Saints hope to witness a similar trend within The Church of Jesus Christ of Latter-day Saints. Will liberals within have their way in moving the Church to adopt the direction and progressivism of the Community of Christ? Regardless of the answer, the association among progressive historians within both denominations has been friendly and congenial, largely due to the work of Leonard Arrington, as Greg Prince observed:

❧❧ Perhaps the highest compliment he could have received came from Paul M. Edwards, a descendant of Joseph Smith and a member of the RLDS hierarchy. While noting that the LDS theology allowing for humans to progress to godhood was a bit

---

46   "Comparison of the Community of Christ and The Church of Jesus Christ of Latter-day Saints," Wikipedia, July 3, 2020, https://en.wikipedia.org/wiki/Comparison_of_the_Community_of_Christ_and_The_Church_of_Jesus_Christ_of_Latter-day_Saints.

47   Community of Christ Doctrine and Covenants Section 163:7a, https://www.cofchrist.org/doctrine-and-covenants-section-163.

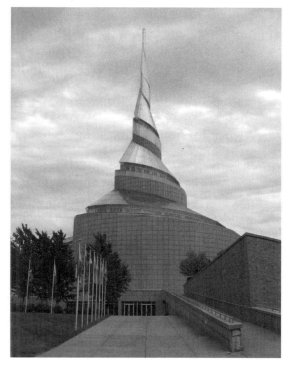

Community of Christ Temple, Independence, Missouri

The RLDS
rejected the
notion of
one true
church and
became the
Community
of Christ

much for the RLDS to swallow, Edwards said to me, in a casual conversation many years ago, "If such a thing is possible, I would like Leonard Arrington to become my God."[48]

Without question, there is a major shift currently picking up momentum toward progressivism among Latter-day Saint historians and thought leaders. John Dehlin of Mormon Stories, who keeps an attentive and rigorous pulse on trends within Mormonism, sums up this turning of the tide:

❝ What we're getting now in Mormonism—whether it is with Spencer Fluhman at the Maxwell Institute, Phil Barlow, Terryl and Fiona Givens, Richard Bushman, Adam Miller, you know, Patrick Mason, any of these kind of neo-apologists within Mormonism—what you're getting now from kind of this

---

48   Gregory A. Prince, *Leonard Arrington and the Writing of Mormon History* (Salt Lake City, UT: Tanner Trust Fund and J. Willard Marriott Library, 2016), 2.

intellectual, privileged, elite is their going around whether it's in their little books, or little presentations to select groups or in these little secret firesides that they hold or in the private one-on-one conversations that they have, it's like:

"Yeah, the Brethren say the Church is true but they should have never really said that. And when Joseph said 'translation,' what does 'translation' mean? Translation shouldn't have been the word that was used.

"And, yeah the Church did set you up with this false binary of true and false, but these are just old guys and, you know, they didn't know any better. And they meant it, but we the neo-apologetic elite Mormon class, progressive liberals [understand that the] . . . Book of Mormon doesn't need to be historical, it can just be a book of myth, a book of good principles to help you live your life.

"And you know, just between you and me, we can't say this publicly because our salaries or our reputation is based on it, but when the brethren say it is about truth and the one true Church, that's not what it's really about. And we apologize that you were kind of set up with that expectation but it's just about finding goodness wherever you can find it . . ."[49]

Did Joseph Smith restore the *true* gospel of Jesus Christ, or is the Restoration nothing more than a false, outdated conception from our intellectually-deficient past? Is the Book of Mormon *true* history, or have we been fed a diet of myth with a bit of goodness intertwined, as the progressive, neo-apologetic elite now popularize—the message now "coming out of the Maxwell Institute and BYU"? The secularized ideology of historians from only a generation ago, including the attestations of Leonard Arrington, appear to have moved into the mainstream.

---

49   John Dehlin and the Pinson Family, "1321-1327: The Excommunication of Mormon Bishop Sam Pinson and His Family in Ammon, Idaho," Mormon Stories, Part 4, 01:14:55, June 9, 2020, https://www.mormonstories.org/podcast/the-excommunication-of-mormon-bishop-sam-pinson-and-his-family-in-ammon-idaho/.

14

Marshall Unwittingly Becomes Arrington's Nemesis

Ronald W. Walker[1] remembered the distressing impact of Richard Marshall's thesis, noting that "[w]hile Marshall's analysis was preliminary and by no means sophisticated, it had the effect of confirming the growing doubts about the historical community."[2] The following year, trouble continued to increase for the History Division, and a frustrated Leonard Arrington felt that his attempts to please the divergent parties and opposing sides were failing.

The "highly orthodox" traditionalists were now watching Arrington's activities carefully, scrutinizing his every move. On January 14, 1978, Arrington confided in his diary his fears that both Tom Truitt and Lauritz Petersen, who had previously served as Church employees, were "spies," planted by concerned parties to watch the goings-on within the division:

❝ ... Tom Truitt (and also [church employee][3] Lauritz Petersen at an earlier stage) is a spy for Elders Benson and Petersen. He reads everything I do or say that he can get his hands on, underlines

---

1   Ronald Walker was a Latter-day Saint progressive historian, author, and professor at Brigham Young University. He worked in Leonard Arrington's History Division beginning in 1976 and later transferred to BYU as a member of the Joseph Fielding Smith Institute for Church History.

2   Ronald W. Walker, "Mormonism's 'Happy Warrior': Appreciating Leonard J. Arrington," *Journal of Mormon History* 25, no. 1 (1999): 123.

3   Brackets in original added by Gary Bergera.

statements which, out of context, will be objectionable to Elders
Benson and Petersen, and sends these on to them.[4]

Moreover, William (Bill) Nelson, Ezra Taft Benson's assistant,
was a "John Bircher who sees an apostate or 'intellectual' (same
thing) under every table . . ."[5] Arrington noted that "intelligent LDS
readers" would accept the New Mormon History; however, there
were three groups, he was certain, which would not. The first group
were the "lunatic fringe" conservatives:

// . . . [T]here are three groups that will not accept professional
history, no matter how carefully, discreetly, and judiciously
written. These are: (1) the lunatic fringe; i.e., members of the
John Birch Society and their sympathizers who do not want even
to try to understand what the professional is saying. They see a
Communist under every bush; a "liberal" in every intelligently
written "fair" book. One cannot please them regardless. (2)
Certain General Authorities who are so protective of the Church
membership, especially the young, that they do not want any
unpleasant facts revealed or acknowledged or repeated. (3)
Certain persons in the church bureaucracy who are fearful that
someone will not like something they read, and they therefore
mention it unfavorably, disapprove it publicly, and refuse to
sanction it for any use.[6]

Arrington and his team's close association with *Dialogue* was
"anathema" for the traditionalist leaders. Despite their concern,
ironically, those leaders likely had only an inkling of how deeply
connected Arrington and his team actually were—with both the
Dialogue publication, and the *Dialogue* worldview. Knowing full
well the implications of their affiliation, Arrington stressed that if
the Brethren became aware of the full truth, "they would press for
our release."[7]

---

4   Leonard J. Arrington Diaries, January 14, 1948; Leonard J. Arrington and
Gary James Bergera, *Confessions of a Mormon Historian: The Diaries of Leonard J.
Arrington*, 1971-1997, vol. 2 (Salt Lake City: Signature Books, 2018), 452.

5   Ibid.

6   Leonard J. Arrington Diaries, November 18, 1948; Ibid., 432.

7   "Dialogue was (is) anathema to Elder [Ezra Taft] Benson and Elder [Mark E.]
Petersen, and they can never forgive us for our associations with them before our

At the same time, Arrington felt disapproval from other progressive historians for not producing history more to their liking; and he felt the keen edge of disrespect from his own colleagues who were feeling the effects of the restraint on their own research. Frustrated by anti-Mormons who were damaging his reputation by citing him as their source for antagonistic material, he also faced the breakdown as progressives began turning on each other—some hurling judgment at Arrington for "caving in, selling out, buckling under, catering to the authorities.... [T]he liberals do not support us," Arrington despaired, pushing him "almost to the point of throwing in the towel."[8]

Conflict among Arrington's own staff continued to add fuel to the flame, and he noted in his diary on March 3, 1978 that, "I sometimes feel that I am going into the lion's den when I have to meet with my own staff."[9] Davis Bitton, James Allen, Jill Derr, Dean Jessee, and Glen Leonard were supportive of Arrington; but others expressed their growing dissatisfaction. Despite the initial call for unity—an essential element needed to succeed in furthering the New History and overcoming the opposition—Arrington's monumental efforts to rally his forces still left many of his own team flailing as they began to lose hope.[10]

An Embarrassing Episode with the Tanners

In the midst of the darkening storm for the New Mormon Historians, two other readers found Richard Marshall's paper particularly intriguing: Jerald and Sandra Tanner. A professional, but anonymous, 63-page-booklet refutation of Jerald and Sandra Tanner's personal work had recently begun circulating among the well-read membership of the Church. Toward the end of 1977, a

---

appointments. If they saw evidence of our association with them today, they would press for our release." Leonard J. Arrington Diaries, February 18, 1978; Ibid., 470; brackets in original.

About seven months later, Arrington noted in his diary, "I regret the ukase [degree] which prevents us from making the contributions we should to Dialogue magazine. Dialogue is making an important contribution to LDS culture and we should be represented in it more than we are." Leonard J. Arrington Diaries, September 14, 1978; Ibid., 617; brackets in original.

8   Leonard J. Arrington Diaries, February 18, 1978; Ibid., 470.

9   Leonard J. Arrington Diaries, March 3, 1978; Ibid., 481.

10   Ibid.

letter, written incognito, had unexpectedly been delivered to Sam Weller, the owner of Zion Bookstore, including certain "details of how he could handle the pamphlet . . . [and] a key to a room in a self storage company on Redwood Road." When Weller arrived at the room, he discovered 1800 copies of the booklet—given entirely free of charge—revealing that whoever the mysterious donor was, they clearly "had a great deal of money to spend."[11]

The Tanners remembered a conversation with a Latter-day Saint singer who had alerted them to rumors that there was a committee at Church Headquarters which was "organized to evaluate" the Tanner's research:

> **//** The committee worked on our material until they received an order From the Prophet—i.e., the President of the Church—that they were to desist from the project. We were unable to learn anything more about this purported committee, but one of the top Mormon historians did tell us in a telephone conversation in Dec. 1976 that a manuscript had been prepared to refute the allegations contained in our work. He was not sure if the Church would actually publish it, but the writing had been done.[12]

When the Tanners obtained a copy of Marshall's thesis, they discovered an unexpected clue—a hint as to the identity of the anonymous critic of their work. According to the thesis:

> **//** [Reed] Durham said he would like to write a book answering the accusations of the Tanners point by point. To do so, however, would require certain admissions that Mormon history is not exactly as the Church has taught it was, that there were things taught and practiced in the nin[e]teenth century of which the general Church membership is unaware. He said that the Church is not ready to admit that yet. He also said that due to the large number of letters the Church Historian's Office is receiving asking for answers to the things the Tanners have published, a certain scholar (name deliberately withheld) was appointed to write a general answer to the Tanners including

---

11   "Blacks Receive LDS Priesthood," Utah Lighthouse Ministry, http://www. utlm.org/newsletters/no39.htm.

12   Ibid.

advice on how to read anti-Mormon literature. This unnamed person solicited the help of Reed Durham on the project. The work is finished but its publication is delayed, according to what Leonard Arrington told Durham, because they can not decide how or where to publish it. Because the article is an open and honest approach to the problem, although it by no means answers all of the questions raised by the Tanners, it will be published anonymously, to avoid any difficulties which could result were such an article connected with an official Church agency.[13]

Jerald and Sandra Tanner's curiosity was piqued. The anonymous rebuttal of their work had begun circulating seven months after Marshall had written his thesis. The Tanners had already suspected that D. Michael Quinn was the secret author as a result of their own comparison of the writing contained within the rebuttal, alongside other of Quinn's publications. Quinn had unequivocally denied any connection with the pamphlet; but the Tanners felt that their suspicions were confirmed, because Marshall's thesis revealed that

JERALD AND SANDRA TANNER'S DISTORTED VIEW OF MORMONISM: A RESPONSE TO **MORMONISM — SHADOW OR REALITY?**

By a Latter-day Saint Historian

Recreation of pamphlet "Jerald and Sandra Tanner's Distorted View of Mormonism"

13   Richard Stephen Marshall, "'The New Mormon History': A Senior Honors Project Summary," May 1, 1977, Department of History, University of Utah Special Collections, Marriott Library, University of Utah, 61-62; photocopy in our possession.

Leonard Arrington, the Church Historian, had been involved. Not surprisingly, the Tanners decided it was time to conduct a little adept detective work of their own.

On January 15, 1978, Arrington received a phone call from Michael Marquardt, a progressive historian and former member of the Church.[14] Marquardt pressed Arrington to reveal the identity of the anonymous historian who had published the "debunking" of Jerald and Sandra Tanner's anti-Joseph Smith book, *Mormonism-Shadow or Reality?* Arrington recorded in his diary that during the phone call, he "denied any involvement and insisted that it was not official in any sense, had nothing to do with our office. And insisted I had no idea who wrote it."[15]

The truth was that Arrington *did* know who wrote the response—the incognito writer was, in fact, D. Michael Quinn—one of Arrington's assistants in the Church History Division. The rebuttal, published under the title, "Jerald and Sandra Tanner's Distorted View of Mormonism," and submitted anonymously as a private project, allowed the Church Historical Department to deny involvement, and retreat from any responsibility for its subject matter.

> *Shortly after his call with Marquardt, Arrington received a call from Jerald Tanner himself.*

Shortly after his call with Marquardt, Arrington received a call from Jerald Tanner himself. Tanner triumphantly explained that he had just spoken with David Mayfield, a former archivist in the Historical Department, and that while on the line, Mayfield had accidentally "spilled the beans."[16] The Tanners had previously stumbled upon information

---

14   Mark A. Kellner, "Mormon History Under Scrutiny," *Christianity Today*, October 3, 1994, https://www.christianitytoday.com/ct/1994/october3/4tb68b.html.

15   Leonard J. Arrington Diaries, January 15, 1978; Leonard J. Arrington and Gary James Bergera, *Confessions of a Mormon Historian: The Diaries of Leonard J. Arrington*, 1971-1997, vol. 2 (Salt Lake City: Signature Books, 2018), 453.

16   Ibid., 453.
    "I then telephoned Dave, who said that Jerald had telephoned him and asked if he had seen a paper by Mike Quinn which was a response to the Tanners. He said

leading them to Mayfield, who accepted their call, not realizing that the Tanners were on the other end of the line. Assuming he was communicating with someone who was in on the 'secret,' Mayfield inadvertently divulged the pertinent information, answering the caller's questions in an open manner later recalled by the Tanners:

// We decided to call Mr. Mayfield and ask him concerning the matter. . . . Our first question to Mr. Mayfield was whether he worked for the Mormon Historical Department. He replied that he had worked there but was not working there at the present time. Then we asked him if he had seen *Michael Quinn's paper* in the typed form before it was published as *Jerald and Sandra['s] Distorted View of Mormonism.* After hesitating slightly, he replied: "*Yes.*" Then we asked if he was sure that it was the typed copy he had seen. The reply: "Yes." The third question we asked was whether it was about a year ago when he saw it. Mr. Mayfield also replied "yes" to that question. Then he began to get uneasy and asked to whom he was speaking. (He apparently thought he was talking to a Mormon who had been initiated into the secret.) Needless to say, he was not too happy when he learned who it was, although he was still very polite. He went on to say that he was told not to reveal the identity of the author because it was supposed to be an anonymous publication. We reminded him, however, that in his answer to an earlier question, he had already revealed the identity of the author. He had replied "yes" to the question of whether he had seen the typed copy of Michael Quinn's paper before it was published.[17]

After finishing their conversation with Mayfield, the Tanners dialed up Leonard Arrington, curious to see if he would continue to deny his indisputable knowledge of the project—even after one of his former employees had now admitted his department was involved, and that Quinn had written the paper:

---

he was 'caught off guard,' and did admit he had seen such a paper. Pretty soon, Jerald Tanner telephoned me again and apologized for becoming angry with me for my denial. I re-denied the whole business again. . . . I telephoned Mike Quinn to tell him this." Ibid., 454.

17   "Blacks Receive LDS Priesthood," Utah Lighthouse Ministry, http://www.utlm.org/newsletters/no39.htm; emphasis in original.

▲▲ ... we called Dr. Arrington, Church Historian, and asked him
if he was still going to stand by his story in the light of David
Mayfield's admission. He emphatically replied that he knew
absolutely nothing about the project and that the charges were
completely untrue. Later that day Dr. Arrington called us and
said he had checked with Mayfield, and that Mayfield told him
he had made a mistake; it was another document that he had
seen. . . . Dr. Arrington continued to deny the whole matter.
Later we called David Mayfield and asked him if he [had] told
Dr. Arrington that he had made a mistake about the document.
Mr. Mayfield did not support Dr. Arrington; he simply replied
that he was "not going to comment" about the matter. . . .

... we called Michael Quinn. The reader will remember that
Dr. Quinn had strongly denied the accusation when we first
called him. This conversation was entirely different from the
first. . . . he replied that he would "neither affirm nor deny" the
allegation. . . . This, of course, was a long step from his original
position. He had moved from an absolute "no" to the compromised
position that he would "neither affirm nor deny" authorship.[18]

The Tanners published their conversations with Arrington and
Quinn in the July 1978 edition of the *Salt Lake City Messenger*,
causing further embarrassment for the scholars. Quinn reportedly
commented to Gary Bergera: "If they want to [attribute] me as the
author, they're free to, just as long as they spell my name right."[19]

Apparently irritated by the "clandestine" approach taken by the
scholars employed by the Church and by BYU, the Tanners gave
voice to the irony that they had been "accused of dishonesty, yet
those responsible for its publication will not admit their connection
with it."

An associate professor at BYU seemed also to disagree with the
approach taken by the History Division, commenting: "Here's
a man who's writing to evaluate the Tanners, yet he doesn't have
enough gumption to put his name on it. The credibility of the
pamphlet, as far as I'm concerned, is nill." The Tanners, on the
other hand, publicly challenged Arrington and Quinn to an open

---

18   Ibid.
19   Ibid.

One issue raised by the Tanners questioned why there are multiple First Vision accounts. Critics argue that these accounts contradict themselves but this is easily explained. www.JosephSmithFoundation.org/FirstVision

debate, declaring, "We will even pay to rent the hall." The Tanners, not surprisingly, received no response.[20]

In retrospect, the humiliating fiasco could have been entirely avoided had there not been an aura of fear and avoidance of hard issues percolating among the bureaucracy working within the Church—perhaps even among Arrington's History Division. The Tanners had raised 'tough' questions surrounding Joseph Smith's alleged money digging, Book of Mormon archaeology, multiple First Vision accounts, Adam-God, plural marriage, blood atonement, freemasonry and the temple ceremony, the Mountain Meadows

---

20   "That the Church Historical Department would publish the rebuttal anonymously is bad enough, but even worse is the fact that those responsible (Church Historian Leonard Arrington and Michael Quinn) would emphatically deny any connection with it. In the rebuttal we have been accused of dishonesty, yet those responsible for its publication will not admit their connection with it. In February, 1978, we challenged 'Leonard Arrington, D. Michael Quinn and everyone else who was involved in this surreptitious plot to come forth and meet us in a public debate. We will even pay to rent the hall.' So far all of the participants have remained silent about the matter." "Blacks Receive LDS Priesthood," Utah Lighthouse Ministry, http://www.utlm.org/newsletters/no39. htm#STONEWALLING.

Joseph Smith as well as many of the Founding Fathers were Freemasons. The Tanners and other critics allege that Joseph Smith plagiarized the temple endowment from freemasonry. For a full refutation, as well as a presentation of the history of Joseph Smith's involvement in masonic activity, see the documentary, "Statesmen & Symbols: Prelude to the Restoration." Contrary to it being a black mark in the Restoration, this is one of the most faith-promoting narratives of early Restoration history.

Massacre, and so forth. Blindsided by the Tanners' logical, albeit misguided claims, members grasped desperately for answers. But instead of approaching these questions with the never-failing aid of inspired truth and God-endowed confidence and wisdom, the far-too-prevalent reaction was to hide. Reed Durham felt the avoidance stemmed from a fear to admit that "there were things taught and practiced in the nin[e]teenth century of which the general Church membership is unaware,"[21] and that these matters should be honestly and openly discussed with the members. Some were shaken; they didn't know how to answer the arguments. Others were deeply embarrassed.

Confident in their origins and testimony, no true traditionalist would subscribe to or endorse covering up history. Why? Because as President J. Reuben Clark Jr. famously proclaimed, "If we have the truth, it cannot be harmed by investigation. If we have not the truth,

---

21   Richard Stephen Marshall, "'The New Mormon History': A Senior Honors Project Summary," May 1, 1977, Department of History, University of Utah Special Collections, Marriott Library, University of Utah, 61; photocopy in our possession.

it ought to be harmed."[22] There is nothing to fear. If the Gospel is true—and we testify that it is—it will bear all the scrutiny of the genuine, earnest investigator. If Joseph Smith was a Prophet of God—and we bear witness that he is—the doctrines he taught, and the conduct of his private and public life, will stand the test of time and honest examination.

We are each called to stand as a witness of God at all times, and in all things, and in all places. Hiding in the shadows, disavowing our history from embarrassment, or clinging to ignorance, is dishonorable—and is causing harm to ever-increasing numbers of men and women facing a personal crisis of faith:

❝ . . . for there are many yet on the earth among all sects, parties, and denominations, who are blinded by the subtle craftiness of men, whereby they lie in wait to deceive, and who are only kept from the truth because they know not where to find it.[23]

Will you pay the price, however steep, to obtain the truth—and will you take a stand to bear testimony of it?

Changes for the Historical Division

On January 20, 1978, progressive historian Stanley B. Kimball arrived at Leonard Arrington's office as the bearer of ill tidings from Deseret Book. The Church's publisher was concerned as a result of the trouble encountered with *The Story of the Latter-day Saints,* and the further hassle brought on by another of Arrington's controversial books—*Building the City of God.* Some progressive writers had been blacklisted, and others speculated over whether the new Church History series overseen by Arrington—the 16-volume sesquicentennial set—would be approved or canceled. It was soon settled that there would be no second printing of *The Story of the Latter-day Saints.* Arrington's friend and the founding editor of *Dialogue,* Eugene England, was disallowed from publishing in the *Ensign* or with Deseret Book.[24]

---

22   D. Michael Quinn, *The Church Years* (Provo, Utah: Brigham Young University Press, 1983), 24.

23   Doctrine and Covenants 123:12.

24   Leonard J. Arrington Diaries, February 2, 1978; Leonard J. Arrington and Gary James Bergera, *Confessions of a Mormon Historian: The Diaries of Leonard J.*

With determined optimism, Arrington held out in the hope that President Benson "may not become president of the Church. And if he does, he may not be vindictive." At this point, President Benson was a consistently resurfacing source of irritating opposition; but what could an "old Dialogue writer" like Arrington do? "Horseflies are inevitably around to irritate the plowing horse," Arrington sighed, reflecting on the analogy. "What can he do but suffer the indignity and continue plowing?"[25]

The cold, foreboding winds of resistance picked up once again, blowing in Arrington's disfavor as sources outside the Historical Division began to implement new adjustments and restrictions. On February 15, 1978, Arrington met with Elder G. Homer Durham, who was exerting greater control over the department after expressing "a number of concerns about . . . the image it [the department] has with certain General Authorities." One of the paramount concerns dealt with "access to archives." Copies of several documents had unsurprisingly found their way into the hands of anti-Mormons and other critics of the Church. Elder Durham stressed "more control over access to archives; more control over xeroxing . . ."[26]

Arrington had been extremely liberal in obtaining and placing the Church's documents into the hands of progressive historians and other scholars staunchly supporting his direction.[27] "Leonard would share everything," one remembered. "He called himself an entrepreneur. He created Mormon historians by sharing his information with them, by pushing them into projects that they didn't know they were interested in, by facilitating the research."[28] Greg Prince observed that Arrington felt an obligation "to make as much information available to a wide circle of scholars as quickly as

---

Arrington, 1971-1997, vol. 2 (Salt Lake City: Signature Books, 2018), 463.

25   Leonard J. Arrington Diaries, January 20, 1978; Ibid., 456-457.

26   Leonard J. Arrington Diaries, February 15, 1978; Ibid., 466-467.

27   For those that have been closely involved in studying and teaching the history of the Church for many years there was always a paradox; why was it that all of the antagonistic authors seemed to have access to the documents, while those sympathetic to the traditionalist Gospel cause did not. Leonard Arrington is the answer.

28   Gregory A. Prince, *Leonard Arrington and the Writing of Mormon History* (Salt Lake City, UT: Tanner Trust Fund and J. Willard Marriott Library, 2016), 222.

possible."[29] Documents had been making their way everywhere, it seemed—into the hands of progressive scholars and even some anti-Mormon writers. Arrington denied responsibility for any breach of custody; but concerns over management of the department still plagued him. Some had other concerns, including the appearance of a strong bias evinced by Arrington. Greg Prince noted:

> Even more troubling was the suggestion that Leonard had taken measures to limit another scholar's access to the Brigham Young papers at the same time that Leonard was working on his biography [*American Moses*]. According to Gene Sessions, who had been employed by the History Division before he joined Weber State's History Department, "Arrington wasn't letting [Don Moorman][30] see the material he wanted to see. Don figured it was all selfishness. Don wanted to write the definitive biography of Brigham Young." Moorman's interest in a biography predated the History Division, and he had a handwritten directive from Joseph Fielding Smith, who stepped up from church historian to church president in 1970, to prove it. While the directive gave him access, it didn't give him cooperation from Leonard. "Leonard refused to let him use the copying machines. He said, 'You can see the Young stuff as long as you hand-copy it.' So Don spent hours and hours and hours sitting in a room in the back of the archives search room. Leonard was letting other people use the copying machine but Don couldn't, because he was working on Brigham Young and Leonard had already announced that he was going to write the definitive biography of Brigham Young."[31]

It seems a common thread among progressives to strenuously complain about openness and transparency; but, more often than not, when the shoe is on the other foot, the liberals are consistently guilty of cutting off conversation, restricting information, and promoting a heavy bias toward their own partisan clan.

---

29   Ibid., 223.

30   Brackets in original added by Gary Bergera.

31   Gregory A. Prince, *Leonard Arrington and the Writing of Mormon History* (Salt Lake City, UT: Tanner Trust Fund and J. Willard Marriott Library, 2016), 401-402.

In 1978, some of the general authorities apparently felt that activities going on within the department were straying from the original purpose intended.[32] Elder Durham explained that Arrington's title would also undergo a change—from Church Historian to "Director, History Division."[33] Arrington took the meeting as "a slap in the face against me and those with whom I work,"[34] and began thinking seriously of resigning and moving to BYU in the next year or two.

Arrington endeavored to conceal the unhappy truth as long as possible. When Sterling McMurrin asked why his title was being changed, Arrington responded that, "on my own request they have given me another title, Director of the History Division of the Church. This gives me a title that's better understood and more secular. . . . I told him I was pleased with the title and welcomed it . . ."[35]

As it was, on February 24, 1978, Elder Durham formally notified Arrington of his title change from 'Church Historian' to the new label, 'Director.' The change was effective immediately, with no announcement made by the First Presidency. Arrington was also instructed that "none of us is to suggest to anybody that they have changed our titles or our functions. . . . If somebody introduces us as Church Historian or Assistant Church Historian, we are to let it pass without any comment. But we are to sign our letters as indicated . . . ."[36] Other changes were made in the same fashion— subtly, quietly, and without publicity. In the end, Richard Marshall's 1977 thesis had instigated an unintentional cascade of events— dramatically and materially affecting Arrington and the progressive quest to rewrite history. The fiasco would haunt liberal historians long into the future.

---

32 Meetings and conversations recorded in Leonard Arrington's diaries document the increasing number of alterations and restrictions being placed on the department. See, for example, Leonard J. Arrington Diaries, February 15, 1978; Leonard J. Arrington and Gary James Bergera, *Confessions of a Mormon Historian: The Diaries of Leonard J. Arrington, 1971-1997*, vol. 2 (Salt Lake City: Signature Books, 2018), 466.

33 Leonard J. Arrington Diaries, February 24, 1978; Ibid., 475.

34 Leonard J. Arrington Diaries, February 15, 1978; Ibid., 468.

35 Leonard J. Arrington Diaries, February 23, 1979; Ibid., 727.

36 Leonard J. Arrington Diaries, February 24, 1978; Ibid., 475.

15

BACKTRACKING ON THE NEW SESQUICENTENNIAL HISTORY

In 1978, with the Church trapped in a legal quandary, Elder Gordon B. Hinckley spoke with Church Legal Department attorneys to explore a lawful means of annulling the agreements the Church had entered into to publish the Sesquicentennial History volumes, an extensive project that had been conducted under the direction of Leonard Arrington. The attorney's grim response was disappointing; the Church was "stuck with the contracts." The original agreements were clear and binding, and if the Church determined to void their obligations, any one of the authors could sue Deseret Book and "almost certainly win."[1] Over the next two years, the battle intensified, resulting in a decisive Elder Hinckley refusing to take 'no' for an answer—asking "the legal department to work out a legal opinion which would enable them to cancel the contracts on the sesquicentennial history."[2]

When Arrington first became Church Historian in 1972, his close friend and future author of *Rough Stone Rolling*, Richard Bushman, proposed a new history series.[3] The concept evolved into the Sesquicentennial History, and was initially projected to comprise 15-16 volumes. To complete the project, Arrington engaged several

---

1   Leonard J. Arrington Diaries, March 23, 1978; Leonard J. Arrington and Gary James Bergera, *Confessions of a Mormon Historian: The Diaries of Leonard J. Arrington*, 1971-1997, vol. 2 (Salt Lake City: Signature Books, 2018), 488.

2   Leonard J. Arrington Diaries, April 21, 1980; Ibid., 3:12.

3   Gregory A. Prince, *Leonard Arrington and the Writing of Mormon History* (Salt Lake City, UT: Tanner Trust Fund and J. Willard Marriott Library, 2016), 168.

liberal New Mormon History scholars and intellectuals, including Richard L. Bushman, T. Edgar Lyon, [4]Eugene E. Campbell, Thomas G. Alexander, James B. Allen, and R. Davis Bitton—commissioning them to write a new history for the Church to publish in commemoration of the 150th anniversary of the April 6, 1830, organization of The Church of Jesus Christ of Latter-day Saints.

Storm clouds began to gather around the ambitious project as manuscripts were submitted to general authorities for approval. Richard Bushman remembered meeting with Lowell M. Durham (general manager of Deseret Book), who bore disappointing news for the historians. During an interview with John Dehlin on the Mormon Stories Podcast, Bushman recalled:

> **"** ... [Leonard Arrington] asked me to write the first volume of the 16, projected 16-volume history of the Church.... And the interesting thing is, the first volume, which was Milt Backman's *The Heavens Resound,* had gone through the committees, had been read by everybody who had to read it, and they were rolling along.
>
> Then came along my volume, [*Joseph Smith and*] *the Beginnings of Mormonism.* And after it was cleared by Leonard, and all his group then it went up to some unknown group of general authorities to read. Never got a word back concerning it. But one day, Leonard and I were—happened to be in Salt Lake and we were called in [to meet with Lowell Durham] ... and the news was delivered that they were cancelling the series. They had given big advances to all the authors so they were into it financially in a big way but they canceled the series. And Leonard was dumbfounded and horrified and it was really a terrible blow to him.[5]

---

4   T. Edgar Lyon was a member of the "Swearing Elders," and believed "that we should examine early Church leaders in the light of their times." He interpreted Joseph Smith's teachings on Zion and the divine mission of America as the result of cultural trends such as Millenarianism and Manifest Destiny, not revelation. Lyon served as a seminary principal, a professor at Ricks College (now BYU-Idaho), president of the Netherlands Mission, as a faculty member of the Salt Lake LDS Institute of Religion, and as a president of the Mormon History Association. He authored a Melchizedek priesthood manual, used in 1960, Introduction to the Doctrine and Covenants.

5   John Dehlin host, "Richard Bushman and *Rough Stone Rolling* Part 1—

Before news that the series would not be published by the Church reached Arrington and Bushman, Arrington had recorded in his diary that "opposition"[6] to the Sesquicentennial History had been raised by President Ezra Taft Benson and Elders Mark E. Petersen, Thomas S. Monson, and Boyd K. Packer. Arrington fought back, writing in his diary that he felt an "important responsibility in staying on this job until the sesquicentennial volumes [were] finally published." A determined Arrington vowed that the Sesquicentennial History would be released, even if he had to form a "private publishing firm and put the books out anyway."[7] When rumors continued to swirl that the volumes were going to be canceled, Arrington again asserted in his diary that "in my own mind there is absolutely no doubt that all of the histories which are turned in by the end of 1980 will be published by Deseret Book . . . ."[8] On January 1, 1979, Arrington recorded his "resolve to make the best books professionally out of the manuscripts turned in for the sesquicentennial history, and not to be swayed by 'expediency,' or by 'Elder [Ezra Taft] Benson['s] and [Mark E.] Petersen['s]' points of view which . . . would not serve the long-run interests of scholarship or the Church."[9]

Bushman's Controversial 'Joseph Smith'

The conflict centered around the first volume of the project that Arrington had assigned to progressive historian Richard Bushman.[10]

Experiences As a Mormon Historian," *Mormon Stories*, January 22, 2007, Part 1, 00:31:10-00:33:16, https://www.mormonstories.org/podcast/richard-bushman-and-rough-stone-rolling-part-1-experiences-as-a-mormon-historian/.

6   Leonard J. Arrington Diaries, March 23, 1978; Leonard J. Arrington and Gary James Bergera, *Confessions of a Mormon Historian: The Diaries of Leonard J. Arrington, 1971-1997*, vol. 2 (Salt Lake City: Signature Books, 2018), 486.

7   Ibid., 488.

8   Leonard J. Arrington Diaries, April 6, 1978; Ibid., 2:503.

9   Leonard J. Arrington Diaries, January 1, 1979; Ibid., 2:696; brackets in original.

10   "While Lowell hoped that some of the volumes might eventually be published by Deseret Book, he was certain that one of them—the one covering the earliest period of Mormonism—would not be and that, indeed, its content was the basis for the divided opinions among the Quorum of the Twelve. 'He cannot publish Richard Bushman's within the foreseeable future, because his was the one which has been the focal point of all the deliberation about the whole series and it will be politically naive for him to propose within two or three years the Bushman manuscript for publication.'" Gregory A. Prince, *Leonard Arrington and the Writing of Mormon History* (Salt Lake City, UT: Tanner Trust Fund and J. Willard Marriott Library, 2016), 337.

Although the Church pulled away from printing the series, Bushman's manuscript would eventually be published independently by the University of Illinois Press in 1984 under the title, *Joseph Smith and the Beginnings of Mormonism*. Although Bushman's manuscript caused some division within the Quorum of the Twelve, the narrative told in *Joseph Smith and the Beginnings of Mormonism* is not nearly as controversial—nor as divisive—as his later work, *Rough Stone Rolling*. In an April 1985 article in *Sunstone Magazine*, Ron Walker claimed that *Joseph Smith and the Beginnings of Mormonism* "defends the traditional Mormon view in a fairly traditional way."[11] However, this diluted version of a new Mormon history set off an alarm for President Ezra Taft Benson, Elder Mark E. Petersen, and Elder Boyd K. Packer, who recognized a serious danger. As they vocalized their opposition to the publication of Bushman's volume, their concerns became "the basis of the divided opinions among the Quorum of the Twelve."[12] Lowell Durham informed Arrington that Richard Bushman's manuscript was "the focal point of all the deliberation about the whole series . . ."[13]

Richard Bushman, the author of the controversial first volume of the proposed sesquicentennial history project, censoriously debated in the late '70s and early '80s at Church headquarters, has since achieved a considerable degree of fame. Bushman is now the chief Latter-day Saint evangelist in the development of a new progressive interpretation of Joseph Smith, particularly through his work, *Joseph Smith: Rough Stone Rolling*. In *Rough Stone Rolling*, Bushman presents a 'Joseph Smith' who was involved in ritual magic, who used peep stones to find treasure, who suffered from "treasure-seeking greed,"[14] "anger,"[15] and "easily-bruised pride,"[16] who possessed

---

11   Peggy Fletcher, "Church Historian: Evolution of a Calling," *Sunstone* 10 (April 1985): 58.

12   Gregory A. Prince, *Leonard Arrington and the Writing of Mormon History* (Salt Lake City, UT: Tanner Trust Fund and J. Willard Marriott Library, 2016), 337.

13   Leonard J. Arrington Diaries, December 30, 1980; Leonard J. Arrington and Gary James Bergera, *Confessions of a Mormon Historian: The Diaries of Leonard J. Arrington, 1971-1997*, vol. 3 (Salt Lake City: Signature Books, 2018), 143.

14   Richard L. Bushman, *Rough Stone Rolling* (New York: Vintage Books, 2007), 51.

15   Ibid., 249-250, 295.

16   Ibid., 295.

"Richard L. Bushman in the film By Study and Also By Faith,"
by BYU's Maxwell Institute under CC BY 3.0

"outrageous confidence,"[17] "[f]rom time to time drank too much,"[18] and grew up with an "oft-defeated, unmoored father"[19]—a father who "partially abdicated family leadership."[20] Today, despite his unfavorable view of Joseph Smith, Bushman serves on the National Advisory Board of the Joseph Smith Papers—and his book, *Rough Stone Rolling,* has sold over 100,000 copies.

In addition to his own revisionist views of the Prophet, Bushman has also expressed admiration for disaffected author Fawn Brodie, proclaiming her biography of Joseph Smith a "classic."[21] "I never had this idealized picture of Joseph," affirmed Bushman in an interview with the antithetical Mormon Stories Podcast. "I knew that Joseph

---

17   Ibid., 132.

18   Ibid., 43.

19   Ibid., 27.

20   Ibid., 42.

21   Dennis Lythgoe, "'Warts and all' in Smith biography," *Deseret News*, October 1, 2005, https://www.deseret.com/2005/10/1/19914955/warts-and-all-in-smith-biography; Neal Conan and Richard L. Bushman, "Book Explores History of the Mormon Church," NPR, December 19, 2005, https://www.npr.org/transcripts/50 61595?storyId=5061595&ft=nprml&f=5061595/?storyId=5061595&ft=nprml &f=5061595.

was a contentious figure from the word 'go' and this [*No Man Knows My History*] was just one more example of him being contentious."[22] In 2005, the *Deseret News* carried a story on Bushman's admiration for Brodie:

❝ Whatever readers or critics think of his book, Bushman remains respectful of older Smith biographies, even Fawn Brodie's controversial "No Man Knows My History," which Bushman considers "a classic, a fabulous piece of journalism. No one will ever match the zing in her writing. Brodie will always be useful in studying Joseph."[23]

Bushman was a close friend of Arrington during the 1970s, and when Arrington became the Church Historian in 1972, he requested that the First Presidency approve Bushman as a third Assistant Church Historian.[24] Bushman would later recall that it was Arrington who encouraged him to write a psychobiographical life story of Joseph Smith that eventually became the book *Rough Stone Rolling*.[25] Bushman would later comment to fellow cynic John Dehlin during a Mormon Stories Podcast interview:

---

22   John Dehlin host, "Richard Bushman and Rough Stone Rolling Part 1—Experiences As a Mormon Historian," Mormon Stories, January 22, 2007, Part 1, 00:27:20, https://www.mormonstories.org/podcast/richard-bushman-and-rough-stone-rolling-part-1-experiences-as-a-mormon-historian/.

23   Dennis Lythgoe, "'Warts and all' in Smith biography," *Deseret News*, October 1, 2005, https://www.deseret.com/2005/10/1/19914955/warts-and-all-in-smith-biography.

24   Leonard J. Arrington Diaries, August 8, 1972; Leonard J. Arrington and Gary James Bergera, *Confessions of a Mormon Historian: The Diaries of Leonard J. Arrington, 1971-1997*, vol. 1 (Salt Lake City: Signature Books, 2018), 227.

25   "On more than one occasion in the 1970s, Leonard Arrington, the founder of this organization, told me I should write a psychological sketch of Joseph Smith. Leonard was probably thinking of Fawn Brodie's brief analysis of Joseph in the second edition of *No Man Knows My History*. Brodie thought Joseph might conform to a psychological type, 'the impostor,' described by psychoanalyst Phyllis Greenacre. A few years earlier, I had spent two years studying psychoanalysis, and Leonard probably thought I was as well prepared as anyone to write about Joseph Smith's psychodynamics. Arrington could not have foreseen the assortment of psychologies studies that would begin appearing after 1976 by T. L. Brink, Jess Groesbeck, William D. Morain, Robert D. Anderson, and Lawrence Foster, most of them describing the Prophet as suffering from one psychological disease or another. After all this work, none of it particularly satisfying to Mormons, Leonard has earned the right to a hearty 'I told you so.'" Richard L. Bushman, "The Inner Joseph Smith," *Journal of Mormon History* 32, no. 1 (Spring 2006): 65.

❦ . . . I knew [Leonard] pretty well. When I—my first job was at BYU—and when I arrived, somehow he got wind of it and knew I was a Ph.D. in history from Harvard and wrote me a personal letter kind of welcoming me to the state of the historical profession. And I realized, this is a guy who takes responsibility for the whole direction of Mormon historiography. And that really was his style.

He was sort of the grandfather, and dean of the whole operation, not just at USU, not just at the Church, but everywhere. And then I worked closely thereafter. . . . I just felt like he was an encompassing figure of a very personal magnitude. I really loved him. I would say he was one of the men I really loved very well.[26]

Joseph Smith and the Beginnings of Mormonism

The essence of *Joseph Smith and the Beginnings of Mormonism* is built upon the premise that Joseph Smith was the "lazy son of a money digger"[27] who struggled to "extricate himself from the schemes of the Palmyra magicians and money diggers."[28] According to Ron Walker, David Whittaker, and James Allen, "Bushman saw Smith both as a youthful treasure hunter and, later, as a divine prophet."[29]

In addition to portraying Joseph Smith and his family as having been involved in money digging and magic, Bushman's representation of Joseph's first visit to Cumorah included claims that "Joseph was not entirely able to suppress his baser motives on the first walk to Cumorah. . . . Joseph spontaneously connected

---

26   John Dehlin host, "Richard Bushman and Rough Stone Rolling Part 1—Experiences As a Mormon Historian", Mormon Stories, January 22, 2007, Part 1, 00:28:37, https://www.mormonstories.org/podcast/richard-bushman-and-rough-stone-rolling-part-1-experiences-as-a-mormon-historian/.

27   Richard Bushman, *Joseph Smith and the Beginnings of Mormonism* (University of Illinois Press, 1984), 127.

28   "Joseph was assaulted from two sides in this struggle between modern rationalism and traditional supernaturalism. He had to . . . extricate himself from the schemes of the Palmyra magicians and money diggers . . . . At times his closest followers and his own family was confused. . . . The perspective of this work is that Joseph Smith is best understood as a person who outgrew his culture." Ibid., 7.

29   Ronald W. Walker, David J. Whittaker, and James B. Allen, *Mormon History* (University of Chicago Press, 2001), 85.

the plates with money-digging lore."[30] According to Bushman, Joseph Smith never "repudiate[d] . . . [the] power to find treasure."[31] Bushman also implied that although Joseph "connected the plates with money-digging lore,"[32] he eventually distanced himself from the occultic hunters, which, he supposed "may have led to a rift in the Smith family over the next few years"[33] because Joseph Smith Sr. "still hoped to find wealth."[34]

In his book, Bushman cites tales that allege Joseph Smith Sr. spent at least four expeditions "hunting for gold and going back to the house to seek further instructions from Joseph Jr."[35] Bushman even blindly asserts that Joseph and his father argued over whether or not to support digging for treasure through the use of magic.[36] Dean Jessee would later comment in *Dialogue* that Bushman's writings portray Joseph Smith as "known for his ability to see in a stone; that he regarded his ability as a gift from God." He also alleged that treasure hunting was "essential to the discussion of Joseph's life." Jessee took it even further, indicating that Joseph received persecution because the "local money diggers" were angry that he was abandoning his former treasure-hunting friends.[37]

Bushman continues his disingenuous portrayal of the Smith family by describing Lucy Mack Smith as "proud,"[38] "belligerent," "capable

---

30   Richard L. Bushman, *Joseph Smith and the Beginnings of Mormonism* (Urbana and Chicago: University of Illinois Press, 1984), 73.

31   Ibid., 74.

32   Ibid., 73.

33   Ibid., 73-74.

34   Ibid., 74.

35   Ibid., 74.

36   Ibid., 74.

37   "Bushman cites evidence that by the mid-1820s Joseph was known for his ability to see in a stone; that he regarded his ability as a gift from God; that he was reluctant to use his gift to hunt for treasure; and that during the process of extricating himself from association with local money diggers he incurred their wrath—which explains some of the violence heaped upon the Smiths during their sojourn in New York." Dean C. Jessee, "The Benefits of Partisanship," *Dialogue: A Journal of Mormon Thought* 18, no. 4 (Winter 1985): 188.

38   Richard L. Bushman, *Joseph Smith and the Beginnings of Mormonism* (Urbana and Chicago: University of Illinois Press, 1984), 10.

of anger,"[39] and claiming that she had a "high-strung temperament"[40] and sensed acutely the "attention and respect which are ever shown to those who live in fine circumstances."[41] He also inferred that Joseph Smith Sr. expressed "diffidence about religion,"[42] although his wife "tr[ied] to interest her husband in religion."[43] Bushman creates a Father Smith who abdicated family leadership and could not hold down a job, and a Mother Smith who imagined her misfortunes as "exemplifications of their character,"[44] while he suggests that it was actually the Smith family's own incompetence that rendered the family financially destitute.

Arrington championed Bushman's new reinterpretation of the Prophet Joseph and his family. When advising Carol Lynn Pearson on a potential screenplay she was writing on the Prophet's life, Arrington advised Pearson to speak with Mary L. Bradford, editor of *Dialogue*, who encouraged Pearson to "make contact with Richard Bushman" for insight into Joseph Smith—especially because of his "training in psychological interpretation."[45] During the meeting, Arrington commented that Joseph Smith "unquestionably had mystical powers and used them."[46]

In 1987, Arrington expressed praise for Bushman's *Joseph Smith and the Beginnings of Mormonism*. After stating his conjecture that Joseph "and other members of the Smith family had at one time engaged in a search for buried treasure," he enthusiastically endorsed Bushman's work:

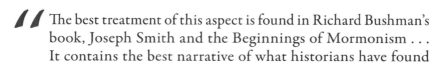 The best treatment of this aspect is found in Richard Bushman's book, Joseph Smith and the Beginnings of Mormonism . . . It contains the best narrative of what historians have found

---

39   Ibid., 10.

40   Ibid., 36.

41   Ibid., 11.

42   Ibid., 36.

43   Ibid., 35.

44   Ibid., 11.

45   Leonard J. Arrington Diaries, August 23, 1979; Leonard J. Arrington and Gary James Bergera, *Confessions of a Mormon Historian: The Diaries of Leonard J. Arrington*, 1971-1997, vol. 2 (Salt Lake City: Signature Books, 2018), 812.

46   Ibid., 2:811.

about Joseph Smith's early life, the family in which he grew up, the translation of the Book of Mormon, and the origins of the Church.[47]

According to Bushman, Arrington—"the patron of virtually all contemporary scholarship in the field of Mormon history"— "sustained and inspired this work [*Joseph Smith and the Beginnings of Mormonism*] from beginning to end."[48] In gratitude, Bushman dedicated the work: "For Leonard Arrington."[49]

Unsurprisingly, other progressive voices soon joined in extreme praise over Bushman's new reconstruing of Mormon origins. Dean Jessee advocated in *Dialogue* that, "Bushman has made a profound contribution to the understanding of Mormonism at its most critical juncture. Written with style and felicity, a product of Bushman's superb analytical powers, *Joseph Smith and the Beginnings of Mormonism* is a major work in Mormon historiography."[50]

What was it that made *Joseph Smith and the Beginnings of Mormonism* such a redefining landmark publication on the shelves of so many Latter-day Saints?

Joseph Smith & the Magic Culture

Both Arrington and Bushman were committed to the advancement of this altogether new history and its accompanying nuanced approach to the Gospel as taught in the Church. Bushman was designated to author the first volume of the Sesquicentennial History, articulating this new, dark portrayal of the early life of Joseph and the founding events of the Restoration, including the coming forth of the Book of Mormon through the deconstructionist lens of New Mormon History. The charge would lay a fresh, neoteric foundation upon which all succeeding volumes would build. The task included answering questions such as: Where did The Church of Jesus Christ of Latter-day Saints come from? What was the environment from which it sprang?

---

47   Leonard J. Arrington Diaries, August 18, 1976; Ibid., 3:462.

48   Richard L. Bushman, *Joseph Smith and the Beginnings of Mormonism* (Urbana and Chicago: University of Illinois Press, 1984), acknowledgments.

49   Ibid., dedication.

50   Dean C. Jessee's review of *Joseph Smith and the Beginnings of Mormonism* by Richard L. Bushman. "The Benefits of Partisanship," *Dialogue: A Journal of Mormon Thought* 18, no. 4 (1985): 189.

Who were Joseph Smith and his family? What are the origins every Latter-day Saint hearkens back to for understanding of their own identity as members of the restored Church in the latter days? Bushman would provide divergent and decidedly misleading answers to these questions; and in doing so, he would introduce a new, contrastingly progressive, 'scholarly' interpretation—a perception so disturbing that no traditionalist leader could possibly accept or countenance. Bushman would transform Joseph Smith from a Christian prophet of God into an occultic, treasure-hunting magician.

Historian Ron Walker, who worked with Arrington both at the Church History Department in the 1970s, and later at BYU, summarized Bushman's portrayal of Joseph Smith:

> *...Joseph Smith and the Beginnings of Mormonism ...* became one of the best sources for Smith's background and early career. Bushman argued that Smith was influenced by "traditional[51] supernaturalism," which included the folk practices of upstate New York. Contesting this influence was Enlightenment rationalism. Bushman believed that Smith eventually outgrew both of these cultural influences and produced something unique. "We can understand Mormonism better," Bushman wrote, "if it is seen as an independent creation, drawing from its environment but also struggling against American culture in an effort to realize itself." If Bushman's conclusion confirmed traditional Mormon belief, he also brought youthful Smith's treasure hunting into the mainstream of LDS scholarship.[52]

Was Joseph Smith born and raised in a family life encompassed by magic, occultism, money digging, and witchcraft? The climate in early America was certainly one of diverse flavors. On the one hand, there were righteous, humble, hardworking, and prayerful colonists. These were the children, grandchildren, great-grandchildren, and so on—the descendants of faithful, pious, and principled New World settlers. These were Pilgrims, Puritans, French Huegenots, Scottish

---

51   Bushman seems to advance a belief in the evolution of social systems and advocates that religion began in a primitive, folk state and therefore the "traditional" religion in America was primitive and essentially superstitious.

52   Ronald W. Walker, David J. Whittaker, and James B. Allen, *Mormon History* (University of Chicago Press, 2001), 124.

Covenanters, and others, having fled maltreatment for conscience sake. These were devout European Reformers who had fled to America to escape torture, death, legal harassment, and other forms of oppression in consequence of principled religious belief. Joseph's ancestors were among these English Pilgrims and Puritans, as well as the Scottish Covenanters.[53] One particularly famous ancestor was John Lathrop. Mark E. Petersen, one of the leaders who endured criticism for opposing Arrington's rewriting of Latter-day Saint history, delivered a tribute to Lathrop in his work, *The Great Prologue*:

// The Reverend Lathrop was a Church of England minister. As he read the Bible carefully, he discovered that there was little harmony between the teachings of that denomination and the scriptures. Being a very conscientious man, he felt that he could not go contrary to the sacred word, so he resigned his position with the state church in 1623 and became the pastor of the First Independent Church of London. In doing so he rejected the state religion and flew in the face of both government and clergy by setting up a separatist group. But he had the courage of his convictions, and he proceeded, regardless of the risks involved.

By direction of the bishop of London, he was arrested and cast into prison. While he was thus incarcerated, his wife died. He was not so much as allowed to attend her funeral, and his children were left with no one to care for them. He made repeated appeals for clemency, but the bishop refused even to listen to him. Finally the orphaned children went to the bishop as a group and personally pleaded for mercy. So pitiful were they in their misery and dejection that the bishop was finally moved, and he released Lathrop on condition that he leave the country. This he did, and, with thirty-two members of his congregation, he went to America.[54]

---

53   "Lucy Mack, daughter of Solomon and Lydia Gates Mack, was descended from John Mack a Scotch immigrant of 1680, who came to Connecticut from Scotland. It is thought that the Mack family dropped their original name, retaining the prefix only because of persecutions on account of religious belief during the religious wars in the British-Isles." Joseph Fielding Smith, *The Life of Joseph F. Smith* (Salt Lake City, Utah: The Deseret News Press, 1938), 30-31.

54   Mark E. Petersen, *The Great Prologue* (Salt Lake City, Utah: Deseret Book Company, 1975), 34-35.

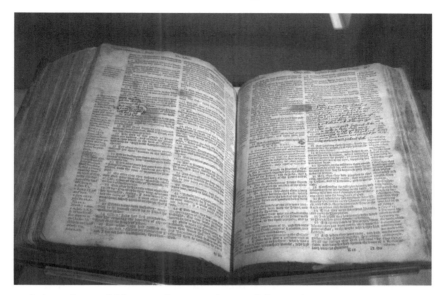

*"The Lothrop Bible"—According to tradition, while traveling to America in 1634,
hot candle wax accidentally fell on Lathrop's Bible, burning holes into several pages.
Lathrop repaired the fragments, rewriting in the passages from memory.*

While Joseph Smith's ancestry hailed from the religious, liberty-infused blood of Israel who emigrated to America from Northern Europe, they lived and toiled side by side with another class of emigrants who could be characterized as the 'Lamans and Lemuels' of the colonies. During the early days of the Nephite civilization, righteous patriarchs Lehi and Nephi, along with their children and followers, lived in righteousness while others of their brethren apostatized from the truth. Those who abandoned the covenants of their fathers served as a "scourge unto thy [Nephi's] seed, to stir them up in the ways of remembrance."[55]

Similarly, leading up to the founding of the Constitutional Republic, the swelling population had become widely diverse in thought and belief, with a broad mixture of both righteous and wicked colonists. Numbers of the descendants of the faithful early stock rejected the virtue and decorum of their fathers, and degenerated into every species of corruption. There were pious, humble followers of Christ; and there was rabble and riffraff, indulging in all manner of debauchery—even Satanic activity— including treasure hunting

---

55   1 Nephi 2:24.

(money digging), divination, conjuring, sorcery, and other forms of the dark arts. These competing societal elements were each grasping for converts throughout the United States during the era of the Prophet Joseph Smith's boyhood.

While progressive history claims that Joseph Smith and his family emerged from drunkenness, extortion, occultism, and the low, degenerate class of early American history, President Gordon B. Hinckley—subsequent to Bushman's new publication— emphatically and explicitly countered Bushman's claims and the allegations of his fellows pressing for this new history:

> ❝ ... [Another phenomenon] is described as the writing of a "new history" of the Church as distinguished from the "old history." It represents, among other things, an effort to ferret out every element of folk magic and the occult in the environment in which Joseph Smith lived to explain what he did and why.
>
> I have no doubt there was folk magic practiced in those days. Without question there were superstitions and the superstitious. I suppose there was some of this in the days when the Savior walked the earth. There is even some in this age of so-called enlightenment.... Similarly, the fact that there were superstitions among the people in the days of Joseph Smith is no evidence whatever that the Church came of such superstition.[56]

Taken in context, President Hinckley's observations are a direct blow to the face of the "new history." President Hinkley had been the point man in negotiations to stop Bushman's book from being published by the Church. He had also not allowed Mark Hofmann's shocking forgeries to soil his faith in our history. Now, he was speaking out graciously—but also publicly and specifically against Arrington's new history movement. While Presidents Hinckley and Benson, along with Elders Packer and Petersen, chose to reject the new sordid history, each of us must study and determine who—and more importantly, *what*—is right.

While it is true there were men and women in early America who practiced magic, witchcraft, occultism, and a variety of other ungodly activities, does this necessarily mean that Joseph Smith and his family were associated with the rabble? Credible sources as well as traditionalists say, NO!

---

56   Gordon B. Hinckley, "Lord, Increase Our Faith," *Ensign*, November 1987.

"the fact that there were [folk magic and] superstitions ... in the days of Joseph Smith is no evidence whatever that the Church came of such"

Gordon B. Hinckley, 1976

The competing narrative of the progressive magical worldview versus the traditional Biblically Christian worldview represents one of the greatest battlegrounds of Latter-day Saint history today. Traditionalists hold that there are no credible historical sources linking Joseph Smith and his family to the alleged use of magic or careers in treasure digging, and that the progressive arguments and alleged historical sources that present such an idea actually spring from slanderous reports published by individuals who circulated rumors, intent on damaging the reputations of the Smiths—and thereby destroying the restored Gospel of Jesus Christ.[57] As the Prophet himself lamented:

---

57 Discussion on the sources cited to portray Joseph Smith and his family as involved in magic and treasure hunting can be found in chapter 16, "Fact-Checking Bushman's Innuendo with Real Data." A thorough investigation and debunking of the claim that Joseph Smith used an occultic seer stone to translate the Book of Mormon can be found in *Seer Stone v. Urim & Thummim: Book of Mormon Translation on Trial* (Joseph Smith Foundation, 2019).

❧❧ ... rumor with her thousand tongues was all the time employed in circulating falsehoods **about my father's family**, and about myself. If I were to relate a thousandth part of them, it would fill up volumes. The persecution ... [became] intolerable ...[58]

The Prophet Joseph Smith has been hounded relentlessly—both during his lifetime and since the event of his death—with every species of lie and defamation that could be invented by the vile and contemptible. He relentlessly pleaded with the Saints, as well as those who knew very little of the Church, to listen to the pure whisperings of the Spirit and reject the disinformation and misrepresentation concerning his life and mission. On one occasion:

❧❧ He commenced by saying, that he knew the prejudices which were abroad in the world against him, but requested us to pay no respect to the rumors which were in circulation respecting him or his doctrines.[59]

While working on his manuscript for the Sesquicentennial History, Richard Bushman previewed the draft for a chapter "on Joseph Smith and the magicians" for the Mormon History Association with Leonard Arrington, Jan Shipps, Marvin Hill, and other MHA members. Arrington later recorded in his diary that the chapter provoked "much discussion as to what kind of history we must write, and for what audience."[60] Bushman would later reflect, when commenting on *Rough Stone Rolling,* that his "shocking" new narrative was "a strain for a lot of people, older people especially."[61] How could these committed progressive historians convert the members to accept their newly revised viewpoint?

---

58   Joseph Smith—History 1:61; emphasis added.

59   Joseph Smith, Discourse, February 5, 1840, p. 1., The Joseph Smith Papers.

60   Leonard J. Arrington Diaries, April 12, 1978; Leonard J. Arrington and Gary James Bergera, *Confessions of a Mormon Historian: The Diaries of Leonard J. Arrington,* 1971-1997, vol. 2 (Salt Lake City: Signature Books, 2018), 507.

61   Blake Bishop, "Richard and Claudia Bushman," YouTube video, 00:45:16, June 12, 2016, https://youtu.be/MA0YS8LWWX4?t=2716.

16

FACT-CHECKING BUSHMAN'S INNUENDO WITH REAL DATA

A careful analysis of the sources used by Bushman in *Joseph Smith and the Beginnings of Mormonism*—as well as other progressive scholarship—reveals that one book appears repeatedly as an authority for the new narrative: *Mormonism Unvailed* [*sic*], published in 1834 by Eber D. Howe.

When first released in 1834 by Howe, *Mormonism Unvailed* included purported affidavits and research collected by Latter-day Saint dissenter Doctor Philastus Hurlbut,[1] who was excommunicated from the Church for immorality less than two years after joining. Hurlbut bragged that "he had deceived Joseph Smith; God, or the Spirit by which he is actuated,"[2] and swore that he would have his "revenge"[3] and would "wash his hands in Joseph Smith's blood."[4]

With that motivation, Hurlbut found support from an anti-Mormon committee who funded him to gather any conceivable evidence to prove the Book of Mormon was a "work of fiction and imagination," and to "completely divest Joseph Smith of all claims to

---

1   Doctor Philastus Hurlbut was not a doctor of medicine or anything else, but rather, carried the name, "Doctor" as his given first name. The Prophet Joseph Smith rightly labeled him, "not so much a doctor of physic, as of falsehood, or by name." Joseph Smith to "the Elders of the Church of the Latter Day Saints," 30 Nov. 1835-1 Dec. 1835, p. 228, The Joseph Smith Papers.

2   Minute Book 1, 21-23 June 1833, p. 22, The Joseph Smith Papers.

3   James Henry Flanigan, *Mormonism Triumphant!* (Liverpool, 1849), 10.

4   George A. Smith, "Historical Discourse," in *Journal of Discourses*, vol. 11 (Liverpool, 1867), 8.

the character of an honest man, and place him at an immeasurable distance from the high station which he pretends to occupy."[5]

Hurlbut journeyed back East to find, or perhaps manufacture, any acquaintance of the Smiths during the time they lived in New York and Pennsylvania who would be willing to excoriate and defame the Smith family. Hurlbut returned to Ohio with his so-called 'affidavits'; but before they could be published, the State of Ohio convicted him on a charge of endangering Joseph Smith's life, and his wife was caught having an affair with a leading member of the Mentor Baptist church. With his reputation as a man of unstable and shady character, and unable to publish himself, Hurlbut delivered his material to E. D. Howe, the anti-Mormon printer who would act as a proxy in the publishing of *Mormonism Unvailed*.

Eventually, Howe would renounce his Christian faith and embrace the growing movement of Spiritualism.[6] As for Hurlbut, many later suspected—and provided evidence and testimony for the assertion—that he robbed and murdered Garrit Brass of Mentor, Ohio, in addition to several other thefts and crimes.[7]

Mormonism Unvailed contained page after page of slanderous material, claiming that the Smith family was lazy, alcoholic, involved in ritual magic and treasure digging, had engaged in occultic animal sacrifice, and a litany of other charges. Upon its publication, Joseph Smith, Oliver Cowdery, and other leaders denounced the book as "all the rediculous [*sic*] stories that could be invented,"[8] and for many decades, faithful Latter-day Saint

---

5   "To the Public," *Painesville Telegraph* (Geauga County), January 31, 1834.

6   Spiritualism was a religious movement identified as beginning in the 1840's in upstate New York, where two sisters, Kate and Margaret Fox, claimed to have established contact with a spirit that communicated through rapping noises. The Fox sisters related that the spirit claimed to have been a murdered peddler. Kate and Margaret became instant sensations as they began to perform as mediums for this "spirit," taking questions from visitors. The idea that spirits were able to communicate with the living through mediums exploded like wildfire on the world's religious stage with converts estimated in the millions. As the Fox sisters' fame as accomplished mediums spread, they began conducting séances for hundreds of eager spectators. Believers in Spiritualism claimed to have "spirit guides," and millions swore to the reality of the phenomena.

7   L. Hannah Stoddard and James F. Stoddard III, *Seer Stone v. Urim & Thummim: Book of Mormon Translation on Trial* (Joseph Smith Foundation, 2019), 129-132.

8   Letter to the Church in Clay County, Missouri, January 22, 1834, in Letterbook 1, p. 81, The Joseph Smith Papers.

Mormonism Unvailed, 1834

historians regarded Hurlbut's affidavits and Howe's publication as nothing worthy of consideration.

Hurlbut's affidavits initially constituted the bedrock for the anti-Mormon attacks on Joseph Smith's character—however, over the past few decades, these controversial allegations have become the foundation for progressive reinterpretations of Joseph Smith. Professor Daniel C. Peterson referred to the affidavits as "an anti-Mormon treasure trove to which generations of critics have turned and returned for years."[9] Succeeding critics of Joseph Smith built on the foundation laid by Hurlbut and the publisher of *Mormonism Unvailed*, E. D. Howe. Without Hurlbut's affidavits, this new image—first painted by and then later adopted by progressives—melts away without support. For years, there have been two competing and entirely contradictory voices: the impugning stories told by the apostates, and the acclamatory

---

9   Daniel Peterson, "Defending the Faith: Were Smiths workers or slackers?" *Deseret News,* May 26, 2011, https://www.deseret.com/2011/5/26/20372831/defending-the-faith-were-smiths-workers-or-slackers.

accounts given by the faithful followers of Joseph Smith. How can we know which of these polarized voices is true?

Fact-Checking the 'Affidavits' with Real Data

Mormonism Unvailed's affidavits present alleged—but extremely suspect and contradictory[10]—signed testimonials from many neighbors of the Smith family who claimed to have been eyewitness to scandalous secrets. According to these accounts, members of the Smith family were reportedly lazy, indolent, beggarly fortune tellers who believed in ghosts and witches; they were an ignorant, superstitious family with no discipline or vested interest in earning an honest income to sustain themselves. Joseph Capron's affidavit imputed that Joseph Smith and "the whole of the family of Smiths, were notorious for indolence, foolery and falsehood. Their great object appeared to be, to live without work."[11] Henry Harris testified that "Joseph Smith, Jr. the pretended Prophet, used to pretend to tell fortunes; he had a stone which he used to put in his hat, by means of which he professed to tell people's fortunes."[12]

> *Enders realized that by evaluating the scientific data, he could either authenticate, or disprove the Hurlbut affidavits*

Was the Prophet indolent and deceptive—an apathetic, inattentive laggard? Could this be proven or disproven with verifiable and quantifiable data?

In 1993, Donald L. Enders published his careful analysis of the available historical data with the intent of fact-checking *Mormonism Unvailed* and other slanderous reports, circulated early on against Joseph Smith and his family. Enders realized that by evaluating the

---

10   Richard L. Anderson, "Joseph Smith's New York Reputation Reappraised," *BYU Studies Quarterly* 10, no. 3 (1970); Richard L. Anderson, "Rodger I. Anderson, Joseph Smith's New York Reputation Reexamined," *Review of Books on the Book of Mormon 1989–2011*, no. 1 (1991).

11   E. D. Howe, *Mormonism Unvailed* (Painesville: E. D. Howe, 1834), 260.

12   Ibid., 251.

Reconstructed Smith family log cabin, by JonRidinger under CC BY 3.0

scientific data he could likely either authenticate or disprove their accounts. In this trailblazing research, he examined "[l]and and tax records, farm account books and correspondence, soil surveys, and interviews with archeological reports, historic building surveys and interviews with agricultural historians and specialists of early nineteenth-century New York."[13]

The long-awaited results of Enders' research would have a decisive impact on the truth claims surrounding Joseph Smith and the Church. If the testable claims in *Mormonism Unvailed* were proven fraudulent, it would serve as a decisive blow to the progressive, New Mormon narrative. Daniel Peterson noted, "If the Hurlbut-Howe affidavits cannot be trusted on matters that can be quantified and tested, there seems little reason to trust their judgments in the less tangible matter of character."[14]

---

13   Donald L. Enders, "The Joseph Smith, Sr., Family: Farmers of the Genesee," in *Joseph Smith: The Prophet, The Man*, ed. Susan Easton Black and Charles D. Tate Jr. (Provo, UT: Religious Studies Center, Brigham Young University, 1993), 213–225.

14   Daniel Peterson, "Defending the Faith: Were Smiths workers or slackers?" *Deseret News,* May 26, 2011, https://www.deseret.com/2011/5/26/20372831/defending-the-faith-were-smiths-workers-or-slackers.

Smith Family Farm in Manchester, New York, by JonRidinger under CC BY 3.0

Enders' work exonerated the traditional narrative after his research concluded "that the Smith version is an honest one." Among the specific questions he sought to answer, the following came to light:

When Enders analyzed New York tax records, he compared the Joseph Smith Sr. farm with 175 farms in the area at the time of their residence there, and found that 71 were valued higher per acre, 14 were valued equally per acre, and 90 had a market value below that of the Smith family farm. In other words, 51.43% of the farms in the area were of lower quality and value as compared with the Smith homestead. Only 40.57% of the farms ranked higher, and 8% were of comparable value. Although revisionist history frequently portrays the Smith family as of lower class, beggarly and impoverished members of their community, the historical data reveals an entirely different story. Based on the stature of the family's farm, these slightly-above-middle-class, respectable citizens persevered in spite of the trials they often faced as external forces repeatedly attempted to crush the family's purpose and future mission related to the Restoration.

Of the 253 farms in Manchester Township, only **24.51%**—merely sixty-two farms—boasted a **larger** acreage than Joseph Smith Sr.'s sizeable spread, while two-thirds, or **66.4%** of the township's other farms were **smaller**—some of them considerably so. Less than a tenth, or 8.7%, of the surrounding farms were of the same size. The final summation of the data reveals that the Smith family farm ranked larger in size, and was better maintained, than the majority of their neighbors. The family built and sustained a valuable homestead, affirming their respectability and civility among their fellow citizens, and refuting claims that they were lower-class residents.

Severe persecution for the Smith family began around the time of the First Vision, intensifying and expanding with the coming forth of later revelations. After the Smith family left the area, increasing sentiment began to emerge, as some neighbors invented accusations and manufactured gossip, accusing the Smith family of being a set of "lazy, indolent," "intemperate," and "worthless men, very much addicted to lying."[15] Paradoxically, a further review of the data reveals that the vindictiveness manifested against the Smith family came primarily from the men and women who owned and worked the farms that were smaller in size and of lower value than the Smith's farm:

// The Staffords, Stoddards,[16] Chases, and Caprons were neighborhood residents who spoke poorly of the Smiths. Only one of the ten families in this four-family group had property assessed more valuable than the Smiths'. Of the five families in the Stafford family group, none had a higher appraisal than the Smiths. . . . In comparison to others in the township and neighborhood, the Smiths' efforts and accomplishments were superior to most. In the township, only 40 percent of the farms were worth more per acre and just 25 percent were larger. In the "neighborhoods," only 29 percent of the farms were worth more and only 26 percent were larger.[17]

What motivated the owners of these lower-class farms to express such contempt toward the Smiths as they fabricated their fallacious misrepresentations about the family, their property, and their work ethic? One can only wonder.

---

15   E. D. Howe, *Mormonism Unvailed* (Painesville: E. D. Howe, 1834), 11, 248.

16   No relation to the authors of this book.

17   Donald L. Enders, "The Joseph Smith, Sr., Family: Farmers of the Genesee," in *Joseph Smith: The Prophet, The Man*, ed. Susan Easton Black and Charles D. Tate Jr. (Provo, UT: Religious Studies Center, Brigham Young University, 1993).

Lazy or Industrious?

A vast host of spurious claims made their debut in chapter 1 of
Mormonism Unvailed—most of which have now made their
reappearance in various New Mormon historical accounts:

> **"** All who became intimate with them during this period, unite
> in representing the general character of old Joseph and wife, the
> parents of the pretended Prophet, as lazy, indolent, ignorant
> and superstitious—having a firm belief in ghosts and witches;
> the telling of fortunes; pretending to believe that the earth
> was filled with hidden treasures, buried there by Kid or the
> Spaniards. Being miserably poor, and not much disposed to
> obtain an honorable livelihood by labor, the energies of their
> minds seemed to be mostly directed towards finding where
> these treasures were concealed, and the best mode of acquiring
> their possession.[18]

David Stafford, one of the Smith's neighbors, swore out an affidavit
that made it into *Mormonism Unvailed*, in which he claimed that:

> **"** It is well known, that the *general employment* of the Smith family
> was money digging and fortune-telling. They kept around them
> *constantly*, a gang of worthless fellows who dug for money [at]
> nights, and were idle in the day time. It was a mystery to their
> neighbors how they got their living.[19]

Contrary to such claims, Enders found, instead, references to
twenty-four specific labors performed by the Smiths in *addition* to
the astonishing work required to account for the improvements they
had made to their own home and farm. The list of tasks included the
following items of manual labor:

- digging and rocking up wells

- mowing

- coopering and repairing barrels (including dye tubs, barrels,
  water and sap buckets)

---

18   E. D. Howe, *Mormonism Unvailed* (Painesville: E. D. Howe, 1834), 11.

19   Ibid., 249; emphasis added.

- constructing cisterns
- harvesting crops
- digging for salt
- constructing stone walls and fireplaces
- flailing grain
- butchering
- digging coal
- hauling stone

Enders also noted that at least "eight wells in three townships are attributed to the Smiths. They likely dug and rocked others, including some of the 11 wells dug on the farm of Lemuel Durfee." Despite their already surprising workload, the Smiths also performed services for hire, and produced items for resale, such as:

- split-wood chairs and baskets
- cordwood
- modest carpentry work
- cider
- garden produce
- bee-gum
- maple syrup
- maple sugar

The exhausting list continues as the Smiths also engaged in activities not listed previously—including, but certainly not limited to:

- hunting and trapping
- teaching school
- providing domestic service
- carting
- washing clothes
- painting oil-cloth coverings
- painting chairs

Lucy Mack Smith recorded in her personal history that "In the spring after we moved onto the farm we commenced making mapel [*sic*] sugar of which we averaged 1000 lbs per year."[20] This was no small feat, as Daniel Peterson commented after calculating that this level of production would require having "tapped more than 500 trees, collected 60,000 pounds of sap and burned 10,000 pounds of wood over perhaps a week of 20-to 24-hour days to boil off the water." "Does that sound lazy?" Peterson asked incredulously.[21] Even the antagonistic Fawn Brodie acknowledged the Smith family's efforts, noting that the family "made seven thousand pounds in one season and won the fifty-dollar bounty for top production in the county."[22]

It would be difficult, and likely impossible, to find a 21st-century family who could boast of comparable productivity and labor like that of Joseph and Lucy Mack Smith, along with their children. In spite of the labor demands imposed on the family, the Smith parents never neglected to prioritize gospel study and family prayer. They held family scripture study or devotionals *twice every day*. Mark L. McConkie noted in his biography of Joseph Smith Sr. that "Father Smith taught them in his own home school and used the Bible as a text." McConkie credited the Smith family with holding what he called the "precursor to the family home evening," except that instead of once a week meetings—a goal aspired to by many Latter-day Saint families—the Smiths held their family gatherings twice each day:

 From the early moments of their marriage, they held daily family devotionals, which continued until their advanced years. These devotionals were held both in the mornings and in the evenings and included singing and prayer.[23]

---

20   Lucy Mack Smith, History, 1844–1845, p. 9, bk. 3, The Joseph Smith Papers.

21   Daniel Peterson, "Did Joseph Smith take the easy path?" *Deseret News*, October 1, 2015, https://www.deseret.com/2015/10/1/20573399/did-joseph-smith-take-the-easy-path.

22   Fawn McKay Brodie, *No Man Knows My History: The Life of Joseph Smith, the Mormon Prophet* (United States: Vintage Books, 1995) 10-11.

23   William remembered that evening prayer, Bible reading and singing occurred daily as far back as he could remember.

"Were your folks religiously inclined before Joseph saw the angel", asked Bro. Briggs.

"Yes we always had family prayer since I can remember. I well remember father

... [O]ur records show that the Smiths raised their children on daily devotionals, in which they prayed and sang, sometimes even upon bended knee. William reports that this practice stretched back as far as he could remember. The family even designated a special spot in the neighboring groves where the family would retire for "offering up their secret devotions to God."[24]

Repackaging Hurlbut

Daniel C. Peterson, a professor of Islamic and Arabic Studies, endorses the progressive position on many aspects of Latter-day Saint history and theology. Some of his conclusions, however, align with traditionalist thought. In an article entitled, "Can the 1834 Affidavits Attacking the Smith Family Be Trusted?" Peterson commented on research controverting and essentially invalidating the anti-Mormon affidavits gathered by Hurlbut as published in *Mormonism Unvailed*. Peterson summarized the study by emphasizing the central issue underlying attacks on the Restoration today:

---

used to carry his spectacles in his vest pocked [*sic*], (feeling in his lower right hand pocket to show us how and where) and when us boys saw him feel for his specks, we knew that was a signal to get ready for prayer, and if we did not notice it mother would say, 'William', or whoever was the negligent one, 'get ready for prayer.' After prayer we had a song we would sing, I remember part of it yet.

"Another day has passed and gone,

"We lay our garments by." "Wm. B. Smith's last Statement," *Zion's Ensign* 5, no. 3 (January 13, 1894): 6; Church History Library, https://catalog.churchofjesuschrist.org/assets?id=b1ab0810-4723-4d54-ac00-2f95725217af&crate=0&index=5.

William also recalled "I was called upon to listen to prayers both night and morning." William Smith, Notes on Chambers' life of Joseph Smith, p. 29, Church History Library, https://catalog.churchofjesuschrist.org/assets?id=7ce89849-3bb8-4ca4-9627-3c283aec0bae&crate=0&index=34. The Smith's held a morning "service, namely, reading, singing and praying" in 1829. Lucy Mack Smith, History, 1845, p. 153, The Joseph Smith Papers. The Smiths held evening devotions at their home in Waterloo, New York in 1830. These evening services were open to their neighbors, often resulting in "some dozen or twenty persons" arriving to join the Smiths in praying and singing. Lucy Mack Smith, History, 1845, p. 189, The Joseph Smith Papers.

24   Mark L. McConkie, *The Father of the Prophet: Stories and Insights from the Life of Joseph Smith, Sr.* (United States: Bookcraft, 1993) 60, 66.

❙❙ The character and claims of Joseph Smith are fundamental to the claims of the Church he founded. Knowing this, critics of the Prophet have contended for more than a century and a half that he and his family were the kind of people from whom nobody would want to buy a used car, much less receive a plan of salvation.[25]

This was not news for the early Saints. For many decades, faithful Latter-day Saint historians considered the affidavits gathered by Hurlbut and published in *Mormonism Unvailed* as nothing more than "false and scandalous reports" that detractors hurled constantly toward the Prophet Joseph Smith, who openly repudiated them while he was alive.

However, during the mid-20th century, Richard Bushman, with the hearty encouragement of Leonard Arrington, decided the 'traditional,' eyewitness, and fact-based Latter-day Saint narrative needed a makeover, with changes especially to what he saw as a 'sanitized' view of the Prophet Joseph Smith. He later recalled:

❙❙ The response of Mormon historians in the 1970s was to deny almost everything. Beyond the Josiah Stowell incident, they argued, all the money digging stories were fabrications of Joseph Smith's enemies. They claimed that the sources for the stories were corrupted and therefore not to be trusted. Most of the accounts came from a set of affidavits collected by Philastus Hurlbut . . .

Church historians thought Hurlbut's motives were too suspect to trust his findings. What reason was there to believe him? . . .

The first thing I [Bushman] decided was that I could not dismiss all of Hurlbut's affidavits with a wave of a hand. Academic historians had taken them seriously, and so should I. . . .

As I read the Hurlbut affidavits, I picked up clues that not only the Smiths but also many of their neighbors were looking for treasure in Palmyra in the 1820s. . . . The Smiths may have been subscribing to folk religion, but in this they were part of

---

25   Daniel Peterson, "Defending the Faith: Were Smiths workers or slackers?" *Deseret News,* May 26, 2011, https://www.deseret.com/2011/5/26/20372831/defending-the-faith-were-smiths-workers-or-slackers.

a culture found virtually everywhere among Yankees of their generation. It may not have been the most uplifting activity, and some scoffed, but it was something like reading astrological charts today—a little goofy but harmless.[26]

Lucy Mack Smith:
Abrac, Magic Circles, & Soothsaying

In the second chapter of *Joseph Smith and the Beginnings of Mormonism,* under the title, "The First Vision," Bushman claimed that Lucy Mack Smith, the mother of the Prophet, had a fluent "knowledge of magic, formulas and rituals." Bushman asserted that when Joseph related his visit with the Angel Moroni to Mother Smith, she "seemed to understand how the story of Moroni might be mistakenly understood as a tale of money digging."[27] Bushman also alleged that Joseph Smith's parents were fascinated with magic, and that "Joseph Smith Sr., stimulated by his son's supernatural experiences, searched for treasure with the help of his family."[28] Moreover, Bushman argued that the Smith family took Moroni's visit as a personal confirmation of "the entire culture of magic."[29]

To support these surly, ignoble claims, Bushman drew from a statement made by Mother Smith as evidence that the Smith family possessed a deep, personal understanding of ritualistic magic. The fact remains that the progressive historian crowd has no contemporaneous Latter-day Saint source providing any indication whatsoever that Joseph Smith involved himself in money-digging activities. Because of this, they frequently resort to misrepresenting and perfidiously misinterpreting a statement from Lucy Smith,[30]

---

26   Richard L. Bushman, "Joseph Smith and Money Digging," in *A Reason for Faith: Navigating LDS Doctrine & Church History,* ed. Laura H. Hales (Provo, UT: Religious Studies Center, Brigham Young University, 2016), 2-3.

27   Richard L. Bushman, *Joseph Smith and the Beginnings of Mormonism* (Urbana and Chicago: University of Illinois Press, 1984), 72.

28   Ibid., 73.

29   Ibid., 73.

30   John Dehlin host, "Folk Magic / Treasure Digging," *Mormon Stories,* February 15, 2019, https://www.mormonstories.org/truth-claims/joseph-smith/treasure/; Richard L. Bushman, *Joseph Smith and the Beginnings of Mormonism* (Urbana and Chicago: University of Illinois Press, 1984), 72-73; Richard L. Bushman, *Rough Stone Rolling* (New York: Vintage Books, 2007), 50-51.

in their attempt to 'create' an alleged Latter-day Saint source. Referencing her autobiography, Bushman quotes Mother Smith, who recorded:

> ❙❙ I shall change my theme for the present, but let not my reader suppose that because I shall pursue another topic for a season that we stopt [*sic*] our labor and went at trying to win the faculty of Abrac drawing Magic circles or sooth saying to the neglect of all kinds of business we never during our lives suffered one important interest to swallow up every other obligation but whilst we worked with our hands we endeavored to remember the service of & the welfare of our souls.[31]

Bushman then uses an entirely twisted *interpretation* of Lucy Smith's words to argue in his antithetic and discrepant *Beginnings of Mormonism* that:

> ❙❙ The Smith family at first was no more able to distinguish true religion from superstition than their neighbors. . . . they were as susceptible to the neighbors' belief in magic as they were to the teachings of orthodox ministers. Joseph's discovery of the seerstone and the revelation of Moroni and the gold plates confused them even further. The visit of the angel seemed to confirm the beliefs of their superstitious neighbors. . . .
>
> [Lucy] revealed a knowledge of magic formulas and rituals. It seems likely that Joseph, Sr., stimulated by his son's supernatural experiences, searched for treasure with the help of his family. Understandably, Moroni's visit and the discovery of the seerstone appeared to confirm the entire culture of magic.[32]

Later, in *Rough Stone Rolling*, Bushman repeats the argument, claiming that Lucy's comment demonstrates, "[t]he Smiths were as susceptible as their neighbors to treasure-seeking folklore. . . . Magic and religion melded in Smith family culture."[33] Did Mother Smith veritably admit to her family's involvement in magic and the occult?

---

31 Lucy Mack Smith, History, 1844–1845, p. 10, bk. 3, The Joseph Smith Papers.

32 Richard L. Bushman, *Joseph Smith and the Beginnings of Mormonism* (Urbana and Chicago: University of Illinois Press, 1984), 72-73.

33 Richard L. Bushman, *Rough Stone Rolling* (New York: Vintage Books, 2007), 50-51.

Lucy Mack Smith, Mother of the Prophet

First, do we understand the true context of what Lucy Smith genuinely stated? The paragraph immediately preceding Bushman's quotation details the Smith family's farm labor, including harvesting 1000 lbs of maple sugar, planting a large orchard, and paying off their debts.[34] Contrary to many false progressive claims, evidence shows that the Smiths were remarkably industrious and hard working.

Lucy Smith's history proceeds with a *denial* of the accusations that her family was involved in "the faculty of Abrac" or spent evenings "drawing Magic circles or sooth saying." She is clear in stating, "**let not my reader suppose** that because I shall pursue another topic for a season that we stopt [*sic*] our labor and went at trying to win the faculty of Abrac drawing Magic circles or sooth saying."[35]

The context of Lucy's denial is her announcement that she is about to "change [her] theme for the present," about to shift from an

---

34   "In the spring after we moved onto the farm we commenced making mapel [*sic*] sugar of which we averaged 1000 lbs per year. we then began to make preparations for building a house as the Land Agent of whom we purchased our farm was dead and we could not make the last payment we also planted a large orchard and made every possible preparation for ease when advanced age should deprive us of the ability to make those pysical [*sic*] exertions of which we were then capable." Lucy Mack Smith, History, 1844–1845, p. 9-10, The Joseph Smith Papers.

35   Lucy Mack Smith, History, 1844–1845, p. 10, bk. 3, The Joseph Smith Papers; emphasis added.

accounting of the Smith family's farm labor to an account detailing the translation and coming forth of the Book of Mormon and other spiritual gifts experienced by her family—not a foray into folk magic. As she changes the focus of her narrative, she wisely appears to be wary that someone could give credence to the lies then circulating about her family; that the tales of "Angel Moroni" and "gold plates" were allegedly part of a magical treasure-digging career within a lazy family that had abandoned their honest farm labor in exchange for a chase after treasure buried in the earth.

The reader will recall that Lucy Mack Smith dictated her history as a 70-year-old widow who had endured decades of vicious ridicule, slander, and the vilest persecution as a direct consequence of her son's testimony and divine mission. Joseph was only fourteen years old when a Methodist minister mocked him for his account of the First Vision, and sneeringly insisted that his vision "was all of the devil, that there were no such things as visions or revelations in these days."[36] Lucy and her family had endured "great persecution, which continued to increase," including the cold shoulders, jealousy, and spite—spewing from their disapproving neighbors. The publishing of lies in local and distant newspapers and books—nearly all of which dismissed the Prophet's testimony—wildly spun and perverted his experiences as occultic. Her beloved husband, Joseph Smith Sr., died a premature death following the effects of the persecution in Missouri. Her eldest living sons, Joseph and Hyrum, were shot and murdered in Carthage Jail. And finally, her sons Don Carlos and Samuel seem to have passed away under questionable circumstances—possibly through sinister means.

Lucy "explicitly denies that they were involved in such things [magic]. She also denies that the Smiths were lazy"

As Lucy sat down to dictate her history in 1844,[37] only a few months after the Carthage martyrdom, persecution in Nauvoo was

---

36   Joseph Smith—History 1:21.

37   Lucy Mack Smith began her manuscript in 1844, concluding in 1845.

intensifying daily. Soon, the Saints would abandon their homes, driven cruelly from their beautiful City of Joseph which they had worked so diligently to build up as a place of refuge—a bastion of freedom where they had hoped to practice their religion according to the dictates of conscience. Sadly, slander and vilification were daily trials in the life of Mother Smith—one undeniably marked by great suffering and sacrifice.

As she prepared to give her eyewitness account of the coming forth of the Book of Mormon, she knew all too well that she was countering the popular, predominant 'magic' spin deeply ingrained in the psyche of the Saint's detractors. To the general public, the story of the Book of Mormon had been horribly twisted by men like Willard Chase and Hurlbut into a demonic account of dealings with the underworld. Now, as Lucy Smith prepared to speak, she rightly felt that she must precede her own eyewitness account by setting the record *straight*. Her husband and sons were *not* indolent men, nor were they obsessed with treasure seeking and magic. Again, her record is emphatically clear on the issue: "let not my reader suppose that . . . we stopt [*sic*] our labor and went at trying to win the faculty of Abrac drawing Magic circles or sooth saying."[38]

William Hamblin (Ph.D. University of Michigan) has likewise concluded that Lucy Mack Smith's statement was clearly a denial—not an admission—of 'magical' activity:

> By the time Lucy Smith wrote this text in 1845, anti-Mormons were alleging that Joseph had been seeking treasure by drawing magic circles. She explicitly denies that they were involved in such things. She also denies that the Smiths were lazy. . . . Lucy Smith's text provides no other mention of the supposedly "important interest" of magical activities but does deal prominently with their religious and business concerns. If magic activities were such an important part of Joseph Smith's life and Lucy was speaking of them in a positive sense as "important interests," why did she not talk about them further in any unambiguous passage?[39]

---

38   Lucy Mack Smith, History, 1844–1845, p. 10, bk. 3, The Joseph Smith Papers.

39   William J. Hamblin, "That Old Black Magic," Review of *Early Mormonism and the Magic World View*, revised and enlarged edition, by D. Michael Quinn, *FARMS Review of Books* 12, no. 2 (2000): 225–394.

The reader should note that positive references—or even allusions—to magic, treasure digging, superstitious tradition, etc. do not appear in *any* of the Smith family's writings, including extended family. It is a point of fact that not one shred of evidence currently exists that any of the Smiths were ever involved in, dabbled with, or even expressed a casual interest in magic.

For a thorough analysis of the doctrinal and scriptural support refuting claims that Joseph Smith and his family engaged in occultic activity, see Chapter 15 "Joseph Smith: 'Village Seer'? Magic?" in *Seer Stone v. Urim & Thummim: Book of Mormon Translation on Trial.*

In addition to the historical record, from a doctrinal and scriptural approach, it should be noted that "sooth-saying" is repeatedly condemned in scripture, specifically in 2 Kings 17:17, Deuteronomy 18:9-14, and Leviticus 19:26. Magic circles that were used in the conjuration of and communion with devils were also strictly forbidden. The Smiths were devout Christians; and such activity was, no doubt, unthinkable. These sordid and debauched pursuits that Richard Bushman and other New Mormon Historians suggest were a "preparatory gospel"[40] for Joseph, were in fact, punishable by death according to the laws revealed by Jehovah in the Old Testament. These dark acts were also denounced as "abominations" by Jesus Christ in the New Testament. Are we to accept the premise adopted by progressive historians that Joseph was an "abomination unto the Lord" just prior to, or even during, the translation of the Book of Mormon? Such a notion defies every sensibility of reason. Scripture declares that the Son of God "is the same yesterday, today, and forever."[41] The same God who unequivocally and unmistakably condemned witchcraft during ancient times is the same God who appeared to the young Joseph in the Sacred Grove. Therefore, while our modernist, 'politically-correct' culture may condone occultic activity—while it may combine magic and heavenly manifestations into the same 'mystic arts' category

40   Richard L. Bushman, *Rough Stone Rolling* (New York: Vintage Books, 2007), 54.

41   1 Nephi 10:18, Mormon 9:9, Hebrews 13:8.

and promote the dark arts in literature, fashion, film, music, games, holidays, and other 'diversions'—the Lord Jehovah has never changed His everlasting position.

Bushman argues that the "polite world" scorned Joseph and his fellow "Palmyra and Manchester money diggers."[42] These disreputable money diggers "dared not openly describe their resort to magic for fear of ridicule from the fashionably educated, and yet they could not overcome their fascination with the lore that seeped through to them from the past."[43] According to the New Mormon History, the Smith family was among those who could not suppress their fascination with magic. Rather, "[t]he Smith family at first was no more able to distinguish true religion from superstition than their neighbors."[44] In fact, their Christian faith "made it easy to believe in guardian spirits and magical powers."[45] According to Bushman, Christianity and the occult walk hand in hand, and the Smith family were apparently not members of polite society.

> *Bushman drew upon the affidavits given by enemies of the Smith family and others who were willing to repeat contemptible rumors.*

To build his case for the new, revised history, Bushman drew upon the affidavits given by enemies of the Smith family and others who were willing to repeat contemptible rumors. The unfortunate and repetitious claim that the Smith family was associated with treasure digging and magic continues to occupy a prominent place at the progressive table, and represents the fundamental message of the New Mormon History.

This theme continues as a common source of anxiety and faith crisis for increasing numbers who feel betrayed by a Church with

---

42   Richard L. Bushman, *Joseph Smith and the Beginnings of Mormonism* (Urbana and Chicago: University of Illinois Press, 1984), 71.

43   Ibid., 71-72.

44   Ibid., 72.

45   Ibid., 72.

a new, incompatible, even repugnant, story—a story no devoted, Bible-honoring Christian can possibly accept. Furthermore, no traditional, faithful Evangelical, Seventh Day Adventist, Jehovah's Witness, Catholic, or otherwise Christian would take seriously an occultic, indolent, drunken ne'er-do-good 'prophet.'

While the progressive message that Joseph Smith and his family dabbled in occult magic and treasure digging has become increasingly widespread and established today—during the 1970s when Bushman was conjuring his manuscript, this revolting concept was foreign to most Latter-day Saints, and intensely repulsive to informed traditionalists, including Ezra Taft Benson.

And yet, a determined Arrington continued to trailblaze through the obstructions of traditionalist position, professing the reception of a heavenly message: "You are doing the right thing. I'm going to involve you in the writing of the history of my church."[46]

Canceling the New History

During the fall of 1978, Lowell Durham, with Deseret Book, spoke with Arrington on the phone, explaining that he had received the green light to proceed with the Sesquicentennial History. All authors were "encouraged to finish their manuscripts," which they would then submit for review—first to Leonard Arrington, then to Elder Homer Durham, and finally to the First Presidency.[47]

After a year of uncertainty—including Elder Gordon B. Hinckley's contact with the Church's legal department—and endless, swirling rumors that the history would never see publication, this welcome news came as a breath of fresh air for Leonard and his downcast team of deconstructionists. Almost immediately, the group submitted four of the manuscripts: Bushman's work, along with three other volumes by Milton V. Backman, Thomas G. Alexander, and Richard O. Cowan.

---

46   Bob Mims, "New Collection of Leonard Arrington's Vast Journals Shows Battles the Mormon Historian Had with LDS Leaders over Telling the Truth about the Church's Past," *The Salt Lake Tribune*, May 9, 2018, https://www.sltrib.com/religion/2018/05/09/new-collection-of-leonard-arringtons-vast-journals-shows-battles-the-mormon-historian-had-with-lds-leaders-over-telling-the-truth-about-the-churchs-past/.

47   Leonard J. Arrington Diaries, May 8, 1978; Leonard J. Arrington and Gary James Bergera, *Confessions of a Mormon Historian: The Diaries of Leonard J. Arrington*, 1971-1997, vol. 2 (Salt Lake City: Signature Books, 2018), 525.

Initial excitement waned, however, as over the next year, a strange, uneasy silence settled over the project. Several months later, in July 1979, Arrington sought for an update from Elder Durham on the status of the project, but was given "the impression that there may be interminable delays on some of the sesquicentennial histories; didn't sound like he had any interest in speeding up the processes, either."[48] Another four months passed while the deafening silence continued to oppress the group. They submitted another volume; but still there was no answer.

An additional four months later, Arrington—pushed to the point of exasperation—finally received information from Lowell Durham who had recently attended a meeting with some members of the Twelve wherein the Sesquicentennial History was discussed. Arrington's takeaway from Durham's report was that "the real obstacles are Elders [Ezra Taft] Benson and [Mark E.] Petersen. Lowell thinks he can win Elder Petersen over, but thinks Elder Benson has such a mind fix about historians that he will never budge."[49] Arrington

> *Bushman's book was the "basis of the divided opinions among the Quorum of the Twelve."*

lamented that cancelling the history would "be taken by many in and out of the Church as an unwillingness to face the facts of our past. . . . It is not fair to the authors to make an agreement and then fail to hold up the Church's side of the bargain."[50]

The silence continued. On August 9, 1980, Arrington recorded his fear that the volumes submitted by Richard Bushman and two other authors "have not been released for publication and it appears

---

48   Leonard J. Arrington Diaries, July 31, 1979; Ibid., 804.

49   Leonard J. Arrington Diaries, April 22, 1980; Ibid., 3:17.

50   Gregory A. Prince, *Leonard Arrington and the Writing of Mormon History* (Salt Lake City, UT: Tanner Trust Fund and J. Willard Marriott Library, 2016), 335. Prince cites Leonard J. Arrington's diary, April 24, 1980. However, although the date, April 24, 1980, does appear in the edited compilation of Arrington's diaries by Gary James Bergera (*Confessions of a Mormon Historian: The Diaries of Leonard J. Arrington*), this quote is not included in that entry.

that they simply sit on the shelf 'until someone dies.'"[51] Eventually, Arrington was informed of disunity among the Twelve, and that the lack of consensus led to a resolution that the authors would be paid for their work on the manuscripts and given the option to find another publisher. The Church's printing of Bushman's volume was an absolute impossibility; it had been "the focal point of all the deliberation about the whole series"[52] and the "basis of the divided opinions among the Quorum of the Twelve."[53] It appeared that for Ezra Taft Benson, Boyd K. Packer, and others, Bushman's portrayal of Joseph Smith as a treasure-digging, greedy, and occultic young derelict was non-negotiable. This history would never be promoted by the Church as long as certain men had the breath to fight. Arrington's mistake, according to his biographer, was that he had underestimated "the existential threat that the series represented to the religious worldview of several apostles," leaving him "genuinely shocked when the series was ultimately canceled in spite of the First Presidency's initial approval . . ."[54]

The Church had formally pulled the plug on the Sesquicentennial History, and Arrington blamed his three nemeses—Benson, Petersen, and Packer, the men responsible for stonewalling his new history. Arrington's son, Carl, later remembered that cancelling the Sesquicentennial History was like "a knife in the heart" for his father.[55]

The cancelling of the history project was not the end of Arrington's woes; he soon had bigger complications to work through. Leonard Arrington and his History Division were about to find themselves eliminated, and—in his mind—exiled to BYU.

---

51   Leonard J. Arrington Diaries, August 9, 1980; Leonard J. Arrington and Gary James Bergera, *Confessions of a Mormon Historian: The Diaries of Leonard J. Arrington*, 1971-1997, vol. 3 (Salt Lake City: Signature Books, 2018), 97.

52   Leonard J. Arrington Diaries, December 30, 1980; Ibid., 143.

53   Gregory A. Prince, *Leonard Arrington and the Writing of Mormon History* (Salt Lake City, UT: Tanner Trust Fund and J. Willard Marriott Library, 2016), 337.

54   Ibid., 170.

55   Ibid., 338.

17

INTERRUPTING THE MYSTICAL CALL
Disassembling His Staff

Several years of controversy and dissention at Church headquarters were taking their toll on the embattled History Division. Still, Leonard Arrington truly believed he had a hallowed, mystical calling from his God to rewrite the history of the Latter-day Saints. Arrington's daughter, Susan Arrington Madsen, recalled that her father told her he had received a heavenly message at some unidentified point wherein "he felt a closeness to God he had never felt before." Arrington felt he received the supernatural message: "You are doing the right thing. I'm going to involve you in the writing of the history of my church."[1]

Ensign Peak Retreat

On June 23, 1978, an enthusiastic Leonard Arrington and his New Mormon History associates in the History Division of the Church hiked to the top of Ensign Peak. With the "breeze ruffling [Arrington's] white hair," participants later remembered their mentor "standing on Ensign Peak and earnestly counseling his colleagues from the Church History Division, in the words of Ezekiel, to 'make these bones live' as they wrote history."[2] Arrington's followers were on a mission to fashion and unfurl a new ensign, a new history—even a new Church. A new

---

1   Bob Mims, "New collection of Leonard Arrington's vast journals shows battles the Mormon historian had with LDS leaders over telling the truth about the church's past," *The Salt Lake Tribune*, May 9, 2018, https://www.sltrib.com/religion/2018/05/09/new-collection-of-leonard-arringtons-vast-journals-shows-battles-the-mormon-historian-had-with-lds-leaders-over-telling-the-truth-about-the-churchs-past/.

2   "In Memoriam, Leonard J. Arrington," *Journal of Mormon History* 25, no. 1 (February 15, 1999): 7.

ensign was indeed in the process of being unfurled.

For those committed to the New Mormon History cause, Arrington stood as their Socrates—their mentor, veritably a father to the movement. Mario De Pillis, a Roman Catholic professor of American Religious history, held Arrington in high regard, referring to him as the "presiding spirit of the community of Mormon scholars."[3] Dean L. May thought of him as a "father to me,"[4] and Klaus Hansen referred to the rising generation of Mormon scholars as "Leonard's 'children.'"[5] When the History Division celebrated Pioneer Day in 1978, the well-attended retreat began with a potluck dinner and program—including a tribute to Arrington's life with a "tape recording of moments from the life of LJA: Aunt Callie (Arrington) [Ward] on LJA as a baby, and Grace, James, and Susan on LJA in later life."[6]

Arrington's drive stemmed, in part, from a mystical epiphany he experienced while working on *Great Basin Kingdom*[7]—which he interpreted as a personal calling from God. Greg Prince commented on what Arrington saw as his divine mandate:

 Reorienting an entire church to a new way of viewing its own history was a daunting challenge, and Leonard had at least some awareness of how difficult the task would be. But he

---

3   Ibid., 14.

4   Ibid., 16. Dean L. May was a history professor at the University of Utah, and served as Mormon History Association president in 2002. He joined the Church Historical Department and worked with Leonard Arrington in 1974. May also served on the Utah State Board of History, edited for the Journal of Mormon History (1982–1985), and wrote nearly 50 articles in publications such as *Journal of Mormon History, Utah Historical Quarterly, Church History, Journal of Family History, Sociology and Social Research, Idaho Yesterdays, Population Studies,* and *Agricultural History.*

5   Ibid., 14.

Klaus Hansen taught history at Queen's University, Ontario for over 30 years. (1968-2001) Hansen was an advocate of New Mormon History, contributing to works such as *The New Mormon History: Revisionist Essays on the Past* and *Joseph Smith, Jr.: Reappraisals After Two Centuries.*

6   Leonard J. Arrington Diaries, June 24, 1978; Leonard J. Arrington and Gary James Bergera, *Confessions of a Mormon Historian: The Diaries of Leonard J. Arrington*, 1971-1997, vol. 2 (Salt Lake City: Signature Books, 2018), 556.

7   See *Faith Crisis, Volume 1*, chapter 11, "Arrington's Epiphany." James and Hannah Stoddard, *Faith Crisis, Volume 1: We Were NOT Betrayed!* (Joseph Smith Foundation, 2020), 141.

also saw his role and that of his colleagues as responding to a divine mandate. . . . According to Ron Esplin . . . Leonard saw himself as racing against time in a narrowing window for his "grand experiment," but "if he could produce enough, quickly enough, the body of evidence, the weight of that evidence would be sufficient to prove the experiment and give some additional time and space for protection."[8]

Disassembling the History Division

It appeared that Arrington's desperate race against time was accelerating as cautious leaders erected defensive walls, and all the while Ezra Taft Benson and others appeared to increase their level of pushback. During the spring of 1978, a letter from the First Presidency's office[9]—drafted by Spencer W. Kimball and N. Eldon Tanner, and addressed to Elder Homer Durham[10]—sent shockwaves through Arrington's division. The letter called for an "altered direction."[11] Instead of a commission to carry on in the work of writing history for the Latter-day Saints, the letter essentially demoted these historians to the role of maintaining archives and conducting supervised research for the use of general authorities. The foreboding letter also contained indirect warnings of impending budget cuts and staff reductions.

For James B. Allen, co-author of *The Story of the Latter-day Saints*, "[Elder] Durham had sounded a death knell, that the 'golden age' of the History Division was now over."[12] Davis Bitton described a pervasive, "dull gloom" that hung over the division: "People quietly go about their work, but the old enthusiasm is gone."[13] Ron Walker

---

8   Gregory A. Prince, *Leonard Arrington and the Writing of Mormon History* (Salt Lake City, UT: Tanner Trust Fund and J. Willard Marriott Library, 2016), 178.

9   See *Faith Crisis, Volume 1*, chapter 11, "Arrington's Epiphany." James and Hannah Stoddard, *Faith Crisis, Volume 1: We Were NOT Betrayed!* (Joseph Smith Foundation, 2020), 141.

10   Ibid.

11   Gregory A. Prince, *Leonard Arrington and the Writing of Mormon History* (Salt Lake City, UT: Tanner Trust Fund and J. Willard Marriott Library, 2016), 302.

12   Leonard J. Arrington Diaries, May 8, 1978; Leonard J. Arrington and Gary James Bergera, *Confessions of a Mormon Historian: The Diaries of Leonard J. Arrington, 1971-1997*, vol. 2 (Salt Lake City: Signature Books, 2018), 530, footnote 59.

13   Ibid., 530, footnote 60.

reflected: "As signs of disapproval accelerated, I recall almost a surreal atmosphere at History Divisions [*sic*]. Leonard, wishing to keep us younger historians on task and our morale at reasonable levels, tried to maintain an outward confidence."[14]

On May 26, 1978, Arrington noted in his diary that Elder Homer Durham was "toying with possibilities of moving us to BYU or setting us up as a separate group at arm's length from the Church but with full access to the archives. This way the Church will not be responsible for what we publish."[15] However, one month later, Elder Durham seemed somewhat more optimistic, counseling Arrington and the History Division to "continue to 'lie low.'"[16] Then, in a surprising twist in August 1978, Elder Durham explained to Arrington that "he continued to feel impressed that one of his responsibilities was to reduce our staff, not this year, but to plan for its elimination in the years to come. That is, say, beginning in 1980."[17] As further evidence of the unwelcome course correction, Arrington recorded a few months later that Durham reaffirmed: "he will not allow us to replace anybody who leaves."[18] Sensing the winds of change, some staff chose to leave of their own accord, while others chose to hold out until the team's final disassembly. On January 1, 1980, Arrington woefully noted: "we are gradually losing strength. . . . Elder Durham seems determined to reduce the work of our division down to the barest minimum." And yet, Arrington continued to resist the change, expressing that he felt:

> **//** . . . assured that future generations will be grateful for all that we do. . . .
>
> Persons tell us that Elders [Ezra Taft] Benson and [Mark E.] Petersen do not like what we are doing and that if and when President Benson becomes president of the Church we might

---

14   Ronald W. Walker, "Mormonism's 'Happy Warrior': Appreciating Leonard J. Arrington," *Journal of Mormon History* 25, no. 1 (Spring 1999): 123.

15   Leonard J. Arrington Diaries, May 26, 1978; Leonard J. Arrington and Gary James Bergera, *Confessions of a Mormon Historian: The Diaries of Leonard J. Arrington, 1971-1997*, vol. 2 (Salt Lake City: Signature Books, 2018), 539-540.

16   Leonard J. Arrington Diaries, June 29, 1978; Ibid., 564.

17   Leonard J. Arrington Diaries, September 6, 1978; Ibid., 611.

18   Gregory A. Prince, *Leonard Arrington and the Writing of Mormon History* (Salt Lake City, UT: Tanner Trust Fund and J. Willard Marriott Library, 2016), 339.

all be relieved of our positions. . . . I am convinced that we are doing what the Lord wants and that the Lord will not permit such a violent end to our work."[19]

Brimming with self confidence and determined in his direction, Arrington remained thoroughly convinced that he had received a commission directly from God to establish his progressive interpretation of history as the dominant narrative for the 20th-century Church of Jesus Christ of Latter-day Saints. Even as signs of disassembly began to swirl around him, Arrington—in full denial—hoped that he was untouchable, backed by a power that likely, he thought, would not allow a disruption to his work.

On the other side of this clash over the dominant narrative, traditionalist defenders tenaciously struggled to stem the inexorable tide of progressive change. Restrictions were newly imposed on who had access to the archives, and furthermore, on November 1, 1979, the responsibility for keeping the Journal History was transferred from Arrington's division to the Library-Archives Division. Ronald O. Barney[20] was assigned to make the transfer; but Arrington noted in his journal on October 15 that he (Arrington) would "probably keep some clippings for our own purposes—items which would not likely be spotted by him and items which we might want to refer to later."[21] Arrington's staff member Scott Kenney was

> *Arrington kept clippings for his 'own purposes'—items not likely to be spotted.*

---

19   Leonard J. Arrington Diaries, January 1, 1980; Leonard J. Arrington and Gary James Bergera, *Confessions of a Mormon Historian: The Diaries of Leonard J. Arrington*, 1971-1997, vol. 2 (Salt Lake City: Signature Books, 2018), 897-898; brackets in original added by Gary Bergera.

20   Ron Barney is Executive Director of the Mormon History Association founded by Leonard Arrington. Barney served as associate editor for the Joseph Smith Papers and as executive producer of the Joseph Smith Papers television series. He expresses admiration for the work of Richard Bushman, including *Rough Stone Rolling*, and has likewise called for a "new era" in how we view Joseph Smith and Church history.

21   Leonard J. Arrington Diaries, October 15, 1979; Leonard J. Arrington and Gary James Bergera, *Confessions of a Mormon Historian: The Diaries of Leonard J. Arrington*, 1971-1997, vol. 2 (Salt Lake City: Signature Books, 2018), 853.

engaged in a biography on Joseph F. Smith, and "worked feverishly while he still had access."[22] Arrington worried: "My main concern is will I be able to get everything I need out before restrictions are tightened? Will Benson be content with this victory, or will he be able to implement even tighter measures?" Arrington persisted in shifting blame onto President Benson for stifling all historical research, jotting down that, "Elder Benson and Petersen are very much in the saddle and they do not want archival material made available to anybody."[23] Meanwhile, Arrington and his key group of progressive personnel, concerned with their ability to assert claim to the records, began laying up "stores of photocopies—'squirreling away things to use when we make the change in offices.'"[24]

Elsewhere, critics of the Church followed the internal conflict attentively for signs of what might happen. Jerald and Sandra Tanner commented in January 1979:

> There is reason to believe that Benson wants to remove Arrington from his position as Church Historian. Some feel that he will gradually be "phased out." It is also reported that it is becoming increasingly difficult for Mormon scholars to get access to documents in the Historical Dept. If Dr. Arrington should survive under the leadership of President Spencer W. Kimball, it is very unlikely that he will remain Church Historian if Ezra Taft Benson becomes President.[25]

"History is on our side—as long as we can control the historians."

When the Sesquicentennial anniversary of the organization of The Church of Jesus Christ of Latter-day Saints arrived in 1980, Leonard Arrington and his department mourned the absence of their new history series, and were disillusioned over rumors of a looming exile. However, the New Mormon Historians still held out hope for a change in their favor.

---

22   Gregory A. Prince, *Leonard Arrington and the Writing of Mormon History* (Salt Lake City, UT: Tanner Trust Fund and J. Willard Marriott Library, 2016), 338.

23   Ibid., 339.

24   Ibid., 393.

25   "MORMONISM—Shadow or Reality?" *Salt Lake City Messenger*, no. 47, March 1982, http://www.utlm.org/newsletters/no47.htm.

Around this time, Carol Lynn Pearson,[26] a friend of Arrington's and a dedicated adherent to the progressive viewpoint, sent a card to Arrington reading: "History is on our side—as long as we can control the historians."[27] Arrington responded to Pearson on January 24, 1980:

// Dear Carol Lynn:

Very thoughtful of you to send that fascinating card. As you wrote, I am using it "judiciously." Some of my colleagues have it and I've sent it to the children, and still have a few left to sprinkle judiciously. Appreciate your thoughtfulness—and concern!

Love,
Leonard[28]

While the battle continued between the traditionalist leaders of the Church and the New Historians, Arrington and his colleagues realized that ultimate triumph would be theirs only if they held the power to train, mentor, and lead the next generation of historians. Surely, history would be on their side "as long as [they could] control the historians."

Confirmed, but Informal, Release

It was not until 1981, however, that Arrington would receive concrete evidence that his position and standing within Church headquarters had changed. On December 21, 1981, Arrington wrote to President Gordon B. Hinckley, an additional counselor in the First Presidency, outlining his confusion as well as his unanswered questions. Was he the Church Historian? Had he been released, and if so—when? Arrington mentioned further: "Many persons continue to refer to me as Church Historian, since there has been no public announcement of any release."[29]

---

26   Carol Lynn Pearson is an advocate of LGBT acceptance, and an outspoken opponent of the teachings on plural marriage taught by Joseph Smith and other leaders. She is the author of the musical *My Turn on Earth*, several screenplays for films produced by Brigham Young University's motion-picture department, and the author of a number of published poems.

27   Leonard J. Arrington to Carol Lynn Pearson, January 24, 1980, LJAHA, Series II, Box 13, fd. 10.

28   Ibid.

29   Gregory A. Prince, *Leonard Arrington and the Writing of Mormon History* (Salt Lake City, UT: Tanner Trust Fund and J. Willard Marriott Library, 2016), 343.

On January 25, 1982, Arrington received a response from the First Presidency, signed by Presidents Spencer W. Kimball, N. Eldon Tanner, Marion G. Romney, and Gordon B. Hinckley:[30]

// We are informed that on February 24, 1978, you were orally advised by Elder G. Homer Durham of the change in your title and status from Church Historian to Director of the History Division. That change was intended to constitute a release from your duties as the Church Historian. However, since you have asked for clarification, it is appropriate now formally to extend to you a release as Church Historian effective as of February 24, 1978. Also in view of your transfer to the Brigham Young University to assume your full duties there, we also hereby extend to you an honorable release as the Director of the History Division.[31]

Arrington later discovered that the Journal History of the Church, as recorded by Ron Barney, stated that Elder G. Homer Durham was "set apart by the First Presidency as Church Historian and Recorder"

---

30   Gordon B. Hinckley was called as third counselor to President Spencer W. Kimball in 1981. "In 1981, President Hinckley was called to serve as a counselor in the First Presidency. During that time, he assumed the bulk of the First Presidency's responsibilities, since all three members of that presidency were experiencing poor health." "Pres. Hinckley dedicated his life to church," *Deseret News*, January 28, 2008, https://www.deseret.com/2008/1/28/20066979/pres-hinckley-dedicated-his-life-to-church#president-hinckley-with-presidents-thomas-s-monson-left-james-e-faust-and-boyd-k-packer-speaks-after-becoming-lds-president.

While the usual precedent is for the President of the Church (or President of the High Priesthood) to choose two counselors, extra counselors have been called on occasion. "Counselors in the First Presidency are almost always apostles, but there are some exceptions — President Clark wasn't ordained an apostle until Oct. 11, 1934, more than 18 months after he became second counselor. . . . Frederick G. Williams, William Law, Daniel H. Wells and Charles W. Nibley were all second counselors in the First Presidency who were not ordained apostles. They were simply high priests.

"In addition, 14 extra counselors have been called to the First Presidency over the years. The most recent extra counselor was President Gordon B. Hinckley, who was called as a third counselor to President Spencer W. Kimball on July 23, 1981, and served until he became second counselor on Dec. 2, 1982." "LDS 2nd counselor vacancy is unusual," *Deseret News*, October 2, 2007, https://www.deseret.com/2007/10/2/20043676/lds-2nd-counselor-vacancy-is-unusual.

31   Gregory A. Prince, *Leonard Arrington and the Writing of Mormon History* (Salt Lake City, UT: Tanner Trust Fund and J. Willard Marriott Library, 2016), 343.

on February 2, 1982.[32] This confusing sequence of events—still unclear today—appears to have caught Arrington unawares. He wrote, "I found out that I was not Church Historian by going down and reading the Journal History of the Church, down in the Church library," Arrington told Dwight Israelsen. "This is the way I found out. They didn't have the guts to come and tell me directly."[33]

In the midst of the disassembly of the History Division, the health of Arrington's wife was also failing, and fast. Grace Arrington struggled with depression, heart issues, stomach troubles, arthritis, edema, and other challenges throughout the entire decade of Arrington's work at Church headquarters. Finally, after a lengthy battle with her many ailments, Grace passed away on March 10, 1982, without her children by her side. In a state of denial, their father had not recognized the gravity of his wife's condition during her last hours, and had neglected to alert the children to the seriousness of their mother's condition until it was too late.

Contemplations

As Leonard Arrington watched the dismantling of the history department he had so eagerly and passionately built, he took the time to reflect in his diary on ideals that had been the source of deep conflict with bureaucracy within the Church. Why the contention and struggle?

Between the April 1978 General Conference sessions, Arrington expressed his frustration with the ill-fated "disadvantages" he believed he was suffering from by not being included or accepted by the mainstream. He concluded that he had "absolutely no desire to

---

32   Leonard J. Arrington Diaries, February 2, 1982; Leonard J. Arrington and Gary James Bergera, *Confessions of a Mormon Historian: The Diaries of Leonard J. Arrington, 1971-1997*, vol. 3 (Salt Lake City: Signature Books, 2018), 240.

Greg Prince notes that during the next General Conference (April 1982), Elder G. Homer Durham's name was not presented for sustaining, nor was Leonard Arrington formally released. "But Hinckley, who was conducting the conference session, slipped the information into a rather awkward sentence that was constructed, bizarrely, to give Durham's birthplace: 'Elder G. Homer Durham, a member of the Presidency of the First Quorum of the Seventy and the Church Historian who, if I remember correctly, was born in Parowan, has now addressed us." Gregory A. Prince, *Leonard Arrington and the Writing of Mormon History* (Salt Lake City, UT: Tanner Trust Fund and J. Willard Marriott Library, 2016), 344.

33   Gregory A. Prince, *Leonard Arrington and the Writing of Mormon History* (Salt Lake City, UT: Tanner Trust Fund and J. Willard Marriott Library, 2016), 344.

be a General Authority," confiding that it was "useless to even think in those terms," and summarily listing his reasons:

❐❐ A. I come from an "outside" family. B. I am too short and ugly. C. I am too much of an intellectual—whatever that means. D. I am too insistent upon straightforwardness and honesty in interpreting our history. E. I have absolutely no interest in spending the remaining weekends of my life visiting stake conferences instead of enjoying the weekend at home reading, watching TV, and enjoying Grace [his wife].[34]

Arrington's list of regrets did not include the issues that led to contention between his department and the traditionalist leaders who opposed him. However, a few months later, on September 25, 1978, Arrington drafted a list of what he perceived to be his "weaknesses" that eventually led to his untimely rejection as Church Historian.[35] The list included certain attributes which would have been a source of serious concern for any traditionalist tasked with selecting the man whom the Church would commission to write the history of the Restoration:

❐❐ Because of my desire to get things done, regardless of regulations— because of the deviousness with which I pursue certain goals—I probably come through as a not-very-religious person, and perhaps to some extent not entirely trustworthy.[36]

It appears that Arrington felt justified in the application of his "deviousness" as a means of effecting the Lord's work in the face of the decided opposition he received from traditionalist leaders and 'suffocating' bureaucratic Church policy. During one History Division retreat organized in 1979, Arrington commented that the division had "a clear conscience: we are all believers, we want to do what the Lord wishes, we want to do what the First Presidency wishes, we have engaged in no conspiracy. We are doing positive things for

---

34   Leonard J. Arrington Diaries, April 5, 1978; Leonard J. Arrington and Gary James Bergera, *Confessions of a Mormon Historian: The Diaries of Leonard J. Arrington*, 1971-1997, vol. 2 (Salt Lake City: Signature Books, 2018), 502. Formatting taken from original in Bergera's publication.

35   Leonard J. Arrington Diaries, September 25, 1978; Ibid., 631-633.

36   Leonard J. Arrington Diaries, September 25, 1978; Ibid., 632.

the Church, and should have absolutely no guilt about anything we have done."[37] However, despite his guiltless altruism and the denial of conspiratorial workings, Arrington admitted in a list of regrets he had written out during the previous year that "it has been necessary in one or two instances to lie." In his diary, Arrington justified the dishonesty by dismissing it as "diplomatic deception," a "tactic [that] was for the good of the Church and kingdom."[38] Arrington's 1978 list of "weaknesses" continued:

- "[I have] . . . many gaps in my knowledge and understanding of Church history. . . . I particularly lack knowledge in Church history before 1847. And in the view of many persons, that is the key period of Church history."

- "I have never been an avid student of Latter-day Saint scriptures. . . . I have read the Book of Mormon through only once, and while I have read portions of it from time to time, I am not a Book of Mormon student. I have read the Doctrine and Covenants several times but have never set any portion of it to memory, and have made no attempt to use it except to support things I was writing or speaking about. In essence I am a bigger user of the index than of the text itself. The same goes for the Pearl of Great Price. To merit the confidence and support of ecclesiastical officials, the Church historian ought to make greater use of the scriptures and ought to be more knowledgeable on the scriptures than I am."

- "I am not as knowledgeable on doctrine as a Church historian ought to be. . . . I realize every Sunday in High Priest and Sunday School classes that I do not know as much doctrine as nine-tenths of the High Priests in the Church. I feel very inadequate discussing doctrine and take the easy way out by simply telling people they ought to talk with a General Authority . . ."[39]

---

37   Leonard J. Arrington Diaries, June 22, 1979; Ibid., 793, footnote 65.

38   Leonard J. Arrington Diaries, September 14, 1978; Ibid., 617-618.

39   Bullet points were not part of the original diary entry, but were added for readability in this volume.

Other attributes Arrington listed included his self-proclaimed misfortune in personal appearance and his ability to work alongside Church leaders. He also shared his perception of being an 'outsider':

- He was not a general authority. A general authority would be "more aware of what is going on . . . [have] direct contact with presiding authorities . . . enjo[y] the full confidence and support of all the General Authorities."[40]

- He had "neither the ambition nor the qualifications to be" a general authority, and therefore did "not enjoy this kind of support or confidence."[41]

- His "long experience outside the Church or on the fringes of the Church," and not having lived "in the Mormon culture," his manner and speech "suggest someone not completely immersed in the culture."

- He was not a relative or "connected in any intimate way" with any general authority.

- He was "short." "People tend to have greater respect for tall people than short people, in administrative positions."

- "I am probably too informal, too afflicted with a sense of humor, too boisterous, too light-minded, too devious [improvisational], too political . . ."[42]

Perhaps in some ways, Arrington's feelings of unappreciated superiority drove him even harder to establish his place in the annals of Church history, even if that meant blurring the lines of historical integrity to accomplish his goals. His deficiency in doctrinal knowledge and understanding of the events surrounding the Restoration did not stop him from exerting his masterful hand in the fomenting of an alternate history. If he could not do it directly as an insider—within the Church's structure—perhaps there was another way.

---

40   Leonard J. Arrington Diaries, September 25, 1978; Leonard J. Arrington and Gary James Bergera, *Confessions of a Mormon Historian: The Diaries of Leonard J. Arrington*, 1971-1997, vol. 2 (Salt Lake City: Signature Books, 2018), 631.

41   Leonard J. Arrington Diaries, September 25, 1978; Ibid., 632.

42   Leonard J. Arrington Diaries, September 25, 1978; Ibid., 631-634.

18

GREENER BYU PASTURES?
The Exile & the Fall of Camelot

When President N. Eldon Tanner first approached Leonard Arrington about accepting the position of Church Historian in 1972, President Tanner also shared that Arrington had been sought after for a position at BYU. Informing him of a recent visit, he related:

" In my office yesterday were Brother Neal Maxwell, Commissioner of Education, and President Dallin [H.] Oaks of BYU. They told me about your fitness for the Chair [Endowed Chair in Western Studies at BYU], and of their desire to have you at BYU.[1]

Learning of two potential, prestigious opportunities coming from leaders seeking him out must have been a satisfaction to the 55-year old historian, and was likely especially pleasing when he learned that he could accept both positions.

When Arrington accepted the appointment as Church Historian, he had also previously accepted the Chair at BYU. President Tanner had informed him, "It simply means that you will have to divide your time in a way you think best between BYU and the Church Historian's Office. President Oaks is willing to support you in both positions, and I am also."[2] A few days later, Arrington received a

---

1   Leonard J. Arrington Diaries, January 7, 1972; Leonard J. Arrington and Gary James Bergera, *Confessions of a Mormon Historian: The Diaries of Leonard J. Arrington*, 1971-1997, vol. 1 (Salt Lake City: Signature Books, 2018), 66-97.

2   Ibid., 98.

personal phone call from President Oaks,[3] and shortly thereafter, the *Church News*, *BYU Universe*, *Provo Herald*, and other papers announced Arrington's appointment to fill both positions.[4]

Now, a decade after his call as Church Historian, the winds of change had altered Arrington's path—and he was headed toward what he hoped would prove to be friendlier skies, with a full-time position at BYU. His friend and colleague, Ron Walker, remembered:

❝ A half dozen years into the enterprise, the staff was downsized. Arrington's scriptural title of Church Historian was exchanged for a more bureaucratic one. Still more, tellingly, the flagship sixteen-volume, sesquicentennial series that Leonard had boosted was canceled; Church leaders honored author contracts and gave permission for the outside publication of ongoing volumes, but they wanted no further connection with the project. In 1980, Leonard and a core of seven historians were administratively transferred to Brigham Young University, where we became members of the newly created [and ironically named] Joseph Fielding Smith Institute for Church History.[5] Two years later in 1982, all of us maintained offices at BYU, and our physical move was complete.[6]

---

3   President Dallin H. Oaks served as the president of Brigham Young University from 1971 to 1980, as well as on the editorial board for *Dialogue* from the first issue in 1966 to the summer issue in 1970.

4   Leonard J. Arrington Diaries, January 13, 1972; Leonard J. Arrington and Gary James Bergera, *Confessions of a Mormon Historian: The Diaries of Leonard J. Arrington, 1971-1997*, vol. 1 (Salt Lake City: Signature Books, 2018), 104; "New Church Historian Called," *Church News*, January 15, 1972, https://news.google.com/newspapers?id=SjMhAAAAIBAJ&sjid=yFgEAAAAIBAJ&pg=4574%2C2972980.

5   The Joseph Fielding Smith Institute for Church History was established in 1980 to provide a place for Leonard Arrington and his remaining staff who were being transferred to BYU. Arrington served as the head of the organization from 1980-1986. He was followed by Ron Esplin and then Jill Derr. It is extremely ironic that the new research organization set up for Leonard Arrington's progressive team was named after the Church Historian, Joseph Fielding Smith, whom Arrington opposed. Joseph Fielding Smith was a traditionalist and his theological beliefs and approach to history were the antithesis to the progressive New Mormon History. In 2005, the Joseph Fielding Smith Institute was dissolved as many of the scholars were transferred to work in Salt Lake City, Utah for the Historical Department of The Church of Jesus Christ of Latter-day Saints.

6   Ronald W. Walker, "Mormonism's 'Happy Warrior': Appreciating Leonard J. Arrington," *Journal of Mormon History* 25, no. 1 (Spring 1999): 123-124.

Moving to BYU

The challenging dilemma Church administration encountered in deciding upon what to do with Arrington and his progressive history voice is evident in a comment Davis Bitton later shared with Arrington's biographer, Greg Prince:

> I believe [G. Homer Durham] thought he was doing everybody a favor. Here was a group of historians that had irritated some people, and there was this bad blood between the historians and some members of the Twelve. Solution: just move them right out of the Church Historian's Office and let them function as a research institute attached to BYU, and let the BYU administrators deal with them. That way, the Church could say, "They don't represent the Church. They are university people."[7]

James Allen shared a similar outlook concerning the move: "I also think that he [Elder Durham] was trying to figure out a way to please Brother Benson and others who were upset about some of the things that they felt might be coming out of the Historical Department."[8]

Ironically, nearly four decades earlier, Arrington had recorded his private sentiment that:

> If I were honest with them [members of the Church] about how I feel, they wouldn't own me. I just wonder how many of the young LDS would agree with me—would think I had the right approach—would want me to teach their children? Probably not very many.[9]

Yet here he was with the nucleus of his department in the summer 1982, ready to move into the Joseph Fielding Smith Institute for Church History at BYU, where he was entrusted with the education and training—in essence, the shaping and molding—of thousands of impressionable, young Latter-day Saints.

---

7   Gregory A. Prince, *Leonard Arrington and the Writing of Mormon History* (Salt Lake City, UT: Tanner Trust Fund and J. Willard Marriott Library, 2016), 382.

8   Ibid.

9   Ibid., 114.

Initially, Arrington viewed the move to BYU as a demotion—an exile of his expertise and that of his fellow expats—from his previously influential role in the Church; but he soon felt renewed energy as the "thought of teaching bright young undergraduate students suddenly appealed to him."[10] In addition to allowing him to continue his research and writing, the revised mission Arrington would undertake at the newly-organized Joseph Fielding Smith Institute for Church History would empower him with the opportunity to "teach courses in history, LDS Church history, and other disciplines related to their fields of expertise and advise student[s] whose major papers, theses, and dissertations address Mormon history topics."[11] Arrington recorded his enthusiasm in his diary on July 27, 1982:

// On the face of it, the move to BYU seems stupid. Why move to BYU, where there are only limited materials on Church history, when we are already located on the Mother Lode? Actually, there are advantages of being placed under the BYU rubric. . . . in the classes we teach at the "Y" we can communicate our findings to students and thus help to educate Church members about our history. We are also in a setting which enables us to earn higher salaries than would be possible under Church employment. In short, if some of the denials of our requests for certain holdover privileges seem petty and humiliating, we are certainly being welcomed and treated generously at BYU. [signed] Leonard Arrington[12]

Just as Arrington had foretold in his personal journal in 1944, the "LDS desire for education & learning is so strong that I think they will accept me & let me teach them in spite of some of my 'radicalism.'"[13] He discovered with joy that unsuspecting Latter-day Saint parents were so trusting, and their children so eager to become "educated," that he could influence and lead them with ease toward embracing

---

10   Ibid., 350.

11   "Joseph Fielding Smith Institute for Latter-day Saint History," Harold B. Lee Library, https://byuorg.lib.byu.edu/index.php/Joseph_Fielding_Smith_Institute_for_Latter-day_Saint_History.

12   Leonard J. Arrington Diaries, July 27, 1982; Leonard J. Arrington and Gary James Bergera, *Confessions of a Mormon Historian: The Diaries of Leonard J. Arrington*, 1971-1997, vol. 3 (Salt Lake City: Signature Books, 2018), 271; brackets in original.

13   Gregory A. Prince, *Leonard Arrington and the Writing of Mormon History* (Salt Lake City, UT: Tanner Trust Fund and J. Willard Marriott Library, 2016), 115.

Brigham Young Academy, forerunner to Brigham Young University
(Endowed by Brigham Young to refute Darwinism, Marxism and socialism,
see Faith Crisis Volume 1, pg. 188-191)

the New Mormon History he and his colleagues evangelized. The older generation were often set in their ways; but the younger, more pliable generation provided the perfect opportunity for shaping the next generation of Latter-day Saint historians and teachers.

Arrington worked as the director of the Joseph Fielding Smith Institute for Church History at BYU-Provo until 1986. He produced a biography of Brigham Young entitled, *Brigham Young: American Moses,* in 1985, as well as additional papers, books, and articles—a publishing effort he maintained after leaving BYU, until his death on February 11, 1999. Leonard Arrington's work left an indelible mark on the realm of Latter-day Saint history—one that would drastically affect the faith of members for generations to come. As for the rest of the New Mormon Historians, Greg Prince noted that "the most important difference from Leonard's era has been the passage of time. His most formidable foes have long since departed this life . . ."[14]

---

14 Ibid., 371.

Ideological Wars

One of those "formidable foes," and certainly the most intimidating and challenging to Arrington—President Ezra Taft Benson—passed away on May 30, 1994, surrounded by his devoted family. Leonard Arrington's subtle—yet seemingly triumphant and contradistinctive response to President Benson's funeral—as recorded in his diary, was an honorific tribute to Darwinism, Freudianism, and historical criticism of the Bible. The entry was significant, as Arrington was keenly aware of President Benson's ideological stance against each of those prevalent and notably progressive ideologies:

> // I was thinking while watching President [Ezra Taft] Benson's funeral [on television], of the four great ideas or movements of the last 150 years . . . Marxism . . . Darwinism . . . Freudianism . . . Historical–critical understanding of the Bible.[15]

Arrington and President Benson were ideologically miles apart on all the major thinkers; the two men shared deeply conflicting points of view. First, Arrington, while not considering himself a Marxist, leaned hard left in politics while President Benson was a staunch conservative. Second, Arrington was an avid supporter of Darwinism, and he included this as one of the four pillars in his reflections inspired by President Benson's funeral:

> // I was early exposed to [Charles] Darwin's theory of evolution in my zoology class as a freshman at the U of I [University of Idaho]. It all sounded reasonable and proven. George S. Tanner helped me to reconcile my faith to it, and I have never had a faith problem with evolution. I believe in the ancient age of the earth, in the existence of dinosaurs, in the existence of pre-Adamites (as they are called), and that all of this is consistent with Mormonism, faith, and good doctrine.[16]

Conversely, President Benson taught that Charles Darwin was one of five antichrists of the latter days, and that the Book of Mormon

---

15   Leonard J. Arrington Diaries, June 4, 1994; Leonard J. Arrington and Gary James Bergera, *Confessions of a Mormon Historian: The Diaries of Leonard J. Arrington*, 1971-1997, vol. 3 (Salt Lake City: Signature Books, 2018), 626-627.

16   Ibid., 626; brackets in original;

Caricature of Darwin's theory in the Punch almanac for 1882

foreshadowed and clearly warned against the false teachings of men like Darwin.[17]

Arrington's third pillar was Freudianism, the outgrowth of which would have Arrington exercising the voice of influence in convincing Richard Bushman to reinterpret Joseph Smith using the principles of psychoanalysis—one of Sigmund Freud's foundational 'contributions.' Such Freudian precepts became foundational guideposts in Arrington's lifeview:

17   Ezra Taft Benson, *Conference Report*, October 1970, 21-25, Church History Library, https://catalog.churchofjesuschrist.org/assets?id=ed9d4987-0610-47ce-ae2e-34a995d0f1c2&crate=0&index=24.

Front row: Sigmund Freud, G. Stanley Hall, Carl Jung; back row: Abraham Brill,
Ernest Jones, Sándor Ferenczi, 1909

❞ [Sigmund] Freud's explanations of the workings of the human psyche have become part of our vocabulary: ego, inferiority complex, passive-aggressive, dream psychology. I never took a course in psychology, but I read several Freudian books, many articles, and listened to some lectures. I finally found an interpreter, influenced by Freud, with whom I could relate: Carl Gustav Jung, the Swiss psychoanalysis consistent with religion, and a theory of the unconscious that seemed reasonable.[18]

The darker side of Freud's influence revealed a definite agenda to destroy the gospel of Jesus Christ. Freud's goal was to undermine and impair Christianity from the inside, through means of inverting Biblical principles throughout civilized culture. His ideas have since become foundational in the modern world as an essential prescript for family life, science, government, education, and every facet of society. In a form typical of many antichrists, Freud was bold in his disgust toward faith in God:

---

18   Leonard J. Arrington Diaries, June 4, 1994; Leonard J. Arrington and Gary James Bergera, *Confessions of a Mormon Historian: The Diaries of Leonard J. Arrington*, 1971-1997, vol. 3 (Salt Lake City: Signature Books, 2018), 626-627.

❝❞ "Religion is comparable to a childhood neurosis [mild mental illness]." (*The Future of an Illusion*[19])

"The whole thing is so patently infantile, so foreign to reality, that to anyone with a friendly attitude to humanity it is painful to think that the great majority of mortals will never be able to rise above this [religious] view of life." (*Civilization and Its Discontents*[20])

"It is still more humiliating to discover how a large number of people living today, who cannot but see that this religion is not tenable, nevertheless try to defend it piece by piece in a series of pitiful rearguard actions." (*Civilization and Its Discontents*[21])

Freud was also one of the primary voices of the sexual revolution leading to the "free love" movement with its accompanying promiscuity, drug use, and anti-patriarchal rhetoric. President Benson, in contrast, was one of the world's chief voices in opposing these radical new movements plaguing the world.

Arrington's fourth pillar, and perhaps most enduring legacy or contravention to the Church—as one views it—was his dogged advancement of historical criticism of the Bible and other scripture.

- "I was introduced to this by George Tanner in 1936, but I have followed it to some extent in the years since."
- "It means understanding the Bible as a collection of writings by many authors over more than a thousand years; they contain different points of view, sometimes contradictory understandings and formulations of the nature of God and our relationship with Him and other human beings."
- "The Bible **may be** the word of God"
- "Moses did not write the first five books of the Bible"
- "David did not write most of the Psalms"

---

19 Sigmund Freud, *The Future of an Illusion* (New York: W. W. Norton & Company, 1961), 53.

20 Sigmund Freud, *Civilization and Its Discontents* (New York: W. W. Norton & Company, 1961), 22.

21 Ibid.

- "Paul did not write the letters to Timothy or Titus"
- "scholars doubt that Peter had anything to do with the books of Peter."
- "Most put aside Joshua, with its horrifying narratives of extermination, and Judges with its accounts of patriarchy and sexual assault"
- "From the point of view of the historically–critical method the Bible can be viewed as a historically conditioned anthology"
- "A series of signposts pointing the way to a goal that its writers, like us, had not yet reached but were moving toward."[22]

Leonard Arrington and Ezra Taft Benson were worlds apart when it came to scripture. For Arrington, scripture was composed of the cultural ideas and theories of men. For the new progressive historians, a literal Adam and Eve, a literal Universal Flood, a literal Exodus with Moses leading ancient Israel, and other such 'artifacts' of the ancient past would become myth and folklore—the foolishness of primitive peoples.

For President Benson, the rock of scripture stood as a solid foundation, and to him, the revelations were the unchangeable, ever-reliable word of God. The scriptures were not a defining influence for Arrington, but these guidebooks most assuredly were for President Benson. During his tenure as President of the Church, Ezra Taft Benson would consistently attempt to refocus obedient members by pointing them back to God's revelations—leading the Church to experience the greatest statistical period of missionary work and general growth in its history,[23] and a clear revival of testimony for the modern Saints.

One example of President Benson's vocal stance against the pillars of Arrington's worldview (liberal progressivism, Darwinism, Freudianism, and Historical criticism of the Bible) can be found

---

22   Leonard J. Arrington Diaries, June 4, 1994; Leonard J. Arrington and Gary James Bergera, *Confessions of a Mormon Historian: The Diaries of Leonard J. Arrington, 1971-1997*, vol. 3 (Salt Lake City: Signature Books, 2018), 627, emphasis added.

23   Image graphic, "LDS Church Growth Rate vs. World Growth Rate," Wikipedia, CC BY-SA 4.0, https://en.wikipedia.org/wiki/The_Church_ of_Jesus_Christ_of_Latter-day_Saints_membership_history#/media/ File:LDSgrowthVSworld2018.png.

in his powerful talk delivered during the October 1970 General Conference. In that straightforward discourse, President Benson warned Latter-day Saint parents of the imminent academic danger posed through the proliferation of antithetical teachings that directly oppose the Gospel of Jesus Christ. The talk categorically identified five specific antichrists whose contemporary influence is currently at work in our educational institutions—namely, Sigmund Freud (father of the sexual revolution and behavioral rationalization through psychology), Charles Darwin (father of evolution), John Dewey (father of progressive education), Karl Marx (father of socialism and communism), and John Keynes (father of government redistribution of wealth). President Benson's talk included specific warnings, even naming individuals:

> As a watchman on the tower, I feel to warn you that one of the chief means of misleading our youth and destroying the family unit is our educational institutions. President Joseph F. Smith referred to false educational ideas as one of the three threatening dangers among our Church members. There is more than one reason why the Church is advising our youth to attend colleges close to their homes where institutes of religion are available. It gives the parents the opportunity to stay close to their children; and if they have become alert and informed as President McKay admonished us last year, these parents can help expose some of the deceptions of men like Sigmund Freud, Charles Darwin, John Dewey, Karl Marx, John Keynes, and others.
>
> Today there are much worse things that can happen to a child than not getting a full college education. In fact, some of the worst things have happened to our children while attending colleges led by administrators who wink at subversion and amorality.[24]

Very few parents heeded President Benson's warning against progressivism. Some felt he was out of touch with the modern direction of scholarship and needed to let go of his out-dated, 19th-century outlook. Others felt that he, and perhaps a few others like

---

24 Ezra Taft Benson, *Conference Report*, October 1970, 21-25, Church History Library, https://catalog.churchofjesuschrist.org/assets?id=ed9d4987-0610-47ce-ae2e-34a995d0f1c2&crate=0&index=24.

Elder Boyd K. Packer, were only one or two witnesses—why was no one else speaking out on these issues? Still, there were others who held firmly to their belief that President Ezra Taft Benson was a leader possessing the spirit of prophecy; and these extremely rare, and often criticized parents, quietly moved forward in testifying and teaching their children of these dangers.

Our best current assessment of available evidence indicates that we may be losing 75% of Millennials in the Church today.[25] This means that for the first time in Church history roughly ¾ of the age group between 25 and 35 could be currently renouncing their faith—a staggering statistic and sign of the time—leaving parents, leaders and even those not of the faith asking the question: *What is happening?* We are witnessing a massive proliferation, even pandemic, of faith crisis, as never before. As we, the authors, have spoken and given presentations over the past decade, scores of pleading parents, siblings, and other relatives have pulled us aside asking and literally crying for help. We have done our best to answer the questions and to reaffirm faith in our traditional, foundational doctrines and history; but even if all of our time and energy could be devoted to reaching

---

25   Personal correspondence with multiple sources confirming the essential accuracy of this statistic. Definitions are important. What does "losing faith" mean? When is faith lost? What age groups are being considered? Are the statistics accurate? Regardless of how optimistically we approach the research, there is unquestionably an increasingly serious problem. Our purpose is not to debate statistics. We should all be able to agree that we are in the midst of a crisis.

Jana Riess has a more positive outlook with 'only' "four or five of every 10" losing faith during their youth. "According to the most recent wave of research in that same study, published earlier this year [2020], 61% of the participants who were Mormon as teenagers still claimed that religious identity as adults. That finding is consistent with other national studies from Pew, the General Social Survey, and the Public Religion Research Institute, in which the Latter-day Saint retention rate in recent years has ranged from a high of 64% to a low of 46%. Losing four or five of every 10 young Latter-day Saints is not something to whitewash . . . ." Jana Riess, "Jana Riess: Controversial Latter-day Saint book pulled from publication," *The Salt Lake Tribune*, September 8, 2020, https://www.sltrib.com/religion/2020/09/08/jana-riess-controversial/.

Riess also explained in 2019, "In 2007, Pew found that Mormons had an overall retention rate of 70%, which is quite good. By 2014, this had dropped to 64% for all generations combined, and to 62% among Millennials. . . . A less rosy picture emerges from the General Social Survey . . . With Generation X we start seeing a drop (62.5%) [retention rate], and with Millennials the drop becomes sharper: for those born after 1981, the GSS finds only a 46% retention rate." Jana Riess, "How many Millennials are really leaving the LDS Church?" ReligionNews.com, March 27, 2019, https://religionnews.com/2019/03/27/how-many-millennials-are-really-leaving-the-lds-church/.

out on a one-on-one basis, there would not nearly be sufficient hours in the day to reach those struggling.

In this light, may we humbly remind readers of some pertinent facts? This age group suffers as the primary casualty of the present faith crisis; the Millennials are typically those either currently attending the universities, or those having attended recently. Many of this age group have responded enthusiastically to the new directive delivered by our Church leaders since the turn of the century to "get all of the education that you can." On the other hand, President Benson's timely warning and plea for parents to become informed of the dangers with respect to progressive innovations within academia, as well as the guidance to keep children close, even while attending college, and to consistently and prayerfully teach and warn them of the dangers of these progressive influences has been almost universally ignored. What consequences should we expect if we neglect the call of the watchman?

President Benson's warnings during the 60s, 70s, and 80s were both consistent and forthright. During the time Arrington served as Church Historian, President Benson issued another resolute denunciation of Darwinian Evolution, Marxist Socialism, Deweyan humanism, and what he would later confront as Arrington's rationalism, as well as other progressive philosophies, during the April 1975 General Conference:

// Now, we have not been using the Book of Mormon as we should. Our homes are not as strong unless we are using it to bring our children to Christ. Our families may be corrupted by worldly trends and teachings unless we know how to use the book to expose and combat the falsehoods in socialism, organic evolution, rationalism, humanism, etc. Our missionaries are not as effective unless they are "hissing forth" with it [Book of Mormon]. . . .

President Benson then delivered one of his strongest prophetic pronouncements, posing the question as to whether the Church was under condemnation:

❞ Some of the early missionaries, on returning home, were reproved by the Lord in section 84 of the Doctrine and Covenants because they had treated lightly the Book of Mormon. As a result, their minds had been darkened. The Lord said that this kind of treatment of the Book of Mormon brought the whole Church under condemnation, even all of the children of Zion. And then the Lord said, "And they shall remain under this condemnation until they repent and remember the new covenant, even the Book of Mormon." (See D&C 84:54–57.) Are we still under that condemnation?[26]

Later, as President of the Church, Ezra Taft Benson would openly declare the Church to be under condemnation in 1986.[27] It is interesting to note that this declaration—stating the Church to be under condemnation—has never been lifted.

Leonard Arrington well regarded and embraced the philosophies and the men of whom President Benson warned his listeners against with an entirely contrasting lens. Arrington's heroes were President Benson's antichrists; the former's protagonists were the latter's antagonists. In 1986, Arrington wrote out his ideas in his journal under the heading, "Concepts or Theories or Intellectual Constructs That Have Molded My Thinking throughout My Life." Among them, Arrington listed the vicarious mentoring effect of the writings of Sigmund Freud, John Maynard Keynes, and Charles Darwin—each of whom appear as one of President Benson's delineated antichrists.[28]

---

26   Ezra Taft Benson, "*The Book of Mormon Is the Word of God,*" General Conference (April 1975), https://www.churchofjesuschrist.org/study/general-conference/1975/04/the-book-of-mormon-is-the-word-of-god?lang=eng.

27   Ezra Taft Benson, "*The Book of Mormon—Keystone of Our Religion,*" General Conference (October 1986), https://www.churchofjesuschrist.org/study/general-conference/1986/10/the-book-of-mormon-keystone-of-our-religion?lang=eng.

28   "3. The law or theory of evolution. The earth is old, always evolving. Plants and animals are old, always evolving. Even man is evolving, with God's blessing toward a better life. Charles Darwin and others.

"4. The theory that the economy may achieve an equilibrium at less than full employment. Special action must be taken, when it does so, to stimulate employment of people, capital, and resources. John Maynard Keynes.

"5. The concept of the unconscious, that our behavior is affected not only by conscious thoughts but by unconscious ones as well. Sigmund Freud and others." Leonard J. Arrington Diaries, November 9, 1986; Leonard J. Arrington and Gary James Bergera, *Confessions of a Mormon Historian: The Diaries of Leonard J. Arrington*, 1971-1997, vol. 3 (Salt Lake City: Signature Books, 2018), 455.

Ezra Taft Benson's Legacy

Ezra Taft Benson was, unquestionably, one traditionalist leader the progressives were not going to miss. But for the thousands of Latter-day Saints who loved and revered him, his loss would be deeply felt. "3,500 mourners attended the [funeral] service in the Tabernacle on Temple Square, while thousands more watched proceedings"[29] on television and broadcasts in meetinghouses. "Perhaps no president of the Church since the Prophet Joseph Smith himself has done more to teach the truths of the Book of Mormon,"[30] President Howard W. Hunter eulogized. President Thomas S. Monson boldly declared, "No one could possibly have had a better role model to follow [than President Benson]. His life has been rich, his love far-reaching, his testimony of the truth ever firm."[31]

As President Benson's casket made its way from Salt Lake City to its final resting place in his beloved hometown of Whitney, Idaho, it seemed almost as though the entire Church paused to honor the beloved leader:

// There was a tribute by members of the Church as they lined the highway and stood on the overpasses along the road. Some were dressed in their Sunday best on a Saturday afternoon. Others paused in respect, stopping their cars and standing reverently, waiting for the prophet to pass. Farmers stood in their fields with their hats over their hearts. Probably more significant were the young boys taking their baseball hats off and putting them over their hearts. Flags waved good-bye as the prophet went by as well. There were signs that read, "We love President Benson." Others said, "Read the Book of Mormon."[32]

President Benson's patriarchal blessing foretold that "if faithful, he would go on a mission to the nations of the earth, that his life would be preserved on land and sea, that he would raise his voice

---

29   Gerry Avant, "President Benson eulogized," *Deseret News*, June 11, 1994, https://www.thechurchnews.com/archives/1994-06-11/president-benson-eulogized-139680.

30   Ibid.

31   Ibid.

32   Robert D. Hales, "A Testimony of Prophets," BYU Speeches, June 5, 1994, https://speeches.byu.edu/talks/robert-d-hales/testimony-prophets/.

Ezra Taft Benson grave site, Whitney, Idaho

in testimony and would grow in favor with the Almighty, and that many would rise up and bless his name."[33] For traditionalists, his long life of service and integrity to Christ, the Prophet Joseph Smith, and the traditional doctrine and principles of God's restored gospel, bear witness to the fulfilment of that blessing.

Rebuilding Camelot

Progressives have lauded Leonard Arrington's decade as Church Historian as a 'grand experiment' they affectionately refer to as "Camelot,"[34] a time reminiscent of the golden age of King Arthur. When Arrington's department was relocated entirely from Church headquarters to BYU, the progressives termed it a self-proclaimed "exile." In their minds, they were martyrs—banished from their

---

33   Sheri L. Dew, *Ezra Taft Benson: A Biography* (Salt Lake City, Utah: Deseret Book Company, 1987), 29.

34   See for example, James B. Allen, review of Gregory A. Prince, *Leonard Arrington and the Writing of Mormon History,* (Salt Lake City, UT: Tanner Trust Fund and J. Willard Marriott Library, 2016), https://byustudies.byu.edu/content/leonard-arrington-and-writing-mormon-history-0.

rightful kingdom by overprotective and passé general authorities who threatened the mission that "God" had called them to perform. While the Church's leaders may have gained a temporary advantage, Arrington's allies quietly waited for the day they knew would come that would vindicate them, restoring them to their former glory for a final triumph. Arrington's extensive army of outcasts hoped for and foresaw a glorious return to finish the work their father and mentor had begun.

On February 13, 1999, in an article in the *New York Times*—lost behind the headline carrying President Bill Clinton's statement that followed his acquittal in the U.S. Senate impeachment trial—was the simple remark: "Leonard James Arrington, the dean of Mormon historians, died on Thursday at his home in Salt Lake City. He was 81."[35] Eclipsed by that statement was the fact that Arrington left behind hundreds of boxes filled with papers, documents, and research—as well as a diary that would soon unleash a voice from the dust to hundreds—perhaps thousands—of future Latter-day Saint historians, scholars, and members. Arrington's daughter told the *Salt Lake Tribune* that "although the diary includes some rich nuggets that will interest researchers, her father did not record history 'warts and all.' 'He had this wisdom,' she says. 'He was cautious what he put in there [the diary] because he knew it would be read.'"[36]

It has been said that "history is written by the victors"; and Arrington evidently intended his diary to be that history. Carol Lynn Pearson remembered that in 1973, Arrington shared with her the diligence he expended in securing his written thoughts:

" . . . he makes two copies of his journal—one that stays in his office, and another that goes home with him. He said that no matter what happens to him, he wants his true story to be preserved. I told him that I also write down all of these details

---

35   Wolfgang Saxon, "Leonard J. Arrington, 81, Mormon Historian," *The New York Times*, February 13, 1999, https://www.nytimes.com/1999/02/13/us/leonard-j-arrington-81-mormon-historian.html.

36   Kristen Moulton, "Diary of famed Mormon historian reveals more of the man," *The Salt Lake Tribune*, September 24, 2010, https://archive.sltrib.com/article.php?id=50275670&itype=cmsid.

in my diary, and we were in agreement that truth has got to be preserved, whatever the cost.[37]

In the years following Leonard Arrington's death, significant changes began to occur; and in 2005, the Joseph Fielding Smith Institute was closed. The historians, who had once thought of themselves as exiled from Church headquarters, eventually did return to Salt Lake City. Their primary product, at the time, was the monumental Joseph Smith Papers Project—an enterprise heralded by many historians, but one that would proceed with the progressive undertones already in motion under Arrington's lasting influence. Many scholars who had worked with Leonard Arrington decades earlier, including Ron Esplin and Richard Bushman, would celebrate this return—and rejoice with the changes they encountered. "Scholars both inside and outside the LDS Church remember the tension between historians and some LDS leaders two decades ago over the tone and content of some scholarship," the *Deseret News* reported. "At that point, access to the archives became more highly restricted and the Smith Institute at BYU was established."[38] Now, however, the winds of change had shifted once again; and today, Arrington's devoted followers look back with satisfaction over the extensive far-reaching success of their mentor's objectives.

One of Arrington's History Division employees, Ron Esplin, succeeded Arrington as director of the Joseph Fielding Smith Institute at BYU. Esplin sung accolades in Arrington's honor, praising his deep-rooted legacy:

 Lots of folks that are not connected in any way to the enterprise right now still trace their roots back to being inspired by, taught by, mentored by, encouraged by him [Leonard Arrington]. All of those things.[39]

---

37   Gregory A. Prince, *Leonard Arrington and the Writing of Mormon History* (Salt Lake City, UT: Tanner Trust Fund and J. Willard Marriott Library, 2016), 2.

38   Carrie A. Moore, "Scholars moving to S.L.: BYU closing research institute dedicated to early LDS history," *Deseret News*, June 21, 2005, https://www.deseret.com/2005/6/21/19898658/scholars-moving-to-s-l.

39   Gregory A. Prince, *Leonard Arrington and the Writing of Mormon History* (Salt Lake City, UT: Tanner Trust Fund and J. Willard Marriott Library, 2016), 451.

Ron Esplin served from 2006 to 2007 as the president of the Mormon History Association—the organization founded by Leonard Arrington around the same time *Dialogue* was established—and later became the managing editor of The Joseph Smith Papers project.

James B. Allen, co-author of *The Story of the Latter-day Saints,* and author of several other works, served with Arrington at BYU after the History Division was moved in 1982, and co-edited *The Joseph Smith Papers, Journals, Vol. 2*. Allen worked side by side with Arrington for many years, explaining:

> [W]e also started or helped enhance the career of many young people. Leonard Arrington brought in people who were working on various kinds of projects and was able to get grants for them. A number of people who later became prominent in various ways did some of their early work through the Historical Department. . . . The whole legacy of the Historical Department experience is very important, I think, and very interesting to me. I was just happy to be a part of that particular legacy, and while I was there I published a few worthwhile things.[40]

Ron Barney spent "most of his career in the Church Archives," and served as Associate Editor of the Joseph Smith Papers and Executive Producer of the Joseph Smith Papers television series. He commented that, "Leonard influenced a generation of thinking. . . . a generation from now nobody is going to remember that. But they will remember the stuff that Leonard produced. And there is a lore about Leonard Arrington, and it will never dissipate."[41] Barney believed that what Arrington started was only the beginning of significant change, and that there was still more to come—especially in our approach to, and our view of Joseph Smith:

---

40   Alex D. Smith and James B. Allen, "James B. Allen," in *Conversations with Mormon Historians* (Provo: Brigham Young University, Religious Studies Center, 2015), https://rsc.byu.edu/conversations-mormon-historians/james-b-allen.

41   Gregory A. Prince, *Leonard Arrington and the Writing of Mormon History* (Salt Lake City, UT: Tanner Trust Fund and J. Willard Marriott Library, 2016), 452.

❝ I think New Mormon history will serve for a period of time but I personally believe we've passed that. . . . I think we are in a new era. . . . I'm working on a book that I've been working on for many, many years on Joseph Smith, and [the] tail end of it is going to be about the historical legacy of Joseph Smith. As I try to look at that, and how Joseph Smith has been represented over time, there is such a clear point of departure in what has happened [in] the last few years [than] all that happened previous to this. I think we will see that distinctly in the future as we cast our eyes back toward this period of time.[42]

Heidi S. Swinton, Leonard Arrington's stepdaughter, served on the Advisory Board of BYU-TV, the BYU Women's Conference Committee, and the General LDS Church Curriculum Writing Committee, authoring many well-known books and television productions. Swinton praised Arrington as having "ears to hear the Lord."[43]

The legacy passed on by Leonard Arrington continues today, its progressive voice now widely accepted—perhaps inadvertently. The *Salt Lake Tribune* commented in 2018 that the "atmosphere has thawed in the years after Benson's death in 1994."[44] One of the managers at Book of Mormon Central, an organization with a public face composed primarily of progressive intellectuals, admitted to a Joseph Smith Foundation contributor that, "if you don't like Arrington . . . you'll have problems with this [Book of Mormon Central Facebook] group."[45]

When the *Salt Lake Tribune* carried the announcement of the release of a new biography on Leonard Arrington, progressive

---

42   Benchmark Books, "Laura Hales & Contributors (A Reason for Faith)--Benchmark Books, 5/11/16," YouTube video, 00:21:30, May 18, 2016, https://youtu.be/zlVGqk5hjlI?t=1290.

43   "In Memoriam, Leonard J. Arrington," *Journal of Mormon History* 25, no. 1 (February 15, 1999), 7, https://digitalcommons.usu.edu/cgi/viewcontent.cgi?article=1032&context=mormonhistory.

44   Bob Mims, "New collection of Leonard Arrington's vast journals shows battles the Mormon historian had with LDS leaders over telling the truth about the church's past," *The Salt Lake Tribune*, May 9, 2018, https://www.sltrib.com/religion/2018/05/09/new-collection-of-leonard-arringtons-vast-journals-shows-battles-the-mormon-historian-had-with-lds-leaders-over-telling-the-truth-about-the-churchs-past/.

45   Documented private conversation, January 1, 2020.

scholars and historians rejoiced at the recognition their old friend was receiving:

// In fact, he laid the foundation for Mormonism's scholarly renaissance—including the groundbreaking "Joseph Smith Papers" about the faith's founder, "The First Fifty Years of Relief Society" about its female leaders, and the church's online Gospel Topics essays about thorny historical and theological issues. Along the way, he nurtured many of today's leading LDS scholars.

Arrington's most durable accomplishment, [Greg] Prince says, is not "what he wrote, but what he did—he mentored hundreds of people at all levels and shaped the future of Mormon studies."[46]

With his time on Earth complete, Arrington's mortal remains lie in repose beneath the fertile Cache Valley loam in the Logan Cemetery only twenty-five miles from President Benson's claimed resting place. Arrington's headstone is inscribed with the final epitaph bestowed by those whom he led: "Beloved Mentor."

Latter-day Saint History in the 21st-Century

For many traditionalists, Ezra Taft Benson's name represents an ideal—an adherence to the Church's foundational tenets and doctrine—a name known throughout the halls of education and in the homes of Latter-day Saints for both good or evil, depending on where one stands in their ideology as it relates to the Church. Truly, for traditionalists, he fought a good fight, he kept the faith, and there can be no doubt that he was greeted by his Savior with a welcoming, "Well done, thou good and faithful servant."

Progressives revere Leonard Arrington as the father of New Mormon History, the mentor of many hundreds of Latter-day Saint historians, and the instigator of a "reconstructed narrative," challenging the traditionalist account and suggesting it is "not true."[47]

---

46 Peggy Fletcher Stack, "New biography tells all about a forthright Mormon historian, Leonard Arrington, who told all," *The Salt Lake Tribune,* June 21, 2016, https://archive.sltrib.com/article.php?id=3988110&itype=CMSID.

47 James F. Stoddard III, "'The dominant [Church history] narrative is not true . . .' LDS scholars encourage new history, new policy, new Church," Latter-day Answers, October 1, 2016, https://ldsanswers.org/dominant-church-history-narrative-not-true-lds-scholars-encourage-new-history-new-policy-new-church/.

Leonard Arrington grave site, Logan, Utah

For the thousands of Latter-day Saints who presently find themselves caught in the crossfire of this desperate struggle over the history and foundation of our faith, the critical message we share is one of reassuring hope. The Church has neither lied to you, nor intentionally betrayed you. Rather, our history has undergone a shift in its interpretation—swinging the message from a conservative, traditionalist point of view to a progressive, permissive understanding. We live in a new, nearly inescapable culture shadowed by degrees of grey, with our reality under constant threat of manipulation. All of us have acquired some traditionalist and some progressive perceptions, and it requires vigilance and honesty to discern between the two and make the choice of where to stand. It is a battle between two opposing narratives, one traditional and the other revisionist—a struggle between two polarized viewpoints. The one that we, as Latter-day Saints, honor most is the direction that will prevail. Where will you stand?

19

RESURRECTING PROGRESSIVE DECONSTRUCTION

". . . [I]n the end, Dad's story was a success story." Susan Arrington Madsen, daughter of Leonard Arrington, reflected on the impact her father's work had on Latter-day Saint history during an interview with the *Salt Lake Tribune* in 2018: "Dad accomplished things that needed to be done [during his tenure], and the proof of that is coming today. He would be ecstatic."[1]

Arrington's expulsion from Church headquarters, and his death nearly two decades later, did not lead to a disintegration of the deconstructionist Latter-day Saint history movement some had expected, or even hoped for. Today, during the 21st century, Arrington's work and vision has expanded exponentially, with little opposition, and has reached a level that dramatically affects the lives of millions of Church members worldwide.

Arrington's Colleagues Return

In 2005, the BYU department that had been created for Leonard Arrington and his team in the 1980s—during their "exile"—was closed. Many of the department's scholars returned to the Family and Church History Department in Salt Lake City, bringing with them a project originally conceived by Arrington's close friend, Dean Jessee. It was called the Joseph Smith Papers Project. It is intriguing

---

1   Bob Mims, "New collection of Leonard Arrington's vast journals shows battles the Mormon historian had with LDS leaders over telling the truth about the church's past," *The Salt Lake Tribune*, May 9, 2018, https://www.sltrib.com/religion/2018/05/09/new-collection-of-leonard-arringtons-vast-journals-shows-battles-the-mormon-historian-had-with-lds-leaders-over-telling-the-truth-about-the-churchs-past/.

to note that the preliminary work of the Joseph Smith Papers project supported Bushman's *Joseph Smith: Rough Stone Rolling*.[2] The current national advisory board of the Joseph Smith Papers project includes: Richard L. Bushman, Terryl L. Givens, and Dean C. Jessee, along with other scholars, who have produced several publications promoting the progressive New Mormon History interpretation of Joseph Smith.

In 2005, Marlin K. Jensen[3] received an appointment to the position of Church Historian and Recorder.[4] Jensen's association with progressive scholars, and his adoption of ideals held by the Democratic Party, earned him the reputation as the "LDS leadership's most visible Democrat. . . . Although his wife tilts Republican or independent, all of his kids lean left."[5] During an interview with the *Salt Lake Tribune* in 1998 he was asked: "Some LDS members subscribe to the notion that it is difficult, if not impossible, to be a faithful Mormon and a Democrat. People point to such things as the gay rights and pro-choice planks of the national Democratic Party. How do you respond?" Jensen replied: "the basic foundational principles of the Democratic Party have appealed to me more. But that's a matter really of personal choice, it has nothing to do with our salvation." However, Jensen also expressed regret over "the decline of the Democratic Party and the notion that may prevail in some areas that you can't be a good Mormon and a good Democrat at the same time."[6] In 2010, during a meeting with gay members of the Church in Oakland, California, Jensen shared with the attending audience: "to the full extent of my capacity . . . I am sorry," in reference to the Church's support of Proposition 8.[7]

---

2   Richard L. Bushman, *Rough Stone Rolling* (New York: Vintage Books, 2007), xxii.

3   We have omitted the use of Marlin K. Jensen's ecclesiastical title here, and elsewhere, because we are documenting his work as a historian, and not commenting on his work as a general authority.

4   Marlin K. Jensen, a Utah attorney with a law degree from the University of Utah, completed his undergraduate work at BYU.

5   Trent Nelson, "Mormon leadership bids farewell to peacemaking progressive," *The Salt Lake Tribune*, October 3, 2012, https://archive.sltrib.com/article. php?id=55011521&itype=CMSID.

6   "Transcript of Marlin Jensen Interview," KevinAshworth.com, http://www. kevinashworth.com/ldr/transcript-of-marlin-jensen-interview/.

7   Trent Nelson, "Mormon leadership bids farewell to peacemaking progressive," *The Salt Lake Tribune*, October 3, 2012, https://archive.sltrib.com/article.

Jensen's desire to see the notion eliminated, that "you can't be a good Mormon and a good Democrat at the same time," was a goal shared by one of his predecessors—Leonard Arrington. Arrington included the following entry in his diary on January 23, 1979:

// Gunn McKay phoned this afternoon to reflect that in the early years the Church gave the appearance of being "up front" or avant-garde, in our enlightened approach to the family, recreation, education, new thought, and so on, and today many people think that the only proper stance is one of ultra conservatism, aka Cleon Skousen. He wanted to know if anyone had reflected on this and written articles or given speeches that might be helpful for him to read. He obviously is feeling a little uncomfortable with the application of labels like liberal or conservative, and wants to demonstrate that a person can be labeled liberal and still be right in line with Mormon tradition.[8]

During Jensen's tenure as Church Historian, he "oversaw the greatest transformation in the church's historical department since the 1970s,"[9] the era of change actuated under Arrington's guiding eye. Jensen harkened back to Arrington, considering him the "the 'founding father' of the scholarly exploration of the Mormon cosmos."[10] During an interview with University of Utah professor Phillip Barlow, Jensen offered due respect to Arrington and the changes he brought to the Historian's office:

// *Barlow*: "I have noticed a shift since the 1980s, you could say, in the mentality and attitude of the Church collectively toward the history. Maybe I am imagining that but you know the First Volume of the Joseph Smith Papers and how widely received

---

php?id=55011521&itype=CMSID.

8   Leonard J. Arrington Diaries, January 23, 1979; Leonard J. Arrington and Gary James Bergera, *Confessions of a Mormon Historian: The Diaries of Leonard J. Arrington, 1971-1997*, vol. 2 (Salt Lake City: Signature Books, 2018), 710.

9   Peggy Fletcher Stack, "Mormon leadership bids farewell to peacemaking progressive," *The Salt Lake Tribune*, October 8, 2012, https://archive.sltrib.com/article.php?id=55011521&itype=cmsid.

10   "LDS Church Gift to USU Continues the Legacy of Leonard J. Arrington," Utah State University, October 13, 2016, https://www.usu.edu/today/story/lds-church-gift-to-usu-continues-the-legacy-of-leonard-j-arrington.

that was by the Church. And I was just wondering if a project such as that and Richard Bushman's *Rough Stone Rolling*, I don't know how well those would have been received in the eighties. I just wondered if a shift has occurred in the attitude towards the Church and history and what accounts for that. What are your thoughts on that?

Jensen: That's a good question. I agree there has been a shift. . . . when [Leonard Arrington] had the job that I now have, he began a tremendous undertaking to share our history. I don't think we have ever had a time that was as productive as those 10 years.[11]

Marlin Jensen was the first general authority to attend an annual conference of the Mormon History Association founded under the leadership of Leonard Arrington in 1965. Jensen's attendance signaled renewed support for New Mormon History, and for liberal progressive scholarship. He oversaw the ongoing Joseph Smith Papers project and facilitated the return of the Joseph Fielding Smith Institute staff to Salt Lake City. Progressive evangelist Terryl Givens said of Jensen's legacy: "Marlin Jensen has done more to further the cause of Mormon history than any person of the current generation." A vocal progressive in his own right, Givens promoted the idea that "much of [the doctrine and teachings of the early brethren] is foolish. Brigham Young said a lot of silly things."[12]

In 2012, following seven years of service, Jensen handed the reins over to Steven E. Snow,[13] who held the title of Church Historian and Recorder until 2019. Four years into his leadership:

❏❏ Elder Steven E. Snow, a USU alumnus and LDS general authority, presented a [$1 million] gift supporting the Leonard J. Arrington Professorship of Mormon History and Culture to USU President Stan L. Albrecht and Humanities Dean Joseph Ward. . . .

11　"Elder Marlin K. Jensen Questions And Answers," audio, 00:18:24, https://archive.org/details/ElderMarlinJensenQuestionsAndAnswers.

12　"Faithful Scholars Address Faith Crisis," ChurchIsTrue.com, PDF, p. 4, https://www.churchistrue.com/wp-content/uploads/2016/10/Faithful-LDS-Scholars-Address-Faith-Crisis.pdf.

13　We have omitted the use of Steven E. Snow's ecclesiastical title here, and elsewhere, because we are documenting his work as a historian, and not commenting on his work as a general authority.

Marlin K. Jensen, a former LDS Church historian and member of the First Quorum of the Seventy . . . said, "[Arrington] mentored a generation of Mormon studies scholars who learned from his model how to foster both faith and intellect."

Jensen said Arrington, who died in 1999, is considered the "founding father" of the scholarly exploration of the Mormon cosmos. He helped establish the Mormon History Association, the Western History Association and the Journal of Mormon History. Such efforts as Arrington's and continued in the USU chair, added Jensen, are "essential to many to foster an informed and sturdy faith."[14]

Snow began his faith journey, questioning and probing Church history, while reading the New Mormon History as interpreted by Juanita Brooks and others:

// Probably what really turned the light on was when I began reading some of the books by Juanita Brooks. She wrote several books about Church history including, of course, *The Mountain Meadow Massacre.*[15]

And the first book Snow read in his search for direction and inspiration, when initially called to be Church Historian, was Arrington's bio-discussion of his own Church Historian years:

// One of the first books I read after being called was *The Adventures of a Church Historian* by Leonard Arrington. I talked to a lot of people, and there is a lot of history with this calling, and it can be a little sensitive, obviously.[16]

During Snow's tenure as Church Historian, he oversaw and was responsible for the new progressive changes in the Church history museum

---

14   "LDS Church Gift to USU Continues the Legacy of Leonard J. Arrington," Utah State University, October 13, 2016, https://www.usu.edu/today/story/lds-church-gift-to-usu-continues-the-legacy-of-leonard-j-arrington.

15   Richard E. Bennett, Steven E. Snow and Dana M. Pike, "Start with Faith: A Conversation with Elder Steven E. Snow," *Religious Educator* 14, no. 3 (2013): 1–11, https://rsc.byu.edu/vol-14-no-3-2013/start-faith-conversation-elder-steven-e-snow.

16   Ibid.

and other historical sites. He was also responsible for the Church's new historical art, reflecting the progressive New Mormon History.

In 2019, Snow commented to the *Salt Lake Tribune* that: "Many of these projects that I worked on were envisioned by him [Marlin K. Jensen] and his folks, and I was able to take them through and finish them."[17] Snow also commented that part of their "good chemistry" may have been "due to the fact that we both loved church history, [and] were Democrats . . ."[18]

Without question, our history and the rising generation is speedily veering toward the progressive left—socially, historically, and politically.[19] At the same time, Millennials primarily—but other age groups as well—are leaving the Church and the faith of their fathers in numbers we have never before seen. Our current state of faith crisis is painfully unprecedented.

Is it possible that political affiliation could be in some way connected to faith? John Dehlin commented in a public Facebook post affiliated with the Mormon Stories Podcast page on June 20, 2020:

" I have a theory that losing one's faith in Mormonism tends (on average) to make people more liberal/progressive politically. Of course there are exceptions. I'm just saying that on average . . . I find this to be true.[20]

---

17   Steven E. Snow detailed some of the projects he oversaw during an interview with Keith A. Erekson. They include the release of the Gospel Topic Essays, changes to the Doctrine and Covenants section headings, a new exhibit at the Church History Museum (*The Heavens are Opened*), and the publication of the *Saints* series. Keith A. Erekson, "The Office of Church Recorder: A Conversation with Elder Steven E. Snow," *BYU Studies Quarterly* 58, no. 3 (2019): 149-185, https://byustudies.byu.edu/content/office-church-recorder-conversation-with-elder-steven-e-snow.

18   Peggy Fletcher Stack, "Mission accomplished: This leader got a more unvarnished LDS history to members, with the blessing of his bosses," *The Salt Lake Tribune,* August 10, 2019, https://www.sltrib.com/religion/2019/08/10/lds-churchs-non/.

19   "[Jana] Riess' research found a 'lot more support for Democrats among young Mormons than [previous surveys] did,' Campbell said. . . . 'more and more young Mormons are turning away from the GOP.'" Peggy Fletcher Stack, "From coffee to gay issues to doctrine, Jana Riess' 'momentous' book shows how LDS millennials view the faith and why more are leaving," *The Salt Lake Tribune*, February 25, 2019, https://www.sltrib.com/religion/2019/02/25/coffee-gay-issues/.

20   Mormon Stories Podcast, Facebook, June 20, 2020, https://www.facebook.com/mormonstories/posts/10158905528869301.

Hundreds of commenters followed his post[21] with story after story of disaffected and faith-estranged members who reported a significant left shift toward liberal thinking and ideology as they embraced progressive Latter-day Saint history, or simply abandoned their faith in the Restoration altogether. Fawn Brodie also veered to the far left politically and socially over the years subsequent to losing her faith and authoring *No Man Knows My History*.[22]

Faith Loss Through Shifting the Narrative

As the Mormon history narrative filtering down to the general membership began shifting from traditional to progressive, multitudes of members experienced a resulting crisis of faith. Kristel Johnson worked for the Church in the office of the Seventy, knew Steven Snow personally, and was raised in an active Latter-day Saint family:

> ... I had always wanted to be an obedient Latter-day Saint. ... [Our family] would have Family Home Evenings every Monday, my dad would get us up in the mornings and we'd do scripture time and sing hymns and we were just very religious and very "in." ... I believed it all, like I *really* believed it all. ... My mom and dad have served four missions. They've been MTC Presidents,

---

21   The following is a small sampling of the comments: "Much more liberal, if that is the correct label. I was raised as a far-right person but cannot stand their human-hostile politics."; "I am much more progressive/liberal than when I was a member. But, I think this is the way I always would have been if the church hadn't actively suppressed it."; "Much more liberal. Raised far right and never thought about it much."; "I[t] is hard to admit that I fell in the follow along category while I was an active member, I didn't give much thought to the impact of some conservative views. I am now much more liberal, preserving my rights should not inhibit or make harder the lives of others."; "It was such a relief to be able to claim my progressive beliefs. I didn't realize how much it was weighing me down ..."; "Yes, went from a pretty hard core conservative to a middle left liberal."; "I noticed the same thing John generally speaking, it seems that initially ex Mormons go from conservative believer to liberal atheist."; "My family was very very conservative right, they didn't lean, they set the standard. Members of the John Birch society, libertarian, Tea Party, Rand Paul, and my mother's favorite, Ann [*sic*] Rand. ... The last two decades I have moved more left and that corresponds with with being out of the church."

22   Brodie also extended a great deal of energy into fighting Ronald Reagon in California, and deconstructing founding fathers including Thomas Jefferson, *Thomas Jefferson: An Intimate History*. Newell G. Bringhurst, *Fawn McKay Brodie: A Biographer's Life* (Norman, University of Oklahoma Press, 1999), 179-181.

mission presidents. They've served in the Area Authorities, they're just very "in."[23]

When her close friend began struggling with her testimony over "Church history," Kristel eagerly stepped in to help. She purchased two books from Deseret Book because she was "going to start on super safe things." One of the 'safe' books she purchased was Richard Bushman's, *Rough Stone Rolling*:

> *There were two things there that disturbed me as I read that. When I was a little girl, when I was in Primary, I was shown pictures of how the Book of Mormon was translated and I swore I had a testimony of the Urim & Thummim as that being the modality of how the Book of Mormon came to be. And I had a testimony on it and I would bear it and I would talk about it. And then when I read in the book [that Joseph Smith translated with a dark seer stone] . . . it confused me. I was very confused how someone could have a revelation, a personal revelation from God while being deceitful because that goes against everything that the Church teaches me. So I really had a hard time with that. . . . I asked my dad if he had read* Rough Stone Rolling*. And he did and all this time as I was learning some things I was trying to talk to my parents about it but my dad [said] "Oh that's just folklore." But it didn't feel like folklore and the person that wrote the book was a Church historian and it's from Deseret Book.*[24]

What members and former members of the Church—including Kristel—are not being told is that *every* account alleging Joseph Smith's use of an occultic, magic seer stone—or any seer stone for that matter—to translate the Book of Mormon originated from ill-disposed, apostatized former-members and other antagonistic anti-Mormons, who actively engaged in seeking to destroy the Church and the work of the Prophet. Although there is some trustworthy evidence that the Prophet did possess one or more seer stones, *no credible history* indicates that those stones were used in the translation

---

23   Mormon Enlightenment, "Truth Seeking w/ Kristel Johnson (The Journey to Find Truth)," YouTube video, 00:04:10, https://youtu.be/7OSuQeL5YIs?t=250.

24   Ibid.

Artistic depiction of interpreters based on J.W. Peterson's influential 1921
recollection of an 1890 interview with Joseph Smith's brother William
by David A. Baird under CC BY-SA 3.0

of the Book of Mormon. Neither is there credible evidence that
Joseph Smith used seer stones for hunting treasure and lost objects,
or that the Smith family pursued, at any time, a career in money
digging. An in-depth investigation of the translation of the Book
of Mormon, and a debunking of the scurrilous seer stone narrative,
can be found in the book, *Seer Stone v. Urim & Thummim: Book of
Mormon Translation on Trial.*

Kristel was not provided accurate history when she read *Rough*

Stone Rolling. Desperate for help, she scheduled a meeting with then-Church Historian, Steven Snow, hoping to find peace with the internal conflict plaguing her mind. Remembering that day, she shared:

❝ ... [I] broke down and I cried to him about the translation of the Book of Mormon and I just said, "It really isn't fair to be fed one narrative and then flip it or all of a sudden change it and have people be okay with that." ...

He was empathetic and he just said, "Well, that narrative would have been kooky."

And I'm like, "Well—but—if it's the truth."[25]

Kristel purchased another book—written by friends and colleagues of Leonard Arrington and encouraged by him[26]—but that work only served to deepen her feelings of betrayal and frustration. One step followed another until eventually, Kristel and her husband Brady—faced with mounting doubt after being unable to find answers about the conflicting narrative—abandoned their fractured testimonies and left the Church.

---

25   Mormon Enlightenment, "Truth Seeking w/ Kristel Johnson (The Journey to Find Truth)," YouTube video, 00:13:35, https://youtu.be/7OSuQeL5YIs?t=815.

26   Linda King Newell and Valeen Tippetts Avery, *Mormon Enigma: Emma Hale Smith* (Chicago: University of Illinois Press, 1984).

20

ICON TOPPLERS OR
AWAKENING DEFENDERS

During the summer of 2020, unprecedented scenes of violence appeared as riots erupted across the United States, unleashing disdain towards anyone not aligned with their own peculiar view. With neither regard for nor understanding of the nation's history, a product of American progressivism, a number of monuments and memorials were removed, vandalized, or destroyed by deconstructionists.

While the protestors claimed entitlement to topple "racist" monuments—targeting many Confederate statues—their fury also zeroed in on prominent Christian figures and heroes. Statues of Christopher Columbus were destroyed or removed; angry mobs defaced and vandalized beloved memorials of George Washington, Thomas Jefferson, and Abraham Lincoln. Puritan preacher George Whitfield, Francis Scott Key, 'The Pioneer Mother,' and even Jesus Christ and the Virgin Mary succumbed to the hateful hands of angry protests.

While these uprisings centered primarily in the United States, other countries also experienced similar attacks on their own historical monuments, giving rise to the *New York Times* headline: "How Statues are Falling Around the World." What few seem to realize is that the tearing down and defacing of the nation's historical statues is not merely a spontaneous reaction to current events; but rather, it is a symptom—a product of the vilification of traditional values that has crept into American classrooms during recent decades.

Christopher Columbus Statue Torn Down at Minnesota State Capitol
by Tony Webster under CC BY 2.0

In his book, *Original Intent*, distinguished historian and author David Barton[1] specifically notes the revisionist strategy to:

> ❝ . . . vilif[y] the historical figures who embraced a position they [the revisionists] reject. . . . [They] portray immorality as indisputable fact. The intended result is for the public's perception of its leaders' integrity and morality to be altered, thus destroying their credibility.[2]

Vicki Jo Anderson discovered the same trend when researching for her work, *The Other Eminent Men of Wilford Woodruff*: "We

---

1   David Barton, who one may consider a traditionalist American historian, is the author of a number of works, including *The Jefferson Lies* and *Original Intent: The Courts, the Constitution of Religion*. He is the founder of WallBuilders. "His exhaustive research has rendered him an expert in historical and constitutional issues and he serves as a consultant to state and federal legislators, has participated in several cases at the Supreme Court, was involved in the development of the History/Social Studies standards for states such as Texas and California, and has helped produce history textbooks now used in schools across the nation." "David Barton's Bio," Wall Builders, https://wallbuilders.com/bios/.

2   David Barton, *Original Intent: The Courts, the Constitution, and Religion* (Aledo: Wallbuilder Press, 2008), 285, 315.

discovered in our years of historical research, that history written prior to 1920 was often written of great men and women who performed great deeds. After 1920, history has highlighted the miseries of men."[3]

Applying this strategy to our Latter-day Saint history and its leaders, the last 100 years have seen a succession of progressive efforts to undermine the credibility of Joseph Smith and Brigham Young, thereby prompting the public to reject their traditionalist doctrines and teachings—those 'disagreeable' aspects of the Restoration that progressives seek to disavow.

Concurrent with the protests that resulted in over 200 monuments and markers being removed, sometime between the late-night hours of Sunday, June 14 and Monday morning, June 15, a statue of Brigham Young located on the BYU-Provo campus was spitefully vandalized:

❝ The word "racist" was spray-painted on the statue in red paint, some of which splattered on to the building sign, BYU Police Lt. Rich Christianson confirmed . . . The student news organization also reported two individuals were found attempting to hang a sign reading "Black Lives Matter" around the neck of the Karl G. Maeser statue on June 16. . . .

It's unknown if the two incidents are related.

. . . This isn't the first time a statue of Brigham Young has been vandalized in Provo, or similar such vandalism has occurred on campus. Back in 2003, a statue at what is now Academy Square and the Provo City Library—the site of the former Brigham Young Academy on University Avenue—was painted with red paint, and the word "sexist" scrawled across the fixture's base.[4]

In his thesis, "New Mormon History," Richard Marshall made the significant observation that the intellectuals engaged in this 'new' history have a "tendency to humanize past leaders of the Church."[5]

---

3   Vicki Jo Anderson, *The Other Eminent Men of Wilford Woodruff* (Malta: Nelson Book, 2000), 4.

4   Sean Walker, "Brigham Young statue vandalized near BYU's Smoot Building," KSL.com, June 19, 2020, https://www.ksl.com/article/46767180/brigham-young-statue-vandalized-near-byus-smoot-building.

5   Richard Stephen Marshall, "'The New Mormon History': A Senior Honors

He noted that Marvin Hill's 1972 *BYU Studies* article, "Joseph Smith and the 1826 Trial: New Evidence and New Difficulties," "is very compromising and shows Joseph Smith in an extremely humanistic light, typical of the New History."[6] Hill announced, "[i]t is time historians began to study this aspect [weaknesses or sins] of Joseph's personality."[7]

The progressive rewriting of Restoration heroes transformed Brigham Young into a blatantly racist, tyrannical autocrat—Joseph Smith into a bumbling, treasure seeking magician—Eliza R. Snow into a cold, dictatorial feminist—Joseph Fielding Smith into a judgmental, incompetent, clumsy historian—and other early Latter-day Saints into superstitious, chauvinist fanatics steeped in mysogynist patriarchy.

Leonard Arrington remarked that one of the differences between his progressive history and President Benson's traditionalist interpretation was that President Benson believed in "revelation direct from on high in pure vessels."[8] In other words, President Benson believed that men and women who are 'great,' must of necessity also be 'good.' Those who speak with God are invariably pure vessels—righteous and holy. The revelations as originally given to the Prophet Joseph and others contain God-like infallibility.

Arrington, on the other hand, published in *Dialogue* that "pro biographies" of Joseph Smith, portraying the Prophet in "pictures of sweetness and light," were guilty of "err[ing] even more on the side of incredibility than the blacker portraits of the anti's."[9] In other words, for Arrington, the anti-Mormon picture of Church history was closer to reality than the faithful Mormon history portrayal given to us by those who worked the hardest and lived the closest to the principles therein espoused. Arrington was adamant in his assertion that Joseph Smith was not the man of blameless character, honor, and integrity

---

Project Summary," May 1, 1977, Department of History, University of Utah Special Collections, Marriott Library, University of Utah, 51; photocopy in our possession.

6   Ibid., 50.

7   Ibid.

8   Leonard J. Arrington Diaries, September 22, 1976; Leonard J. Arrington and Gary James Bergera, *Confessions of a Mormon Historian: The Diaries of Leonard J. Arrington*, 1971-1997, vol. 2 (Salt Lake City: Signature Books, 2018), 241.

9   Leonard Arrington, "Scholarly Studies of Mormonism in the Twentieth Century," *Dialogue: A Journal of Mormon Thought* 1, no. 1 (1966): 25.

that the Church portrayed for over 100 years; and therefore, the revelations he provided to the Church are only cultural 'products of his time,' with perhaps some inspirational worth.

Other progressives have expressed their feeling that to depict the Prophet as a paragon of virtue and honor is both naive and unrealistic. When commenting on his biography, *Rough Stone Rolling,* Richard Bushman explained that: "People are ready for a realistic picture of Joseph Smith. They want to know him straight, not as someone lifted two or three feet off the ground."[10] Or, as Bushman admitted during a 2005 FAIR Mormon conference, ". . . I do not feel that we have to protect Joseph Smith. . . . I take great pleasure in his flaws and in his weaknesses—they make him more appealing."[11] Nevertheless, as one honest reviewer of *Rough Stone Rolling* warned, "Those looking for a faith-promoting view of the prophet's life may want to look elsewhere . . . ."[12]

Another progressive scholar, Henry Eyring, shared his own corresponding sentiment about a mistake-prone 'Joseph' in *Reflections of a Mormon Scientist*:

❦ I've often said that I would be delighted to have someone point out some flaw in the Book of Mormon that proved that Joseph Smith made an error in translating or inserted some idea of his own that wasn't on the plates. Of course, he might have been inspired to deviate. But even if I thought otherwise, that would merely prove that he was human, a fact about which I was already quite sure. It would also show that the Creator is tolerant of a mistake now and then. These seem quite hopeful ideas to me . . . .[13]

What is the cause of this compulsion among revisionist scholars to seek out deficiency and weakness in the heroes of Latter-day Saint, American, and even world history? Why are they determined to reject the possibility

---

10   Lee Benson, "Quite a ride for author of 'Rolling,'" *Deseret News*, March 6, 2008, https://www.deseret.com/2008/3/6/20381170/quite-a-ride-for-author-of-rolling.

11   Richard Bushman, "A Joseph Smith Miscellany," FairMormon, August 2005, https://www.fairmormon.org/conference/august-2005/a-joseph-smith-miscellany.

12   "Joseph Smith: Rough Stone Rolling," Amazon.com reviews, https://www.amazon.com/Joseph-Smith-Rough-Stone-Rolling/dp/1400077532.

13   Henry Eyring, *Reflections of a Scientist* (Salt Lake City: Deseret Book, 1983), 45.

that there could be men, such as Joseph, who are far greater than they can comprehend? Our early leaders accepted and taught that Joseph Smith stood immediately next in holiness to our Lord Jesus Christ. Why do progressives distastefully challenge and vehemently protest the contemporary witnesses of the Prophet's nobility?

Progressive historian and author James Goldberg recently shared his cynical belief with the *Salt Lake Tribune* that moderns were "tired of heroes":

❝❞ To James Goldberg, a Utah-based writer, "*Saints*" represents "a seismic shift in how Latter-day Saints are approaching our history.

"... [W]e started packag[ing] the history more and more for those media.... Writers [during the 1900s, who were predominantly traditionalist and] compressed the story into a simple heroic arc with leaders like Joseph Smith and Brigham Young acting not only as historical figures but also as mascots for Mormon virtues of righteousness, spirituality and industry."

The rise of the internet toppled that thinking.

"Once people had a way to hear from multiple voices, we developed a thirst for complexity and authenticity," he says. "We didn't believe in (or, quite frankly, find ourselves interested in) the mascot versions of early saints."

Mormons "got tired of heroes," Goldberg says. "We wanted real people."

"Saints" is full of them.[14]

While the views, and consequently new narrative, offered by deconstructionists like Bushman and Goldberg differ widely from those of traditionalists, one can accept the premise that both—progressives and traditionalists alike—genuinely believe their personal interpretation represents an accurate portrayal of the past.

It seems logical to infer that the toppling of the icons of virtue and integrity in our history has led to an overall mediocrity in our

---

14   Peggy Fletcher Stack, "New volume of 'Saints' reveals the many sides of Brigham Young," *The Salt Lake Tribune*, February 12, 2020, https://www.sltrib.com/religion/2020/02/12/racism-polygamy-colonizer/; brackets in original.

culture, and an age which has divested itself of true heroes. Without an ideal to achieve—a heroic example to emulate—it is common in our time to promote the belittling of past heroes in an attempt to self-justify our own mediocrity and increasingly lower moral standards. In his 1997 Freedom Festival address, President Gordon B. Hinckley quoted Charles Malek:

> " I respect all men, and it is from disrespect for none that I say there are no great leaders in the world today. In fact, greatness itself is laughed to scorn. You should not be great today—you should sink yourself into the herd, you should not be distinguished from the crowd, you should simply be one of the many.
>
> The commanding voice is lacking. The voice which speaks little, but which when it speaks, speaks with compelling moral authority—this kind of voice is not congenial to this age. The age flattens and levels down every distinction into drab uniformity. Respect for the high, the noble, the great, the rare, the specimen that appears once every hundred or every thousand years, is gone. Respect at all is gone! If you ask whom and what people do respect, the answer is literally nobody and nothing. This is simply an unrespecting age—it is the age of utter mediocrity. To become a leader today, even a mediocre leader, is a most uphill struggle. You are constantly and in every way and from every side pulled down. One wonders who of those living today will be remembered a thousand years from now . . .
>
> If you believe in prayer, my friends, and I know you do, then pray that God sends great leaders, especially great leaders of the spirit.[15]

In every child there exists a desire to look up to someone for nobleness, purpose, and example. The Master taught, "Come follow Me"; and traditionalists seek to identify and to emulate those true heroes who have sought to follow His example—doing so with all their might, mind, and strength. Those who possess a sacred witness know that Joseph Smith was indeed such a man. Some have sought to depict the Prophet Joseph as an ordinary man with typical weaknesses, allowing for an uncommon gift of leadership—and perhaps, at times,

---

15   Gordon B. Hinckley, "Stand Up for Truth", BYU Speeches, September 17, 1996, https://speeches.byu.edu/talks/gordon-b-hinckley/stand-truth/.

the gift of inspiration. However, this grossly slanted view dismisses the fact that a prophet of God is no greater than the degree his life mirrors that of the Master he serves. Righteousness and character are the sure measuring rods of greatness—or the lack thereof—in all individuals. For every hero of morality and righteousness, detractors will arise who feel that the best way to lift themselves to a higher level is to ridicule and debase those who exemplify Christlike traits.

The more one truly studies the life and works of the Prophet Joseph, the more one comes to know and love the Master, the Son of God. The Prophet is a window to the Son of Righteousness, the Savior of all. No greater, nor more righteous man has lived on this Earth—with the exception of the Lord Jesus Christ—and the life of the Prophet reflects corresponding honor, love, and faithful devotion to the Father. If one desires to follow Christ or to instill a love of truth and godliness in his or her family, the traditionalist voice resolutely persists in advocating a dedicated study of the true life and original teachings of the Prophet of this dispensation—and through this study, a commitment to follow the principles he revealed and vigorously espoused.

Does 'Private' Morality Matter?

The dismantling of national and Restoration heroes coincides with the growing progressive philosophy that personal morality is not a determining factor in the success of an individual's mission, accomplishments, or level of greatness.

During the 1992 Presidential campaign, American singer and actress Gennifer Flowers came forward, accusing Bill Clinton of a 12-year sexual relationship. CNN later admitted that "Clinton had a well-known reputation for womanizing."[16] Clinton initially denied the allegations—in spite of suggestive tapes released by Flowers—until six years later, in the course of the Paula Jones' sexual harassment lawsuit against the U.S. President. Clinton finally confessed that he had had a "sexual encounter" with Flowers two years into his marriage with Hillary.

In 1992, shortly after Bill Clinton was elected as President of

---

16   Julian Zelizer, "Bill Clinton's nearly forgotten 1992 sex scandal," *CNN*, April 6, 2016, https://www.cnn.com/2016/04/06/opinions/zelizer-presidential-election-campaign-scandals-bill-clinton/index.html.

Arrington did not feel Clinton's immorality had any relevance when it came to his leadership or standing as a Christian.

Bill Clinton, 1993

the United States, notwithstanding Gennifer Flowers' accusations, Arrington journaled his belief that Clinton's personal morality had no bearing on, and would not affect his public life or political work. Arrington didn't care about Clinton's affairs—nor did he feel his immorality had any relevance when it came to his leadership abilities or his standing as a "good American" and a Christian:

❝ ... I think Clinton will make a good president. I was never impressed with the "character" charges against Clinton. . . . Who ever cared about the "affairs" of [Thomas] Jefferson,[17] FDR [Franklin Delano Roosevelt], LBJ [Lyndon B. Johnson], Dwight Eisenhower. Clinton must have real leadership qualities. . . . Clinton is intelligent, experienced in political organization, and is a good American . . . . the speech that Clinton gave . . .

---

17   The charge that Thomas Jefferson maintained an affair with one of his slaves, Sally Hemmings, has been proven to be false. Interestingly, while the allegations have been in existence for over a century, Fawn Brodie (the author of the defamatory Joseph Smith biography, *No Man Knows My History*) "was the first to set forth a convincing case that Thomas Jefferson was the father of children by his slave Sally Hemings." Book description for *Thomas Jefferson: An Intimate History* by W. W. Norton, https://wwnorton.com/books/9780393338331. This revisionist history has been essentially debunked. For more information, see David Barton's work, *The Jefferson Lies*, documenting the origins of the Hemings accusation, along with contradictory evidence.

revealed Clinton as an unabashed Christian and a man of strong religious sensibility.[18]

In light of more recent accusations involving both Bill and Hillary Clinton attempting to cover up and intimidate Bill's victims—as well as the revelations concerning the proven Clinton connection with child sex trafficker Jeffrey Epstein—one wonders where Arrington would have finally drawn the line. If depraved immorality—a sin next to murder[19]—is acceptable, would child sex trafficking—a sin very possibly more serious than murder—also be tolerable?

The New Mormon Historians applied this same reasoning to the life of the Prophet Joseph Smith, presenting a progressive version of the Prophet as a money digger, a magician, likely an immoral adulterer and liar, and a man who struggled with arrogance, pride, anger, and vengeance. And yet, the historians argue—employing the same reasoning Arrington used for Clinton—that we should care nothing about Joseph's private life. After all, he still had leadership qualities and intelligence; he was just an ordinary man whom God called to an extraordinary calling.

In the words of Richard Bushman, "I'm not sure I want 'Joseph Smith' to be balanced. Prophets have a right to be wild."[20] According to Brant A. Gardner, another popular Latter-day Saint author, God used the weak occultic elements of early American society (of which the Smiths were supposedly a part) to bring forward the Book of Mormon. Traditionally, "weak things" in the Church's doctrine and tradition have been the humble and meek who listen to the promptings of the Spirit of God and do the Lord's work without worldly accolades. Gardner changes all of this:

❯❯ Joseph couldn't learn to read the text on the plates—there was no Nephite dictionary available. What God used to effect the transformation was yet another **weak thing**. God used the **folk beliefs of the rural population** . . .

---

18   Leonard J. Arrington Diaries, November 3, 1992; Leonard J. Arrington and Gary James Bergera, *Confessions of a Mormon Historian: The Diaries of Leonard J. Arrington*, 1971-1997, vol. 3 (Salt Lake City: Signature Books, 2018), 608-609; brackets in original.

19   Alma 39:5.

20   Dennis Lythgoe, "'Warts and all' in Smith biography," *Deseret News*, October 1, 2005, https://www.deseret.com/2005/10/1/19914955/warts-and-all-in-smith-biography.

Joseph was only one of several seers in that region. As a local seer, he was consulted to find things that were lost or to see into the future. . . .

It was Joseph's belief that he could see the unseeable that the Lord used as the fulcrum to **leverage the village seer into a translator** and then into a prophet of God.[21]

For Gardner, "weak things" are superstitions, involvement in magical rituals and fortune telling, the use of peep stones, and other occultic activities traditionally considered anti-Christian. Gardner continues by explaining his beliefs that in 1828-29, Joseph used the same occultic "skills" he used as the "village seer" to dictate the Book of Mormon.[22]

The prophet-historian Mormon taught the Nephite remnant of believers during the closing era of the Nephite civilization that "the way to judge is as plain, that ye may know with a perfect knowledge."[23] So how does one know if an individual's character or work is righteous? The Scriptures provide an answer:

// Wherefore, a man being evil <u>cannot</u> do that which is good; neither will he give a good gift. For behold, a bitter fountain <u>cannot</u> bring forth good water; neither can a good fountain bring forth bitter water; wherefore, a man being a servant of the devil <u>cannot</u> follow Christ; and if he follow Christ he <u>cannot</u> be a servant of the devil.[24]

For traditionalists, the Book of Mormon represents the word of God—and Mormon's teachings in regard to character, as directly and inescapably relating to a person's works and true accomplishment—good or bad—stand as a prophetic avowal sanctioned and affirmed by God. Conversely, progressives value the revelations and the Book of Mormon, not necessarily as inspired utterance, and certainly not as

---

21   Brant A. Gardner, "Translating the Book of Mormon," in *A Reason for Faith: Navigating LDS Doctrine & Church History* (Provo: Religious Studies Center, Brigham Young University, 2016), 22-23; emphasis added.

22   "The meaning on the plates was certainly hidden and lost. Joseph could not translate as the scholars did. However, with God's help, he would do so using the instrument and methods he had successfully used before. This time he wasn't finding a lost object, but rather a lost meaning." Ibid., 23; emphasis added.

23   Moroni 7:15.

24   Moroni 7:10-11; emphasis added.

the definitive word of God—but more as utterances influenced by the deliverer's cultural environment. Thus, we can understand *Rough Stone Rolling's* subtitle: "A cultural biography of Mormonism's founder."

Traditionalists view Mormon's instructions as a straightforward way—a natural law, in fact—to test the character of Joseph Smith. Was his work good or bitter? Did he produce righteous fruit or conversely evil fruit? If the answer is that the Prophet's fruit was good, then we can conclude that he was a "pure fountain." He was righteous, honorable, and great to the degree that his work was righteous, honorable, and great. If his fruit was evil, then we must suppose that he was a "bitter fountain," and we should reject the Restoration he led, the Book of Mormon he brought forth, and the teachings he left for us, because, "A bitter fountain *cannot* bring forth good water."[25]

The Nephite prophet Alma provided an additional witness for determining whether one can safely trust a man's teachings or philosophies. ". . . trust *no one* to be your teacher nor your minister, except he be a man of God, walking in his ways and keeping his commandments."[26] Alma experienced what it was like to live under the ecclesiastical and political leadership of someone who did not fit this prerequisite. Because of what he observed through the medium of his wicked leader, Noah, he knew firsthand the danger of trusting the teachings of a man whose private moral character was not virtuous. True traditionalists hold to this standard as an essential measuring stick before trusting *any* man or group of men.

The Book of Mormon is replete with examples of men who were committed to tearing down righteous prophets, or the doctrines taught by these holy men. Are there men committed to the same purpose in our day, and can we identify their destructive nature and objectives? If so, are the insidious consequences for Latter-day Saint testimonies far more to be feared in this day than in Book of Mormon times?

---

25 Moroni 7:11; emphasis added.

The same test must be put forward to the fruits of the progressive revision of Mormon history. What are the fruits? President Ezra Taft Benson was deeply concerned that if this narrative were allowed to continue, we would lose our young people. Is this happening? Did President Benson speak prophetically?

26 Mosiah 23:14.

Bruce R. McConkie's Survey

In 1984—the same year Richard Bushman published *Joseph Smith and the Beginnings of Mormonism,* the manuscript originally intended for the Sesquicentennial History—Elder Bruce R. McConkie shared the shocking results of a "testimony survey" conducted at the Missionary Training Center in Provo, Utah, with faculty members at BYU. In Elder McConkie's own words, he admitted the results "about bowled me over."[27] The anonymous survey presented at the MTC asked the missionaries to indicate the strength of their certain knowledge in regard to the following statements:

1. God is my Father, the Father of my spirit.

2. Jesus is the Christ, the Son of God.

3. Joseph Smith is a prophet of God.

4. The Book of Mormon is the word of God.

5. Spencer W. Kimball is a prophet of God today.[28]

The survey asked participants to choose from a list of responses that included the following:

A. I know this to be true because I have received a spiritual witness of its truthfulness.

B. I believe this to be true, but I have not received a spiritual witness.

C. I do not know whether this is true.

D. I doubt whether this is true.[29]

Elder McConkie revealed the shocking results of the survey, which exposed the areas of greatest weakness in the testimonies of the elders, sisters, and couples then residing at the MTC. The weakest areas were:

---

27   Joseph Fielding McConkie, *The Bruce R. McConkie Story: Reflections of a Son* (Salt Lake City, UT: Deseret Book, 2003), 304.

28   Ibid., 305.

29   Ibid.

3. Joseph Smith is a prophet of God.

4. The Book of Mormon is the word of God.[30]

Bruce R. McConkie's son, Joseph Fielding McConkie, was present during his father's address to the BYU faculty members, and he remembered the stunned silence and the shock that permeated the room as he divulged the results of the survey:

> The effect upon the whole group was visible. It was as though someone had hit us in the stomach with a baseball bat. We were stunned-shocked, for these matters were fundamental to what the missionaries would soon be proclaiming. Elder McConkie raised his voice and said: "Something's wrong. Something's terribly wrong! Maybe it's something I've done wrong. Maybe it's something the Brethren have done wrong. Perhaps it's something we've done wrong here at BYU or in our Church Educational System, but clearly something's wrong."[31]

Elder McConkie subsequently counseled with the BYU faculty, reading passages from the Doctrine and Covenants "that state powerfully our need to be loyal to the Restoration and to the truths delivered through the Prophet Joseph Smith."[32] Then, he turned with them to Doctrine & Covenants 84:54-61, urging a course correction as they read the revealed "condemnation, scourge and judgment that still rest[s] upon the Church because of our neglect of the Book of Mormon and latter-day revelation."[33]

"Maybe in our efforts as a Church to ensure that everyone knows we're Christian, we have gone too far," Elder McConkie advised:

> A while back we changed our missionary discussions to make our first discussion a message about Christ. It seemed at the time a good thing to do, given that Jesus is the Head of the Church. But what was the result? A decrease in convert baptisms and a decrease in the number of copies of the Book of Mormon placed

---

30   Ibid.

31   Ibid.

32   Elder McConkie cited Doctrine & Covenants 5:10; 20:11-17; 31:3-4; 49:1-4.

33   Joseph Fielding McConkie, *The Bruce R. McConkie Story: Reflections of a Son* (Salt Lake City, UT: Deseret Book, 2003), 306.

> *"Something's terribly wrong! ... We are not teaching the Restoration as we ought to."*
> (Bruce R. McConkie)

Bruce R. McConkie, used with permission

by full-time missionaries from one million per year to 500,000. We are *not teaching the Restoration as we ought to.*[34]

Elder McConkie sought to strengthen weakened testimonies by upholding and unfolding the righteous character of Joseph Smith, and the centrality of the Prophet's mission and teachings to the Gospel of Jesus Christ. His son recorded:

> The more [Elder McConkie] studied the revelations of the Restoration, the more convinced he became that we will never have the success in missionary work that we should have until we as a people come to the realization that we cannot present that message independent of the testimony of Joseph Smith. That is, for instance, we cannot simply go out into the world and profess our faith in Christ; we must, rather, profess our faith in that Christ revealed to the Prophet Joseph Smith. In his judgment, to attempt to teach of Christ without reference to the Book of Mormon or without drawing upon the revelations given to us by

---

34   Ibid., 305-306, emphasis added.

the Prophet Joseph Smith was to offend the Spirit. "Joseph Smith is the revealer of the knowledge of Christ for our dispensation. If it were not for him and the witness and testimony he has given, we would not have more knowledge than the sectarian world has; hence, we bear testimony of Joseph Smith." . . .

I think we've got a message, and it ought to be delivered. It's a worldwide message, and our centering should be on Joseph Smith. Here is Joseph Smith and he revealed Christ, and here is Christ, and here is salvation through this system.[35]

For Elder McConkie and for traditionalists who embrace his understanding and possess his witness, to malign Joseph's character and work is to cut the life support from the Gospel of Jesus Christ. It is to cut the vine, leaving the branches to whither. Is it an accident that a primary thrust of the new progressive history intentionally demeans the Prophet and the authenticity and reliability of his revelations? Elder McConkie feared that moving away from the Prophet Joseph and the foundation he laid would result in a weakening of the Church. What have we to think today—do our statistics justify his fears? We are losing a plurality of our Millennials—possibly roughly 75%[36] of

---

35   Ibid., 302-303.

36   Personal correspondence with multiple sources confirming the essential accuracy of this statistic. Definitions are important. What does "losing faith" mean? When is faith lost? What age groups are being considered? Are the statistics accurate? Regardless of how optimistically we approach the research, there is unquestionably an increasingly serious problem. Our purpose is not to debate statistics. We should all be able to agree that we are in the midst of a crisis.

Jana Riess has a more positive outlook with 'only' "four or five of every 10" losing faith during their youth. "According to the most recent wave of research in that same study, published earlier this year [2020], 61% of the participants who were Mormon as teenagers still claimed that religious identity as adults. That finding is consistent with other national studies from Pew, the General Social Survey, and the Public Religion Research Institute, in which the Latter-day Saint retention rate in recent years has ranged from a high of 64% to a low of 46%. Losing four or five of every 10 young Latter-day Saints is not something to whitewash . . . ." Jana Riess, "Jana Riess: Controversial Latter-day Saint book pulled from publication," *The Salt Lake Tribune*, September 8, 2020, https://www.sltrib.com/religion/2020/09/08/jana-riess-controversial/.

Riess also explained in 2019, "In 2007, Pew found that Mormons had an overall retention rate of 70%, which is quite good. By 2014, this had dropped to 64% for all generations combined, and to 62% among Millennials. . . . A less rosy picture emerges from the General Social Survey . . . With Generation X we start seeing a drop (62.5%) [retention rate], and with Millennials the drop becomes sharper: for those born after 1981, the GSS finds only a 46% retention rate." Jana Riess, "How

those confronting and investigating this new history. We have never faced an exodus like this before. Is something "terribly wrong!"?

Defending

During the month of September 1835 in Kirtland Ohio, Oliver Cowdery gave Joseph Smith a blessing which was very much like an additional patriarchal blessing.[37] Oliver's prophecy was revealed to him while he was enraptured in a powerful vision. "[W]hile in the heavenly vision, I wrote the following blessing," Oliver recorded, "which is a part of that which was shown and declared should come upon my brother." The blessing spoke of the Prophet Joseph's enemies, but promised that in the future, "thousands shall stand up to defend him from the hand of his enemies, and put forth the hand and ward off the blow were it needful . . . ."[38]

Moroni promised Joseph when he was only seventeen years old, that his "name should be had for good and evil among all nations, kindreds, and tongues, or that it should be both good and evil spoken of among all people."[39] The fulfillment of this prophecy has seen, and continues to see, its realization today. Joseph Smith's patriarchal blessing, given by his father, quoted Isaiah's prophecy of the Latter-day servant, linking that long-foreseen, preeminent messenger to the Prophet Joseph Smith, that the wicked would "mar him for a little season."[40] Truly we are living in a day when the Prophet's visage, his

---

many Millennials are really leaving the LDS Church?" ReligionNews.com, March 27, 2019, https://religionnews.com/2019/03/27/how-many-millennials-are-really-leaving-the-lds-church/.

37   Copies of the patriarchal blessings given to the Prophet Joseph Smith are available for free viewing at Latter-day Answers: "What can we learn from Joseph Smith's patriarchal blessings?" Latter-day Answers, June 27, 2018, https://ldsanswers.org/what-can-we-learn-from-joseph-smiths-patriarchal-blessings/.

38   Blessing from Oliver Cowdery, September 22, 1835, p. 15, The Joseph Smith Papers.

39   Joseph Smith—History 1:33.

40   The prophet Isaiah foretold the coming of a servant of the son of God in the latter-days. Many have asked, "Who is this servant?" When the Son of God visited the Nephite people, He identified the latter-day servant as the declarer of the marvelous work and a wonder.

"For in that day, for my sake shall the Father work a work, which shall be a great and a marvelous work among them; and there shall be among them those who will not believe it, although a man shall declare it unto them.

"But behold, the life of my servant shall be in my hand; therefore they shall not hurt him, although he shall be marred because of them. Yet I will heal him, for I

character, his image, his appearance to those searching for the truth has been marred, distorted, defaced, injured, and disfigured more than any other prophet of the Lord Jesus Christ.

One mother shared that during a fast and testimony meeting, a descendant of Hyrum Smith and member of the Church arose and, from the podium, began to characterize Joseph Smith as a "bumbling idiot," and to speak of his having been a "rough stone needing to

---

will show unto them that my wisdom is greater than the cunning of the devil." 3 Nephi 21:9-10

Joseph Smith's patriarchal blessing identifies him as the man who performs the marvelous work and a wonder in the Latter-day.

> "Thou hast been called, even in thy youth to the great work of the Lord: to do a work in this generation which no man would do as thyself, in all things according to the will of the Lord. A marvelous work and a wonder has the Lord wrought by thy hand, even that which shall prepare the way for the remnants of his people to come in among the Gentiles, with their fullness, as the tribes of Israel are restored." Blessing from Joseph Smith Sr., December 9, 1834, p. 3, The Joseph Smith Papers.

According to Oliver Cowdery, the Angel Moroni also identified Joseph Smith as this chosen instrument, "He has therefore chosen you as an instrument in his hand to bring to light that which shall perform his act, his strange act, and bring to pass a marvelous work and a wonder." Oliver Cowdery, *Messenger and Advocate* 1, no. 5 (February 1835): 79.

Note that Joseph Smith's patriarchal blessing also identifies him as a fulfillment of the "marred" servant foretold in Isaiah 52.

> "His feet shall stand upon the neck of his enemies, and he shall walk upon the ashes of those who seek his destruction . . . No weapon formed against him shall prosper, and though the wicked mar him for a little season, he shall be like one rising up in the heat of wine—he shall roar in his strength, and the Lord shall put to flight his persecutors . . ." Blessing from Joseph Smith Sr., December 9, 1834, p. 4, The Joseph Smith Papers.

See Isaiah 52: "Behold, my servant shall deal prudently, he shall be exalted and extolled, and be very high. As many were astonied at thee; his visage was so marred more than any man, and his form more than the sons of men:" Isaiah 52:13-14

Joseph Fielding McConkie observed, ". . . Isaiah 49, one of the suffering servant prophecies, is also descriptive of Joseph Smith and his role as the great prophet of the latter-day restoration. . . . it has traditionally been interpreted as a description of the life and ministry of Christ. . . . It is a common thing for prophecies of the scriptures to have various levels of meaning and for them to be fulfilled again and again. . . . All prophesies are fulfilled in Christ, yet many have a dual meaning; such is apparently the case with the 'servant' spoken of in Isaiah 49." Joseph Fielding McConkie, "Joseph Smith as Found in Ancient Manuscripts," *Isaiah and the Prophets: Inspired Voices from the Old Testament*, ed. by Monte S. Nyman (Provo, UT: Religious Studies Center, Brigham Young University, 1984), 11–31.

Additional study of the Prophet Joseph Smith's life and future mission connects him to every requirement for the latter-day Servant as specified in Isaiah, Ezekiel, Jeremiah and so forth.

be polished," (undoubtedly a reference to Richard Bushman's book, *Rough Stone Rolling*). The member justified that this depiction "made him feel better about himself with his own weaknesses." The mother shared her teenage son's reaction:

/ / My seventeen-year-old son and I couldn't help looking at each other at the words "bumbling idiot," and probably couldn't hide our shock, sitting on the second row that week. I knew instantly that someone needed to go up and defend the Prophet, and was trying to prepare myself, wondering what I ought to say so as not to cause conflict in the meeting. As the brother sat down, I saw my son get up to go up to the stand. Then I worried just a little, and prayed to myself that he would say the right thing since I absolutely knew what it was that he was going up to do; he had a very determined and upset look on his face. He began by bearing his testimony of the Church, the Book of Mormon, etc., and didn't get right to the point immediately. Then he bore a powerful testimony of the Prophet Joseph Smith, and said that he would defend him to anyone who said that he was not the magnificent prophet that he was. Afterward, my husband, son, and I received many comments and expressions of gratitude that he had done that, and for how it had "fixed what needed to be fixed."

Elder Bruce R. McConkie taught that "the measure of a person's spiritual maturity is found in his or her loyalty to the Prophet Joseph Smith."[41] So we might ask ourselves: Where do I stand on the loyalty meter? What have I done personally to stand against the attacks of those who now mar the character of the Prophet Joseph?

Another parent shared with us that after their fourteen-year-old son recently found a new group of friends, he began exhibiting anger and rebelliousness. "I knew there was something going on," the mother explained:

/ / To make a long story short, last week, our son came to us and wanted to speak to us alone. He completely broke down and became hysterical. He confided in us and told us that this group

---

41   Joseph Fielding McConkie, *The Bruce R. McConkie Story: Reflections of a Son* (Salt Lake City: Deseret Book, 2003), 256. See also Bruce R. McConkie, "Joseph Smith: A Revealer of Christ," BYU Devotional Address, September 3, 1978, 6.

of kids have been getting together to "bash Joseph Smith" and talk about how soon they will leave the church. They also have been encouraging him to "follow his heart to be happy" and that they are all bi-sexual and he should try it. My poor son was so broken as he explained how hard it has been to avoid all the temptations. Defending Joseph Smith is so important right now! These poor young people are not being taught truths so they can't discern what's real and what is not. I can't blame people for bashing Joseph when they really believe he was into magic and the occult!

While Joseph Smith languished in the bitter cold of Liberty Jail, he was promised that 'his people' would never be turned against him "by the testimony of traitors,"[42] but would stand to defend his name, his character, his doctrine, and his mission. Who are 'his people'? President Heber C. Kimball also prophesied that while many of the Prophet's "boys" are asleep, they will one day rise up and "bear testimony" to the "true character of Joseph [Smith]":

> At present the Prophet Joseph's boys lay apparently in a state of slumber, everything seems to be perfectly calm with them, but by and bye [sic] God will wake them up, and they will roar like the thunders of Mount Sinai.
>
> There is much work to be done: God is not asleep, and He will wake up our children and they will bear off this kingdom to the nations of the earth, and will bear testimony to the truth of this work, and of the **integrity** and **true character** of Joseph . . . .[43]

We bear solemn witness that it is time to wake up! Joseph Smith's character is currently being marred by those within, who dishonor and defile as never before. Where are the voices who will stand up and be counted in defense of the Prophet of the Restoration, the architect of the Marvelous Work and Wonder? Where are those possessing both a spiritual witness and an intellectual understanding?

Will your voice be among the awakened?

Will you sink into the crowd, or stand up to be counted?

---

42   Doctrine and Covenants 122:3.

43   Heber C. Kimball, "The Saints Should Prepare for Future Emergencies," in *Journal of Discourses*, vol. 4 (Liverpool, 1860), 6. Discourse given on June 29, 1857; emphasis added.

INDEX

L. Hannah Stoddard, author

L. Hannah Stoddard is the lead author of *Faith Crisis, Volume 1: We Were NOT Betrayed!* and *Seer Stone v. Urim & Thummim: Book of Mormon Translation on Trial.* She is the executive director of the Joseph Smith Foundation and the producer or director of seven documentary feature films.

- Nephites in Europe (Episodes 1 & 2, Quest for the Nephite Remnant) (2019)
- Hidden Bloodlines: The Grail & the Lost Tribes in the Lands of the North (2017)
- Unlocking the Mystery of the Two Prophets: Revelation 11 (2017)
- The Prophet Joseph: More than we know (2015)
- Statesmen & Symbols: Prelude to the Restoration (2014)
- For Our Day: Divinely Sanctioned Governments (2013)
- For Our Day: Covenant on the Land (2013)

In addition to directing Joseph Smith Foundation projects for over a decade, she is often invited to speak on various radio and video programs. Beginning at age 16, Hannah helped direct her first documentary film. She has worked as a history and literature teacher, graphic design artist, software developer, videographer, project manager, agriculturist, and research assistant. Her work focuses on Church history and doctrine, answers to Latter-day Saint faith crisis questions, educational philosophy, culture, and defending the Prophet Joseph Smith. Hannah's research supports the writings and teachings of ancient and latter-day prophets.

James F. Stoddard III, author

James F. Stoddard is a film producer, author, entrepreneur, and father of 10 children. James is the executive strategist for the Joseph Smith Foundation. He is a direct descendant of Asael and Mary Duty Smith, the Prophet Joseph Smith's grandparents, and other Latter-day Saint Church history figures. James is the co-author of *Faith Crisis, Volume 1: We Were NOT Betrayed!* and *Seer Stone v. Urim & Thummim: Book of Mormon Translation on Trial* and the producer or executive producer of eight documentary films:

- Nephites in Europe (Episodes 1 & 2, Quest for the Nephite Remnant) (2019)
- Hidden Bloodlines: The Grail & the Lost Tribes in the Lands of the North (2017)
- Unlocking the Mystery of the Two Prophets: Revelation 11 (2017)
- The Prophet Joseph: More than we know (2015)
- Statesmen & Symbols: Prelude to the Restoration (2014)
- For Our Day: Divinely Sanctioned Governments (2013)
- For Our Day: Covenant on the Land (2013)
- Creation and Evolution: A Witness of Prophets (2007)

James has worked in private, public, religious, corporate and home education as well as engineering, videography, property development, and natural health. He has started and helps operate several family businesses and enjoys working with his kids. James spends any free moments working on Highland Cathedral Estate, a planned family retreat and learning facility with perennial gardens and walking trails specializing in experimental farming techniques and four-season food production. James has worked as a release time Seminary teacher and as an instructor at the Provo Missionary Training Center (MTC). His research supports the writings and teachings of ancient and latter-day prophets.

Nephites in Europe Documentary
(Episodes 1 & 2) Quest for the Nephite Remnant
Winner, 2nd Place—LDS Film Festival Feature Documentary—2020

For over a century and a half, we assumed the Nephites struggled to extinction. What if remnants escaped to Europe, Japan, New Zealand, Burma, etc.–to become nations, kindreds, tongues, and people? An ancient Icelandic text records a royal family in Northern Europe descending from a prince by the name of Nefi or Nephi. Another Northern European tribe was known by a name that likely means the "people of Nephi." Did Nephites travel to Europe?

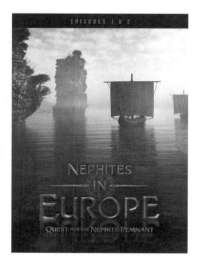

Episode 1: Nephites in Europe

An ancient Icelandic text records a royal family in Northern Europe descending from a prince by the name of Nefi or Nephi. Another Northern European tribe was known by a name that likely means the "people of Nephi." Did Nephites travel to Europe?

Episode 2: Nephite Survivors in Prophecy

Did righteous Nephite families escape and spread throughout the world? Was Joseph Smith a descendant of Joseph, son of Lehi? Why did the Lord tell Joseph Smith that the Book of Mormon would be given to Latter-day Nephites, Jacobites, Josephites, and Zoramites as well as Lamanites, Lemuelites, and Ishmaelites?

Guest Appearances: John D. Nelson, Scott N. Bradley, Timothy Ballard
RUNTIME: 1 HR 2 MIN

Order now at www.JosephSmithFoundation.org
or watch on Amazon Prime

JOSEPH SMITH FOUNDATION DOCUMENTARIES

www.JosephSmithFoundation.org

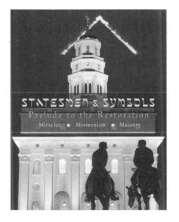

Statesmen & Symbols: Prelude to the Restoration

What do LDS temples have in common with the Great Pyramid of Giza, Stonehenge, and the Hopewell mounds in North America? Why are some of the sacred symbols used by the Founding Fathers also found on tapestries in China that date to the time of the flood? What are the details of American Founding Father Benjamin Rush's vision concerning Thomas Jefferson and John Adams?

Unlocking the Mystery of the Two Prophets: Revelation 11

Who are the two prophets in Revelation 11, the two messengers who lie dead in the great city? An assassination by enemies, a forbidden burial by persecutors, and bodies lying in the street for three and a half days are only a few of the clues found in scripture revealing their identity. The two prophets have generally been shrouded in mystery . . . until now.

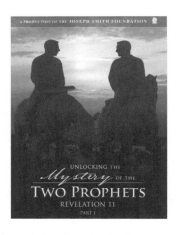

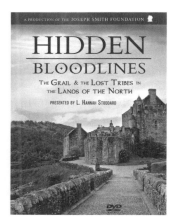

Hidden Bloodlines: The Grail & the Lost Tribes in the Lands of the North

Winner, 3rd Place
LDS Film Festival Feature Documentary—2018

The legendary search for the Holy Grail has resonated with millions for centuries! What is the Holy Grail, and why is this legendary symbol important to the lives of Joseph Smith and the Son of God? Was Jesus Christ married and did He have children? Discover your own heritage, your own royal birthright, in a way you may never have imagined!

Book of Mormon Parallel Events Timeline
Posters (20x30", 12x18", 8x12")

This timeline overlays the Book of Mormon history with Latter-day prophetic history and organizes the matching events.

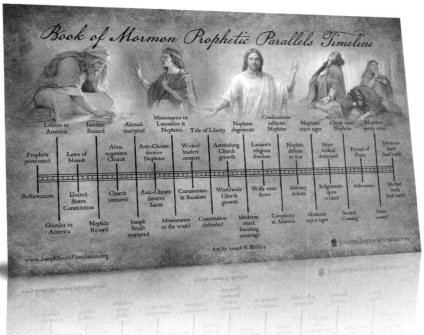

- Is the entire latter day history laid out and foreshadowed in the Book of Mormon?
- What if we were to take the most fundamental and key prophetic events of the Latter-days and organize them chronologically, and then take this model and lay out the Book of Mormon history on top of it?
- How does this help us better understand the Latter-day Signs of the Times?
- What can this tell us of the challenges that lie ahead, and more importantly, the solutions to those challenges?
- This timeline overlays the Book of Mormon history with Latter-day prophetic history and organizes the matching events.

Order now at www.JosephSmithFoundation.org

For Our Day Parallel Model
Posters (20x30", 12x18", 8x12")

What if we stepped through the Book of Mormon history and paralleled it with the latter-day Signs of the Times, as detailed by inspired prophets? Even more, what if we could find these Signs of the Times foreshadowed in the Book of Mormon chronology in the correct sequence?

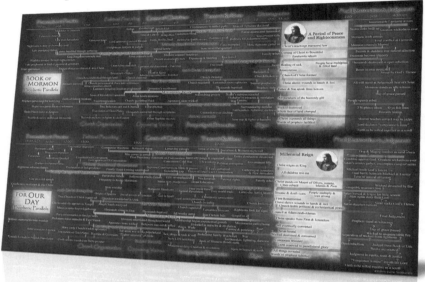

In both the Book of Mormon record and in latter day prophecy, major calamity and destruction follow the Saviour's appearance. In both accounts the whole face of the land is changed. In both, Christ appears to the people, shows the marks in His hands and feet, the sick are healed, and the righteous are resurrected. Cities are rebuilt and the people multiply exceedingly and enjoy great prosperity.

In both the Book of Mormon and latter-day prophecy, the Church is re-established by Alma (Mosiah 18) and the Prophet Joseph Smith, respectively. Inspired seers, Mosiah (Mosiah 8, 28) and the Prophet Joseph Smith translate ancient records from plates of gold. Additionally, is it an accident that the principles of the Nephite republican form of government—the Laws of Mosiah—can be found in the Constitutional law upon which this nation, the United States of America, was established? What about Latter-day antichrists? President Benson taught, "The type of apostates in the Book of Mormon is similar to the type we have today."

Order now at www.JosephSmithFoundation.org

For Our Day: Covenant on the Land

This film discusses the covenant on the Promised Land for both ancient and modern inhabitants, presenting inspiring history from the American colonization, paralleling the Puritans, Pilgrims and other righteous forebears with Lehi, Nephi and the first part of the Book of Mormon. Is latter-day history laid out and foreshadowed in the Book of Mormon?

For Our Day: Divinely Sanctioned Governments

This film compares the Nephite and Latter-day governments of liberty, covering principles of liberty including: Unalienable Rights, Oath of Office, Federalism, the U.S. and Hebrew connection, as well as the Laws of Mosiah. This feature documentary adds an understanding of governmental principles as they are taught in the most correct book, the Book of Mormon.

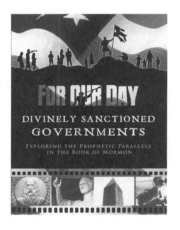

The Prophet Joseph: More than we know

Ground-breaking research on latter-day prophecy! Is the Prophet Joseph the Angel in Revelation 14, the designator of Zion inheritances, the Messenger in Malachi, the Servant in Isaiah, the passport to Celestial glory, the Voice crying in the wilderness? Discover the Prophet Joseph Smith in a way you have never imagined!